The Central Banks

The Central Banks

MARJORIE DEANE AND ROBERT PRINGLE

WITH A FOREWORD BY PAUL VOLCKER

VIKING

VIKING
Published by the Penguin Group
Penguin Books USA Inc., 375 Hudson Street,
New York, New York 10014, U.S.A.
Penguin Books Ltd, 27 Wrights Lane,
London W8 5TZ, England
Penguin Books Australia Ltd, Ringwood,
Victoria, Australia
Penguin Books Canada Ltd, 10 Alcorn Avenue,
Toronto, Ontario, Canada M4V 3B2
Penguin Books (N.Z.) Ltd, 182–190 Wairau Road,
Auckland 10, New Zealand

Penguin Books Ltd, Registered Offices:
Harmondsworth, Middlesex, England

First American edition
Published in 1995 by Viking Penguin,
a division of Penguin Books USA Inc.

10 9 8 7 6 5 4 3 2 1

Copyright © Marjorie Deane and Robert Pringle, 1994
Foreword copyright © Paul Volcker, 1994
All rights reserved

LIBRARY OF CONGRESS CATALOGING IN PUBLICATION DATA

Deane, Marjorie.
The central banks/Marjorie Deane and Robert Pringle.
p. cm.
Includes bibliographical references and index.
ISBN 0-670-84823-9
1. Banks and banking, Central.   I. Pringle, Robert.   II. Title.
HG1811.D423   1994
332.1′1—dc20   94-23017

This book is printed on acid-free paper.

Contents

Foreword

A few years ago, asked to 'keynote' a conference on central banking in what these days are called emerging markets, I felt at a loss as to what to say. I was, after all, to be addressing the faithful: a group made up largely of central bankers, old and new, generally enthusiastic about the role that central banks must play in promoting stability and developing financial markets. Nor could there be any doubt that, throughout Central and Eastern Europe, governments were already placing a great deal of emphasis on the formation of new central banks.

To one who has spent so much of his own working life either in a central bank or working alongside central bankers, that was a happy state of affairs. But, in the circumstances, another address by me affirming the glories of central banking, or even a lecture on the importance of price stability, seemed redundant at best and hardly challenging.

Instead, I had the nagging thought that maybe the more useful message would be to restrain the sense of enthusiasm, to emphasize the natural and inevitable limits on central banks acting alone to achieve the goal of sustained growth and stability – in sum, to remind central bankers themselves of what they are wont to warn others about: excesses of zeal and confidence. Among other things, I found myself reminding my fellow conferees that history provided little support for the simple proposition that the creation of a central bank, in and of itself, would provide much assurance against inflation. Nor was there much evidence that we could look towards any simple rule book to determine when to ease or when to tighten, and the unknowns could only multiply in less developed economies with poorly functioning markets.

We sometimes forget that central banking, as we know it today, is, in fact, largely an invention of the past hundred years or so, even though a few central banks can trace their ancestry back to the early nineteenth century or before. It is a sobering fact that the prominence of central banks in this century has coincided with a general tendency towards more inflation, not less. By and large, if the overriding objective is price stability, we did better with the nineteenth-century gold standard and passive central banks, with currency boards, or even with 'free banking'.

The truly unique power of a central bank, after all, is the power to create money, and ultimately the power to create is the power to destroy.

My point then and now is not to denigrate the importance of central banks. On the contrary, they are today typically among the institutions of prime importance in governments of all nations, large and small, economically well developed or not. Their efforts to restore and sustain price stability, which are now achieving a substantial measure of success, will, in my view, help enormously in shoring up the foundation for sustained growth. On a purely personal level, my experiences with central banks and those who run and staff them have been the most satisfying of my professional life. It is precisely their significance, and the complex amalgam of factors, human and otherwise, that underlies their performances and their success, that makes this treatise on central banking so timely.

Marjorie Deane and Robert Pringle have that rare facility of writing, at one and the same time, for both the expert and the curious layman. Readers who have felt that central banks are mysterious and inexplicable institutions – somehow almost inhuman – will no longer have grounds for complaint. For specialists, the authors have brought to bear a combination of broad scholarship, historical perspective, and sensitive personal observation that simply has no contemporary counterpart in the world of central banking.

Writing at a time when central banking is at a pinnacle of influence and respect, the tone of questioning and even scepticism that pervades much of the book is surely justified. We are reminded again and again that central banks are human institutions, with all the limitations of understanding and foresight which that implies. The authors are well aware of the point that the mere existence of central banks provides no assurance of price stability. They accept the importance of a substantial degree of autonomy in decision-making in countering political pressures for excessive money creation, but they also emphasize the inherent limitations on the functional independence of a central bank in an interdependent world, a world of open markets and of enormous flows of capital across national borders. The sometimes underrated role of central banks in fostering efficient and reliable financial systems and in protecting their stability receives proper emphasis, balanced by concerns about spreading responsibilities too widely, at the risk of ineffectiveness and political interference. Not least, they worry about accountability, without which central banks will ultimately lose their capacity to serve a democratic society.

For all the questions raised, for all the doubts expressed, there can be no mistaking the key role that central banks play in a modern economy. That role is frequently related entirely, or almost so, to the importance of monetary policy – the decisions about the appropriate supply of money and credit or the direction and level of interest rates. Especially at a time when other instruments of national economic policy, and especially fiscal policy, seem inflexible or frozen in political debate, that emphasis may be understandable. But one of the contributions of Deane and Pringle is to make clear that the importance and influence of central banks is rooted in a broader tradition than monetary management alone.

At the most fundamental level, central banks are institutions that, by their nature, provide support for the principles of a market system, of competition, and of openness. Whether fully recognized or not, in acting as lender of last resort, they are part of the essential underpinning of modern financial markets. Characteristically, central banks provide their governments with a bastion of professionalism and continuity, and the tradition of avoiding partisanship typically and usefully becomes a leavening influence in the political process. Indeed, there have been times in various countries, when other public institutions are in question, fragmented, and unable to command support, that central banks have provided an important centre of stability, contributing to the larger enterprise of government.

Marjorie Deane and Robert Pringle have not shied away from emphasizing the dilemma and conflicts inherent in the exercise of the large responsibilities of central banks. They have correctly placed the emotive question of 'independence' in the context of the large political and market forces that inescapably impinge upon, and set limits on, autonomy. They emphasize the demands for more openness in decision-making, however uncomfortable that may be, in democratic societies.

To this reader at least, these seasoned observers of the financial scene have achieved a balanced, comprehensive and comprehensible assessment of the state of central banking. In the process, one senses that it is the authors' hope – it is certainly mine – that this book will also help to reinforce the best traditions and values of central banking, and in so doing further solidify its legitimate and critically important role in democratic societies.

Paul Volcker, July 1994

Acknowledgements

Many people have given help and advice. Rupert Pennant-Rea, while editor of *The Economist*, provided initial encouragement and useful suggestions. Special thanks go to Andrew Franklin, the publishing director of Hamish Hamilton whose enthusiasm and perception have been invaluable. Peter Bakstansky, Francis Cassell, John Footman, Alexandre Lamfalussy, Luigi Marini, Lord O'Brien, Robert Raymond and Wolfgang Rieke all generously agreed to read parts of the draft for factual accuracy and we are grateful for their comments.

As to the chores involved, we owe a special debt to Alex Allan and Rhiannon Davidge for transforming untidy manuscripts into neat transcripts, patiently and efficiently, and to David Turnbull for the Appendix.

I   *A Huddle of Central Bankers*

According to the American writer Joyce Carol Oates, the only people who claim that money is not important are people who have sufficient money that they are relieved of the ugly burden of thinking about it. So perhaps this book, which, quite simply, is about the business of central banking, at the very heart of the money game, is not for the ultra-rich. For the rest of us, the remarkable transformation of central banks and their potential new power over the supply and use of our money are very much our concern.

From being a remote, dry-as-dust business that mere mortals could not be expected to understand, and it mattered little if they did not, central banking has become a cult. Every country in the world now possesses, or intends to possess, a central bank, be it Russia, China, an emerging democracy in Eastern Europe or a new nation that has spun itself off. When the last of Africa's states gained independence in 1990, it was only a matter of months before the Bank of Namibia opened its doors. Yet Namibia is certainly not a wealthy country and the style in which a central bank expects to operate does not come cheap. What is this thing that everybody wants so much? Do central banks do anything worthwhile – or anything which could not be done in other ways? Does it make sense for everyone to be so keen to have a central bank?

Some seasoned hands in the business are not sure it does. Central banks, they say, are an expensive luxury. Fashion is fickle and for high-flyers the fall can be a hard one. While flattered by the attention they are commanding, their concern is that their institutions are being portrayed as too powerful, the current wisdom being that if a country's central bank is made independent of political pressure, all its economic ills will be cured.

This is arrant nonsense. We cannot help but recall the comments ten or so years ago of a recently retired statesman who had played a leading role in European affairs. He told us, in confidence, that he regarded central bankers as generally reactionary, cowardly types. 'They are oblivious to the effect of their policies on unemployment for they know they will never be on the job market. They are always safe,' he said, this last quip coming with a snort.

But, prejudice apart, far too little is understood generally about the role and responsibilities, let alone the capabilities, of contemporary central banks. Nor does it seem widely appreciated how little history can be drawn on to judge their behaviour. Nor, again, how idiosyncratic they can be.

No two major central banks are alike in structure or functions; in fact, there are astonishing differences between them. They even use different methods in preparing their own accounts, reflecting national traditions and laws. Moreover, despite the distinguished pedigrees some boast, a central bank as we know it today is a twentieth-century phenomenon – a Johnny-come-lately. So unlike its ancestors is it, that it must be classed as an entirely distinct species.

Yet it is to these newish creatures (and rare ones at that – there being only one per country) that so much enhanced power is being given to shape the destinies of all of us. Nobody can afford to ignore what this is all about.

In from the cold

There are three main threads to the story of how and why the status and real influence of central banks have risen over the past decade. First, and most important, the big powers shifted their economic priorities; monetary policy became virtually the only game in town and monetary policy is the province of central banks – an area where many of them can lay claims to special technical expertise. Second, initiatives to establish new central banking institutions by the European Community and the emerging democracies in Central and Eastern Europe required governments to spell out explicitly what their relations with the new institutions would be – a process that laid bare the pivotal role being attached to them in market economies. And third, the deregulated, globalized, technologically driven financial markets discovered that they need nannying, that they cannot do without the monetary authorities even if at times they despise them.

All three strands are interlocked by a new folk dream of 'stability'. Listen to Gerald Corrigan, the thoughtful man who for eight years until the summer of 1993 ran the New York end of America's central banking, the Federal Reserve System, and who had no doubts about the value of his work. 'The single theme of a contemporary central bank's functions,' he says, 'is to provide stability – stability in the purchasing power of the currency of the country and stability in the workings of the financial system, including the payments system.' That is a far cry from the mundane way a central bank used to see itself, little more than an issuer of the nation's currency and as banker to the government. Yet central bankers, through carelessness or arrogance or maybe confusion of thought, have neglected to sell their new ideology to the public, other than glibly. They have been slow to explain what 'stability' means in a market-oriented world that is, by definition, geared to movement.

But we have run too far ahead in our story. Let us turn back to the three main threads – monetary policy, relations with government and supervision of markets. We look briefly at them in turn.

Switch in policy objectives

If a date is sought for when central banks started to come in from the cold, it must be put around 1980, or, more cautiously, sometime in the second half of the 1970s. It was then that the major industrial powers retreated from the belief that economic policymaking should focus on the avoidance of unemployment by targeting specified growth rates of output. It was then that they turned instead to inflation control through the management of credit, interest rates and exchange rates. And since the one thing certain about central banks is that they are concerned with monetary conditions, their time had begun.

Many say governments had no choice but to switch their priorities as they did; it was dictated not by a conscious change in ideology but by the appalling record of the 1970s, in such sharp contrast to the 'golden' 1960s. Inflation, it will be remembered, was in double digits in 1973–74 throughout the industrialized world. But some countries – the United States, Britain — suffered far worse inflation than others – Japan, Germany – and people drew lessons from this. The countries that had relied on traditional methods of avoiding recession – boosting demand and money supply – suffered worse inflation than others. Those countries had ruled out drastic action because it was thought that losses entailed in output and jobs would be unacceptably high. However, by the end of the decade, even these governments were realizing that the welfare costs of inflation were endangering their political existence; they had to act. Faith had been undermined, if not totally destroyed, in the fine tuning of aggregate demand on which post-Keynesian economists had built a profession.

Governments have not abandoned the goal of economic growth, but they now target it implicitly rather than explicitly. With varying shades of conviction, they have accepted the free-market philosophy that growth – or 'quality' growth as they like to call it – will come about given the right incentives. And the biggest incentive of all, as they see it, is low inflation, or 'price stability' as it is more popularly called in a misuse of the language.

If any single time and place is to be chosen for this decisive change, it is 1979 in Belgrade. It was there that Paul Volcker abruptly left a meeting of the International Monetary Fund to return home to do something about inflation. The domestic action taken against inflation in the United States from that time onwards, orchestrated by Volcker in his first years running the Federal Reserve in Washington, did more for central banks' reputations than anything else before or since – although it had the dismaying international consequence of precipitating the third-world debt crisis. Certainly Volcker became a hero to many of his fellow countrymen. One of the authors of this book was present at the social climax of an international banking conference in Boston in June 1986 – a Harvard/Radcliffe 'night at the Pops', also attended by white-haired men and women from the class of '36. Standing up to stretch his legs in the interval, the 6 foot 7 inch round-shouldered, balding figure of the world's top central banker was quickly spotted. One Harvard veteran approached him with outstretched hand. 'Mr Volcker,' he said, 'I want to thank you for saving our country.' A dozen or more of his class mates eagerly pressed behind him to pay their homage too.

But if Volcker knew the right questions to ask, he did not know all the answers. It is one thing for central bankers to see a price stability anchor as essential, quite another to ride at anchor over any length of time. Operating procedures may have been transformed in the past decade but, as we discuss in this book, experience with them has not been wholly encouraging. There are both theoretical and practical obstacles to turning central bankers' dreams into reality.

Going for independence

In their relations with governments, the second strand in the story, central banks aspire to 'independence' and in the past few years events have finally been moving their way. Back in the 1920s, the then Governor of the Bank of England, Montagu Norman, took every opportunity to emphasize the need for all countries to establish 'autonomous' central banks. Nobody listened. At home, thirty years on, the Labour Chancellor of the Exchequer, Stafford Cripps, took great pleasure in describing the Bank of England as *his* bank. And the Treasury's bank it has remained ever since, and never more so than in the years when Margaret Thatcher was Prime Minister (1979–90).

It is not easy to line up public opinion behind this issue. Independence does not give a central bank a noticeably different face. To most intents and purposes, the American and British central banks are seen as look-alikes. One day the Fed may be operating in the American markets to signal that it wants interest rates nudged up, the next day the Bank of England may be doing likewise in the London markets. Who stops to think that in the one instance the action is taken as a result of an internal decision, in the other under instructions from outside, from the executive branch of government? In both countries, when mortgage rates rise the central bank and government are likely to share the blame indiscriminately.

Nevertheless, the British public's imagination was caught in 1989 when Nigel Lawson, as he resigned from the Chancellorship at the Treasury, made a startling revelation. He had recommended to Prime Minister Margaret Thatcher that the Bank of England should be given a free rein to run monetary policy. It was not an off-the-cuff remark. Lawson had detached a senior Treasury man from his normal duties for several months to prepare, with the help of colleagues, a paper detailing how it could be done. The disclosure certainly caught the Bank by surprise – for not since Stafford Cripps had it been treated so brutally as by Nigel Lawson.

But even someone as clever as Lawson cannot produce an open-and-shut case for central bank independence. Evidence is mixed. True, countries with 'strong' (i.e., largely independent) central banks – America, Germany, Switzerland – have done well in keeping inflation low or at least better than average. But so, too, has Japan, whose central bank, although less under the thumbs of the finance ministry in practice than it is on paper, is still far from a free agent. Also France, with a central bank then totally controlled by the government and notoriously subject to political influences, has managed from time to time to get its inflation rate below Germany's.

On the face of it, it is easier to make out a case *against* independence. Surely monetary policy in a democracy should be in the hands of elected representatives? Why should monetary policy be hived off any more than, say, industrial or trade or nuclear energy policy? Isn't it naïve to argue that money *is* different and *does* merit special treatment?

That last question makes us a little uncomfortable, but as we develop the arguments in this book, we conclude that, because money is the most politically sensitive commodity conceivable, its management does need some protection from political misuse. Allow governments total say in the setting of interest rates and they will use that power to produce booms just before political elections, carefully timed so that the inflationary bursts, which will follow as night does day, come after the electors have voted. On the other hand, an astute and educated electorate could learn to see through such manoeuvres – just as they learnt to distrust the unions. So the question – Why is money so special? – can't be disposed of too easily.

Electioneering aside, the priority attached to anti-inflationary policies tends to be called into question whenever recession threatens; it is just too tempting, because it is so easy, to reduce interest rates so as to boost activity. Resistance requires courage. Alan Greenspan, Volcker's successor, was slated by the Bush administration for reducing interest rates in 1990 more slowly than it was demanding. Not all central bankers would have been as resolute as Greenspan was then, even if it were within their power to be so. That is why, as we shall stress in later pages, if a central bank is given some freedom from government, it should be by way of a very specific mandate that puts its reputation on the line. It is imperative that the demarcation lines are very clear.

If a tug-of-war develops between a Prime Minister or finance ministry and a central bank, it is probably helpful if the game is played out publicly, so long as the rulebook has been agreed. The Deutsche Bundesbank saw in 1990 that its famed independence, mandated by law, offers it very little protection against political forces on big questions. Disagreement with Chancellor Kohl over the financing of German reunification made the Bundesbank feel it had lost face and caused the central banking stage to lose one of its most colourful players, Karl Otto Pöhl, who resigned after the clash. Even the Bundesbank had to accept that, in the end, there must be limits to the influence of any monetary agency.

The Federal Reserve likes to say that it is independent *within* government. It rolls off the tongue a little too glibly, but at least it suggests that the Fed is aware there are boundaries to the game. In fact, the Fed is careful not to push its luck too far. It does not complain, for instance, because it does not have control of America's exchange-rate policy. But then exchange-rate policy matters less – for domestic inflation – in the United States than in the more open economies of Europe. By contrast, the Bundesbank's influence on Germany's exchange-rate policy was demonstrated in the European currency crises of October 1992 and July 1993 when its refusal to go on supporting weaker currencies indefinitely caused the Exchange Rate Mechanism to collapse, despite the Bonn government's desire to keep it going (see Chapter 13 on exchange rates).

If the question of independence for existing well-established central banks can be left to work itself out in the flow of events and debate, this is not possible in the case of new institutions. Nothing is having a

greater impact on the world of central banking than the political drive
to establish new central banks, above all in Europe.

Even if the European Central Bank should never actually come about,
even if it were to remain just out of reach, central banking has been
changed irrevocably as a result of the preparations for it – a reason in
itself for taking a fresh look at the profession. That European central
bankers were able to agree – in large measure at least – on the shape of
an institution that would inevitably make almost redundant the ones
they were then running shows a remarkable meeting of minds. Their
smartness lay in insistence that the first step towards the creation of such
an institution should be to make the existing central banks independent
– which France did in 1994.

The European Union is not alone in planning a new central bank.
The restructuring countries of Central and Eastern Europe are also
attaching much importance to developing central banks; some progress
in that direction is underway in the republics of the former Soviet
Union, not to mention the Baltic states. China, too, says it wants a
stronger central bank, as do countries in Latin America that now show
signs of 'getting it right' on economic policies. Africa will soon catch the
bug.

An industry has grown up in response to the technical needs involved
in this creative process. Western central banks, with the Austrian one in
the lead, have been almost falling over each other to help Eastern
Europe on this score – with an eye, one has to add, to some benefits for
their own country. The Bank of England has established a special
training unit and sent a number of staff to provide specialized help; it
considers it beneficial to the City of London's reputation if it is seen as
the centre of expertise. What is remarkable is that everyone is teaching
that the pursuit of price stability is the centrepiece of economic policy –
a consensus inconceivable even a few years ago.

Supervision of financial markets

There is much less unanimity among the fraternity over the third aspect
of their role, the regulation and supervision of banks and other financial
institutions. But nowadays, whatever the formal position, no central
bank can distance itself from the running of the financial markets if it is
to make a decent job of executing monetary policy. Gerald Corrigan
was surely right when he said the integrity and stability of the financial
system, which encompasses such technicalities as payment and settlement
systems, is very much a central bank's concern. What is in important

debate is whether it should also be the authority examining each cog in the wheel as it were, vetting individual banks' management, performance and balance sheets.

For many Continental bankers it is natural that banking supervision should be the responsibility of a specific separate organization. It is equally hard for the British to realize that the Bundesbank is not the supervisory body in Germany and that the Federal Reserve shares responsibilities with several other agencies in the United States. In its relationship with Whitehall, the Bank of England may play a conspicuously more servile role than its German or American counterpart, but within the bounds of the so-called Square Mile it dominates the banking scene in a way no other central bank in the industrialized world can match. True, it no longer rules through an informal system of 'nods and winks', but the legislation that has formalized the Bank's authority still gives it considerable flexibility to wield its truncheon – and, likewise, plenty of opportunity to get egg on its face.

Supervision is a big yawn – until things go wrong. When, from time to time, supervisors are perceived as having done a substandard job, the public howls for revenge and for changes in the system, whatever type that may be. When an American commercial bank goes under without warning, the cry comes that there is a hole in the supervisory net that can only be closed by giving sole authority to the Fed, which is best placed to know what's going on. But when the Bank of England closed the corrupt Bank of Credit and Commerce International in London in July 1991, indignant voices were heard asking for the regulatory and monetary functions in Britain to be officially divided, the implication being that because the central bank gives too much attention to the latter to the detriment of the former, it had failed to spot irregularities at BCCI as soon as it should have done.

If this last contention were true, the remedy could lie in better organization at the Bank. It does not afford a conclusive argument for two separate authorities. But more and more it looks as if banking supervisors have to be highly skilled in detecting fraud – not really a central banker's talent.

Financial regulation, whether or not they actually administer it, is going to take up more and more of central bankers' time just when they have exciting intellectual challenges in other fields – which is why we are giving it such an airing in this introductory chapter. Ironically, this is happening at a time when market forces are supposed to bring their own discipline. But the fear of losing money creates panic on just as widespread a scale in market-based economies as in more controlled ones – probably more so, since there is more nervous money around.

Liberalization – a word we prefer to deregulation to describe the main financial trend of the past decade – has made it very difficult indeed to keep track of money flows. With capital controls lifted, savings can move around the world at the press of a button. Restrictive policies that prevented banks from being stockbrokers or selling life insurance have been swept away entirely in some countries, eased in others. A plastic card gives access to cash at home or in Timbuktu. The headline 'One world, one market, one crisis' has surely come to haunt central bankers.

The extent to which technical innovation would bring greater risks was probably not foreseen. Initially, when freedom seemed so sweet, the markets thought they could look after themselves, with only a very light touch of authority. When they were given new rulebooks for the brave new world, they grumbled incessantly. There was dismay in some quarters at what was seen as an objectionable amount of reregulation. London, in particular, feared it might lose business to centres allowed more freedom. But such fears have receded in the past year or so. The perception is growing that professionals want markets that are 'properly' regulated, and precisely what that means is much debated.

It is a tough challenge to devise supervisory regimes that strike the right balance between market efficiency and overall safety and soundness. In most countries, different money businesses – banking, stockbroking, insurance, etc. – have been regulated quite separately and vested interests want to keep it that way. The walls between markets have come down, but not between the regulators. And, of course, as markets have gone global, this brings in yet another dimension – external cooperation in supervision.

No country's financial system operates in a vacuum. The fashionable derivatives business alone – the dealings in fancy financial instruments such as futures, swaps and options – represents thousands of billions of dollars in capital and regularly crosses national borders. But this is only the latest chapter in the long history of global money trading. Yet even with banking, the oldest money business of all, international cooperation in supervision is fairly new. Twenty years ago it didn't exist; there was little contact between those responsible for banking supervision in major countries. As in so much else in financial history, it took a crisis to remedy a shameful neglect.

That particular crisis came in the summer of 1974, after a huge growth in international banking and particularly in the Euromarkets. Spectacular foreign-exchange losses at a private bank headquartered in Cologne, the Herstatt Bank, suddenly shook confidence throughout banking the world over. It took that shock for central bankers to realize they needed to exchange more information about their national banking systems and to establish some common codes of practice. Accordingly they set up a standing committee of supervisory experts to get on with the job, which still has a hefty workload today.

Progress in policing international banking through the efforts of that special committee, which has been neither spectacular nor negligible, is discussed in a subsequent chapter. We cannot pretend it makes as good reading as stories of trying to control drugs rings, but there are parallels. It does little good to stamp out bad practices in money management in one place if they just resurface in another; a level playing field across countries is essential to make any lasting impact.

The idea, it is said, is to create a level playing field so that banks compete on broadly similar terms under similar rules of the game. Like the Scarlet Pimpernel, however, that level playing field is proving damned elusive. Differences in cultures, backgrounds, legal systems, accounting codes and taxation are only some of the obstacles. Inevitably, too, central bankers, however well informed, will always be running behind today's markets in techniques, desperately trying to catch up. It is the markets that make the innovations, the overseers can only react.

Birds of a feather

Central bankers like to huddle together. Their camaraderie, we dare to suggest, is cemented by resentment. Even in a country like Germany, where the central bank is almost worshipped by the public, there is no doubt who ranks first in any official delegation; the central bank governor always plays second fiddle to the finance minister. At some international meetings he may not even get a back seat, he may be barred altogether from discussions. This riles, especially when the minister is a politician first and foremost, rated rather low in technical expertise. Especially, too, when he is new to the job and the central bank governor is an old hand, which is often the case, since politicians come and go much more frequently. Central bankers therefore take an almost malicious joy in the exclusiveness of their club.

The solid town of Basle – the Swiss Philadelphia, as some call it – is far away from political clamour. The Bank for International Settlements – the BIS, pronounced 'Biss' – was set up there in 1930 and takes pride in being the world's oldest international financial institution. It was created to deal with national payment problems arising from German reparations after the 1914–18 war and to provide services to the central banks, looking after some of their gold and dollar reserves. But right from the start, its special role was to promote the cooperation of central bankers. There they can huddle to their hearts' content.

One weekend each month, central bankers eagerly converge on the BIS in Basle from all the European capitals and from Washington, Ottawa, Tokyo and New York. The big names nearly always attend – not Alan Greenspan, maybe, but the Fed man closest to the American markets and banks, the boss in New York, is a faithful attender. Basle has some quaint charm; it offers the choice between old-fashioned Swiss hotels and a stereotype Hilton, excellent restaurants and tennis courts for some dignified exercise; but it is hardly a place worth travelling half-way round the world to get to. Something goes on at those weekends that seems vital to these busy people: huddling.

Their gatherings begin with dinner on Sunday evening – or rather dinners, for they separate into cliques. What they discuss over the Cognac and cigars is their affair, they say, and there are few leaks. Long gone are the times when they made headlines as, grey-faced, they juggled with their national finances to support their currencies within the narrow bands of the fixed exchange-rate system of the 1960s. No story of these meetings today can match the well-worn tale of how Leslie O'Brien of the Bank of England was nearly run over by a tramcar as he fled from a pack of excited journalists across the Basle Bahnhofplatz – and how, incidentally, he would have incurred a fine from the orderly Swiss had misfortune actually befallen him crossing the road at an unauthorized place.

But behind the impenetrable BIS we know that much goes on that offers greater rewards and demands greater cooperation, as we hope to persuade our readers in the course of this book, than the headline-grabbing rescues that put Basle on the map. Propping up the pound sterling against speculative attacks in the 1960s was, in retrospect, a useless and costly exercise, even if it was skilfully handled. And the cooperation of those days was forced. Central banks then worked under the harsh discipline of explicit rules and very precise goals; they couldn't help but coordinate.

Today, central banks are internationally involved in much else besides foreign exchange. It is at the BIS that the Basle Committee on Banking Supervision, famous for forcing banks to have adequate capital behind them, and at the time of writing chaired by Tommaso Padoa-Schioppa from the Bank of Italy, beavers away at near-intractable problems. It is there, too, that other groups of experts discuss a wide range of mutual concerns, from traditional issues of monetary policy and currency markets to the technical wizardry of computers and payments systems.

But the most remarkable meetings hosted by the BIS have been those of the European Community's central bankers. Remarkable, because for all the years since it was formed in 1964 until the beginning of 1994, this group met on territory *outside* the Community, tucked well away from the reach of either political masters or Brussels bureaucrats. It was here that the statutes of the European Central Bank were agreed before they were passed to the official negotiators of European economic and monetary union. It was here, too, that the first steps were taken towards a consensus on how a common European monetary policy might work in practice and on what would be involved in creating a common currency. Now, however, with the setting up of the European Monetary Institute in Frankfurt, Basle has lost these meetings. Does the BIS go more global, turn away from Europe, change constitutionally? It is certainly time to take a fresh look at this élitist club. With new leadership from the start of 1994, it falls on ex-Bank of England executive director Andrew Crockett to ensure that history continues to be made in Basle.

Custodians and watchdogs

This book in part tells a historical tale, and examines the lessons to be learnt from it, but it is as much about where the business of central banking is now heading. The next chapter offers our analysis of some of the social and economic forces at work. Our story leads us to believe that powerful monetary institutions are in the making. They will be custodians of money's purchasing power and, whether they like it or not, the lead watchdogs of the world's financial system. They will make mistakes, fall short of our hopes, fail to act as forcefully as they should, but we are enthusiastic about the evolution.

The potential returns are high, but so are the risks. We hope this book will help to increase public awareness of what is at stake. Although central bankers' influence won't go on rising for ever, they constitute a powerful force in democratic society – but one that in our view can be expected to be a force for good only if more open and more accountable. Not just because their performance should be subject to rating, but also because, as the philosopher Jeremy Bentham said some two centuries ago, 'without publicity, no good is permanent'.

Accountability is a matter of individual responsibility. We have said little in this introduction about personalities, though they play a big part in our story. Confidence in a central bank depends almost indecently on the reputation of the few at the top who are allowed public faces. This makes them, to say the least of it, ultra self-conscious. But in Basle, away from the trappings of office and the solemnity of their ornate sanctums, they loosen up. What would an innocent tourist in that Swiss town on the Rhine make of them as they wander between the BIS and their hotels? A woman among them will be a rare sight; if she is from one of the big central banks, she will be American, for the Fed is alone among the key group in having women in high slots, though never at the pinnacle. The men won't be as uniformly dark-suited or display trouser-creases quite as knife-edged as the private bankers they lord it over; a spot of individuality doesn't come amiss in this group and their wallets are so much slimmer than those of their charges that they may not rise to high fashion. They will be likeable-looking fellows. Many, if not most, will be economists by training, but that's hard to detect. Perhaps our bystander could be heard muttering 'Neither fish nor fowl. Neither academics nor bankers.'

Born central bankers they are not. It is rare for a governor to rise through the ranks. The selection system in some countries is rather hit-or-miss. That may change. We have a dream that perhaps some day central banks will be staffed by an international corps, and officials will climb a career ladder by moving from one central bank to another. Sometimes the top job will be filled by a career man, sometimes – as in a national diplomatic corps – by a distinguished outsider.

But that is fanciful for now. Meanwhile, let's hope the talent flows in, and that it can be said, as did the eighteenth-century poet Oliver Goldsmith of the French, that

> They please, are pleased; they give to get esteem
> Till, seeming blessed, they grow to what they seem.

2   The Widening Domain

In January 1994, the Banque de France, which ever since its foundation by Napoleon had been fully subordinate to the government, was made fully independent, its top policymakers forbidden by law to accept instructions from any outside party. At the ceremony to mark the handover of monetary policy to the bank, Governor Jean-Claude Trichet said that the change symbolized the attachment of the French people, who were often thought to be 'flighty' and 'inconstant', to the stability of their currency. All very high-minded. But he also hinted at a more venal motive behind the divestiture. Acknowledging that French interest rates beyond the very short-term were set by international investors, he added that the independence of the central bank would impress these investors:

> Your credibility and stability – if they are perceived as real by investors – give you an immediate advantage in the market. Independence is a plus for this credibility and stability.

Trichet added: 'In a democracy, I believe that an independent institution should both listen and explain itself.'

Investors, markets and the general public – these are the key constituencies of the modern central banker. As Trichet suggests, the central banker now has wider responsibilities than those to the government of the day. He wishes to impress investors by offering them a stable currency and the public by promising that its money and savings will hold their purchasing power. To do this, he cultivates public opinion. Like anybody else in business life today, he has to market his services. With the tacit approval of the politicians, he appeals for support over their heads to the general public and to the markets. But could this evolution give him real political muscle? Where, if anywhere, is his power base? Is he the servant or the master of the markets? Of governments? Of the public? These are the questions we explore in this chapter, before plunging into the detailed story of how central bankers came to their present prominent positions in economic and political life.

Market prices and money

The roots of the central banks' new role are to be found in the shift from centralized to decentralized structures, from large enterprises to small, from planning to markets, not just within each country but worldwide.

Around the world, markets rule. Never before has the doctrine of the free market spread so widely across the globe. Communism is dead. Statism, which prevailed in most developing countries, is dead or dying. New countries born from the debris of the communist system are frantically trying to build the infrastructure of a market economy. Older developing countries – the legacy of empire – are still in many cases building the institutions of capitalism. All are desperate to attract new capital from outside. Even more important for them is to mobilize their domestic savings more effectively.

The collapse of the command economy, where much, if not all, of everyone's daily activity was decided by bureaucrats, was dramatic in the former communist countries. But a comparable change took place in democratic societies. All the leading industrial countries have also come to rely on a 'spontaneous order' (to use the expression of Friedrich von Hayek, the Nobel prize-winning philosopher and economist), where individual actions are coordinated through the market system. Even the modish 1990s word 'empowerment' meant giving people more responsibility to decide for themselves the best course of action – implicitly, in a market setting. During the 1980s, big structures, whether of the state or business life, were decaying. Big business was busy divesting, selling off peripheral business. Many people found new occupations, often as self-employed or in small firms. Instead of going to work for a big company and being told what to do, these people started selling their services or products directly to customers. Millions of people throughout Europe and North America suddenly discovered by direct personal experience what markets were all about.

Decentralized, the activity of each family and each business enterprise is coordinated with that of other families and enterprises through markets, guided by the price mechanism. Money is the common denominator of this coordinating mechanism; as markets have taken over from centralized decision-making at the national level and as small business takes over as the engine of growth and employment, money has become that much more important. Without a good money, markets can scarcely function at all, and certainly not well.

True, governments can still intervene in specific markets, such as those for housing and food, giving or taking away subsidies – though they have to be able to finance the cost of those subsidies. More usefully, they can seek to preserve competition – all markets suffer from rigidities or monopolistic practices that reduce their effectiveness and distort prices. Governments can also take measures to improve the way markets function – they can improve education facilities, for example; or reduce obstacles to labour mobility such as the lack of rental accommodation; or legislate against restrictive practices by unions or professional bodies; or ensure that there are sufficient firms in a sector to produce a competitive environment. But all such measures are aimed at improving or supporting markets, not at superimposing another level of decision-making. Indeed, if the measures are successful in freeing markets, it becomes all the more crucial that the monetary unit in terms of which prices are expressed is trusted and stable.

A non-nuclear threat

The message that prices have become much more important as markets take over from centralized decision-making does not itself imply that the price level has to be absolutely flat. What it does require is an acceptable means of payment, i.e., functioning money. When economies have no central planning mechanism, and the monetary unit collapses, then the standard of living is likely to fall very steeply. There is a return to barter, when each enterprise can sell only in its immediate neighbourhood, or to a small trusted circle. Such breakdowns have been a frequent occurrence in the twentieth century – the most recent cases taking place in the former Yugoslavia and in some of the successor states of the former Soviet Union. Currency collapses have led to precipitous falls in living standards, the disintegration of society and, all too frequently, to civil unrest. Whether the currency breakdown was cause or consequence is a chicken-and-egg question.

But whatever the causal sequence may have been, there can be no adequate money without means of controlling its issue – and in modern conditions, that means in practice a central bank or currency board. By the same token, a badly run central bank, like that in Germany in 1923 or Russia seventy years later, can cause immense damage. This is another reason why central bankers are treated with new respect. Central banking is an invention, like nuclear energy, with huge potential. Its power can be used either constructively or destructively, either to assure a functioning money, or to bring about a total breakdown of society. Indeed, the consequences of the lack of functioning money can even be comparable in some cases to those of a nuclear war – a catastrophic collapse in living standards and famine, as in China in 1947.

Both sides of central banking's Jekyll and Hyde personality have been witnessed during this century. The great inflations of the Roman empire or of sixteenth-century Europe were as nothing to the inflations of this century, produced with the help of central banks. But proper monetary control was equally out of reach; the nineteenth-century gold standard provided long-term price stability, but at the cost of severe fluctuations in prices and ouput. The true goal of central bankers should be to produce the benefits of the gold standard without its costs. If central bankers have such a key job to do, they must be properly trained and selected, and offered the appropriate incentives to perform well when in office. They need to keep their eye on the ball.

The past hundred years have been one long experiment in learning how to control the new power of central banks. As we shall see later in this chapter, the classical eighteenth-century economists warned in the strongest possible terms of the risks of paper money and central banks, and nineteenth-century reformers such as the British Prime Minister Robert Peel, set tight limits to their power to create credit. Under the gold standard, the explosive potential of the new central banks was kept firmly under wraps. But with the end of that era in 1914, the covers came off. Ever since, one country or another has been suffering from either excessive inflation or excessive deflation, caused by bad central banking.

Discipline of the markets

By the 1990s, with inflation in the leading countries at low levels, it seemed as if the leading powers had learnt how to control the worst excesses and easiest temptations offered by the seductive charms of central banking. This was not due to any sudden conversion to virtue and self-restraint but to far-reaching changes in the political and market environment. Until the 1980s, governments generally benefited from inflation, and thus had an incentive to create it by telling their captive central banks to print money. Historically, governments had always financed overspending and reduced the real value of their outstanding debt by inflating; central banks had been used to enable them to overspend more and inflate faster. But as people got wise to this, so it became harder to impose this inflation tax. The financial markets became extremely sensitive to the slightest hint of lax monetary policies. Moreover, as we note later in this chapter, the political clout of sound money lobbies had also increased.

Denied easy option of the the inflation tax, governments still needed money. Despite the rhetoric, the Reagan–Thatcher era did little to reduce the share of government spending in national output, and, with tax revenues failing to keep in step, most countries were piling up debts. But they were having little trouble financing the deficits. The new globalized financial markets, plus the new credibility of monetary policies, were actually creating a worldwide boom in government bond prices and a fall in interest rates – at least until early in 1994, when a tightening of policy by the Fed set off a worldwide fall in bond prices.

In short, the political and financial equations changed simultaneously. There was less political attraction in inflating; and reduced means for doing so. Because of these changes, governments looked to obtain more of their financing needs direct from the markets, and less through the back door in the form of the inflation tax. They started to demand a better performance in terms of price stability from their monetary policymakers. Governments also still wanted their central banks to guard against the danger of financial panics. In other words they wanted general financial stability. But markets exacted a price. Markets wanted deregulation, a level playing field, an assurance that the state stood firmly behind the banking system. And the resourcees that could be mobilized through the markets were far larger than those of the central banks.

In these changed conditions, are governments merely making a virtue of necessity in granting independence to central banks? Trichet's comments imply as much. The markets want a demonstration of a society's commitment to long-term price stability; separating central banks from the government and handing over monetary policy to them provides such a demonstration. However, looked at another way, giving central banks their independence represents merely a change of tactics rather than strategy. To the extent that governments now look to the financial and capital markets for their borrowing needs, the objectives of state policy can be more effectively pursued if central banks appear to be independent.

Where are the limits to these demands by the markets? Is this the end of the welfare state – or even of the nation-state? Much would depend on what happened when governments reached the limit of their ready financing from the markets. Then the real power struggle could come into the open. Already it seems clear that giving monetary policy to central banks means also giving it priority over fiscal policy (tax policy); in a conflict, monetary policy would prevail. And it wasn't just monetary policy that governments had given up, but all instruments for steering the economy. As the quotation from Trichet suggests, France was acknowledging that it could do nothing effective to stimulate the domestic economy, at least by traditional instruments of policy.

In principle, France in 1994 could of course have reduced interest rates, and many economists were urging it to do so. After its ignominious exit from the fixed D-mark link (the so-called 'narrow band' of the exchange rate system) in August 1993, what was the purpose of keeping interest rates high? Just to hold its head up in competition with the D-mark? Yet the French government disregarded such arguments. It feared that a sharp cut in rates would immediately be punished by the markets, with a collapse of the franc, a rise in import prices and a resurgence of inflation. Denmark and other European countries felt the same apprehensions. So they felt compelled to shadow the D-mark, reducing interest rates only in step with declines in German rates, despite the risks of worsening the recession at home.

If governments had thought they could reduce unemployment by cutting interest rates or taxes, they would never have given independence to their central banks with a mandate to pursue the different objective of price stability. Instead, governments conceded defeat. In effect, they admitted that, even if they could reduce unemployment in the short term, the costs in terms of undermining their other objectives (especially price stability) would be too high. Instead, they had to argue that price stability is a precondition of reaching full employment but that, as they were apparently unable to achieve price stability on their own, they would hand over the means of attaining it to a separate agency, the central bank. History probably would see it as a stage in the decline of the nation-state. As for the welfare state, that was on the retreat anyway.

So in the complex power-play between governments, central banks and markets, the last two were coming out on top. Governments, increasingly, were seen as market participants − just another group of borrowers competing with other borrowers and flaunting their wares to attract the all-powerful institutional investors. Indeed, as economic activity was coordinated more by markets within each country, so it was also, by extension, coordinated by markets internationally. The state, increasingly, was simply being bypassed. Governments' authority over the markets steadily diminished. As Richard O'Brien, chief economist at American Express Bank in London, expressed it in a booklet he wrote in 1992:

A truly global market knows no internal boundaries, can be offered throughout the globe and pays scant attention to national aspects. The nation becomes irrelevant, even though it will still exist.

But while nations may have become irrelevant, currencies are still national. The problem is how to ensure proper control over currency issue (now called monetary growth) within each country. The main lesson from this century's experience is that national governments cannot be entrusted to use the power of currency issue wisely. The big development of the past ten years is that many more governments have been forced to acknowledge that. Whether the gambit of giving real control over currency issue back to the central banks – in whose name currencies were always nominally issued – would provide price stability at acceptable cost remains to be seen.

The exchange rate option

There is an alternative means of applying discipline – to move back to a system of fixed exchange rates. The exchange-rate regime has a crucial influence on monetary policy. Indeed, it is the main factor in setting the context within which monetary policy decisions are made and is often considered an integral part of monetary policy. Decisions over the exchange rate have nearly always been kept firmly in the hands of governments (the Bundesbank's control over exchange market intervention is exceptional, and even in Germany decisions over the exchange-rate regime are made by the government). A country with a fixed exchange rate adopts the monetary policy of the country to whose currency it is linked. If that country has a stable policy, others can import it.

The pervasive influence of the exchange-rate regime on central banks is a thread that will run through virtually all the chapters of this book. The pendulum has moved from fixed exchange rates to flexible rates and back about once every generation or so during this century. At times when most countries have fixed rates, as in the gold standard or in the fixed-rate system after the Second World War, only the dominant country can follow an independent monetary policy; the role of the central banks is to cooperate with each other, by extending credit and in other ways, to bolster the fixed-rate regime. In contrast, when flexible exchange rates are the norm, as in the past twenty years, each country has more freedom to run an independent monetary policy, and its central bank obviously has greater potential influence in shaping that policy. Central bankers often prefer to operate within systems of fixed rules – for a start, international cooperation is then easier as everybody knows their rights and obligations; but they have more power under flexible, discretionary regimes (see Chapters 5 and 13).

Fixed exchange rates have been found very useful in helping to bring inflation down quickly in high-inflation countries, because of their effect in disciplining policymakers, and in small, open economies; but larger countries, including larger developing countries, generally prefer more flexible rates. And there is no chance of a return to fixed rates at the worldwide level. Any counter-attack by governments on central banks from this angle seems unlikely to succeed.

When currencies compete

So central banks will enjoy greater autonomy. Will they manage money well? By 1994 some independent observers were already sounding the alarm bells. Few mourn the passing of the all-powerful state. Besides its other faults and inefficiencies, it had proved, in every country, to be inflationary. Even in Germany, the country with the best recent record of price stability, annual inflation of 3.8 per cent between 1972 and 1992 cut the purchasing power of the 1972 D-mark to only 0.47 D-mark twenty years later; in the United States, one 1972 dollar would buy only 30 cents' worth of goods in 1992; and in several countries inflation had rendered the currency totally worthless. But would the regime of independent central banks suffer from the opposite danger – excessive deflation? By 1993–94 in some countries, such as Japan, the growth of the money supply appeared to be inadequate to support a reasonable, non-inflationary, expansion of output – shades of the Great Depression of the 1930s, the depth of which is blamed by monetarists mainly on the failure of the central banks to prevent a disastrous fall in the stock of money.

A regime of independent central banks could develop into a regime of currency competition. Even now, national currencies enter into competition in the world market-place for goods, services and money (or financial assets). Central bankers are naturally proud to have strong currencies, like fathers with healthy infants. The very language of central banking suggests a paternal link between the bank and currency; printing bank notes is called 'monetary emission' and a central bank is a 'bank of issue'. Now that they are free to nurture their offspring, they could overdo it, and measure their health entirely by their success in competing with other currencies – as evidenced for example by their exchange rates.

Friedrich von Hayek, whose writings contain so many of the seminal ideas of the second half of the century, extolled the notion of currency competition. This reflected his profound hostility to the state:

> It is wholly impossible for a central bank subject to political control, or even exposed to serious political pressure, to regulate the quantity of money in a way conducive to a smoothly functioning market order.

But what he advocated was competition among privately owned note-issuing banks, banks that would not have any right to support from public funds. For all their independence, central banks are still very much public-sector institutions, with privileges such as the exclusive right to issue notes in a given country, and indeed in many cases the right to close down commercial banks in certain circumstances. Currency competition among national central banks is therefore very different from the kind of competition von Hayek advocated (if the regime of independent central banks fails, then privatization and 'free banking' may indeed come on to the agenda as discussed in Chapter 21 – but that is a long way off).

Such competition between newly independent central banks could in time be a potential threat to monetary stability, rather than a support for it. As if to counter such fears, Eddie George, Governor of the Bank of England, went out of his way to deny that he was 'an inflation nut'. Other central banks may be nuttier. In any case they face a real dilemma. A central bank that has a poor track record, and is then given independence, has to convince the market that it has kicked its old inflationary habits. This can best be accomplished by squeezing the money supply over a prolonged period. Yet if all newly independent central banks with poor records were to do that, the world would rapidly be squeezed into slump.

The new risk of a downward slide caused by central banks' excessive anti-inflationary zeal could be reduced by cooperation – and fortunately, that is likely to be forthcoming. But again, such cooperation would be between central banks rather than governments. For now governments could enforce their will, even supposing they could agree among themselves on what to do, only by taking away the independence of their central banks – and that would immediately destroy their credibility in the markets. Thus a heavy responsibility will lie on institutions where central banks coordinate their policies, such as the European Monetary Institute and the Bank for International Settlements. But again the ball is in the court of the central banks.

The small business constituency

Whichever way the balance tilts, now that central bankers have in many countries taken over the reins of monetary policy, they face the need to develop public support for their policies. How are they setting about that? What chances do they have of securing such support? In short, how good are they at politics?

Whatever the governments' motives in giving central banks operational autonomy, it soon became clear that, far from removing central banks from the political arena, their newly acquired powers over policy would plunge them into the maelstrom of the political debate. After all, interest rates are in every country a highly sensitive issue, affecting all mortgage holders and other borrowers as well as investors. The people who set interest rates can expect to come under almost continuous sniping fire. More generally, central banks have to show they are fulfilling the mandate that society (not just the government) seems to have given them – to safeguard the currency. This is bound to put them at times in opposition to the wishes of the government of the day. Increasingly, central banks will argue that they have a responsibility to society which is above that to the government (see Chapter 23).

So there is a need 'to listen and explain'. But the message that prices have become much more important now that markets have taken over from planning is not the simplest to get across. For the most part, central bankers think that if they keep repeating that inflation is addictive, that price stability promotes long-term growth in jobs, this will become the accepted wisdom. But as Eddie George has put it, it cannot actually be proved 'any more than one can prove anything else in the field of economics – it is a behavioural science, if it is a science at all'.

One constituency – and a growing one – on which central banks could appeal, especially if they understood it better, is that of smaller businesses. Why? Because they are much more vulnerable to inflation than larger firms. Large companies usually have what economists call 'market power'; being in a monopoly or near-monopoly position, they can pass some or all of an increase in their costs on to the consumer. More important, large firms enjoy much better access to the capital market – by borrowing at fixed rates, they can pass the risk of inflation back on to the lender, and sometimes they can even raise risk (equity) capital, whereas small business owners generally have their own money at risk in their business. So stable prices are especially important to them. Moreover, smaller firms and individual entrepreneurs have more political clout than they used to have, as the role of big firms and trade unions has declined. After all, small firms provided most of the net new jobs created in the 1980s in most industrial countries.

One reason for the power of the Bundesbank in Germany is that the German economy has since the war been more dependent on small and medium-sized businesses than most other economies. The family business is still the bedrock of the German economy. Politicians are aware that the *Mittelstand* will not tolerate inflation; this curbs at source politicians' natural inclination to promise more than they can deliver. Politicians in all industrial countries are realizing that the only hope of reducing unemployment over the remainder of the 1990s is through job-creation by small firms. The bourgeoisie is back in business.

Long-term savers

Pensioners and all those saving for retirement form another natural lobby for sound-money policies. Here also there has been a big change. Until the 1970s, most people counted on the welfare state or their employer to provide their retirement pension; and they expected that to be enough for their needs. Normally, they did not calculate on the erosion of these fixed pensions by inflation. Some had index-linked pensions. However, with the rapid increase of inflationary expectations in the 1970s, people realized that the state or occupational pension might not be enough. With budget finances under strain, people realized they should make their own provision, and soon discovered that to purchase pensions linked to the cost of living through the market was prohibitively expensive. The only way to maintain income in real terms after retirement was for the state to ensure reasonable stability in prices.

As soon as this was realized, a huge new pressure group in favour of sound money was created. First, the electoral influence of older people ('grey power') is growing fast. The number of people aged over 65 as a percentage of those aged 16–65 is forecast to rise from 19 per cent in 1990 to 28 per cent in 2020 and to 37 per cent in 2040 in the twenty-four OECD member countries; the numbers over 65 will soar from 100 million in 1990 to 231 million in 2010. Second, the change affected younger people as well: they would now have to make their own provision since the state was scaling down the provision of pension benefits as quickly as it decently could.

Distrust of politicians

In their campaign to spread the message of price stability, central banks can also count on massive public distrust of politicians and all their works. Politicians dislike owning up to the true cost of their programmes and policies. True, conservative politicians are often opposed to government spending and to deficit financing in rhetoric – but only very rarely in practice. Because of the class basis of their support, left-leaning governments have to promise more, but once in office have often been more responsible fiscally and financially than right-wing governments; witness recent 'socialist' governments in France and Spain. The last thing politicians, as a group, want is for the public to understand the connection between their earlier promises and present inflation. Their motto is '*pas devant les enfants*'.

The cynicism of political approaches has, however, dawned on the general public in the past few years. Now some blunt truths are being revealed. To take just one example, in 1993 Sir Peter Middleton, formerly chief mandarin at the British Treasury, told a parliamentary committee investigating the role of the Bank of England that heretofore the manipulation of the money supply had been regarded as one of the legitimate tools available to the Treasury. 'If all else fails,' he admitted, 'you raise money by inflation. From the Treasury point of view it is simply another form of taxation, and one that you certainly do not have to come to parliament to get approval for.'

Demand for financial security

If small firms and savers are natural lobbies for sound money, they are also natural supporters of those who attempt to keep the financial system free of criminals, smart-alecs , and shysters. These types are attracted to banking like moths to a flame – and always have been. The public demands protection from them, and from any threat to the whole banking system, from whatever quarter.

This increased demand for security is a natural reflection of the accumulation of wealth and the greater stake in financial stability. The 1980s witnessed a massive increase in personal financial assets – by the beginning of the 1990s, for example, it is estimated that the average Japanese household had financial savings worth about $100,000. The average holding of marketable financial assets in Germany was put at DM100,000 per household (about $70,000). The Japanese, Germans and others needed substantial savings, for they were also more aware than their parents of risks.

Where have all the bankers gone?

Yet the banking markets where most people held the bulk of their savings had been changing fast – and, arguably, becoming more unstable. The role of traditional banking structures and operations – deposit-taking and lending – was declining. At the same time, there was an increase in alternative forms of financing – notably through the issues of securities by firms and sovereign governments and parastatal enterprises able to tap these markets. Meanwhile, banks were pushed into higher-margin, higher-risk activities. We return to this subject several times in the chapters that follow.

By the early 1990s, the financial markets facing central banks were very different from those they had been used to since the Second World War. The new markets were slippery, shadowy, hard to define and yet harder to control; full of pitfalls and strange devices. The globalization of services was led by banks, securities markets and other financial services companies. So firms everywhere had access to highly liquid international markets – both depositing money and borrowing (assuming they had sufficient credit), and availing themselves of the new products developed on the basis of 'derivatives' – such as options and futures.

Even though the worst fears of world finance as a Frankenstein's monster devouring its controllers had abated, by the early 1990s two things had become reasonably clear: first, nobody really could say whether these markets had increased the risks of the financial system; and second, the markets had far greater resources than any government or central bank. This discrepancy meant in turn that a return to fixed exchange rates was out of the question (except perhaps in clearly defined regional blocs). Given these market realities, governments were dependent on central banks to tell them both how to safeguard financial stability in the new market environment and how to conduct monetary policy.

Money's mysterious inertia

Although governments in many countries have given up the power to decide interest rates, and have reason to fear the new financial markets (to which they have lost much taxpayers' money in ill-timed interventions), they love fiddling with money. Whenever you see a politician launching some proposal to reform money, you know he has run out of ideas. The latter half of the twentieth century was filled with currency plans. Initially, these were aimed mainly at reforming the international monetary system. They got nowhere. The would-be reformers turned their attention to Europe. We tell the story of central-bank involvement in this later in the book. Here we merely point out that politicians continue to believe finance can be used for direct political purposes – like the building of Europe. Yet it remains very questionable whether this is feasible.

Because money markets are so quick to evolve when left alone, it is very tempting to believe that their evolution can be steered from above, can be made to run in channels decided by governments. Yet just as important as the accelerating speed of change in some areas of finance – as of social life generally – is the agonizingly slow pace of change in others. Blithely, all finance is assumed to be in the fast lane; yet some elements of finance prove to be in the crawler lane – the lane marked 'Slow Vehicles Only'. For instance, it proves much harder than expected to change a people's deep-rooted attachment to its national currency. Even in 'basket case' economies with apparently worthless currencies, like Russia, residents still use their familiar currency.

With successful economies, and economies with good records of price stability, the attachment goes deep. This is certainly true of the attachment of the Japanese people to the yen, the Germans to the D-mark and the Swiss to the Swiss franc. The attachment of countries with middling performance on the inflation front, such as the French and British, has yet to be really tested. But over the very long run the British have had the most stable currency in the world, and it is possible that they will simply refuse to let politicians – or central bankers, come to that – take it away from them. Rather like the popular revolt against the poll tax which so weakened Margaret Thatcher's political position in the 1980s, the public may have deep-rooted habits and attitudes about money that politicians ignore at their peril.

One big problem facing governments planning the European Central Banking System was that they did not really know the extent of their peoples' attachments to their separate currencies, and thus the political costs of switching to a single EC currency. In this area governments were vulnerable to criticism for making grandiose plans to unify Europe's currencies. As evidence of popular resistance to giving up their familiar national currencies grew, governments were taking the blame for misunderstanding popular feelings about their currencies (we return to this subject in Chapter 22).

Related to this inertia was another aspect of international finance where people seemed slow to change – their use of the dollar. Despite two decades of US currency instability, depreciation and payments deficits, the dollar remained the number one world trading, reserve and investment currency. Above all, it remained the currency at the hub of the world's foreign-exchange and derivative markets.

This special combination of inertia in some areas and accelerating pace of change in others presented governments with a perplexing mix of opportunities, threats and constraints. Who did they ask to lead them through the maze? Who else but the central bankers; financial expertise was at a premium.

Academe's swings and roundabouts

Economists have played a leading role in shaping public and political opinion about the function of central banks and what should be their relationship to governments. Traditionally, states had always claimed the right to determine what counts as money in their realms and to vary it at will. Starting in the eighteenth century the silver and then gold standards gradually subjected monarchs, parliaments and citizens to the same rules. Classical economists rationalized the gold standard, which, among other things, reassured the middle classes that their money would not be eroded by inflation and so made the world safe for long-term private savings and investment. The twentieth century witnessed the birth of 'discretionary' monetary policy, and the British economist Maynard Keynes, confronted in the 1930s with mass unemployment, argued that full employment rather than price stability should be the key goal of policy. However, the last twenty years have witnessed a reaction against these Keynesian notions.

Now for a little more detail, as background to the story told in following chapters. Classical eighteenth-century economists, notably David Hume and Adam Smith, were very interested in understanding the role of money in its social context. Both saw state borrowing as a road to serfdom. Hume's diatribes against the national debt, which he called 'the source of degeneracy which may be remarked in free governments', seem remarkably fresh today. Smith believed default to be inevitable: 'When national debts have once been accumulated to a certain degree, there is scarce, I believe, a single instance of their having been fairly and completely paid. The liberation of the public revenue, if it has ever been brought about at all, has always been brought about by a bankruptcy.' Smith added that this default was sometimes open, sometimes disguised, but always real. The usual expedient by which a bankruptcy is disguised, he said, was by raising the denomination of the coin of a given weight in gold, thus allowing debtors to pay off their debts with less gold.

Adam Smith was alive to the political role of central banking. The Bank of England, said Smith, 'acts not only as an ordinary bank, but as a great engine of state'. And his insight carried him unerringly to an appreciation of the true social function of banking. Its real value was to help make capital active and productive: the banking system provides, he said, 'a sort of waggon-way through the air', allowing all the produce of the country to be carried to market. Smith not only shared Hume's distrust of paper money but issued a prophetic warning against bad central banking. Commerce and industry are, he said, 'exposed' to 'accidents' from the 'unskilfulness of the conductors of this paper money'. Smith advocated 'free banking' as a way of guarding against the abuse of power by central banks (See Chapter 21).

Just as the work of these economists and their successors laid the basis for the movement towards free trade, so did it also serve to curtail the power of the state in the monetary realm. One of the most influential in this respect was David Ricardo, whose *Principles of Political Economy* published in 1818 was quite clear about the rationale for the gold standard:

> Experience . . . shows, that neither a State nor a Bank ever have had the unrestricted power of issuing paper money, without abusing that power: in all States, therefore, the issue of paper money ought to be under some check and control; and none seems so proper for that purpose, as that of subjecting the issuers of paper money to the obligation of paying their notes, either in gold coin or in bullion.

Significantly, Ricardo was as anxious to point to the dangers of excessive deflation: 'When I contemplate the evil consequences which might ensue from a sudden and great reduction of the circulation [of money], as well as from a great addition to it, I cannot but deprecate the facility with which the State has armed the Bank with so formidable a prerogative.' Ricardo himself advocated abolishing the Bank of England to ensure the issue of paper money rigidly followed gold standard rules. Instead, Robert Peel in his Bank Charter Act of 1844 merely made sure the Bank of England would follow them, though he anticipated there would have to be suspensions of convertibility as a safety valve (see Chapter 4).

The great revolutionary was of course Maynard Keynes, who as early as 1923 drew people's attention to the fact that a 'managed' monetary system had come into being. 'It exists,' he said, and should therefore be managed properly by the central bank. He was sceptical about the case for a statutory mandate: 'One would not expect that the rules of wise behaviour by a central bank could be conveniently laid down – having regard to the immense complexity of its problems and their varying character in varying circumstances – by Act of Parliaments.' Although many countries had enacted legislation in a bid to limit the discretionary powers of the central bank, he called this a 'very ineffective method of curtailing the powers of a government'. In a conflict, the government would always prevail. Keynes urged that policy should be left to the 'unfettered discretion' of the central bank, as the agent of the state.

As he pointed out, money had usually in the past been a matter of state policy. In his *Treatise on Money*, he stated that for 4,000 years the state has 'claimed the right' to determine what counts as final settlement of debts. He also saw money as barren: 'Money is only important for what it will procure' (for a contrasting view of money, see Chapter 23).

The objective of the central bank's monetary policy should be to promote full employment. Unfortunately, the central bank had no means of reducing real wages directly; this may be possible in communist Russia or fascist Italy but not under capitalist individualism. Some commentators regard the whole apparatus which Keynes erected in his *General Theory* as an elaborate smokescreen for reducing real wages (the classical remedy for unemployment) by reducing the value of money, while pretending to do nothing of the kind. The following quote, which pokes fun at central banks, gives colour to this view:

> Unemployment develops . . . because people want the moon; men cannot be employed when the object of desire (i.e., money) is something which cannot be produced and the demand for which cannot be readily choked off. There is no remedy but to persuade the public that green cheese is practically the same thing and to have a green cheese factory (i.e., a central bank) under public control.

The idea is that the greed for money is so great that nothing else is produced; if money were produced in a factory, then people could be employed. However, as Keynes's biographer Robert Skidelsky points out, the paradox has lost its punch, 'for since the war the monetary authorities have amply proved their ability to make money go as bad as cheese'.

With a few notable exceptions, later twentieth-century economists have not shown much interest in analysing the constitutional, political and social environment of central banks. Interest increased, however, with the collapse of socialism in the late 1980s. In developing countries and formerly communist countries, the role of the central bank was very quickly seen to be crucial to their success. But this actually served to highlight the neglect by Western economists of the role of money and banking in a capitalist system. In their advice to Russia and its former satellites, Western economists did not give enough attention to the institutions needed to make a go of capitalism, or to the examples of countries like China which had chosen the gradual road to modernization to give new institutions time to develop and old ones time to decay.

A transformation of almost equal magnitude was required in the central banks of many developing countries. True, these had functioned more nearly as central banks in the accepted sense of the word since their foundation (mostly in the 1940s to 1960s) but virtually all remained wholly subordinate to the government of the day. Moreover, many had been sorely abused by governments and by sectional interests exploiting the 'public good' of money for their private ends (in some countries, commercial companies bought banks merely to obtain access to deposit insurance provided by the state); as a result the banking systems of many developing countries were bankrupt, as was the state itself. But by the early 1990s, there were signs of a far-reaching change, and the movement to give independence to central banks rippled out from Europe to Asia, Latin America and Africa (the story is told in Chapters 17 and 19).

The situation is changing rapidly. Ten, even five, years ago, anybody who suggested that many European governments would soon hand over a large part of their economic policy decisions to unelected central bankers would have been laughed out of court. Now they are virtually all doing just that. But we expect the escalator to continue to move. The dynamic forces that have pushed central bankers to their positions are still at work, and the direction of the changes to come is clear even if the detail remains obscure.

Strengths and weaknesses

This chapter has sketched out some of the wider influences that have changed the life of the central banker; it has also provided some illustrations of how central bankers are exploring the limits of their domain. It has looked at the scoresheet in the power struggle between their institutions and governments on the one hand, financial markets on the other. Sitting in the middle – and with a powerful voice in the international financial institutions as well – central bankers are exerting growing influence on shaping policies in wider fields outside their specific professional responsibilities as regulators of the money supply and overseers of the financial system.

What are their resources and their weaknesses as a group or 'community'? Among their strengths we would place first their ability to move quickly and discreetly, though this may decline as they assume a more prominent public role. They have long tenures of office (on average five years) and often serve two terms, so they get to know each other well. These relationships, often of long standing, are cemented by frequent meetings both formal and informal – notably in the Bank for International Settlements but in many other gatherings as well.

They have weaknesses. Some are politically naïve. Many are still not skilled in presenting themselves and their institutions to the media. They lack a power base of a traditional sort – which in the past has been based on class differences. They lack a direct mandate from the people or in many cases from parliament. They are identified in the popular mind with high finance and banking interests and can expect to be at most respected, rather than popular, figures.

But, having replaced the planners of East and West, the money they issue is the stuff that enables society to function without centralized planning. Their financial expertise is more in demand than ever before. While their resources are dwarfed by those that can be mustered by the anonymous markets, at least they know their way around these markets. Politicians will continue to look to central bankers to protect them – and the wider society – from financial instability. And academic opinion has swung in their favour.

Central bankers also have the rudiments of a real power base in society's demand for greater financial security, greater stability in the value of money, and in the widespread distrust of politicians. They have placed themselves in a position to play a growing role in wider policy issues, such as the reconstruction of former socialist countries, and the construction of the European Union. To quote Larry Summers, Undersecretary for Economic Policy at the US Treasury and a very bright economist: 'Monetary policy is destiny. The prospect for peace and prosperity for the rest of this century and beyond depends as much on monetary policies as on any other factor.' If he is right, central bankers' responsibilities are awesome indeed.

3 *How it all Began*

On 15 May 1968, nearly 800 people attended a banquet in Stockholm City Hall in the presence of King Gustav and other members of the Swedish royal family. Among the 150 or so foreign guests were distinguished central bankers with their wives, and others high and mighty in financial circles. In the brightly lit, stately scene could be spotted Karl Blessing, Otmar Emminger, Erik Hoffmeyer, Marius Holtrop, Bill Martin, Sir Leslie (later Lord) O'Brien, Louis Rasminsky, Bob Roosa, Pierre-Paul Schweitzer, Erwin Stopper and Jelle Zijlstra, star players in the fast-moving monetary drama of that time. Six months earlier, sterling's fall from grace, its 14 per cent devaluation against the dollar, had sent them all into a tizzy. Just two months earlier, they had been in the thick of yet another crisis as speculators raided the London gold market, that one ending, after deeply divided discussions, in the momentous decision to free the London gold price, which set the stage for President Nixon three years later to kill off gold as a currency once and for all.

Yet they showed no sign of weariness with each other on that May evening in 1968, when they came together to celebrate the 300th anniversary of the founding of the Bank of Sweden, the Sveriges Riksbank. On the contrary, the occasion provided a pageant of the extraordinary solidarity of the central banking species, always obeying its unwritten rules of exuding confidence and of suggesting, rather slyly, that it alone knows the real secrets.

Monkishness, tribalism, how to describe it? When, earlier in the Swedish celebrations, the foreign visitors had been received by the Riksbank's then chief, Per Asbrink, they proffered gifts as if endowing the custodian of a sacred shrine. A grandfather clock, an exquisite antique bronze, a choice piece of Charles I silver (this from Governor O'Brien of the Bank of England), the reception room came to look like a Sotheby's sorting depot. Nothing was too good to bestow on the Methuselah among them.

The Riksbank can certainly claim to be the oldest central bank in the world, beating the Bank of England by a generation. It did not get its present name, however, until 1867, and even by then it had little of the character and few of the functions associated with a modern central bank. Like other early central banks – a name, incidentally, not applied to them at that time – the Riksbank was simply a public bank with a special relationship to the state, in its case, the unusual one of being governed exclusively by the Swedish parliament. It still is today, a distinguishing arrangement (another example is the Bank of Finland) that has considerable bearing on the current debate about central bank autonomy.

You may be surprised to learn that Sweden is the birthplace of central banking. As schoolchildren are taught, banking belongs to the Italians. But the banking houses of Venice and Genoa were little more than money-changers or deposit-takers in the seventeenth century. They came and went quickly too, without developing into proper banks. The first public bank that survived for any length of time was created in response to the needs of the merchants of booming Amsterdam, who had great trouble sorting out debased gold and silver coins (with less than the full bullion content) from the real thing. Standardization there was not. The Dutch parliament in 1606 listed 341 silver and 505 gold coins; and as many as fourteen mints in the Dutch republic were churning out coins.

Early collapses

Help was at hand. Three years later, in 1609, the Bank of Amsterdam was established under the city's guarantee. It took in a merchant's coinage, weighed it, assessed the valid metal and, after an appropriate commission, gave him a credit on its books and stored the metal away. On instruction from the owner of the deposit, the bank could transfer sums to others in settlement of accounts. For a long time it flourished on this simple, risk-free, traders' business. But as it became more ambitious and moved towards the present-day concept of banking, making loans out of the funds on deposit to the account of others, it got into trouble. Lending to the Dutch East India Company in the eighteenth century, especially after heavy losses entailed in the war with England in 1780, proved even more calamitous than lending to Latin American governments was to be for so many banks two centuries later. The Bank of Amsterdam folded in 1819, leaving its Swedish counterpart the longest survivor of any national bank.

In its early days, the stability and prestige of the Bank of Amsterdam fired imaginations in other European trading centres. In 1619, Sweden's Lord High Chancellor, Count Axel Oxenstierna, first proposed the establishment of a bank in his country, but nothing came of his ideas.

Other Swedish proposals followed quickly, but not until 1656 was one accepted. A Royal licence that year gave one Johan Palmstruch the right to establish a 'lending bank' and an 'exchange bank'. Not two separate banks, as might be supposed, but an entitlement to carry out functions roughly akin to those performed by the loan and deposit departments of a modern commercial bank. Through the lending side, the new bank could advance money against collateral in real estate and other tangible assets. The Stockholms Banco, as it was called, though formally a private business, was effectively a state institution; the government appointed the managers under Palmstruch and one half of the bank's net profit went to the Crown, the other half being divided equally between the community of Stockholm and the bank company itself.

Palmstruch came unstuck when the Swedish authorities played a dirty trick and tampered with the famous *platmynt*, the enormously cumbersome copper coins which formed the principal means of payment in the country and which his bank held on deposit in large quantities. In theory, they were worth their weight in copper but then in 1660 a decree was passed which debased the value of newly minted coins. The old *platmynts* became worth more as raw copper than as coin, and there was a stampede to withdraw them from the bank and put them in the melting pot.

Palmstruch was obviously a fellow full of initiative who didn't give up easily. Faced with demand for coins outstripping the stock in his vaults, in 1661 he started issuing *kreditivsedlar*, 'notes of credit'. Non-interest-bearing for fixed sums, they were effectively banknotes in the modern sense, the first in the world. To begin with, the system of notes was a huge success. But, then, following the same old pattern that has persisted through the centuries, Stockholms Banco lent imprudently. In the autumn of 1663, it found itself unable to redeem its notes. When they started to change hands at a big discount, the government stepped in and appointed a commission of inquiry. Taking three years to report, during which time the bank's business was virtually at a standstill, the commission declared that the bank's accounting had been negligent and that there was a substantial cash shortfall. Palmstruch was held responsible for the bank's losses and sentenced to death, though the order was never carried out.

A parliament-owned bank

Despite this bruising introduction to the risks of banking, Sweden did not abandon the idea. It was then at the height of its political and military strength, one of the world's great powers; the Baltic had become virtually a Swedish inland sea, so extensive had been the conquests in neighbouring states. Commitments and tax-raising in foreign currencies in occupied territories, not to mention traders' needs, might have been enough to convince a majority of the Swedish parliament in 1668 to have another go. But what clinched the argument was the need for a vehicle to finance an apparently insatiable appetite for war.

This time the Swedish parliament didn't look for another Palmstruch; it took sole charge of the new bank – the Bank of the Estates of the Realm. But only three of the four 'Estates' represented in parliament – the nobility, the clergy and the burghers – appointed its management and were represented on the parliamentary banking committee that controlled its activities. The fourth, the peasants who made up 80 per cent of the population, would have nothing to do with the bank until very much later, 1800, presumably seeing it as a rip-off for the rich. Suspicion of banking, central or otherwise, clearly has a long pedigree. And it is no coincidence that it surfaces most often today in the American Congress, which, as we shall relate later, while not owning the country's central bank as in Sweden, legally has more power over it than does the executive branch of government. Parliamentarians or congressmen are subjected to persistent, though by no means consistent, lobbying by their constituents over the business of making money out of money, and feelings can run very high.

Back to our pioneering tale, the odd thing about the Bank of the Estates of the Realm was that it had no capital of its own. And the fact that its deposit base was much enlarged by taking over the Crown's holdings was a mixed blessing. From the day the bank opened its doors, the Crown was an active borrower. It wasn't long before demands to finance a war – this one against Denmark – nearly broke the bank, the first of many similar crises that were to mark its history throughout the eighteenth century and beyond. A parliament-owned bank is also prey to political pressures to lend cheaply to favoured industries – agriculture and the ironworks in Sweden's case in those early days.

Like its predecessor, the Estates Bank was divided into two. Paying no interest on its deposits of copper coins, the exchange department was not supposed to lend them out—it was the 'core' or 'narrow' bank, in today's jargon – but actually did to some extent. The lending department advanced money against six-month interest-bearing deposits or tangible assets as collateral – unfortunately, however, operating very clumsily on a stop-go basis since nobody had cottoned on to what seems obvious today, the use of interest rates to balance the supply and demand of money. So the loan business was cut off when deposits were thin and, vice versa, when too much money was around, the deposit window was slammed down.

Nor did the parliamentarians running the Estates Bank make life easy for Swedish traders when they expressly prohibited notes of credit, scared by what had happened in Palmstruch's day. This was over-timid; something more convenient had to be found than bagfuls of heavy *platmynts* for settlements. So resort was made to what paper there was around, such as deposit receipts and payment orders, a much less efficient system than Palmstruch's should have been. However, by 1726 'transfer notes' – deposit receipts – were declared legal tender for tax payments and in 1743 the Estates Bank began to issue notes for fixed denominations of copper money which shortly afterwards became legal tender for all payments.

The first banknotes

With the Estates Bank printing its own banknotes, redeemable in silver coin, there came bouts of inflation that nobody knew how to control. An Act of 1779 required it to try to keep the volume of notes in circulation backed to the extent of 75 per cent by cash reserves, but who would bother about that injunction when it came to war with Russia? The Swedish bank is often credited with being ahead of its time in financial innovation, but it was lucky that public confidence in it was never completely destroyed, although at times it was very badly shaken.

In any case, trail-blazing for central banking soon passed out of the Swedes' hands as their power in the world waned. So we do not need to stay much longer with the Riksbank, the name given to the Estates Bank in 1867. But before leaving it, reflect a moment on how its experience bears on our story. Much of its history relates to getting a national currency system running. It was not until 1855 that a single unit was adopted for the Swedish currency and only at the turn of the last century was the Riksbank given a monopoly of the note issue, private banks having come into being in Sweden in the 1830s with the right to issue their own banknotes. Such slow progress towards uniformity was by no means untypical of the time; indeed, England took even longer. The surprise – or disappointment – is that Sweden did not manage to build on its initiative in introducing banknotes to Europe as early as 1661.

For the rest, the Riksbank evolved, like most early forerunners of central banks, as a commercial bank with the government its biggest customer. True, by the beginning of this century, it was experimenting with credit control, a discount market and a system of interbank clearing. But by then – and in some cases long before – seventeen other commercial nations had set up similar banks, some of which have played a bigger part in our story. And one of them above all.

No great admirer of central bankers – indeed, he once suggested their reputation will be the greater, the less responsibility they assume – the American liberal economist, John Kenneth Galbraith, has nevertheless said of the Bank of England: 'It is, in all respects, to money as St Peter's is to the Faith. And the reputation is deserved, for most of the art as well as much of the mystery associated with the management of money originated there.' There was nothing saintlike about its origins, however. The Bank of England was created even more explicitly than the Riksbank to finance wars, in its case the Nine Years' War with France, which started in 1688.

Over to the Bank of England

The revolution of that year, which would bring William and Mary to the English throne, unleashed a wave of financial creativity. Among a score of schemes for a national bank was one from a young Scot, William Paterson. He had travelled extensively in continental Europe, knew all about the Bank of Amsterdam and probably also about the Bank of Sweden's banknotes launched in 1661. Backed by a powerful group of merchants in the City of London who were afraid that the new Protestant king might capitulate to the French because he could not afford to fight them, Paterson offered to arrange a loan to the government of £1.2 million at 8 per cent interest. In return, the subscribers to the loan were to be incorporated as the Governor and Company of the Bank of England, the first joint stock (i.e., capitalized by public subscription) bank in the country, and the Bank was to be given certain privileges.

The scheme received parliamentary approval, after some strong opposition, and the subscription to the Bank's capital proved highly popular, the money being raised in a mere 11 days. The charter was sealed on 27 July 1694 and the Bank opened for business a few days later with a staff of just seventeen clerks and two doormen – or gatekeepers, as they are known to this day. The Court of Directors responsible for its management was headed by Governor Sir John Houblon, grandson of a French Protestant refugee and a wealthy City merchant who subsequently became Lord Mayor of London – whose portrait appears on the £50 banknotes issued in 1994, the year of the Bank's 300th anniversary.

Paterson was one of the directors for a short time only, before he took off to launch a rival bank, but this time his scheme flopped disastrously.

The Bank's privileges were considerable. It was given a monopoly of joint stock banking, the handling of the government's account, the right to deal in bullion, to discount approved bills of exchange (these IOUs were already a common means of settling international trade payments) and to issue notes. Handsome interest on its government loans was secured against duties on shipping and alcohol, which led to it often being referred to as the Tunnage Bank. With the government's promise to pay behind it, the Bank could issue notes to match the sum lent to the government. Though these notes bore the name of the Bank of England, they were not banknotes as we know them today; they were for variable amounts, the sum involved being hand-written on them by the cashier, and went out as loans to suitable private borrowers. So interest was earned twice over, both from the government and from the private sector. The more the Bank lent the government (it raised additional capital quite quickly), the more notes it would issue and the more profits it would earn. Every pound invested in the Tunnage Bank earned its keep twice over – a wondrous system based on faith that, surprisingly, worked, though not without frequent alarms.

The ease with which money could be raised in the City of London reflected a lack of boltholes for savings and the power of the merchants who acted as bankers. Wealthy individuals had little choice but to entrust them with their money. The merchants then stored their deposits with the London goldsmiths, who, in turn, could be persuaded – usually at a heavy price – to lend on to the government. This was the system the Bank of England was to 'modernize', and much of its longstanding reputation rests on the skills it developed in money management as a commercial bank.

Conflicting interests

Not as a normal commercial bank, though. Throughout the eighteenth century, about four-fifths of the Bank of England's business and profits came from the government connection. In addition to keeping the accounts of most of the government departments, it managed the national debt, which, after a series of military campaigns, had ballooned to £850 million (£22 billion in today's money) by the end of the Napoleonic Wars in 1815. Right from the start, the Bank had to balance the demands of shareholders looking for profits in a private company with a requirement to pay attention to public benefit. And, perhaps almost without realizing it, the Bank also became not only the City of London's protector but champion of its interests as well, a role which it retains today, though in reduced measure after successive British governments worked to make the Bank their creature rather than the City's.

Guardianship was an inborn instinct. As early as 1720, the Bank was readying itself – mistakenly as it so happened – to rescue the South Sea Company, only to find its work cut out to save itself, as panic spread among its own depositors. Though that episode was clouded by the Bank's public–private conflicts of interest, it exposed an awkward question that bothers central bankers even today: when is it their duty, if ever, to rescue companies which deserve to go bust yet in so doing may create a financial panic that could destabilize the whole monetary system? As it looks back today, the Bank likes to boast of its leadership in averting what it saw as just such a threat at the time of the Baring 'crisis' over Argentinian debt in 1890, when it organized a City cooperative bail-out that involved borrowing gold from France and Russia. But the *Economist* magazine commented at the time that a dangerous precedent might have been set if bad management can count on being saved. It is a criticism that has been widely echoed many times subsequently, not least when the Bank stepped in to rescue a subsidiary of a leading gold-bullion dealer, Johnson Matthey Bankers, in 1984. The Bank's judgement was very questionable in that instance. All the experience developed over the two and a half centuries since the South Sea Bubble stood it in no great stead; a snap decision had to be made and it is arguable that its nerve failed.

The Bank, of course, had changed considerably over that long time span. The last century found it at the centre of many political debates over banking in England. For a start there was the question of whether it could protect the nation's gold reserve and at the same time honour a citizen's right to convert its paper money into gold on demand – a right that had to be suspended during the Napoleonic Wars. The 'restriction period' lasted, in fact, from 1797 until 1821 and the public debate that preceded the decision to restore convertibility at the old rate of exchange between notes and gold brought forth differences of opinion that persist even today. As noted in the previous chapter, one voice preaching the merits of convertibility was that of the stockbroker-cum-economist, David Ricardo, whose success in this instance was to draw the sharp comment from Keynes in the 1930s that Ricardo had conquered England 'as completely as the Holy Inquisition in Spain'.

Reshaping the Old Lady

But it was the Victorians who did most to transform the Bank of England. They inherited a banking structure that was horrifyingly unstable. With the Bank of England having virtually scooped the profitable note-issue business in the London area and alone being allowed joint stock status, small, inadequately resourced banks had spawned elsewhere. Confidence in the notes of these country banks was shaky at best and there were persistent runs on them; some 300 are said to have crashed in the first quarter of the century. So Westminster finally decided enough was enough; it cut back the Bank's retail banking powers and moulded it more into a state bank.

Three pieces of nineteenth-century legislation were particularly important. The Country Bankers Act of 1826 broke the Bank's monopoly of joint stock banking by allowing other such banks, with note-issuing power, to set up outside a sixty-five mile radius of London. (The Bank – naughtily, some said – responded by branching throughout the country.) Then an Act of 1833 opened the door to joint stock banks within the sixty-five mile radius, but they were not allowed to issue notes. The Bank Charter Act (Peel's Act), which followed in 1844, did something more thoughtful – it tried to limit the supply of money at source and, at the same time, meet the wishes of those who wanted the Bank's note issue tied to its gold reserve. The Bank could continue its existing issue of £14 million in notes not backed by gold (the fiduciary issue), but notes in excess of that sum had to be fully covered. The Act also ordered the Bank to keep its accounts of the note issue separate from those of its banking operations and to produce a weekly summary of both. (The Bank Return is still published every Thursday.) At the same time, the Act moved to centralize the note issue; whenever a private bank's right of issue lapsed for any reason, that right had to pass to the Bank of England – a gradual elimination that ran its course until 1921, when the Bank of England gained sole control of note circulation in England and Wales.

In shaping the 1844 Act, the British parliament understood that money supply and price inflation are linked, but not what constitutes money; there was no recognition that it included not only cash-in-hand but also bank deposits. All the same, even though the note issue was not yet centralized, the Bank of England began to test ways of regulating the lending of commercial banks. And the Act did ensure price stability in the long term.

In developing techniques in the latter half of the nineteenth century that were to become the pattern for central banks the world over, the

Bank had, of course, enormous advantages at that time. London was unchallenged as a trade financing centre, its money markets were the best and sterling was virtually a world currency. The Bank was not only the government's bank but had become the bankers' bank too; other commercial banks used accounts with it to settle claims between themselves and kept their reserves with it. And it was exercising some control by raising or lowering the discount or Bank rate – the rate at which it supplies funds to the market by discounting bills – to maintain the gold value of sterling. It was also experimenting with the other historic instrument of central bank control, open-market operations: the buying and selling of government securities in the open market. But it operated by rule of thumb, and commercial banks saw little connection between the Bank rate and their own lending rates in the high street, a state of affairs that lasted until after the First World War.

Nevertheless, the Bank of England was well ahead of the pack in groping towards central banking as we know it today. And, unwittingly, the Victorian legislators widened its lead when they opened the gates to other big banks in Britain. Not that this was immediately obvious; on the contrary, they thought they were cutting back the Bank's powers – which, of course, they were on the commercial side. But that is just what made it unique among its kind.

Most of the other countries with central banks before this century, with the notable exception of Japan, were in continental Europe and these banks also combined public responsibilities, especially with regard to the note issue, with commercial interests. Spain claims the third-oldest central bank, but this was not formed until 1782 – nearly a century after the Bank of England – when it was required to provide finance so the country could join in the American War of Independence. However, it was not until 28 January 1856, after an overhaul and a merger with another bank, that it was officially named the Bank of Spain, by royal decree.

So the Bank of France likes to think it is the older, having been created, with that name, in 1800 especially to satisfy Napoleon's wartime financial needs; within three years, it was combining a note-issuing monopoly in Paris (and later elsewhere) with ordinary banking activities. Though a private institution, the governor and his two deputies were state appointees from the start. The Dutch central bank stands out as having been the sole bank of issue from its start in 1814, though only *de facto* until its monopoly was legalized in 1948.

The Italian experience is particularly interesting. At the time of political unification in 1861, the Italian government pursued the idea of unifying the note issue – though there was no consensus in the country that this was particularly desirable. It thought this did not require a new institution, but could be brought about by giving special privileges to the largest of the existing banks of issue. However, this didn't do the trick, so – still with the same aim – the Bank of Italy was formed in 1893 as a public institution, though through the merger of three existing banks. Even then, for various reasons the unification of the currency issue in Italy was postponed until the 1920s.

As many as fifteen continental European countries boasted some kind of central bank by the end of the last century. A mixed bunch in constitution, they mostly had one common trait which the Bank of England lacked: they conducted quite a large part of their country's banking business. Thus they could influence monetary and credit conditions directly, simply by the way they conducted their own business, whereas the Bank of England had to resort to indirect techniques as modern central banks do. It was no matter of chance that the Bank of France hardly moved its discount rate in periods when the Bank of England was repeatedly manipulating its own.

All for gold

Manipulating to what purpose? Bank spokesmen were not very articulate in those days, but there is no doubt they felt its first duty was to maintain the fixed gold price. For that they needed a gold reserve, the defence of which came before its commitment to finance the government or to earn money for its shareholders. First and foremost, it had to provide assurance that claims in pounds sterling were convertible on demand into gold at the fixed price of £3. 17s. 10½d. per standard ounce, set in 1717 by Sir Isaac Newton as Master of the Mint.

The Bank was not just running a domestic gold standard, though that was tricky enough after the 1844 Act set such a tiny fiduciary issue that any run on the bullion reserve could quickly reduce it to the level at which the Bank could no longer provide any more banknotes – indeed, the Act had to be set aside on several occasions. But London had also become a clearing house for foreign settlements, which became more and more centred on it as the century wore on. By the 1870s, Britain's gold standard system had been adopted by all the trading nations that mattered; the bimetallic silver and gold system that most of continental Europe, including Russia, as well as the United States had retained for so long after Britain discarded it in 1774 was no more. The Bank of England was at the centre of an international gold standard world.

It was a deceptively simple system. Participating countries defined their currency in a certain weight of gold and holders could always obtain gold in exchange at a fixed price. So these countries' currencies were fixed to one another through gold payments (or nearly so, allowing a slight margin for transaction costs) and payments across frontiers could be settled in gold. A country in external deficit would have to mend its ways to stop the drain on its gold. Today we would say it must contract its money supply to reflect the loss of gold so that the deflationary impact on its economy would correct its balance of payments. Conversely, a surplus country would expand its money supply. (But temporary deficits could easily be financed through capital movements because of total confidence that exchange rates would remain fixed.)

The Victorians didn't use such language but they knew that Bank rate had to be moved up and down in step with the gold flows. And they soon discovered that while it was prestigious to have a reserve currency that foreigners wanted to hold, there were penalties too. In 1873, the banker-cum-economist-turned-journalist, Walter Bagehot, editor of *The Economist* from 1861 to 1877, wrote in his most famous text, *Lombard Street*, that the periods of internal panic and external demand for bullion commonly occurred together. However, he thought that experience by then had dictated the prescription: raise the rate of interest high enough to stop the foreign drain, which would allay the domestic alarm, and then lend freely from the banking reserves to restore confidence in the money markets. 'But though the rule is clear,' Bagehot warned, 'the greatest delicacy, the finest and best skilled judgement, are needed to deal at once with such great and contrary evils.'

Did Bagehot trust the Bank of England to have that kind of judgement? It would hardly seem so. He worried about Britain's banking reserves being concentrated with the Bank, though he recognized it was too late to do anything about that. He worried, too, about the Bank being run by a board of merchants, named by shareholders, 'who might be called amateurs' and on whose wisdom 'it depends whether England shall be solvent or insolvent'. On the other hand, the French option of having state appointees at the head was not on. 'No English statesman,' he declared, 'would consent to be responsible for the choice of the Governor of the Bank of England.' Why not? Because the opposition in parliament would blame every 'panic' – a word he was fond of – on the misconduct of a man appointed by the ministry. Moreover, such an idea 'would seem to an Englishman of business palpably absurd; he would not consider it, he would not think it worth considering'.

A man of many misgivings, Bagehot also offered prescriptions, none more repeatedly or more consistently than those for crisis medicine. He saw a clear need for the Bank to act as lender of last resort and upbraided it for not admitting a duty in that respect. 'The Bank has never laid down very clear and broad policy on the subject,' he grumbled. He described a 'panic' – he had experienced at least three, in 1847, 1857 and 1866 – as 'a species of neuralgia, and according to the rules of science you must not starve it'. To stop the panic, the Bank must advance 'freely and rigorously' to the public out of the reserve. Then, although he had admitted on another occasion that rigid rules were apt to be dangerous, he proceeded to stipulate two: 'First, that these loans should only be made at a very high rate of interest... Secondly, that at this rate these advances should be made on all good banking securities, and as largely as the public ask for them.'

Poor Bagehot. That particular prescription, involving hiking up interest rates, has come to be blamed, in hindsight, for the poor showing central bankers made of coping with the troubles of the Depression years in the 1920s and 1930s. Flattered though he would have been that his words had carried so much weight fifty years on, he might well have protested that his 'panics' were very different from a prolonged recession in a business cycle – though the 1866 one, caused by the crash of a respected bill broker, Overend's, was certainly not over in a matter of days. But that is a subject for a later chapter. Here we want to emphasize that in Bagehot's day a central bank came to assume most significance because it could be empowered to deal with sudden monetary panics. This function weighed quite heavily in the debate preceding the creation of the three central banks that are the most powerful today, those belonging to the United States, Germany and Japan. All three were set up in response to failings in the national banking systems.

Japan and Germany take different routes

The Bank of Japan emerged in 1882 at the initiation of the Ministry of Finance – and remained very much its creature until recently. As part of the modernization plans of the Meiji government, which replaced the Tokugawa Shogunate feudal regime, a national banking system had been set up in 1872 based on that in the United States at the time. Some 150 banks were given the right to issue their own banknotes, which resulted in a rapid growth in the money supply. The government, already overextended in its development commitments, incurred extra expenditures in putting down an uprising in Kyushu in the late 1870s. Rapid inflation, inconvertibility of banknotes and bank failures led the Ministry of Finance in 1881 to start planning a central bank with the sole right of issuing banknotes, convertible to gold (and with the power to withdraw existing inconvertible national banknotes). The Bank of Japan

Act was passed the following year and the central bank began as a deliberate government creation, in contrast to the Bank of England founded 200 years earlier as a public company. It had a mandate to bring inflation under control and to implement monetary policy, but, even after a reorganization in 1942 under the Bank of Japan Law, it remained first and foremost the financial arm of the government. In Chapter 16, we see how recent changes in financial markets and instruments of monetary policy are pushing the Bank of Japan into a more independent position.

The history of German central banking starts in the 1870s following political unification at the end of the Franco-German War. The German empire, or Reich, inherited a money system that was still closer to one of the Middle Ages than modern times, silver coinage making up about three-quarters of the money in circulation. While the coinage system had been largely – though not entirely – standardized, there were more than 140 different sorts of denominations of paper in use, none of it legal tender. The individual states guarded the rights of their treasuries and banks to produce their own versions as jealously as Margaret Thatcher tried to protect the pound from takeover by a European currency unit.

However, one bank, the Prussian Bank in Berlin, a sort of central bank for the most powerful of the German states, was by far the largest issuer of banknotes in the country. Not surprisingly, then, it was this bank that was transformed into the Reichsbank in 1876, intended to be as strong as the Bank of England. But, unlike the English model, the Reichsbank was subordinated to the government, even though its capital was in private hands. The Reich Chancellor presided over the bank's directorate and the government shared the profits with the shareholders. Though legislation prohibited the government from using the Reichsbank for its own fiscal needs, this proved no protection against war financing.

At the start, the Reichsbank was given the lion's share of note issuance but there were still four other note-issuing banks even by 1906 and it took another three years to squeeze them out of the business and declare the Reichsbank's notes legal tender. On the outbreak of the First World War, gold convertibility was abolished and regulations relaxed; the Reichsbank became virtually an executive branch of the Ministry of Finance (much as in Japan) and printed money with total abandon. Thus started the galloping inflation that made the gold coin of the Kaiserreich almost worthless by the early 1920s.

Germany's monetary affairs were hopelessly mishandled after the First World War. A lunatic overprinting of money by the Weimar Republic in 1923 led to hyperinflation on such a scale that prices quadrupled every month. It was a sobering demonstration of how a central bank can be put to bad use and, worse, that only a country with a central bank can suffer real hyperinflation. That experience led to the Reichsbank being delinked from the government. But by 1937 independence had been lost again; once more the bank's directorate was directly responsible to the Reich Chancellor. And as Hitler's war effort grew so too did the inflationary pressures. The final legal nationalization of the bank came in 1939; the gold cover was withdrawn and the amount of credit granted by the Reichsbank to the state was simply a matter for the Führer to decide with a stroke of his pen.

Hyperinflation induces independence

The postwar monetary mess in Germany was better handled the second time round. In 1948 the Allies set up a two-tier central banking system in West Germany, modelled on the regional structure of America's Federal Reserve. It consisted of legally independent Land central banks, which operated in the individual Länder of the Western-occupied zones, and a joint subsidiary, the Bank deutscher Länder in Frankfurt, which was independent of the federal government and was to achieve full autonomy vis-à-vis the Allies in 1951. It was responsible for the issue of banknotes and given some modern central bank functions, such as determination of the discount rate and − a new feature − the power to require minimum reserves from commercial banks.

Whether or not the plan announced on 20 June 1948 that called for a 10 : 1 conversion of the currency and all debts − replacing ten Reichsmarks with one new Deutschmark − was his work or not (it is open to dispute), West Germany was lucky to have Ludwig Erhard as Minister of Economics (later to become Chancellor) to carry it through with the firmness he did. Aptly described by the American economist, Charles Kindleberger, as 'one of the great feats of social engineering of all time', the monetary reform paved the way for Erhard to implement his free-market ideas, abolish price controls and accept strikes rather than wage increases. The way a devastated country became one of the strongest European economies in less than a decade still seems little short of a miracle.

Nine years on, in 1957, the federal government replaced the occupying powers' legislation by German law, creating a unified central bank, the Bundesbank as we know it today, and turning the Land central banks into offices of the Bundesbank, though they still have some leeway in administration. We have now moved into today's central banking world, which is the concern of later chapters of this book. But as the tale unfolds in them keep in mind just why the Bundesbank obtained its high degree of autonomy.

There was no doubt in German minds after the Second World War that their new central bank must be as independent as possible of political pressures. They had twice experienced the horrors of a world of worthless paper, and twice they had blamed the hyperinflation on a government-dominated central bank. Even as memory dims and the war-shocked become a smaller and smaller proportion of the population, German fears of inflation are still coloured – perhaps, overly coloured – by the consequences of its military history in the first half of this century. Because the Bundesbank – whether one dates it from 1957 or 1948 – is the newest of the big central banks, it is reasonable to suppose that it should be best designed for today's needs. It certainly persuaded its fellow central banks that it should be the model for the proposed new European Central Bank.

But in assessing the Bundesbank's performance, it is important to remember that it has been supported not just by the public's horror of inflation, but also by reasonable fiscal policies, limited budget deficits (until very recently) and a consensus style of government. So could the Bundesbank be just a shade too independent or, some would say, too arrogant? Not that it asserts its dignity in any outward show; its offices are modern, modest and soulless, with none of the trappings or manifestations of solid substance that characterize those of most other big central banks. But, as we shall describe later, there are fewer visible checks on what it does than in the American system, which it resembles in many other ways.

America has two tries

If it seems surprising that the Federal Reserve System dates only from 1913, after over a century of quite vigorous American economic development, we must remember that suspicion of banking of any sort in the United States is deep rooted. The Constitution not only expressly forbade the states to issue paper money but the federal government as well – a ban that was to be treated flexibly from the start, informally abrogated in the 1812 war and set aside completely during the Civil War, when Lincoln's Secretary of the Treasury, Salmon Chase, repeatedly asked Congress to authorize issues of 'greenbacks' (notes printed with green ink). Nevertheless, those clauses in the Constitution encouraged public suspicion of banks in general – and, as it turned out, large ones in particular. They also helped to explain why America had two false starts in central banking.

Among the many recommendations of the innovative Alexander Hamilton, America's first Secretary of the Treasury, was one he put to Congress in December 1790 for a national bank modelled on the Bank of England, for which he had considerable respect. The proposed Bank of the United States was to be a place of deposit for government funds, a source of loans to both government and private concerns through its issue of banknotes, and a dealer in bullion and bills of exchange. Two months later, George Washington signed a twenty-year charter for the bank; it was established in Philadelphia, then the financial and commercial centre of the country, with a capital of $10 million, one-fifth subscribed by the government and four-fifths by individuals, partnerships and corporations. The government, instead of paying in its share, immediately borrowed $2 million from the bank. No matter. Over the years it became an important financial institution with eight branches – and a very sound one, highly liquid with deposits greatly exceeding its banknote issue. It competed as a commercial bank but it also exercised some discipline on other banks by sending their notes back promptly for redemption. Neither activity made it popular and it made few friends in high places. One school of thought had it that the bank was unconstitutional, another that it was controlled by British interests while a third considered it a dangerous monopoly. The bill renewing its charter, which expired in February 1811, was defeated.

War was again to play its part in central banking history. The 1812 American war with Britain drained the exchequer and the ensuing monetary disorder was exacerbated by the multitude of small banks that set up in the postwar boom, whose notes went to discounts going as high as 50 per cent for some. So a second Bank of the United States was chartered in 1816, again in Philadelphia, with a similar division of ownership and functions but this time larger; it had a capital of $35 million – a sum worth $280 million today. Perhaps it was over confident for it did much less well than its predecessor.

Indeed, it was not long before the second Bank of the United States overextended itself, particularly in real estate. In 1818, its Baltimore branch went bust; so loose were the ties, however, that the main bank survived. But this scare resulted in over-retrenchment which created just as much panic. It took the ingenuity of a new head of the bank, Nicholas Biddle – the first name to conjure with in American central banking – to set things straight. He increased the number of branches to twenty-nine and emphasized the commercial side of the bank – short-term commercial loans, discounting of bills of exchange, foreign exchange and so forth. At the same time, under Biddle the bank again exercised discipline on the state banks and was also set to become the most important note-issuing bank in the country (partly through a fiddle, whereby endorsed cheques were used to counter Congress's refusal to allow the bank's branches to issue notes). It therefore became just as unpopular as its predecessor.

Although a bill to recharter the bank was passed by Congress well ahead of time, in July 1832, it was vetoed by President Andrew Jackson, who, ever since learning about the South Sea Bubble, had taken against banks in general and the Bank of the United States in particular. The Senate failed to override the veto. When its charter expired in February 1836, the second Bank of the United States was turned into a state bank, the United States Bank of Pennsylvania. More than likely embittered, Biddle, who remained its head, seems to have thrown caution to the winds. The bank began speculating in stocks and commodities; it failed in February 1841. Private shareholders lost everything, Biddle was arrested and charged with fraud. He was luckier than another bright banker, Palmstruch, had been in Sweden nearly 200 years earlier; the evidence against Biddle was deemed insufficient and he escaped sentence. But the country's experiment with a central bank ended, not to be revived for more than seventy years.

The Fed's gainful birth

Those seventy years contained little to boast about in American monetary history, though the record has its defenders among advocates of free banking. As the country opened up, there was a stampede to set up banks under a wide variety of states laws – some of them very lax – and there was no central bank to test their ability to redeem their notes. Not only did individuals lose their money when banks failed, but so too might the government. An independent Treasury, established from 1847, spread government funds too thinly among the state banks; even if deposits were not actually at risk, there were transfer difficulties that often immobilized them.

But it took the financial demands of the Civil War to stir Congress into action. In 1863, it voted in a system of national banks – so–called not because they operated nationwide but because they were chartered and regulated by the federal government rather than, as up to then, the states. The new banks could issue notes to the extent of 90 per cent of their holdings of federal bonds (deposited with the Treasury) within a combined ceiling of $300 million for the national banknote issue.

Unhappy though the new competition made them, state banks fought back even when Congress, trying to squeeze them out, imposed a 10 per cent tax on their note issue after mid-1866; they began providing credit in the form of deposits (drawable by cheques) rather than notes.

However, by 1870, national banks outnumbered state banks by five to one, and could boast assets seven times as large. Yet the state banks were to mushroom and overtake their new rivals in the following twenty years as bankers chose to escape the stricter supervision of a nationally chartered bank – higher reserves, tougher capital requirements (based on the population of the city in which it was located) and the constraint that no single borrower could obtain credit in excess of 10 per cent of the bank's capital stock. The return to the predominance of state banking coincided with an increased incidence of 'panics' in the United States – they were actually called that – in the latter part of the last century and the early years of the present one. After occurring roughly every twenty years – in 1819, 1837, and 1857 – they became twice as frequent, coming in 1873, 1884, 1893 and again in 1907. It was this last one which proved, some might say, a blessing in disguise. For it tested to the limit the custom that had grown up of large commercial banks – clearing houses – providing central banking functions such as leadership to protect sound banks in a panic.

For a week in October 1907 a team of New York bankers, led by the seventy-year-old Pierpont Morgan, struggled to save the American financial structure. Because of a carelessly drawn-up New York state law, trust companies had near-banking powers without being subject to banking supervision and several of these were in trouble, unable to meet their obligations. As the news spread, there were runs on weaker banks and the panic then threatened to spread to Wall Street securities firms. The syndicate of bankers put together a $40 million rescue package and in the end catastrophe was averted. But, as one historian put it, it was a near-run thing. Six years later, President Woodrow Wilson would create the Federal Reserve System and one of Pierpont Morgan's most assiduous assistants in the 1907 rescue – lent by Bankers Trust Company – would shortly afterwards start making his mark on central banking. His name was Benjamin Strong, and we have more to say about him soon.

When Congress eventually concluded from hearings on the 1907 crisis that a central bank was needed to eliminate the defects in American banking and give it stability, rather paradoxically, or so it might seem, it gave it the task of furnishing an 'elastic' currency. Never properly defined, this attractive-sounding commodity reflected vague concepts of the need for both a managed money supply and an official lender of last resort. They were the principles that Democratic leaders started to formulate in the spring of 1912, confident of the success of their candidate, Woodrow Wilson, in the presidential election later that year. It was not an easy piece of legislation to negotiate, but, on 23 December 1913, Wilson signed the Federal Reserve Act and nearly a year later, on 16 November 1914, the Federal Reserve Banks opened for business.

Banks in the plural, because what had been created was not a single central bank, but twelve, one for each region or district. The Democrats had baulked at the idea of a monolithic central bank, and even though the coordinating body in Washington, the Federal Reserve Board, the first members of which had been sworn in on 10 August 1914, was ostensibly an independent bureau, it included the Secretary of the Treasury and the Comptroller of the Currency as *ex officio* members. All national banks had to belong to the System; membership fees, set at 6 per cent of a bank's capital, formed the capital of the regional Reserve Banks, half of it paid up. Member banks – as they were by then called – had to maintain a specified minimum of reserves against deposits, keeping at least a third at the local Reserve Bank. In return, member banks enjoyed the privilege of borrowing against collateral from their Reserve Bank – rediscounting, as it is called. Backing up the whole system, each Reserve Bank had to keep gold or gold certificates at the Treasury.

To begin with, the Washington Board had nothing like the power or prestige it has today. It could try to persuade a Reserve Bank to move its discount rate up or down, but did not necessarily succeed. It lacked power to alter member-bank reserve requirements. Moreover, while it could make recommendations to Reserve Banks about their open-market operations – the buying and selling of government securities – they were not compelled to accept them. It was not until the Banking Act of 1935 established the Federal Open Market Committee that a national point of view came to bear effectively on credit problems. That same Act also strengthened the Board's standing and removed the Treasury officers from it.

A worldwide corps

Flawed though it was, the arrival of the Federal Reserve was nevertheless a significant milestone in central banking progress. It was important that it was created to serve only commercial banks and government, not individuals and businesses too, so avoiding the conflicts of interest that dogged older central banks. It was also the first attempt to create such a creature for a large diversified country with a range of regional and special interests (a much wider range than in Switzerland, for instance, which also had to accommodate regional demands when setting up its National Bank in 1907). And the Fed came just in time to throw its weight into international efforts to restore monetary confidence after the 1914–18 war and to help deal with German reparations. It was in these postwar years that a cooperative role for central banks was perceived. And it was only then, in fact, that the term 'central bank' came into common use.

4   *Making a Name for Themselves*

In 1834, a French traveller in America is said to have referred to the Bank of the United States as a *banque centrale*. Forty years on, Walter Bagehot used the term – in English – to describe a bank, headquartered in a nation's capital, that had a monopoly of the note issue throughout the country. But until the last seventy years or so, national banks were nearly always referred to individually by their name; or, occasionally, as note-issuing banks, reflecting the role that attracted most attention even up to the early part of this century. There seemed little cause to group them in any other capacity.

To say there was no collective action between those early central banks would not, however, be quite true. There could be mutual support, in a simple way, in times of trouble. Between the French and the British this dates back to 1825, when the Bank of France helped out with a shipment of gold sovereigns to the Bank of England, swapped against silver, to stem a run on gold in London. On another occasion, in 1860, there was a reverse swap when the French were in straits. And in the spectacular 1890 crisis in London, when the City trembled because the highly respected merchant bank, Barings, was sitting on a pile of worthless Argentinian bonds and facing bankruptcy, the Bank of England drew gold from both the Bank of France and the Russian State Bank. But such 'accommodations' – there were others – were little publicized, no doubt because the borrowing national bank felt humiliated. It was far too premature to consider such operations as a way of central banking life, let alone something to boast about.

Moreover, the international gold standard seemed set to run itself with the minimum of hand-holding. In its 'classical' period, in the three decades up to 1914, it worked remarkably well. The rules were clear, the stability of exchange rates was maintained with little conscious effort. Only in hindsight can it be seen how much its success owed to the stability of the key currency, the pound sterling, and the willingness of the City to create credit – lend – on a narrow base of gold reserves. With sterling considered as good as gold, it was used in lieu of it in international transactions, so masking the sensitivity of the system to changes in the world's supply of gold, a feature that made it far from ideal as time went on.

What turned those nascent central banks into a distinctive species of some substance was the hole blown in the world's financial system by the First World War. In the course of it, all the fighting nations fully or partly suspended the gold standard, *de jure* or *de facto*. Austria-Hungary, France, Germany and Russia all came off it completely almost at the outset. And five months after the United States entered the war in April 1917, President Wilson put an embargo on the export of gold from his country, removing it only in June 1919.

The sly British

Britain was the joker in the pack. Formally, it never suspended convertibility at home. Nor did it prohibit gold exports until the war was over. Although private bankers urged suspension at the outset, the Bank of England did not; its governor at the time, Walter (Lord) Cunliffe, strongly supported the Treasury's view, expressed by Maynard Keynes shortly before he joined it as a junior adviser, in this warning: 'The future position of the City of London as a free gold market will be seriously injured if at the first sign of emergency specie payment is suspended.' But the Bank was tongue-in-cheek. It saw to it that every obstacle was put in the way of the man in the street getting gold sovereigns, that patriotism was fully exploited and that London gold dealers would trade abroad only on reciprocal arrangements.

The nations at war needed their gold. But it could purchase only a fraction of their wants. Domestic spending could be financed by printing money, new taxes, fresh government debt – all were used to finance the war. To pay for imports, governments had to turn abroad, selling foreign assets or borrowing from neutrals. As the volume of external debt rose, so did the intricacy of the network of international lending. To some extent, it served to defend the exchange-rate parities, but only by so much.

After going on a roller-coaster, the pound was pegged to the dollar at a rate of $4.76 from early in 1916, just marginally below its parity of $4.86, but only with considerable help from funds raised in New York, principally by bankers J. P. Morgan, acting as an agent of the British Treasury. Then, in the spring of 1919, Britain changed policy and let the exchange rate go. The Bank of England, guardian of a dwindling gold reserve, had bowed to the inevitable.

At the pegged exchange rate, gold shipments from London were extremely profitable and it had become increasingly difficult to stop them. So, at last, on 1 April 1919, an embargo was put on the export of gold coin and bullion from Britain. It was intended to be short-lived. It was to last six years.

'An unprecedented orgy of extravagance'

After the war, Britain and all the European countries assumed that, like the United States, they would go back fully to the gold standard. This seemed never in question – only how to stabilize conditions to make the return possible. Four years of printing money had left the money markets awash and sent prices soaring, despite controls on many items. Removal of those controls added yet another twist to the inflationary spiral and a speculative boom became scary.

By 1920, wholesale prices were five times their prewar level in France and had trebled in Britain. Currencies had tumbled. The French franc, which, like the pound, had been pegged in New York during the war but then let loose, had reeled to little more than a third of its prewar parity against the dollar, and the pound to little more than two-thirds of its. America was scarcely any happier; prices there had doubled and, with the embargo lifted, gold was flowing out. In its annual report for 1920, the seven-year-old Federal Reserve Board declared that the year had been 'characterized by an unprecedented orgy of extravagance, a mania for speculative, overextended business in nearly all lines and in every section of the country, and general demoralization of the agencies of production and distribution'.

It was time to do something. Fresh and eager, the League of Nations offered an umbrella for talks; its International Financial Conference, held in Brussels from 24 September to 8 October 1920, attracted finance ministry officials, central bankers and private bankers from nearly forty countries. In the history books, it rates as a flop; it brought no visible action, no quick remedy. But it has an important place in our story for two reasons. First, by calling for every country to have a central bank, it started the crusade for central banking that the legendary Montagu Norman, who had just taken over at the Bank of England, was to lead throughout the decade and beyond; one of its resolutions was that banks of issue (as they were still called then) should be autonomous, free from political pressure, as Norman was to preach time and time again. Second, the Bank of England's dear money policy won over credit rationing as the weapon to be used against the current excesses, but it was quite strongly attacked by the Dutch central bank. One of central banking's controversial themes had been flagged.

Dear money in those days meant a 7 per cent discount rate, imposed by the Bank of England for just over a year from April 1920 and by leading Federal Reserve Banks in America for nearly as long from June. Alas, the timing was unfortunate; the boom had already cracked when the final hike was given to the rates. With other countries also aiming at deflation by one method or another, boom quickly turned into depression everywhere and world prices collapsed. Chaos again, and time for another conference, with an eye to economic recovery.

Old billed as new

This time it was the Supreme Council of the Allies that did the inviting to the International Economic Conference, held in Genoa in April 1922. Again attendance was good, coming from thirty-nine countries. But no American delegates. Their absence raises a number of intriguing questions. Did the United States simply shy away from being dragged into European political affairs, determined on isolationism? Or did it resent a perceived European cliqueness? Was it sensitive to Europe's reluctance to recognize how much financial power had shifted into America's hands, to admit that there was no turning the clock back? Or did the United States itself not fully appreciate the magnitude of the change?

From today's vantage, it may seem surprising that in those early postwar years continental European countries chose to peg their currencies to the pound, rather than to the dollar and gold, waiting until Britain resumed the gold standard before following it. But America had only just been transformed from a debtor nation to a creditor nation after exporting $11 billion of capital during the war, and Britain, despite losing three-quarters of its foreign assets, was still a creditor of tried status. A dollar world was not yet in European sights. However, blinkered though they were, the Europeans recognized that their gold reserves were so depleted that it would be essential to economize on their use when back on gold – still the undisputed aim. So the Genoa conference voted for the so-called gold exchange standard; there would be gold centres, such as London and New York, but countries other than the major ones would be encouraged to hold gold-based assets denominated in national currencies – claims on the gold centres rather than gold itself – which would serve as reserves.

The concept was billed as new. In fact, it was an extension of the prewar sterling exchange standard. But an important extension, for it brought in other currencies. When the system eventually got going in the mid-1920s, the build-up of foreign-exchange reserves (mainly dollars in addition to sterling) was much more rapid than the Genoa delegates ever envisaged; they trebled in just four years to $2.5 billion by the end of 1928. And governments had been encouraged to let their central banks back their note issue with foreign exchange as well as gold – thus relaxing but not dissolving the link between international reserves and domestic money supplies.

The Genoa conference also called for international cooperation between central bankers in running the new gold system. Specifics were to be decided by them at a follow-up meeting which the Bank of England was asked to convene. That meeting, however, never came about. Continued uncertainties over reparations and war debts, as well as the collapse of the German mark after June 1922, got in the way. But two remarkable central bankers, Montagu Norman at the Bank of England and Benjamin Strong, by then president of the Federal Reserve Bank of New York, spread the gospel from the Brussels and Genoa conferences with great zeal through the 1920s. Of today's central banks, fourteen were founded in the decade following the First World War (six of them in Latin America). Most of the affluent countries had been persuaded. And by the end of that decade, the central bankers' own bank had come about, dedicated to promoting cooperation among them.

Autonomy is elusive

But Norman had little success in getting the doctrine of autonomy for central banks accepted in practice for all time, even though it was enshrined in the resolutions of two international conferences. The chances are that he did his cause no good by childish parades of his attitude. In his official history of the Bank of England of that time, Richard Sayers notes that Norman would refuse all contact with overseas ministers or their officials; 'if some were in the same room when he met central bankers, he would confine his conversation to the latter'. Like Bagehot, he was particularly disdainful of the Bank of France's subservience to politicians, yet his own relationship with the British government was ambivalent. He was always courteous with British ministers and considered it his duty to give them advice, but no more. There was no question in his mind but that Britain's return to the gold standard must be a political decision. Already, seventy years ago, in a much simpler monetary world than today's, the concept of central bank independence was defying clear definition.

As Strong and his colleagues soon found out. Although the Federal Reserve was intended to be insulated from partisan politics, the Secretary of the Treasury and another Treasury officer, the Comptroller of the Currency, sat on the Washington Board in its early days. They could exert considerable influence. It seems they did so in April 1919, when the Board dismissed suggestions by several Reserve Banks that it was time to raise the discount rate – as it undoubtedly was. Because the Treasury wanted to float a victory loan at low cost, no move was made until January 1920 and the final hike to 7 per cent, as we have already noted, not until mid-year. So much blame for the subsequent short, sharp recession in the United States was laid at the Fed's door that a congressional commission investigated. It concluded that the Fed should have acted sooner. (Strong, in testimony, said it would have been desirable to have raised discount rates in the first quarter of 1919.) More important, it stressed that it should answer, not to the Treasury, but to Congress. So began that jealous guarding by the American Congress of its right to take the Federal Reserve to task, a right that today makes considerable demands on the time of the world's top central banker.

Another muddy area in the Federal Reserve's early constitution was the division of powers between the Board and the regional Reserve Banks. In formal dealings with the American central bank, Norman was careful to preserve the niceties and involve the Washington institution, but it was to the New York Federal Reserve Bank that he and other European central bankers looked in practice. Its lead in international affairs might well have come about anyway – Wall Street bankers wanted it to be of 'commanding importance' – but with Benjamin Strong at its head, this was never in doubt. In international financial expertise and experience, he was head and shoulders above anyone else around. Moreover, his appetite for travel and personal contacts almost matched Norman's.

The rapport between the two men developed into a close friendship, which extended even to taking holidays together. Their earlier backgrounds in banking were similar – Norman, too, had had a spell in Wall Street as well as with merchant bankers Brown Shipley in London – and they prided themselves on being practical men. But there were some marked differences. Slightly the younger of the two, though he was to die much earlier, in 1928, Strong was the more intellectual, more ready to explore monetary techniques and their impact on the domestic economy. He was way ahead of Norman in recognizing the power of open-market operations – i.e., the buying and selling of government stock, now a classical central banking tool. He saw how these operations can be used to inject cash into the system or drain cash from it, thus influencing interest rates and, through them, economic activity and prices. It was Strong's efforts, beginning in 1920, to coordinate the open market operations of the twelve Federal Reserve Banks – and, typically, have his own bank execute their orders – that sowed the seeds of today's famous system run by the Federal Open Market Committee.

But Norman, in the immediate postwar years, wanted to turn the clock back, to relegate Treasury bills to their former insignificance before they had been used to finance war, and to confine the Bank's discounting to commercial bills. Of course, it was impossible; British government debt was set to grow and the Bank did develop its open-market operations. But it was still underrating their importance even at the end of the 1920s. And Norman was still saying that Bank rate policy was mainly decided by international considerations.

It was not that Norman lacked curiosity about domestic issues; he seems to have had more than his fair share of inquisitiveness. But he set store by judgement, not rules. Though he could spell out his views in letter-writing, he disliked having to testify in public and made a poor go of it. For a man who revelled in international affairs, in having contacts with bankers throughout the world, he was notoriously secretive inside the Bank, a quality that again seems at odds with Strong's more balanced personality. However, it paid off handsomely for Norman in a way he did not deserve. The Bank's directors decided in 1924 to reinstate the prewar habit of rotating the governorship and planned for Norman to be replaced in 1927 by the newly appointed deputy governor, one Sir Alan Anderson. But, two years on, fed up at being unable to find out what was going on even though he had often to stand in for his boss, Anderson resigned. From then on, the post was Norman's for as long as he wanted it – which turned out to be until 1944, when he had held it for almost a quarter of a century.

Destruction of the mark

Norman's phenomenally long tenure got off to a splendid start. He was the right man at the right time; Europe's desperate financial chaos in the early 1920s, which took the better part of the decade to sort out, was just his meat. The official rescuer was the League of Nations, or more specifically its Financial Committee, but political suspicions slowed its work and, anyway, it needed the help of bankers to provide new foreign money for reconstruction. Norman was only too ready to get the Bank of England involved, though not its own money in any big way – it was, after all, still a private bank with commercial instincts. Apart from a genuine personal commitment to getting the war-ravaged countries back on their feet, Norman was egged on by the hope of seeing that new or renovated central banks were set up on his model, preferably headed by men of his choice.

His scheming was successful. To get the world's bankers even to consider lending to debt-ridden countries like Austria, created out of a vacuum, and Hungary, precariously governed within artificially drawn boundaries, the League of Nations had to arrange for economic programmes to be accepted and monitored. First on its prescription was that an independent bank of issue had to be established, coming even before budget reform. With that agreed, a triumphant Norman then energetically used his personal influence to help these countries raise loans and credits not only in London but also on continental European and American capital markets.

It was all very new, that provision of financial help under international auspices and surveillance. With the difference that it had no cash of its own to lend, the League of Nations can be seen in those initiatives as a forerunner of the International Monetary Fund, which today provides credit to around fifty countries on condition that they stick to an agreed economic reform programme. Techniques are more sophisticated today, but the principle of conditional lending was set in the 1920s.

Speed, however, was not the essence of those early collaborative efforts. Before the rescue was settled of either Austria or Hungary, the first countries on the list, the spotlight had turned on Germany. There is no word which adequately describes the staggering rapidity with which prices were rising in that country in 1922–23. To most people, rapid inflation conjures up a trebling, quadrupling, maybe even a twenty-fold increase of prices in a year, the pace of Latin American inflation in the 1970s and 1980s. All the defeated European countries experienced that degree of inflation and worse in the early 1920s, but in the Weimar Republic it knew no bounds. Prices there went up about seven-fold in the year to July 1922, another 185-fold in the next twelve months and then an unbelievable 850,000-fold between July and November 1923.

View any precise figures with some suspicion, but the order of their magnitude is not in doubt; prices in Germany by November 1923 stood at around 1.5 million times their pre-1914 level. The mark was worthless; it had tumbled to nothing. Any form of financial savings – bonds, mortgages, pensions – had lost all its real value. The German middle class was all but wiped out.

The great German hyperinflation – we have no better term for it – will stay in the history books as a warning that nobody wins if creditors try to extract the last ounce of flesh from their debtors, of which some notice was taken the next time round after the Second World War and, again, in the handling of the Latin American peacetime sovereign debt crisis in the 1980s. The Allies bungled reparations under the Versailles Treaty. The demands made on Germany, set in terms of gold or prewar marks at France's insistence, were impossible to meet. Germany already had a large overhang of wartime debt and a depreciated currency; it was obvious from the start that the payments, or what part of them could be met, would strain the exchange rate further. Keynes said they were undesirable, Norman repeatedly argued for a moratorium, Strong forecast a currency collapse.

To no avail. To avoid unemployment, the German government kept expanding the money supply and fell more and more into default over its foreign debt. The French, aided by the Belgians, made things worse by occupying the Ruhr in January 1923, bent on obtaining overdue reparations in kind, mainly in coal; the miners went on strike, the government felt obliged to pay them, the money-printing presses rolled even faster.

But it was not until the autumn of 1923 that the French caved in and agreed to a reconsideration of the reparations question by a special committee under the chairmanship of Charles Dawes, a Chicago banker who had been ambassador to Britain at one time and later became Vice-President of the United States. Germany took heart – and action. On 20 November that year, the old mark died an inglorious death, and the Rentenmark was born, one new unit being given for a billion old ones. Ingeniously, the Rentenmark was said to be backed by a mortgage on all the land of the Reich. It was a trick, but it worked surprisingly well; the German people accepted it. What really established the new currency was that supply was kept under firm control.

Enter Hitler's magician

Instead of being entrusted to the Reichsbank, well established and of forty-seven years' standing, the currency transition – the 'miracle of the Rentenmark' – was put in the hands of a forty-six-year-old private banker, Hjalmar Schacht. By an odd twist of fate, however, the head of the Reichsbank died just at the same time and Schacht was appointed his successor. So there arrived on the central banking stage another star player. Schacht was to return Germany to importance in the international monetary scene in a remarkably short space of time. He was also destined to become the genius behind Hitler's initial economic success, in the dual role of economics minister and central bank governor.

Intelligent, technically brilliant, self-confident and urbane, Schacht was summed up by Per Jacobsson, the lifelong internationalist, as 'clear-sighted but short-sighted'. That he had principles were demonstrated when he resigned from the Reichsbank in 1930 on the grounds that Germany was giving away too much in reparations. But after he was reinstated in 1933, he played a curiously enigmatic part in Nazi history, flattering Hitler yet not always telling him what he wanted to know. Eventually Schacht was removed from office on 20 January 1939, implicated in the 20 July 1944 plan to assassinate Hitler and ended the war in a camp. At Nuremberg he was acquitted on all charges.

No such foreboding could have troubled Schacht when, nine days after being appointed to the Reichsbank and just before taking up his post, he visited Norman in London on 31 December 1923. Ostensibly, he wanted to ensure that any financial help London could give to stabilize the German economy should be directed to his institution rather than to a proposed new bank to provide trade finance which the separatist Rhinelanders were demanding. In fact, Schacht was to scotch this plan by setting up his own Gold Discount Bank (Goldiskontobank) to finance foreign trade for the country as a whole, backed by gold and foreign exchange – to which the Bank of England advanced £5 million in March 1924. What Schacht was really after from his early visit to London, repeated two months later, was to establish a connection to the Norman–Strong alliance before the time came for Germany to raise the big credits he knew would be essential.

He did not have long to cement relationships. The Dawes Plan was ready by April 1924; in addition to scaling reparations over a five-year period, it called for an external loan for the German government, a recycling of dues to prime the pump of an indebted country on a scale not seen before. Norman thought the Dawes loan (the equivalent of 800 million Reichsmarks) would be difficult to raise. But, impressed by Schacht, he had the Bank of England work like a demon to see it wasn't. Indeed, the loan was an astounding success. Tranches were taken by six European countries and the London issue, nearly a quarter of the total conducted through the Bank of England, was oversubscribed thirteen times, a performance almost matched by J. P. Morgan with the American tranche of nearly half the total. The strings attached to this loan, which apparently encouraged investors, were that the Reichsbank had to be made completely independent of government, accept a General Council half of whose members would be foreigners, and eventually replace the oddball Rentenmark with a new Reichsmark nominally convertible into gold.

Back on gold

The Dawes scheme not only gave Germany relatively stable money but also generated enough international confidence for Britain to decide the time had come to restore the gold standard. Strong helped by having the New York Federal Reserve Bank cut its discount rate three times in the second half of 1924, so that funds flowed to London, although the American economy was already pulling out of a moderate recession – which made it overheat, necessitating a reversal of the policy early in 1925. Announced by Winston Churchill, then Chancellor of the Exchequer, in the course of a budget speech on 28 April 1925 and enacted by parliament on 13 May, the Bank of England was again obliged to sell gold bullion in exchange for notes (but only for large quantities of them, gold coins not being available as before for small quantities) at the prewar value of £4 7s. 5d. per ounce. So the pound sterling was again convertible at the old parity of $4.86. Nearly thirty years later, Professor Galbraith was to write: 'In 1925 began the long series of exchange crises which, like the lions in Trafalgar Square and the streetwalkers in Piccadilly, are now an established part of the British scene.'

As most students of economics know, Keynes dubbed gold a 'barbarous relic'. But he accepted the inevitable and reserved his main criticism of the 1925 decision to his contention that the pound was overvalued – by at least 10 per cent. And so it clearly was. But there is no record that anyone at the Bank of England was saying so.

However, while Norman, backed by Strong, was fixed on looking the dollar in the face, he had enough unease to arrange two lines of credit in New York, one from Strong's bank, the other from a private placement by J. P. Morgan. Though these credits were never drawn on, they suggest that perhaps Norman was glimpsing the potential trouble he was storing up by his continual urging of other central banks to hold sterling balances at the Bank of England. Tiny though these balances were to begin with, already by 1925 some twenty central banks had complied and the sums involved were to multiply rapidly over the rest of the decade. Hot money had found an open-door home.

Others followed Britain on to gold. At the end of 1925, thirty-nine countries had established parities for their currencies with the dollar, some at the old rate, more at a depreciated one. Notably not among their number was France. With heavy war debts owed to its Allies, predominantly the United States, France had run large budget deficits and the Bank of France had been forced to print money. As the franc slithered down, helped on by German and Austrian speculators, the French poured their savings into London and New York, while in Paris one government after another was toppled, sometimes after only a few days.

Then, in the middle of 1924, came one of those near-miracles that swiftly changes a country's fortunes. The veteran politician Raymond Poincaré, earlier overthrown after his Ruhr invasion plan backfired, was re-elected and pledged to save the franc. His right-of-centre coalition government, in which he served as his own finance minister, restored confidence by having the temerity to raise taxes. It helped that there was a new man heading the Bank of France; Emile Moreau may not rank as an outstanding central banker but he was canny. Soon French money that had fled was being repatriated, too much of it for Poincaré's and Moreau's liking; they had watched Britain's overvalued currency leading to depression and unemployment. The Bank of France was empowered to buy gold and foreign exchange to hold down the franc – and did so once Moreau ensured that it was indemnified against any losses incurred in the interventions. The franc was eventually stabilized at the end of 1926 around twenty-five francs to the dollar – 80 per cent devalued from its 1914 rate – though France did not formally return to the gold standard until 1928.

Boom and bust

A much undervalued French franc, a noticeably overvalued British pound, two men in charge who were deeply suspicious of each other: trouble was guaranteed. Moreau resented Norman's assumed leadership of the central banking fraternity, his pro-German sentiment, his closeness to Schacht. Norman could never warm to a man heading a non-autonomous central bank and he particularly disliked French politicians. Then, in May 1927, Moreau threatened to convert his bank's large sterling balances in London into gold unless the Bank of England raised interest rates so as to slow down the return of French private funds, which was driving up the franc. This led to a historic meeting three months later on New York's Long Island between Norman, Strong, Schacht and Moreau's deputy, Charles Rist.

Norman, backed up by Schacht and Rist, sought American help to relieve the persistent strain on Britain's weak reserves. Strong obliged in two ways. He agreed to make gold available to Europe in New York at the London price. And, rather than have Europe raise interest rates, he lowered them in New York, so diverting the French demand for reserves from Britain to the United States. On 5 August the New York Federal Reserve Bank's discount rate fell from 4 per cent to 3.5 per cent.

That action on interest rates is now regarded by many observers as having been largely responsible for the boom and bust culminating in the stock-market crash of October 1929, perhaps even leading to America's subsequent 'Great Depression'. This judgement is probably too harsh. Some distinguished economists, such as Charles Kindleberger, point out that 1927 was a year of recession in America and that Strong's easy money policy was appropriate domestically at the time. Nevertheless, the move came during the final stages of recession and, in a repeat of the 1924–25 episode, was reversed early the following year.

So, at best, that meeting in July 1927 between Strong and the Old World bankers, as the *New York Times* called them, bought time. That time was not used effectively. As Kindleberger has put it, it would be difficult to call the central bank cooperation forthcoming from that meeting 'a brilliant success'. Strong died in 1928; his successor, George Harrison, was able enough but let the power within the Federal Reserve System slip away from New York to Washington. Franco-British squabbles continued. And coming to an end was the reconstruction of Europe, which had provided a heaven-sent platform on which central banks could display solidarity – no fewer than sixteen of them, for instance, combined to offer credits totalling £15 million to support Italy's stabilization plan in 1927 (though these were never used).

Yet, as the 1920s closed, central bank cooperation was to be institutionalized – another consequence of war. As the five-year coverage of the Dawes Plan ran out, another committee under another American, Owen Young, later chairman of General Motors, re-examined the reparations arrangements and, after some acrimonious sessions, the Germans (whose negotiations were led by Schacht) agreed a blueprint to settle their debts over fifty-nine years.

The Young Plan included setting up a new international bank through which reparations could be channelled, but which had the potential to be something much more. Norman saw to it that it was. Planning for the Bank for International Settlements began after the idea was broadly endorsed by the Hague Conference of creditor nations in August 1929. Norman and Schacht lobbied vigorously to scotch a widely held view that it should be an offspring of a political organization like the League of Nations. Unexpectedly, Moreau, too, supported 'absolute independence' from governments. Considering its origins, however, politics could not be ignored; inevitably the initial board of directors was drawn predominantly from the reparations-receiving countries.

The final go-ahead was given at a second Hague Conference in

January 1930. Suitably located in Basle in neutral Switzerland, the BIS was told it should be a bank which above all was to promote cooperation among central banks. So a central bankers' club had been created. Modern central banking could be said to start from 17 May 1930, the day the Bank for International Settlements opened its doors.

The BIS was immediately involved in a big operation, arranging, as part of the new reparations scheme, the Young loan of $300 million, two-thirds of which went to the creditors and one-third to Germany. The loan was not easy to raise in those distressed times, but it was done. Equally quickly, the BIS began to develop a deposit business for central banks. This had the good effect that some of its customers, notably the Bank of England, alarmed at the BIS's inexperience, lent their own experts on both short- and long-term placements during the 1930s.

The goings-on in Basle rate a separate chapter later on. But how ironic it was that a vehicle should have been created for the cooperative approaches initiated by Norman and Strong just when these were to be swept aside by economic mayhem. The BIS, after a glorious start, was crippled; the war-debts agreement broke down in the slump years, the new institution's basic job disappeared. True, it functioned as an intellectual sounding-post and Norman insisted it was the duty of governors to attend the monthly meetings. True, too, that with the arrival as top economist in September 1931 of Per Jacobsson – who had worked in the 1920s on European reconstruction with the Financial Committee of the League of Nations – the annual reports quickly established a reputation as masterly accounts of major economic and financial developments, and problems. But by 1947, the BIS had barely a hundred staff, fewer than at its inauguration. The Americans even wanted to close it down when the International Monetary Fund was created. Marshall aid for Europe saved it; the BIS became the agent for intra-European payments agreements and subsequently for the European Payments Union in the 1950s, a big postwar job. But that comes later. We need now to mark a few events in the dismal 1930s, especially a turning point in monetary history, the 1931 crisis in Europe.

A battle lost ingloriously

Ironically, Wall Street's stock-market crash in 1929 helped Britain's defence of sterling as funds fled New York to London. But then, in May 1931, a run developed on Austria's largest bank, Credit Anstalt – precipitated, ironically again, by the announcement of support by the central bank, the government and the House of Rothschild. Two credits, hastily arranged by the BIS, were quickly exhausted. The pressure then spilled over on to German banks, which, in a panic, scrambled to switch their sterling in London into gold. At the same time, foreign investors wanted out from Germany, and as talks dragged on about a moratorium on the country's war debts, the Reichsbank was drained of foreign currency and gold; in June alone, it lost a third of its reserves.

Looking back more than half a century later, a former head of the Bundesbank, Otmar Emminger, was to reflect:

> During the banking crisis of July 1931, which initiated a whole series of disasters, the governor of the German central bank flew in vain to London and Paris to obtain a helping hand. In June 1976 a small group of central banks put up about $5½ billion of short-term credit for the sinking pound sterling in a blitz operation through European calls over a telephone.

Emminger was not being quite fair in his recollections; central banks, including the Federal Reserve Bank of New York, did extend credit to the besieged Reichsbank in June 1931, but to nothing like the extent sought. The Bank of England contributed a mere £5 million to a total rescue line of about £100 million. The consequences of this failure of central bank cooperation were far-reaching.

But the Old Lady couldn't afford to take on anyone else's worries. A weak position, with Britain's short-term liabilities abroad already exceeding its reserves, had been made worse by the freezing of London's claims on both Vienna and Berlin. Supported by credits from the New York Fed and the Bank of France, and anxious to preserve the gold standard, the Bank of England struggled on through August trying to barricade gold reserves against foreign raiders. Heightening the drama, Ramsay MacDonald was forced to replace his Labour government by a National one on 25 August. The political change, viewed favourably, brought only temporary relief. Britain gave up the struggle to defend sterling and abandoned the gold standard on 21 September 1931. In the previous two months it had lost £200 million in gold and foreign exchanges.

Even at the time, the Bank of England did not escape criticism for its handling of that 1931 crisis – for acting belatedly to raise interest rates, for being inconsistent in its strategy. Some liked to think it would have turned out differently had Norman been around – he was on sick leave from end-July until just after the collapse. But no. The timing might have been different, the eventual outcome not so. An overvalued currency had become vulnerable to recurring poor trade figures and to waning confidence; unemployment in Britain was about 20 per cent and had never been below 8.5 per cent since Churchill had returned to gold.

Wage costs could no longer be reduced in order to make the exchange rate stick – in Britain over the next sixty years, whenever the two conflicted, it was the exchange rate that usually gave way.

It had always been an illusion that the pound could be returned to its former supremacy. The dollar was now the gold exchange standard's major reserve currency and the Federal Reserve faced a conflict. Its new international responsibilities and the threat of gold exports called for a tightening of credit, recession and unemployment begged for stimulus. The Fed dithered, and went on dithering. President Roosevelt solved its dilemma for it. Less than two months after his inauguration, on 19 April 1933, he took the dollar off gold – not because it was under pressure but because he put the domestic interests of his New Deal first. When the gold price had risen suitably, he fixed a new parity on 31 January 1934: $35 an ounce, up from $20.67. The dollar had been devalued by just over 40 per cent and the Roosevelt administration had given itself a windfall paper profit of over $3 billion, the official value of the American gold stock having jumped from $4 billion to $7.4 billion.

Was America back on the gold exchange standard? Not exactly. A new Act gave the President power to change the gold content of the dollar, within limits, at any time. And American citizens could no longer redeem dollars for gold; gold sales were obligatory only for international settlements. The Federal Reserve called it 'our modified gold standard'.

Name it what you will, the new system brought back gold as the primary source of money growth in the United States for several years. Its new price was high enough to attract gold from abroad, which the Treasury monetized by issuing gold certificates to the Federal Reserve and the latter simply let the money supply grow accordingly. With the new deposit insurance restoring the public's confidence in the banks as the place for its money, unprecedented holdings of excess reserves built up in the system. The banks just sat on their cash mountains, either because there were no borrowers around or because they didn't want to lend. A perplexed Fed, worried about inflation being set up even after the Treasury stopped issuing gold certificates in 1936, resorted to levying reserve requirements on banks. But it could hardly be said to have been exercising an active monetary policy; from the summer of 1932 until the end of the decade, it made almost no use of open-market operations or the discount window, its traditional policy tools.

Meanwhile, Roosevelt's dollar devaluation devastated the efforts of countries off the gold standard, like Britain, that were coaxing exports to pull them out of economic misery. It also forced the remaining gold-bloc countries in Europe – France, Italy, Switzerland, Belgium, the

Netherlands and Poland – to abandon their anchor one by one, Poland first, France in 1936 after a fearsome struggle. Almost everyone then had floating currencies and some played the silly, self-defeating game of 'competitive devaluation'. Research by the leading economic historian Barry Eichengreen suggests that hoarding of gold by France and the United States (which in 1931 between them had 60 per cent of the global stock of gold) exerted a severely deflationary effect on the world economy, since other countries reduced their money supplies as they lost gold.

Exchange controls were also brought in during the 1930s where it suited – particularly strongly by Germany. Nationalism did not stop with currencies. Fortress communities were formed behind trade barriers. The imperial preference system, created at the Ottawa Conference in 1932, was but one example. Schacht, wily as ever, devised his own trading weapon for the Reichsmark bloc. Germany bought goods from the likes of the Balkans at prices well above world level but paid for them in heavily overvalued 'blocked' marks which could be spent only on German goods.

Central banks did not cover themselves with glory in the 1930s. Monetary policy was relatively inactive in the key countries, there was no concept of using it collectively to counter the slump. External matters still predominated, particularly as rumours of impending war became insistent. European central banks like the Bank of England, which had only toyed with restrictions on foreign exchange, had to prepare hurriedly for statutory exchange control. During the war itself, their main task, of course, was wartime housekeeping, the financing of the war itself. Across the Atlantic the United States, unlike most of its trading partners, continued to maintain a fixed price for gold – $35 an ounce – although it restricted gold exports.

A brand new rulebook

While it was shaming that it took the blast of war to restore any international monetary arrangements, the Allies' determination to plan ahead and avoid repeating the appalling mistakes made after the First World War must be admired. On the New Dealers' part, it was perhaps strengthened by contriteness that they had scotched the one hope of restoring financial order that might have come from the bizarre World Economic Conference in London back in the summer of 1933, a League of Nations initiative. A tripartite agreement between the United States, Britain and France to stabilize exchange rates between each other, if only temporarily, had been ready to initial when Roosevelt suddenly decided to keep his options open. In a famous telegram to 'the greatest conference of nations' (over sixty attended), he referred to the 'old fetishes of so-called international bankers' and advised delegates not to 'be diverted by the proposal of a purely artificial and temporary experiment affecting the monetary exchange of a few nations only'. The telegram broke up the conference.

Even so, even if consciences were heavy and history had taught its lessons, it was still something of a miracle that an international conference in July 1944 at the Mount Washington Hotel in a small American mountain resort, Bretton Woods in New Hampshire, could lay the foundations, during wartime, for two mould-setting multilateral institutions and a brand new monetary system. It was nearly as broad a conference as the 1933 one had been – forty-four countries attended – but this time an Anglo-American deal had been struck before it began. The miracle was that this was accepted by the others with scarcely any amendments.

Behind that Bretton Woods deal, long negotiations had stretched over two years between two talented men, John Maynard Keynes and Harry Dexter White, Assistant Secretary of the American Treasury. White came out on top; the American plan for what eventually became the IMF and World Bank won over Keynes's vision of a single Clearing Union, a world clearing bank. Britain was negotiating from weakness; it would badly need postwar American aid. But the two men bounced ideas off each other and Keynes got much of what he wanted. Conspicuously absent was any sign that either the Fed or the Bank of England had much influence on the plan; the latter, indeed, had taken a very negative attitude to the whole idea.

Keynes had a less happy time negotiating Britain's postwar loan from the United States. The $3.75 billion finally agreed in December 1945, and ratified by the American Congress in July 1946, committed Britain to full sterling convertibility by July 1947. That string led to one of the country's many humiliating financial experiences; in just over five weeks after introducing it, convertibility had to be repudiated, legally breaching the loan agreement after reserves had been drained of $650 million (over $5 billion in today's money). Convertibility was not to be restored until 1958.

For the most part, however, catastrophes were avoided in Europe's financial rehabilitation after the Second World War. Though it was awash with currency as it had been in 1919, currency reforms were initiated fairly promptly. In West Germany, the Allied military government in 1948 replaced the old Reichsmark with the present currency, the D-mark – at a rate of one new mark for every ten old ones for large amounts. It also set up a new central banking system to bolster confidence, modelled on a federal structure. Reparations were not pressed impossibly as they had been in the 1920s. And, best of all, America's Marshall Plan – named after the then Secretary of State, George Marshall, who proposed the European Recovery Programme in 1947 – provided grants, not credit. As noted earlier in this chapter, it was this generous American support that brought the central bankers' club, the BIS, back to life.

But the sun was rising only fitfully over central banks. The better handling by governments of European reconstruction robbed the banks of the star part they had played in this in the 1920s. True, they had a currency rulebook again after the IMF opened its doors on 1 March 1947, and a more explicit one than the gold or gold-exchange standard had provided. And central bankers at that time – and possibly even today – seemed to think that essential to any cooperative approach. So the Bank of England's Harry Siepmann certainly implied when, long before he had the misfortune to be the executive director on the international side at the time of the 1947 sterling crisis, he commented that by 1932, following Britain's departure from the gold standard, 'the Bank's business relations with other central banks had dwindled to insignificant proportions and practical cooperation, whether directly or through the BIS, was not a reality'.

But if the IMF gave central banks a rulebook, it was also a monument to the ascendancy of governments; it was, and is, their creature. Its birth shattered any dreams the BIS might have had of becoming the sort of international central bank that Keynes had in mind.

Almost everywhere outside North America, governments took wide-ranging powers over their national economies. Central banks were also coming under state ownership, and although this has not proved restrictive (or even necessarily very relevant to their operations) in practice, it was not evident at the time. Before 1936, only five European central banks – those in Sweden, Finland, Russia, Bulgaria and Iceland – were state-owned. During and after the Second World War, nationalization proceeded quickly. Today all except nine of the world's 170 central banks are fully or largely government-owned, the notable exceptions being the Federal Reserve, the Swiss National Bank, the Bank of Italy and the South African Reserve Bank – a group that includes, coincidentally, some of the world's most successful central banks.

So as this chapter ends and our story moves on to the Bretton Woods era, central banks were in lower key than they had been fifteen or twenty years earlier – not that they had much to shout about in the 1930s either – and not, perhaps, much the wiser. Nevertheless, the idea was catching on. Even in the dismal 1930s, six countries set up central banks including, as a result of Norman's crusade, New Zealand, Canada and India. By the middle of this century, fifty-six countries boasted a central bank, a number that was to double in the following twenty years and now has trebled.

5 Reign of the Rulebook

It is understandable, in retrospect, that the Bretton Woods era, at least from the early 1950s to 1971, is sometimes called a golden age. Certainly by comparison with the decades before and after, the label may seem justified. Preceded by the depression of the 1930s, the Second World War and immediate postwar reconstruction, it was followed by the 'climacteric' of the 1970s, with its oil-price shocks and wild currency gyrations, then the recessions of the early 1980s and 1990s. But even viewed in isolation, the period was remarkable for good economic growth, low unemployment and, at least for the greater part of it, relative stability of prices, exchange rates and business conditions. Universal stability is every central banker's idea of paradise. So why was it not a golden age for central banks?

That it wasn't has already been implied in earlier chapters. True, the 1950s and 1960s were not without their attractions for central bankers. 'Our life was relatively simple under the Bretton Woods system of fixed parities,' recalled Jelle Zijlstra in 1981, when he headed the Dutch central bank after having served as his country's minister of finance and then Prime Minister. Nannying the reserve currencies, the dollar and sterling, also gave the leading central bankers public importance (see Chapter 18). But real power they had not. However well they played it, they had only a minor role in the grand scheme of things. The vision some had of a world central bank emerging was never more than that, a dream. Governments ran the show and new international institutions stole some of what might have been the central banks' thunder.

Yet the discipline imposed by rules, which Bretton Woods provided, has a natural appeal to central bankers and many of them like to think it may be possible to return to some sort of rule-based system one day. So it is important to our story to explore how central banks of the leading industrial countries of Europe and North America – the core countries of the Bretton Woods system – functioned during those years, the legacy of their experience and why breakdown eventually became inevitable.

How the system worked

First some history. Bretton Woods is, of course, shorthand for the system, designed by the United States and Britain, that governed international monetary and economic relations in the decades following the First World War. Had the more recent practice been adopted of tagging international monetary agreements with the name of the building in which they were hatched – Smithsonian, Louvre, Plaza – it would have been called the Mount Washington system, after the luxurious summer hotel in New Hampshire that housed the negotiators in July 1944. It would have been an appropriate name for the launch of the postwar phase of super-dominance of the United States and the dollar.

However, it was not perceived as such at the start. Public opinion accepted that the United States had made a genuine effort to construct a system that would be fair to all participants and subject to international control. All member countries pledged themselves to play by an internationally agreed set of rules. It was the first attempt to give the world economy a written constitution, comparable in some ways to the constitutions of nation-states. It said, in effect, that economic freedom is desirable, but that in order to make such freedom socially productive the actions of individual states and other parties have to be constrained by rules to which they commit themselves in advance and which make their behaviour predictable.

These rules were quite strict, and enforced by a new world economic policeman, the International Monetary Fund. Countries had to declare a 'par value' – an exchange rate – of their currency in terms of the American dollar and/or gold, and change it only after consultation with the IMF. Various forms of currency manipulation were banned in what proved to be a successful effort to prevent a return to the competitive devaluations and currency chaos of the 1930s. While countries could keep some controls on movements of capital, they basically undertook gradually to dismantle the wartime systems of exchange and trade controls and to move towards free convertibility of their currencies (first allowing foreigners to buy and sell the national currency against foreign currencies, then gradually extending the freedom to a country's own residents). They also pledged themselves to adhere to the rules of the multilateral trade and payments system. 'Multilateralism' was indeed one of the system's key components; 'bilateral' government-to-government agreements, which in effect always ended up discriminating against third countries, were another disreputable practice of the 1930s that America was determined to banish.

Maynard Keynes hoped that it would increase the ability of countries to follow economic policies for full employment. Given occasional changes in par exchange rates and access to IMF credit, it was believed there would be no conflict between the objective of full employment on the one hand and a fixed exchange rate on the other. As it turned out, there was.

With the need to justify internationally any proposed change in parities, these were increasingly resisted, partly because they came to be seen as 'immoral', partly because they always hurt some sectoral interests, either exporters or importers. Governments were rarely criticized for sticking to their par value, but a change in it was a politically difficult move that not only brought complaints from groups that were injured by it, but invited press and opposition attacks about speculators' gains, international repercussions and so on. For the most part, therefore, a government would respond to an impending payments deficit by tightening fiscal policy or putting up interest rates; and a country with a surplus would ease fiscal policy or lower interest rates. Of the major countries, only France resorted regularly to devaluation as a way of maintaining its export competitiveness and growth.

The United States was also a force behind parity defence. As the major creditor country, it wanted to apply fairly tight discipline on other countries' policies so as to reduce the demand for further international credit, for what was the equivalent of an overdraft from a bank. It also saw its own interests as being closely bound up with the survival of an open international trade and monetary system, and its relative power was so great that it was in a position to insist that others followed the rules. Anyway, they were willing to obey voluntarily because, by the time they had recovered sufficiently from the war to have any say in the matter, they could see that the system was bringing benefits all round. Moreover, the United States had, it seemed, also submitted to discipline by its agreement to convert into gold any dollar balances presented to it by overseas central banks at the fixed price of $35 an ounce. The United States was the only country to accept such a gold convertibility obligation and the only one in a position to do so, having ended the war owning about two-thirds of the world's stock of monetary gold.

In these conditions national central banks of countries other than the United States had little influence on policy decisions. Domestic monetary and economic policy came to be dominated by one objective – the maintenance of the fixed exchange rate against the dollar – and exchange-rate policy was, of course, entirely a matter for governments. Central bankers provided technical advice and in many countries also administered exchange controls as agents of the government. They busied themselves intervening in the currency markets to maintain fixed exchange rates. They also kept domestic banking systems under tight control. But policymakers didn't need them.

The subordination of domestic objectives to external ones worked – that is to say, its cost was low – as long as two requirements were met: first, monetary stability in the United States; and, second, widespread government controls on financial markets and international capital movements. Given these, the Bretton Woods system delivered a stable and low inflation rate, its prime benefit.

Those years also witnessed a relatively rapid rate of economic growth, though there are many other explanations for this without bringing in the international monetary system – such as the rapid productivity gains of European countries and Japan as they hastened to catch up with much higher levels of productivity in the United States and the release of labour from agriculture to manufacturing. However, good growth rates also owed much to the multilateral trading system of the GATT (General Agreement on Tariffs and Trade) and that could not have been sustained in the absence of a stable multilateral payments system. Just how much of the period's rising prosperity can be attributed to the Bretton Woods system is a question that will never be fully answered.

There is also room for dispute as to just how long the Bretton Woods system delivered its promise. Some will say until the mid-1960s, since, until then, meeting its objective did not pose insurmountable difficulties for most countries. Money and capital markets (domestic and international) were relatively underdeveloped and could be kept largely under official control. And American policy was broadly consistent with the interests of its major partners. The dollar was nearly as good as gold and performed much the same function as an anchor for price stability as gold had done under the old gold standard.

But a stricter view of Bretton Woods, demanding the best from it, would be that it actually worked only for a few years, in its heyday. For central bankers or other officials involved, the problems of operating within the system were often more apparent than its munificent achievements. And in the last decade of the system many economists had turned against it; a majority had come to believe it could not long survive.

Erosion of exchange controls

There had been no need, however, to turn to learned economic journals to see the writing on the wall. It was apparent to the perceptive between the lines of an official British document that was widely circulated among central banks: the Radcliffe Report. This was the outcome of a Royal Commission set up under Lord Radcliffe after the sterling crisis of 1957 to examine the working of the British banking and monetary system. The report was published in 1959, a year which probably, in retrospect, saw the high point of achievement of the Bretton Woods system; with the advent of full convertibility for most European currencies in that year, the task of postwar reconstruction could be said finally to have been completed. Yet the seeds of the destruction of the monetary system on which that reconstruction was based had already been planted.

The report's formal recommendations supported the maintenance and even extension of direct controls on financial transactions. But its analysis clearly pointed in a very different direction; it showed that financial markets were already pushing at the artificial boundaries and limits imposed on them. In particular, the segmentation into different types of markets, with no overlap, which had facilitated postwar direct controls on lending or investing by banks and other financial institutions, was becoming blurred. Members of the Radcliffe Committee had a heated debate about whether, for example, instalment credit firms took business away from banks or whether banks remained 'unique' because they provided transactions services. The answer was that banks remained unique but certainly lost lending business to the new competitors. The implications for central banks were clear. If continued, as observers were quick to point out, these dynamic market processes would erode the effectiveness of official policies, which were directed mainly at the banks and implemented by them.

There were more specific implications for the Bretton Woods system in the Radcliffe Report. While regarding currency and credit controls as legitimate policy instruments, it also made clear that, even in the 1950s, before the invasion of American banks and the growth of international money markets, these controls could not prevent large-scale cross-border capital flows (called 'hot money' in those days). Countries holding sterling balances in London could draw down these balances to make payments, instead of purchasing foreign exchange by selling their currencies in the markets. Multinational corporations could borrow in Britain and run down their borrowings abroad. Long-term overseas investment by British companies also continued on a considerable scale and there was large and unavoidable scope for traders to alter the timing of current payments – the 'leads and lags'. These could all cause a large drain on the central reserves in London – reserves which in those days also acted as the central reserve for the entire sterling area. Nearly all other European countries also enforced controls on capital flows, and until 1959 on current payments also.

The support provided to Bretton Woods by exchange controls was weakened by social changes as well as by financial innovation. The 1960s saw the rise of a class of internationally mobile people – corporate executives and professionals involved in services such as insurance, ship and air chartering, civil engineering, medicine, law, banking and the new inter-governmental agencies – for whom it was increasingly a matter of choice where they called home. As they joined the ranks of the old rich, the pool of internationally mobile (and tax-avoiding) funds rose, swelled further by capital flight from developing countries. It was this pool that the Euromarkets would tap, from the early 1960s, in addition to the funds of the corporations themselves, and exchange controls couldn't touch it.

Chafing against discipline

The Radcliffe Report had noted the possibility of conflict between Britain's international obligations and policies to secure full employment but took the view that there was enough latitude in the Bretton Woods system, so that only moderate sacrifices of national objectives would be called for. Membership of the International Monetary Fund, it said, gave 'reality' to the nation's duties and aspirations as a member of the international community. Any policy measures taken by Britain must 'not only be reconcilable with the rules of these organizations but should foster the spirit of mutual aid that underlies them all'. The advantages, it lectured, were clear: being part of this international community allowed Britain 'to pursue in active cooperation with them the objectives of economic growth'.

But what was a source of respectability, even pride, in 1959 had become an irritant only a few years later. It was a country in surplus, Germany, that was the first to feel the unwanted side-effects of exchange-rate rigidity when it was faced with an influx of hot money as speculators bet on a revaluation of the D-mark – a revaluation that duly took place in 1961. Faced with a chronic balance of payments deficit, Britain's Labour government ruled out devaluation of sterling when it came to power in 1964 but, after a dour battle that drained the energies of the government, admitted defeat three years later – though the Prime Minister, Harold Wilson, having made the defence of the pound a moral issue, told the people in a television address that the 'pound in your pocket' had not been devalued. He fooled nobody. Devaluation of sterling put the spotlight on the dollar itself – the lynchpin of the system.

America slips anchor

But America was no longer fulfilling its assigned role; it was letting inflation accelerate. President Johnson had tried to keep the long economic boom of the Kennedy years going by expanding monetary creation to finance the Vietnam War, rather than raising taxes. This proved fatal for the Bretton Woods system; the fixed rate to the dollar no longer provided an anchor of stability for other countries' currencies and price levels. Yet it was natural that he should have taken advantage of the new room for manoeuvre being offered borrowers everywhere by the expansion of international money markets and especially the Eurodollar market during the 1960s. He tapped the markets on a large scale to finance the war, and then speculators turned the liquid resources of the enlarged market against the United States, engineering massive speculative attacks on the dollar, which by that time, after several years of relatively rapid inflation, was perceived to be fundamentally weak. President Nixon finally cut the ship adrift by suspending the convertibility of the dollar into gold in August 1971. Unpegged from gold, the dollar fell sharply against other currencies.

Ultimately, the system broke down because it could no longer contain the new forces, opportunities and problems unleashed by the growth of international financial markets and governments' desire for greater policy independence. It had moved a long way from the one conceived in the Mount Washington Hotel. It had changed partly with regard to the degree of flexibility of exchange rates, more so in the freedom of capital movements. The presumption at Bretton Woods was that capital movements could not be freed or left subject only to standards of good behaviour, but it had virtually ignored how the normal flows of capital among nations should be dealt with.

Comments from two distinguished economists in the central banking fraternity before the dust had settled are illustrative of early diagnosis. In September 1972, just one year after the débâcle, Henry Wallich, then professor of economics at Yale before joining the Federal Reserve Board (he had earlier headed the New York Fed's research division), outlined to an international audience in Washington the circumstances that led to dollar inconvertibility. He then went on:

This sequence of events dramatically illustrates a fact well known to economists, but never recognized in our institutional arrangements or avowed principles of national policy: fixed exchange rates, free capital movements, and independent national monetary policies are inconsistent. In certain situations, such as those of 1969–71, one of the three has to give.

Wallich was to return again and again to what he called the 'inconsistent trinity'. But in his shoes a year later (that is to say, giving the annual Per Jacobsson lecture), Otmar Emminger, then deputy governor of the Bundesbank, put a rather different slant on the Bretton Woods collapse, if only in emphasis. It broke down, he said categorically, 'because of its inflationary implications'. He elaborated:

> The former regime did not break down merely because of the unrest in exchange markets. It is remarkable that, in spite of the currency disorders, world trade has continued to expand by leaps and bounds; and in spite of a rush of controls against disequilibrating capital flows, international investment – in particular, direct investment – is flourishing. Nor did the system break down because of a lack of financing facilities – European central banks have no lack of their own currency with which to buy up incoming dollars. It broke down because the limit of tolerance for the inflationary effect of such currency inflows had been reached.

In those few sentences, Emminger had voiced in no uncertain terms Germany's desire for more freedom to insulate itself from the unwanted inflows of 'hot money' that were undermining its monetary policies and threatening the country with inflation. But he also acknowledged that the Bretton Woods epitaph should sing some praise. Trade and investment had flourished, as he said. In general, the great ideals that inspired the American founders of the system, with some help from the British, were achieved – indeed, to an astounding degree. Virtually all countries of Western Europe were persuaded voluntarily to join the club and abide by its rules, and the benefits they reaped convinced them of the virtues of a free trading and open monetary system, with all the implications that those rules have for politics, foreign policy and the whole way of life of a people. Recent research by American economist Michael Bordo and others confirms that the performance of the world economy was better during the Bretton Woods period, and especially during its heyday, than during other international monetary regimes such as the gold standard, the interwar period or the flexible exchange rate period of the 1970s and 1980s. Inflation was low and stable, and economic growth rapid. International capitalism was put on a firm foundation.

Why central bankers ran scared

The new 'regime' (it can hardly be called a system) of floating exchange rates among the major currencies has proved much more durable than anybody thought in 1971 to 1973, when there were frantic efforts to put Humpty Dumpty together again – that is to say, restore the former fixed-rate system (see Chapter 13). Indeed, in 1994, after the collapse of the European semi-fixed system it looks as if this at first scary regime could last longer than the Bretton Woods system had done.

Scary is not too strong a word. Remember that countries had for nearly thirty years given up the freedom to pursue independent monetary policies and relied on membership of a club of like-minded countries committed to open trade and payments policies. What was so frightening about the plunge into the turbulent seas was the uncertainty about whether, once each of the ships became detached from the convoy, they would be able to look after themselves or whether they would succumb to forces which they could not control. Would they float or would they sink?

Most private bankers were initially opposed to free floating. For one thing, it brought back disagreeable memories of the 1930s. So attempts were made to construct a new fixed-rate system which would provide for greater 'symmetry' among countries, so that the burden of running the system was not placed on America alone, and create a new method of increasing international liquidity – total foreign exchange reserves – in amounts needed to match the growth of world trade. But these efforts failed, as neither the United States nor the European countries were willing to bind themselves to a new system of rules constraining their domestic policies – nor were they ready to hand the job over to the International Monetary Fund.

By the time it was clear the floating system would last, central bankers had got used to it, and the much-feared collapse of the world trading currency systems had not occurred. Then came the massive dislocation from the oil-price increase, though whether the Arab action in quadrupling the price of oil in 1973 was the real cause or merely the trigger is still debated – the oil price had been kept artificially low for many years. There was no alternative but for each country to react to the new situation as best it saw fit.

For central banks, this was a crucial stage in their evolution, for it placed monetary policy at the forefront of national economic policies generally. Under Bretton Woods, countries in effect contracted out their monetary policies to the United States. The Federal Reserve was everybody's central bank, because it was the central bank of the anchor country. With floating exchange rates, each country could formulate its own monetary policy. It could choose to increase the money supply, in the hope of bringing down unemployment and increasing growth, but at the risk of inflation and a lower exchange rate. Or it could keep a tight rein on monetary growth, let its exchange rate rise and hold down inflation even at the risk of higher unemployment. Controversy raged about which was the better approach; in the event, national policies were decided by politics rather than by discussion among economists. But central banks for the first time since the Second World War were in the thick of the battle.

The climacteric

We discuss the events of the 1970s at many other points in this book. In a few words, they were crucial years of transition, years when governments, central bankers, firms and consumers were learning to live with the powerful forces unleashed by the advent of flexible rates. They did not make a good start; while some countries struggled to overcome the inflationary legacy of the fixed-rate period, others reacted to their new freedom by telling their central banks to pump up the money supply. The idea was to promote full employment and growth. The underlying issues were muddled by the impact of the oil price increase; why, it was asked, should consuming countries deflate their economies just because some rich Arab sheikhs wanted to get still richer? Calling in the International Monetary Fund, governments demanded that the oil monies be 'recycled', if necessary with the help of massive new international credits.

Average money supply growth in industrial countries (developing countries are discussed in the next chapter) was between 9 and 12 per cent in every year of the decade except 1974, when it dipped briefly to 7.8 per cent. In some countries such as Britain, Italy, Spain, Ireland and Finland money growth exceeded 20 per cent in one or more years – as measured by growth of 'narrow' money (see Chapter 8). Even in Germany and France, the money supply in some years grew by 14–15 per cent. Prices rose steeply – in Britain consumer prices rose 24 per cent in 1975. In many countries the stock of money and the level of consumer prices doubled within a few years. Even people who had previously denied there was any link between money and prices started having second thoughts.

Central bankers found the ground shifting under their feet. Nearly all of them remained dependent on governments, and few governments understood that they and their economies had entered a new world. With economic growth uneven at best, and governments expanding the welfare state, budget deficits yawned open, and central bankers were told to fill any financing gap that was left after trying to sell government bonds at interest rates fixed by the government. Yet unemployment rose along with inflation. Central bankers were bitterly criticized for letting money grow out of control. But instead of taking responsibility, all too many had resort to specious explanations of inflation – attributing it to pressure from trade unions for higher wages. Many called for more effective control over wages so as to allow growth to continue with low inflation. But that world, if it ever existed, had gone. Central bankers were called on to attend to their responsibility for something they could influence – money – rather than things that were beyond their competence. The accompanying changes in economic doctrine are discussed in Chapter 8.

The sea change that took place in the 1970s is illustrated by the very different response to the second oil crisis in 1979–80. During the first oil shock, in 1972–73, some countries had adjusted to the changed real price of oil while others tried to borrow their way out of the problem. By the second oil shock, it was agreed that countries which had adjusted had performed better, while countries that had borrowed (like Britain) had merely saddled themselves with unsustainable levels of debt. As a report by the Group of Thirty think-tank, signed by one of the authors, commented at the time, 'the policy response to the second oil shock was shaped by the main lesson drawn from the first oil shock, namely that countries which acted in practice promptly to effect their adjustment also adjusted more successfully than others'. Monetary policy had become the only game in town. It was the start of a new era.

6   Currency Boards and their Legacy

Thirty, even twenty years ago, we might have approached a discussion of central banking in the third world with less than enthusiasm. After all, it has never been in the vanguard of the profession's progress. Ever since colonial days, the monetary systems of developing countries have been largely determined by the influence of the centre powers, notably Britain, France and the United States; even after they cut loose and went their own ways, these countries (or most of them) were still ready to take advice about their central banks from the leading industrial nations. So why has their evolution, and where they are heading, now become a fascinating element in our story?

It is not just because these central banks are now so thick on the ground, although the growth is remarkable – over sixty added to their number since 1970 alone. More important is the shift in wealth creation in the world. 'My power is as great as the power of money.' Those were the words of Karl Marx, but they might have been said by any central banker. The countries that are now getting richer fastest are in Asia, Latin America, Southern Europe and Central Europe. It is among the newly industrialized and reforming countries in those regions, not in the advanced world, that foreign-exchange reserves are piling up. That extra wealth brings scores of investment bankers to the doors of the central banks in these countries, bowing and scraping in hope of a part in managing it. Inevitably as they gain confidence, these central banks will be propelled into a bigger role in the international fraternity. Maybe in time the pupils will be showing teacher a thing or two.

More curious things can happen. It has been suggested that in its pre-natal state central banking in the third world has lessons for today. In 1992 some advisers were advocating that East European countries, and in particular the successor states of the former Soviet Union, which urgently needed a stable monetary unit but lacked the money markets to make a go of open-market operations, should base their monetary systems on currency boards – as the colonizing powers did in dependent territories in the first instance. We feel there is considerable merit in this proposal – at least for some countries in special circumstances. Certainly it made topical a subject that had long been buried and whose resurrection cannot be dismissed out of hand.

The essential feature of currency boards was that they kept control of the value of the local currency unit by rigidly fixing its value to the 'mother currency'. In the case of a British currency board – most boards, though not all, were in the British empire – it issued local currency (notes and coins) only in exchange for sterling, at a rate of exchange fixed by legislation. It was legally obliged to make such an exchange on demand, and, in reverse, to supply sterling on demand in exchange for local currency. Investing its reserves in British bonds or bills, it held at least 100 per cent cover in assets denominated in sterling for all the local currency issued. There was no exchange risk, no exchange control; no discretion for the currency board manned by a small number of commissioners appointed by the British government, to follow an independent monetary policy; no control over the note issue.

As deposit banking gradually developed at branches of British overseas banks in the colonial territories, bank deposits came to form a growing part of the money supply, but in most cases this was small and thus the note issue determined the price level. The amount (face value) of local notes issued, being determined by the amount of sterling presented or demanded, was a function largely of the trade balance; importers demanded sterling to pay for imports while exporters exchanged sterling receipts for local currency to pay for wages and other local costs. Notes remained in circulation until demand for sterling by importers and others absorbed them.

A trade surplus naturally led to an increase in the volume of local money in circulation and thus a rise in prices, and a trade deficit to a fall in the local money supply and prices. This rigid link automatically kept the prices of goods and services that were traded internationally by the colony at the British level of prices for them. (If the local price increased above the British price, traders would import goods and make an excess profit until the additional supply brought prices into line.) Currency boards were quite profitable institutions; interest on the reserves they invested in British securities exceeded the relatively small costs of administering the board and paying for the printing of notes and minting of coins. Needless to say, profits went to the British government.

In practice, only commercial banks operating in the territory – mainly the branches of British overseas banks – dealt directly with the currency board. Individuals, traders and the colonial government normally had accounts with local banks, and banks were legally obliged to redeem deposits on demand in local legal tender. They therefore needed assets that could easily be converted into local currency; these were held in the form of marketable securities in London. Anna Schwartz (the American economist best known for the monetary history of the United States she co-authored with Milton Friedman some thirty years ago) describes the process:

> A colonial bank that wanted additional currency transferred funds from its own London accounts to the board's headquarters in London or to the Crown Agents – the link between the colonial governments and the London money market – for the account of the board. As soon as the London payment was confirmed, local agents of the board supplied the currency to the bank.

Although a few currency boards were established in the second half of the nineteenth century, most were set up between 1912 and 1945, modelled on the West African Currency Board, formed in 1912 to serve the four territories of Gambia, Gold Coast, Nigeria and Sierra Leone. They nearly all folded up in the 1960s when the vast majority of former colonial territories gained their political independence. (The most notable survivor, though in a modified form, is in Hong Kong.) Economists of a monetarist persuasion believe the currency boards worked well during the hundred years or so in which they operated. In her paper *Do Currency Boards Have a Future?* Schwartz concluded:

> The boards limited monetary growth. Home-grown inflation was not a problem. A local lender of last resort was not needed. The head office of an expatriate bank had resources to support a troubled local branch. Effects on confidence of a local indigenous bank failure were contained by the cooperative actions of the bank community. The bank community acted in this way because indigenous banks were only a small part of the banking system. Currency boards did not extend loans to governments, banks or non-financial firms. If colonial governments borrowed, they did so in London where they were held to international standards of creditworthiness.

In other words, on this view they worked to the advantage of the local economy as well as serving the interests of the colonial power. Nevertheless, the first thing every colony did on achieving independence was to abolish the currency board. A central bank was as proud a symbol of its independence as a state airline. Yet all too often, the airline made a loss and the central bank had to finance it – and much else besides.

Independent countries, dependent banks

As currency boards were abandoned one by one, the orthodoxy that an independent country had to have its own central bank was little challenged. By 1965 the East African Currency Union was the last politically independent area in the world not to have one, and the break up of the union in 1966 led to the introduction of new currency systems in Kenya, Uganda and Tanzania, each with its own central bank. Earlier, Nigeria had established a central bank under colonial rule, Ghana did so at the same time as independence, while the dissolution of the Rhodesian Federation in 1963 resulted in the separate monetary systems of Rhodesia (later Zimbabwe), Zambia and Malawi, each with its own central bank. These are just a few instances of the transformation.

The dependent central banks created by newly independent countries existed to serve the interests of the state, as defined by local politicians and dictators. Unfortunately, in almost all such countries, they were to become efficient engines of inflationary finance, holding back rather than accelerating their countries' economic development. The worst cases occurred in Africa, but few countries elsewhere escaped the trap.

These effects were longer-term, and unexpected. The central banks which were to cause so much damage were in nearly all cases established with the active assistance from central banks of developed countries or from the international agencies set up after the Second World War, notably the IMF. The thinking in all these institutions was strongly influenced by the dominant trends in intellectual fashions. The advice offered by Western economists was well meaning but breathtakingly naïve. They assumed, for a start, that all these countries would remain faithful pupils of Westminster democracy – when a few transitional difficulties inherited from the bad old colonial system had been surmounted.

Like Polonius, they were full of wise old saws, offered to the new central banks and governments which, they fondly believed, would work harmoniously to produce economic growth, more developed banking systems and welfare provisions for the citizens. They had simply no idea of the horrors that were to come, especially in Africa but also in parts of Latin America and Asia: the systematic debasement of the currency, the incapacity of many countries to provide stable legal systems, or provide law and order, or prevent a regression to more primitive forms of social and economic behaviour. Lacking constitutional constraints, monetary expansion came to depend almost entirely on the whim of political rulers, except in countries such as those of East Asia where an entrenched bureaucracy was partially insulated from political pressure. The power of corruption was also enhanced by the availability of central bank credit. Out of control, average inflation rose steadily decade by decade to hyperinflation in some countries.

Latin American style

Hyperinflation is most often associated historically with Latin America. Chronologically, we should have said more about this region earlier in the chapter, since it boasts the first fully fledged central banks in developing countries, apart from the Bank of Indonesia, set up in 1828. But the monetary history of Latin America is very much its own; although it cast off colonial dependence so much earlier, it seemed to offer few monetary lessons to those colonies that did so only this century. It never experimented with currency boards, it had a lingering flirtation with gold and what cues it took from the industrialized world came mainly from its northern neighbour. Just a decade after the Federal Reserve had been formed, Latin America – at least some countries there – decided that what was needed to achieve currency stability and strengthen the banking industry was the creation of central banks.

During the 1920s central banks were set up in Colombia, Peru, Chile, Mexico, Ecuador and Bolivia. In the 1930s it was the turn of El Salvador and Argentina; in 1940, Venezuela. The smaller Central American countries followed in the 1940s and 1950s. Brazil waited until 1965. A little history explains why the establishment of these central banks bunched so heavily in the period between the two world wars, a century or more after most of the countries achieved independence from Spain.

The typical characteristics of the financial history of the region were established very early. Although the caricatures painted by North Europeans and Americans of the indolence of the Spaniards should be discounted, it can hardly be argued that the colonial societies of Spanish America were well suited to achieve autonomous economic progress. As David Joslin, a leading historian, puts it:

> They still bore the heavy imprint of the conquering aristocracy of the sixteenth century. A renaissance love of splendour had endowed the imperial cities with fine town houses and elegant palaces, and their cathedrals and monasteries proclaimed the power and wealth of the Church. Among the richer landowners a love of luxury too often dissipated in unproductive display the limited surpluses of wealth produced by poor communities.

Already by the 1830s, every country of the region had borrowed heavily abroad and defaulted on its loans. Yet trade with North America and Europe flourished despite repeated financial crises and widely fluctuating exchange rates. And some banks were granted note-issuing rights. Paper currency, which was not convertible into gold or silver, was in general use, with silver as its basis until about the middle of the nineteenth century. Then, in the latter half of the century some countries linked their currency to gold, following the trend in Europe. Argentina's attempt to do so in 1883 lasted only eighteen months. Uruguay was much more stable. Chile spent only three years on the gold standard (1895–98), and thereafter reverted to paper. Brazil stabilized the value of its currency by opening a Conversion Office at which notes could be converted into gold in 1906.

In the first decade of this century several other countries succeeded in fixing their exchange rates to gold, mainly due to very favourable trading conditions and a massive inflow of capital not only from Europe but, increasingly, from the United States. At one time the Argentina Stabilization Fund held more gold than the Bank of England. However, the system was fragile; the inflow of capital contributed to domestic inflation as gold was converted into local currency, but when the flow went into reverse, bank reserves were drained, loans were called in, there were widespread defaults and in 1912–13 banking crises engulfed Argentina, Brazil and Uruguay. As recent research has shown, countries at the periphery of the gold standard received some benefits from the system, notably easier access to capital, but also remained acutely vulnerable to sudden changes in confidence and interest rates in the financial centre.

Dogged by financial crises, it was hardly surprising that Latin America joined in the worldwide attempt in the 1920s to restore financial stability after the slump and rapid inflation that followed the First World War. The crusade by Benjamin Strong and Montagu Norman bore fruit. The creation of central banks in the region did not, of course, prevent further financial crises. But, perversely, that may have been all to their good in terms of recognition as we discuss later in this chapter; crises bring central banks into prominence.

Asia the exception

Looking round the globe at the early efforts of the third world to provide central banking services it seems these were performed best in two kinds of circumstances. Either where the central bank was part of the official apparatus of a country with a coherent, outward-oriented strategy for export-led growth and competitiveness, such as Singapore, South Korea, and Taiwan. Or where there was no central bank as such, as in Hong Kong. These examples suggest that central banks are not needed when the government knows what it wants, has a reasonable strategy to attain its goals, and is committed to price stability or fairly low inflation. Before an economy has reached a certain stage of maturity and integration, central banks have a subsidiary position.

But even in Asia, or especially in Asia, central banks have become more important, and even independent to some extent. This, of course, is because of the spreading influence of financial markets in dynamic economies, the need to watch over them, develop policies for them, respond to them, fix or vary exchange rates, liberalize or tighten exchange controls and so on. There has to be an institution set apart from the government, in contact with these developing markets, which can advise the government on matters of financial policy, help to formulate policy and then carry it out.

So although central banks did not play a large part in the early stages of Asia's astonishing economic leapfrogging of the West, they will in future. One Asian central bank – Taiwan's – has had at times the world's largest foreign-exchange reserves. Others, notably Malaysia's central bank, have been among the most active official participants in the foreign-exchange markets (though the Malaysian Central Bank revealed in 1994 that it had made huge losses on its reserves and its Govenor resigned). All are attending to the development of their domestic banking systems.

Unfortunately, many also have been faced with severe losses in commercial banking, requiring them to develop recapitalization and restructuring policies. This is true of the Philippines and Indonesia – and most of the Indian sub-continent.

The abuse of central banks

We carry on the story of central banking in countries with underdeveloped financial systems in Chapter 17 (where the focus is on smaller central banks) and in Chapter 19 (with the focus on newly established central banks and central banks that have undergone radical restructuring). But although generalizations about setting up and running central banks in countries at very different stages of development can obviously be misleading, a little more needs to be said about why so many received poor advice when currency boards were abolished.

The writings, admired at the time, of contemporary economists provide a forceful reminder of the risks run by economists when they make policy recommendations. Even those who were aware of the damage that excessive credit creation could cause assumed that the leaders of the newly independent countries would use the power wisely. Many badly underestimated the risks involved. One influential British monetary economist of the time, Edward Nevin, attacked the scepticism expressed by some central bankers in developed countries about the usefulness of fully fledged central banks in developing countries. In *Capital Funds in Underdeveloped Countries* (published in 1961), he asserted that even those prepared to welcome the newcomers saw them in 'traditional' terms, whereas the role of a central bank in a developing economy should be 'fundamentally different' from its role in developed economies. The main purpose should not be the control of the money supply but the encouragement of economic development. To promote this, the central bank should control not only the note issue but also the commercial banks. It should also act as banker to the government and, on its behalf, manage the public debt. Techniques of credit control should be developed in the form of statutory reserve ratios, giving the central bank resources 'which form part of the total assets available to it for the finance of development and other purposes'.

Central banks should not be independent, Nevin said. Governments were responsible for the level of employment – and thus for the levels of prices, income and output. So a 'parallel narrowing of the freedom of action which could be allowed to a central bank' was inevitable. Whatever the risks may be, the advantages of a central bank in contributing to development outweighed the disadvantages. It would finance development first, from its own capital and reserves; second, from the investible portion of the currency backing; and third, from the use of at least a part of the commercial bank deposits placed with it.

In conclusion Nevin launched a diatribe against conservative central bankers who were unable to perceive the need for such a policy: 'All too often the desire of dependent territories to carry out monetary reforms is treated in terms normally reserved for a child wishing to play with a lethal weapon.' In practice, however, all too often the weapons did prove to be lethal. Without the restraints imposed by the fixed exchange-rate regime, or by the currency board system, there was a systematic tendency towards excessive monetary expansion resulting in either inflation or chronic payments crises – or, more commonly, both. But the greatest omission of writers like Nevin is their total naïvety in presuming that the governments would use the 'commanding' powers accorded to them to benefit society rather than to consolidate their own power.

As a result of excess monetary expansion, inflation in many developing countries was worsening even before the oil price hike of November 1973. In a sample of twenty-six developing countries analysed by Surjity

Bhalla for the Institute for International Economics, a Washington think-tank, the main cause of the 'universal and synchronous' inflation of 1973–74 was monetary expansion in 1970–72. True, this particular boost was spurred principally by increases in reserves, which developing countries were unable effectively to sterilize. But after this acceleration, inflation remained at very high levels in many countries – domestic credit creation took over from international influences as the main engine. Average inflation in developing countries remained at or above 20 per cent in every year from 1973 to 1993. Only a handful of countries contained inflation rates to below 10 per cent; while an increasing number suffered the ultimate fate of hyperinflation. Central banks were not the sole cause: what is clear is that in the absence of central banks with money-creation powers, inflation could not have remained at such high levels as it did in much of the third world in the 1970s and 1980s.

One of the main motives behind the abuse of central banks was governments' desire to raise revenue. Central banking is, or at least should be, an enormously profitable business, because people need money and the central bank has a monopoly over the supply of currency and bank reserves. The profits from this business, or seigniorage, reflect the difference between the costs of printing notes or minting coins (it usually pays no interest on reserves that private banks are required to keep with it) and the interest the central bank receives on the corresponding assets. Calculations by Maxwell Fry of Birmingham University suggest that in 1984 seigniorage tax revenue in Argentina, Mexico, Peru and Yugoslavia accounted for more than one-third of government current revenue, equivalent to between 5 per cent and 10 per cent of GNP. When the government sets out to maximize the revenue it can squeeze out of its central bank, the tax received can even rise for a short period to 25 per cent of GNP, as in Chile in the early 1970s, before the resulting inflation brings about economic collapse.

Governments developed many other ways of using central banks as tax collectors. These include rigging the financial markets in favour of government borrowing by placing ceilings on interest rates on assets that compete with government paper, increasing reserve requirements on commercial banks beyond what is necessary for monetary control, requiring importers to place deposits with the central bank, and forcing exporters to sell their foreign exchange receipts to the central bank at lower prices than the central bank makes foreign exchange available to importers. As Fry, in his study 'The Fiscal Abuse of Central Banks', pointed out, central banks collect revenues in forms that closely resemble conventional taxes, but are well concealed – they do not appear in any tax codes, or in the government's budget.

Revival of interest in currency boards

After such a sorry performance, it is not surprising that currency boards, which are tightly restricted in the range of activities they may undertake as well as subject to binding rules restraining currency issue, became a topical subject again. They died with imperialism, because the British, French and Dutch had to relinquish their possessions, rather than because of technical inefficiency. But they relied on being able to tie their local currency to a relatively stable reserve currency that also dominated their trade. (Usually the mother currency, but a few British colonies linked to the American dollar or rupee.) The obvious choice for a central European country today would be to peg to the D-mark, and by 1994 most countries of the area were targeting their exchange rate on the D-mark; thus even though these countries had central banks rather than currency boards, they wanted the main benefit of the currency board system – the firm anchor to a major stable currency.

In the more primitive systems of the countries of the former Soviet Union, there was a stronger case for the currency board system, not only to provide a stable currency but, more importantly, to provide a degree of financial protection from Russian nationalist revanchism. It was only too easy to reincorporate weak currencies issued by fledgling central banks in a new rouble area, which would be no more than an instrument of financial exploitation by the stronger power. In the view of many economists, international agencies like the International Monetary Fund were mistaken in recommending these countries to set up central banks rather than currency boards. But at least the Fund had come to recognize the great potential value of an exchange-rate link to a strong currency as an anchor for monetary policy in developing countries and those in transition.

Subordinated but unbowed

For the most part, central banks in developing countries have had little independence. Almost everywhere, they remained legally and *de facto* part of the government apparatus. But there are exceptions and there are signs of a more general change – though this runs ahead of our story. Mexico in 1993 announced plans to make its central bank independent. Chile has long had a tradition of autonomy for its central bank. A new law of the Central Bank of Venezuela, which came into effect in December 1992, made it solely responsible for designing and implementing monetary and exchange policies, though this was swept away in the banking crisis of 1994. In India, the governor of the central bank is a figure of considerable prestige and influence – such as I. G. Patel in the 1960s, a distinguished international economist who later became the director of the London School of Economics. More recently, the Pakistani government headed by Moeen Qureshi, former director of the World Bank, announced plans to make the State Bank of Pakistan independent.

While lacking independence, in many countries the central bank has long been the best source of economic and financial data. For visiting financial journalists, it is usually the first port of call. Their officials are generally much more open and friendly than the bureaucrats of the economics, planning or finance ministry. Most have good statistics departments. And after the international financial markets opened up in the 1970s, they became involved in negotiating terms of syndicated loans with merchant bankers in London and New York, and in hiring bright new graduates from top universities.

When a country opens up to foreign banks, the range of contacts also naturally grows. Permissions and licences have to be sought. Friendships are formed. This helps to speed the flow of new ideas as well as finance. Then there is involvement in regional central banking associations, such as those for Southeast Asia, the Pacific, and Latin America. Central bankers from countries with any appeal to foreign investors, or any money to be managed by City merchant banks, will be invited to conferences in the world's more pleasant watering holes. And through such informal channels, Western influence on the evolution of central banking in developing countries – and later in countries of the former Soviet Union – has remained strong.

Many central banks also became prominent in helping to clear up the mess after the debt débâcle in Latin America. In the early 1980s, the names of their governors would trip off the tongue of anyone in the international financial community – names such as Julio Gonzalez del Solar of Argentina, a Harvard-educated man with international experience including spells at the IMF, and the Brazilian Carlos Langoni, a Chicago-trained economist of Peruvian–Scottish descent who had served at the World Bank. Another familiar name at the time was that of Courtney Blackman, a Columbia Business School graduate with experience in Wall Street, who headed the central bank in Barbados.

Recently, the advice from the centre countries is: make your central bank strong and independent; also, do not use it to collect taxes, or spend money in ways that have nothing to do with its monetary policy responsibilities. So within a space of thirty years we have seen a 180-degree turnround; where before central banks had to be dependent on the Ministry of Finance, now they have to be independent. Where before they had to help finance development, now they must have nothing to do with it. This all caused mighty confusion.

Fortunately, central bankers tend to be more relaxed people than finance ministry officials. Even though developing-country central banks were constitutionally under the thumbs of their finance ministries and political leaders, they have throughout had a different spirit – more open, and often more realistic. Most of them kept in touch with events outside. Through the work of some of the leading central banks, notably the Bank of England with its annual informal gatherings of central banks of Commonwealth countries and former members, the distinctive character of the traditional central bankers brushed off on the bankers from newly independent countries. Often, as happened in Zimbabwe, the central bank remained relatively liberal despite the socialist temper of their governments (in this case, of President Mugabe) so that they jumped at the chance to implement liberalization programmes when the political climate became ready for them. It would seem that a central banker is a central banker, whether he comes from a developing country or a developed country, and whatever his formal constitutional position may be.

The 1979 meeting of the International Monetary Fund and World Bank, held in Belgrade in late September and early October, may seem best forgotten. All the sweat, tears and taxpayers' money that this vast annual convention involves – many times more so when it is outside Washington every third year – yielded not a single decision on that occasion. Yet that conspicuous lack of success, the sheer impotence of the world's financial community in the face of a dangerously deteriorating economic situation, may have been the best of all possible outcomes. For it left no doubt in the mind of the newly elected top central banker that America needed a more effective monetary policy. And his determination to bring that about heralded an era marked by a new assertiveness among central banks and a surprising degree of consensus among them that the main objective of their monetary policy should be price stability.

Economic malaise in the autumn of 1979 belied the optimism of officials a year earlier. Unemployment in industrial countries was unacceptably high, there was a danger of recession turning into slump, imbalances in international payments were overblown and the volatility of key currencies had got out of hand. Just days before the Belgrade meeting, the European Community's semi-fixed exchange-rate system had failed; only six months after the European Monetary System had been inaugurated, there was a general realignment involving a 2 per cent upvaluation of the D-mark against the other five currencies and an extra 3 per cent devaluation for the Danish krone.

At the 1979 meeting there was also particular concern about the dollar, which wasn't behaving as it had been expected to do. In the earlier part of the year, it had faced the D-mark at the level which the heads of both the American and German central banks had, very rashly, declared was about right – DM1.85–1.90. But it had stayed there only with the help of massive central bank intervention. By the autumn the rate was down to DM1.75, close to the weakness that had triggered off President Jimmy Carter's rescue package in November 1978, which had included the issue of $10 billion worth of foreign currency bonds – 'Carter bonds' – carrying a dollar exchange guarantee. So America couldn't control the mighty dollar? No wonder the barometer of currency temperature in those days, the gold price, was flashing feverish signals, surging to new heights above $400 an ounce.

On top of everything else, inflation in the industrialized world was in double digits. And rising. And rising hand in hand with unemployment, which was as eerie as if the laws of gravity were being defied, as if water were running uphill. But although that link might be weird, the soaring inflation was largely home-grown, with central banks having had more than a hand in producing it. Even the Geneva-based General Agreement on Tariffs and Trade had dared to argue that the latest oil price hike was not the major cause of high inflation, and that its impact could be made relatively small if only oil-importing countries carried out the right policies. And from the universities, where the monetarists were busy shoving out the old generation of Keynesians, the calls for better monetary policies were deafening.

Yet, unnervingly, precisely nothing happened when all the world's moneymen were brought together in Belgrade. Only one new idea was floated and that had nothing to do with the root problem of inflation, being aimed at better currency management by way of a substitution account. This would have allowed central banks to swap their surplus dollars, which were overhanging the market, into the IMF's 'funny money', the special drawing right (SDR). But, at best, such a scheme would have been for the long term, offering nothing for the present. As it turned out, the Americans were fooling everyone at Belgrade. Much to the secret relief of central banks, which didn't want the IMF nuzzling into their business, they were never really prepared to have dollars dumped. The plan was summarily ditched – officially, 'postponed' – at the first opportunity after Belgrade, at the IMF's spring meeting in Hamburg in April 1980.

Volcker skips Belgrade

With the substitution account long forgotten, the Belgrade meeting is remembered chiefly today for the flurry of excitement when, before the main proceedings had even started, delegates realized that the bulky figure of the Federal Reserve chairman, so tall that he could never be overlooked, was no longer in their midst. Paul Volcker had departed for home.

Volcker had been in the job for only two months, appointed after President Carter had switched Bill Miller from the central bank to be Treasury Secretary. There had been a number of possible candidates for the prestigious post, but Tony Solomon, then Treasury Undersecretary and one of the architects of the dollar rescue the previous November, had recommended Volcker to the President. Carter's response – Who's he?' – says something about his interests, for Volcker had then completed four years as president of the New York Federal Reserve Bank. Ironically, in a Machiavellian twist, Solomon was to slip into the shoes left empty in Liberty Street five and half months after Volcker was installed in the Fed chair on 6 August 1979. Ironically, too, Solomon was then way ahead of his nominee in pay. In moving to Washington, Volcker paid a penalty for power; his salary halved to less than that of a yuppie, dropping from $116,000 to a miserly $57,500. Maybe that financial sacrifice strengthened his resolve to stifle inflation and make sure his stipend didn't shrink further.

Though not expansive when interrogated, preferring questioning to being questioned, Volcker had been a public servant long enough for his views to be quite widely known by the time he reached Belgrade. At the congressional confirmation hearings for the Fed chairmanship he had said that the most fundamental way to stabilize the dollar overseas was to develop a policy to control domestic inflation. Interest rates, he went on, would not return to lower levels until this problem was solved. The markets took note and prepared for a tougher stance, remembering that Volcker, as New York president, had twice voted hawkishly against the chairman, Bill Miller, at policymaking meetings.

Volcker left no doubt at those congressional hearings that he considered a stable dollar essential for the United States to deal with its domestic problems. But on earlier occasions he had shown himself opposed to exchange-rate targeting. All he wanted was an understanding among a few leading nations of 'what extremes of fluctuations are mutually tolerable, and which should be strongly resisted'. He has never budged from his simple philosophy that you can know the wrong rate for a currency without knowing the right one.

In his own chronicles, Volcker denies a common assumption that he fled Belgrade because the sour atmosphere of the IMF meeting convinced him America had an emergency on its hands. 'The more prosaic fact,' he wrote, 'is that I went home because there was nothing more for me to do in Belgrade.' Quite so. But a little more explanation is called for. Volcker's departure dramatically exposed, for all to see, what the IMF would prefer to hide, which is that to all intents and purposes the annual meeting is over before it begins; any decisions are taken in the committee and group meetings that precede the formal sessions. And to Volcker, cynical about the likelihood of any good coming out of international forums larger than twos or threes, going to Belgrade at all was a waste of time, once the American mission to West Germany had failed.

The Germans also had a hand in the change of American policy. Just as was to happen thirteen years later, in 1992, their central bank was being blamed for pursuing a tight money policy without consideration of others – a criticism that dismayed and hurt the Bundesbank's chief at the time, Otmar Emminger, as it was to do Helmut Schlesinger a decade and more later. To the Americans in 1979, having to explain why their recession was going to be deeper and longer than expected, it was worth buttering up the Germans. By stopping off on their way to Belgrade at Hamburg, home town of Chancellor Helmut Schmidt, the American delegates raised hopes of a deal.

False hopes, however, for although Volcker, along with Miller and Charles Schultze, chairman of the Council of Economic Advisers, talked with Schmidt and Emminger, explaining that they had come not to badger the Germans to reflate but to press them not to overreact on the deflationary side, they got short shrift. Volcker records that Schmidt, 'at his irascible worst', left his visitors in no doubt that 'his impatience with what he saw as American neglect and irresolution about the dollar had run out'. It was then that Volcker knew it was time to get back to his desk.

A revolutionary change in monetary policy?

The upshot was that the Fed chairman called a secret meeting of the central bank's policymaking body, the Open Market Committee, followed by one of Board members, for Saturday, 6 October, just two days after the Belgrade meeting ended. That evening a package of restrictions was delivered. It would move the United States more firmly towards recession in the near term and more firmly away from inflation in the longer term. The discount rate was raised another percentage point to a record 12 per cent, special reserve requirements were imposed on the growth of commercial time deposits and – most important of all – far-reaching changes were announced in operating techniques for controlling money growth. The Fed's previous focus on short-term interest rates – specifically, the federal funds rate, the price at which American banks lend overnight to each other – was jettisoned for more direct control of money supply through a focus on bank reserves. In short, the Federal Reserve shifted from controlling the price of money to controlling its quantity.

This was a significant bow towards the rigid monetarists of the

Chicago school of economists, whose guru is Professor Milton Friedman. The most well-known of Friedman's proposals is that the one and only cure for inflation is to pump money into the system at a steady and predictable rate on automatic pilot, never tightening or slackening the tap once it is set, no matter what. For a time many assumed that this was what Volcker was set on doing.

But Volcker and his colleagues, while plainly influenced by the change of opinion that the monetarists had brought about among economists, bankers and the media, were not embracing Friedmanism wholeheartedly. The Fed would continue to declare its objectives, as required by law, in terms of the growth it was seeking in various measures of the money supply, still allowing itself room for manoeuvre by targeting a range rather than a single figure. On the surface, all it was doing was using another guide to try to hit those targets. Nevertheless, the man who was to succeed Volcker at the Federal Reserve, Alan Greenspan, commented at the time that if the Fed was serious about controlling the money supply exclusively and abandoning all semblance of control over interest rates – which is close to the policy urged by monetarists – it would be the most revolutionary change in monetary policy in the central bank's history.

Greenspan knew better than most that, by letting interest rates go where the market took them, the Fed would not only be inviting more volatility in them but also accepting that they might run up sharply, risking deep recession, before America's inflation rate – then at an annual 13 per cent – was brought under control. Hardly a scenario with political appeal. The top dogs in the Carter administration, including the President, who knew in advance what the new Federal Reserve chairman had in mind, were decidedly unenthusiastic. Volcker went ahead against their instincts and preferences. It was a gamble of no small order.

It paid off, in that the inflation genie was largely put back into the bottle. But not before America had experienced its worst recession since the war. And not before the Federal Reserve had to accept that its new monetary technique wasn't working all that well. Interest rates bounced about in unprecedented fashion, much more than Volcker or anyone else had expected. Making things worse, marketmen continued to focus on these ups and downs and react to them, misreading the new thrust of policy; they simply didn't believe the Fed could be indifferent to the big gyrations in the federal funds rate. They helped to ensure it wasn't. Before 1982 was out, the Open Market Committee was indeed slipping back into its old ways, or at least using a hybrid approach to steering money supply growth.

No stopping the bandwagon

But the Fed had set in train soul-searching at other central banks. As inflation soared in the 1970s, many had adopted monetary targetry, though none – except perhaps for the Bundesbank – had managed to convince the markets of their commitment to it. Now, at last, they were sharing problems. Charles Goodhart, then chief adviser in the Bank of England's economic division, commented in the spring of 1982:

> If the number of conferences held to discuss a particular topic was a good indicator of concern about that subject, then the thermometer would be registering a fever of anxiety about American monetary control techniques. I would doubt whether any major policy change has been so quickly, repeatedly and thoroughly analysed as the changes in monetary control arrangements introduced in October 1979.

The British authorities at that time had been kick-started into introspection more directly. Margaret Thatcher, on becoming Prime Minister, had abolished exchange controls and ordered a review of monetary policy. Her Chancellor of the Exchequer, Sir Geoffrey Howe, did away with the infamous 'corset' which had controlled credit directly. Although a joint study by the Treasury and the Bank of England in March 1980 (a year in which British inflation peaked at nearly 22 per cent) decided against following the Fed's lead and switching to direct control of the quantity of banking reserves, it led to major changes in operational techniques to reinforce control over interest rates. Even more telling, the Bank of Japan, the most reluctant of the big central banks (other than the Bank of England) to adopt even a whiff of monetarism, was catching up in the early 1980s, beginning operations in short-term government bills and relinquishing its direct control on individual banks' lending – its so-called 'window guidance'.

If the results of all this introspection were none too happy, technical disappointments did not stop a bandwagon theory, initiated by the monetarism debate, gathering momentum among central bankers in the 1980s. Almost to a man, they decided that price stability is essential to the efficient functioning of an economy and attaining it should be the primary goal of monetary policy. The decade began with the Federal Reserve showing the way, it ended with European central bankers writing the principle firmly into their blueprint for a European Central Bank. That a central bank can only effectively carry out an anti-inflationary policy if it is independent of political control is, of course, delightfully convenient. Any means which secured such an end might seem justifiable to some central banks, and to have found one with a moral overtone may seem too good to be true. Yet the 1980s provided one of the most striking examples of how bitter-sweet a central banker's power can be.

Slings and arrows

Independence has a price – at least for those at the top. The more independent a central bank becomes, the more it is personalized, identified with its boss. The Fed's switch in operating techniques was not something Volcker had conceived on his own; some of its staff and some of its regional presidents had been itching to do it long before Volcker arrived on the scene. Yet the package of October 1979 was 'Volcker's Saturday Night Special', the subsequent tightening 'Volcker's squeeze'. The consequences for Volcker were not all pleasant. The Bank for International Settlements gave him, indirectly, its stamp of approval; its 1980 annual report welcomed the arrival of the American recession as a dampener of world inflation. America's senior citizens hailed Volcker as the man who made their pensions mean something again. But many younger Americans judged his tough measures and high interest rates very differently, as did master builders and the like whose firms went under in a year-long slump which brought unemployment approaching 11 per cent and record bankruptcies.

By the spring of 1982, Volcker's critics were baying. The cover of a Tennessee construction trade journal consisted of a WANTED poster of Volcker and the other six governors of the Federal Reserve (THE MALEFICENT 7), charging them with 'premeditated and cold-blooded murder of millions of small businesses' and 'kidnapping (and holding for ransom) the American dream of home ownership'. A cattle rancher in Florida had a simple solution: 'Take a stick and run Mr Volcker out of the country.'

More worrisome to the man at the centre of the row were the squawks in Washington. After Reagan took office in January 1981, a monetarist, Beryl Sprinkel, became undersecretary for monetary affairs at the American Treasury and barked continually at Volcker, like a terrier at his ankles, about the jerkiness of monetary growth while supporting the broad monetarist thrust of his policy. Up on Capitol Hill, one Democratic congressman, tired of his constituents' complaints, called for Volcker's impeachment, while the majority leader of the Republican-controlled Senate, Howard Baker – who later became President Reagan's Chief of Staff at the White House – proclaimed that the

Federal Reserve 'should get its boot off the neck of the economy'. By the autumn of 1982, three separate pieces of legislation had been introduced aimed at forcing the Fed to be more responsive to congressional concerns – though they were destined to get nowhere in the end.

So how was it that Volcker not only survived all these attacks but was reappointed by Reagan for another four years in August 1983? The answer is three-fold. First, Reagan's monetarists fundamentally supported Volcker's approach, despite all the much-publicized tiffs. Second, judging by the seat of his pants, Volcker had relaxed the Fed's monetary grip just a little from mid-1982 in order to spur economic recovery. Third, American banks looked so vulnerable in the early stages of the Latin American debt crisis that Reagan was probably advised to keep Volcker, if only to have a scapegoat ready if the worst happened and the country's financial network fell apart.

Mexico drops a bomb

It didn't. But fears for its safety – and for that of the whole international financial and trading system – were only too real for a considerable time. Mexico started the ball rolling on 20 August 1982 by telling its international bankers it could not repay them. They knew a dozen or more other big borrowers in the third world, without the advantage of being oil exporters, were stretched to their limits financially. A widespread default, which would have bust their banks – and some very big ones – threatened to turn nightmare into horrible reality.

To stop that happening, Mexico had to be convinced quickly of the folly of a debtors' cartel and shown it could secure better treatment by bargaining on its own. Luckily for the banks, America's political sensitivity towards a country on its doorstep made that imperative – as they had always counted on. Even so, the Mexican deal was no pushover.

Less than two weeks after the Mexican 'bombshell', as blinkered officials perceived it, the main characters in the drama came together at the IMF annual meeting in Toronto. A sort of partnership between them developed remarkably quickly, orchestrated by Paul Volcker and Jacques de Larosière, then heading the IMF. But only central banks, along with the American government, came up with what Mexico needed at that moment: money. Against oil as collateral and under the aegis of the Bank for International Settlements, Group of Ten central banks, joined by the Bank of Spain, put together a short-term bridging loan of $1.85 billion, counting in a contribution from the American

Treasury. The American government also promised another $2 billion in credits and advance payments for oil.

For their part, the Mexicans agreed in Toronto to start negotiating an economic programme with the IMF, while the creditor banks, overwhelmingly American, were persuaded to help that programme work, once it was in place, by not only stretching out payments due on old debt but providing some new money as well. Amid all the razzmatazz of the financial community's annual jamboree, a strategy was hatched that, country by country, was to be applied, reapplied and revamped repeatedly to solve the debt crisis, painfully, stumblingly. That it was such a lengthy business shades its success. 'You squirm because it took ten years', Volcker told a newspaper in 1992.

Volcker dropped out in 1987, halfway through that ten-year haul. But not before he had sold some new ideas to the American Treasury Secretary, Jim Baker, who announced them with much fanfare as his own at the IMF meeting in Seoul in October 1985. By then, the debt strategy was clearly not living up to its original promise. Mexico was missing targets – as, too, was the other big debtor, Brazil – and banks were nowhere near resuming voluntary lending to it, as had been hoped. Hurt by harsh recession and high international interest rates, debtors were ready for open confrontation with their creditors as they arrived in Seoul. The 'Baker initiative' defused a potentially explosive situation.

'Adjustment with growth' was the new slogan. Some fifteen heavily indebted developing countries, Jim Baker said, must step up economic reforms and then 'grow' their way out of the mess they were in – with the help of additional outside financing. The World Bank and the Inter-American Development Bank were to step up their disbursements by nearly 50 per cent to $9 billion a year, while banks were to pledge $20 billion in new money over the three years 1986–88. Sir Jeremy Morse, then chairman of Lloyds Bank, called the scheme one of the great political initiatives of the postwar period.

But most banks refused to participate. The twelve months that followed Baker's proposals was a lost year in the debt calendar. With the threat to the world's banking system, if it had ever existed, by that time contained, the banks began to assert themselves. They were peeved that when a new IMF deal was eventually struck with the Mexicans, Volcker and de Larosière had offered concessions without, as the banks saw it, adequate reference to themselves. The feeling grew that the Volcker–Baker approach was fundamentally flawed. Maybe the debtors were not just broke, but bankrupt.

Insolvency demands debt relief. Calling it anything but that name, which isn't in their vocabulary, banks began to practise it. When world leaders and finance ministers talked debt at the economic summit in Venice in June 1987, they encouraged flexibility, a 'menu of options', innovations like debt-equity swaps and buybacks. This inspired a blue-blooded American bank, J. P. Morgan, to pioneer a scheme at the end of that year which allowed the 500-odd banks owed money by Mexico to swap their loans for bonds guaranteed by the American Treasury if they offered a sufficiently deep discount. Not many were prepared to do so at that stage, however, and what Volcker grudgingly called 'a rather ingenious and complicated way out for those who want to exit' relieved Mexico of little more than $1 billion, or 2 per cent, of its bank debt.

But to the American Treasury it was a 'breakthrough' and it led, in March 1989, to its then Secretary, Nicholas Brady, floating a much broader Morgan-style scheme. Its novelty was bringing in official money (mainly from the IMF and World Bank, but also the Japanese government) to back debt relief – provide 'enhancement', in the jargon – as part of an IMF reform programme. Creditor banks could sell back their debt at a discount to debtors. Or swap it for bonds that either paid less interest or were set at less than the original face value, their attraction being that both interest and principal were guaranteed by American Treasury bonds held by the Federal Reserve. The 'Brady plan' lived on. It fuelled a tiny market in third-world debt into big business by 1994. And Brady-style deals were still being struck, though the debt saga for the larger debtors, essentially in Latin America, was more or less over.

Who was to blame?

If the third-world debt crisis taught anything, it is that belief is fallible. It suited the financial community to go along with Walter Wriston, chief executive of Citicorp in its mighty days, when he wisecracked that only companies go bust, sovereign countries don't. As the poet Robert Lowell put it in a memorable line, 'experience is what you do not want to experience'. For too long, the disruption of international payments was considered purely a cashflow problem, whereas it went much deeper. As to initial blame, banks get their share for falling over themselves to recycle huge amounts of oil money without ensuring it was put to good use. And developing countries get theirs for economic mismanagement, corruption, poor housekeeping, you name it. But what about central banks? Success in fire-fighting does not excuse them from fire prevention.

There were warnings and mutterings going back to June 1976. At the annual meeting of the Bank for International Settlements that month its

Dutch president, Jelle Zijlstra, questioned whether banks might not be 'running excessive risks in their international lending', while large international banks were uneasy enough to ask the BIS to collect statistics about their exposure to the third world. By 1980, even the more reckless bankers were calling for the IMF to do more third-world lending and contemplating their own safety net in case of emergency. Celebrating its 50th annual meeting in June that year, the BIS commented on how highly concentrated the debt problem was, picking out Brazil, Mexico, South Korea and the Philippines. On the other hand, its head manager, René Larre, on the eve of his retirement at that meeting, saw nothing wrong with lending simply to refinance existing debts; bankers, he said, had to realize that governments' international loans were no more likely to be repaid than their domestic ones. Moreover, he felt American banks still had a good deal of spare capacity for developing-country finance, a view Volcker seemed then to endorse in general, though worried about some individual banks.

Larre's economic adviser at the start of the 1980s, Alexandre Lamfalussy, insists that BIS figures were spelling Mexico's default at least a year before it happened. But against a background of industrial sluggishness that could have turned into world slump, his institution shilly-shallied when it reported in June 1982. On the one hand, it was urging stricter prudential guidelines on banks, on the other warning that the banks' 'growing caution' over sovereign lending might extend 'too widely and too indiscriminately to whole groups of countries'. The central bankers' bank was running scared, but it didn't know what should be done and it was too late to do it anyway. The market had opened the lending tap too much and for too long; now the worry was that it would shut it down altogether.

Leading governments also had a lot to answer for in encouraging banks to overlend. It was always unrealistic to have expected them to provide official channels for recycling the huge oil profits that flowed from the first oil-price rise in the early 1970s, but finance ministers who run institutions like the IMF were too ready to let banks step into the breach. All concerned averted their gaze from the central question: were banks lending too much?

But central bankers were best placed to see the answer was 'yes'. Instead, they equivocated. It shouldn't have needed world debt worries to focus attention on an alarming decline in banks' capital compared with their assets, so persistent and so worldwide, though most acute in America, that it stuck out like a sore thumb. Alas, that is how banking regulation comes about, reluctantly, trailing the markets, driven by crises, as our story of it in Chapter 10 relates. It is only because there was so much bad financial news in the 1980s, so many shocks, that international guidelines for the conduct of the banking industry and payment systems have taken on some substance. Central bankers, it seems, only cooperate when cornered.

Where coordination counted

It was not a banking crisis, however, that arguably gave central banks their best moment of coordinated glory in the 1980s, but something outside their responsibility, the stock-market crash of October 1987. Led by Alan Greenspan at the Federal Reserve, leading central banks acted promptly to contain the damage, by relaxing their monetary policies and pumping liquidity into the system, the opposite of the disastrous curtailment after the 1929 crash. That the British and Japanese authorities failed to reverse the action at the appropriate time does not detract from the smartness of the original move, though their subsequent ineptitude turned it into a hollow victory – indeed, in their cases, a disaster. Again, the Bundesbank followed the right course – joining in the initial measures to reassure the markets, but quickly regaining monetary control as soon as the alarm was over.

Central bank coordination in a more familiar area, the currency markets, demanded particular skill in two episodes in the 1980s. We return in Chapter 13 to the outcome of the Plaza and Louvre agreements of September 1985 and February 1987, the one to help an overvalued dollar decline and the other to steady it. More important than where it settled was America's acceptance that its currency, while still the dominant world money, is no longer in a class of its own. From having no exchange reserves worth speaking of, relying on short-term borrowing on the rare occasions it did want to intervene in the markets to influence the dollar rate, the United States started to accumulate reserves in the latter part of the 1980s. By the 1990s they were comparable in size to those of other key-currency countries like Germany and Japan. And the Federal Reserve could talk intervention like any other big central bank.

As the 1990s began, the signposts were pointing towards a tripolar currency world, based on the dollar, yen and a European currency, the D-mark standing in until Europe's monetary union was forged. The smoothness of East Germany's switch in July 1990 to the D-mark, as part of Germany's reunification, and the way the foreign-exchange markets took it in their stride helped to strengthen this view. Even the rebellious president of the Bundesbank, Karl Otto Pöhl, was upbeat about the event. In a particularly jolly mood on the evening of 3 July, he told a top-notch gathering in London, which included the Bank of England's stars, Robin Leigh-Pemberton and Eddie George, that even if monetary targetry would be more difficult initially, 'this should not materially affect the Bundesbank's ability to stay its course of price stability'. He could not hide the disagreeable fact that the German government would have to borrow, borrow and borrow again to pay for the rebuilding of eastern Germany, but he was confident this would be only a temporary state of affairs. However, in his impish way, Pöhl added 'you will not expect me to stress the risks of the exercise unduly'.

Before these risks had built up and pessimism had set in Pöhl announced on 16 May 1991 that he would step down prematurely as president of the Bundesbank. He was doing so partly for personal reasons, but he had been vexed by Chancellor Kohl's failure to tell him early of the decision to rush into reunification, ignoring his misgivings about a one-to-one conversion rate between the Ostmark and the D-mark, and by the disregard of his warnings that it was essential to cut back public spending and subsidies in western Germany.

Germany had problems peculiar to reunification in the early 1990s, but most of the industrialized world was in an economic morass. It is a sobering thought that thirteen years after the Belgrade meeting, where we started this chapter, at the 1992 annual meeting of the same worthy institutions (this time on their own ground in Washington), Group of Seven officials were again sheepish, concerned with many of the same symptoms of economic failure. Their earlier optimism about growth had again been misguided, unemployment remained too high, there were European currency troubles again, sterling having been forced out of the Exchange Rate Mechanism only days before the meeting on 'Black Wednesday' (16 September). What made 1992 so different, though, was that at least inflation was low and expected to stay that way.

That was the difference the 1980s had made. The pursuit of price stability had been established as the overriding objective of central banks. And, in that pursuit, many countries were to commit their central banks to a degree of independence in the running of monetary policy. It was a turning point in economic management of enormous significance.

A classic mid-twentieth-century work on banking pronounced that 'the fundamental business of a central bank is to control the commercial banks in such a way as to support the monetary policy directed by the State'. We would rephrase this statement by Richard Sayers (in his book *Modern Banking*) to read, equally categorically, that 'the fundamental task of a central bank is to regulate the supply of money so as to provide society with price stability'.

Price stability is secured when the monetary unit – pound, dollar, D-mark or whatever the national money may be – holds its value in terms of purchasing power, i.e. what it can buy over the whole range of a nation's goods and services. And is expected to continue to hold its value. Not all prices have to stay unchanged; some can rise, others fall. But market forces work best when the general level of prices is stable.

A society that has lost confidence in its money is close to losing confidence in itself. In this century hyperinflation has often given an advance warning of social and political collapse, the most recent examples being Yugoslavia in 1989–91 and Russia in 1992–93. At the extreme, inflation leads to a fragmentation of a monetary area with people increasingly switching to other currencies or even to barter, where they refuse to accept money and trade goods and services directly against other goods and services. Either of these leads to a severe cut in living standards because the market in goods and services that can be directly exchanged is much smaller than the market available through the use of money, so production of goods and services collapses. But even a gradual inflation will impair the efficient working of the economy by blurring the signals that changes in market prices give to producers and consumers. It benefits the government at the expense of the private sector and unfairly redistributes wealth from creditors to debtors.

Monetary policy can stop inflation and keep it at low levels and this is now considered to be its principal objective. This conception of monetary policy is not new, but the consensus on it is. As the above quotation shows, the dominant 1940s-1970s view held that monetary policy only had a subsidiary role to play anyway – fiscal policy was what really mattered – and that it should support the general economic policies of the government. If the government demanded credit on a scale so large as to cause inflation, that was its right. As we saw in Chapter 6, providing credit to support development was viewed as the main duty of central banks in developing countries.

What put paid to that conception was the experience of the 1970s, when inflation reached 20 per cent or more in some countries while unemployment remained high. Injecting huge amounts of money into the system did nothing to bring down unemployment. Other influences were important too: one was the growing prestige and power of the Bundesbank (established in 1957), which was obliged by law to put price stability first. Another factor was the intellectual revolution of economics associated with the work of monetarist economists such as Milton Friedman and Karl Brunner. Central bankers, who need sensitive economic antennae, picked up the shifting winds in the late 1970s.

The monetarist rebellion

The basic contribution of this school was to help make price stability the objective of monetary policy – the central thesis of Friedman's presidential address to the American Economic Association in 1967. To do this they had to convince economists and policymakers that persistent inflation was caused by something which was in principle under the control of monetary policy – the money supply – rather than by things like wage increases, which were obviously not. Of course the intellectual case was not decisive; when politicians decided to make price stability their goal, they were swayed by other factors; but it was nevertheless important for the case to be made.

Any debate about inflation starts with a tautology. Inflation is caused by an increase in the demand for goods and services in excess of an economy's ability to produce those goods and services without generating inflation, or by a reduction in the supply of goods and services with unchanged demand. Where does money come in? Through its effect on demand. But is money the only factor that can bring about a sustained increase in demand? The answer is still in dispute. Some economists believe that it is. Others say that there may be other causes, such as increases in government spending. How do wage increases affect inflation? Rather than saying they directly cause rising prices by increasing costs, people now tend to say that a rise in wages reduces the supply of goods and services relative to the demand. With unchanged money supply and less produced, prices will tend to rise. But again, monetarists would say – and most economists now agree with them – that prices are unlikely to rise for a prolonged period (say, a year or two at most) unless the money supply increases.

Monetarists believe that persistent inflation is caused mainly by monetary expansion and can be reduced by monetary policy. According to Samuelson and Nordhaus, not themselves 'monetarist' economists, 'monetarism holds that the money supply is the major determinant of short-run movements in nominal GNP and of long-run movements in prices'. This echoes the classic statement by David Hume, the eighteenth-century Scots pioneer of economics, that 'money, when increasing, gives encouragement to industry, during the interval between the increase of money and rise of the prices'. Perhaps the most famous of all definitions is that of Hugh Dalton, Britain's Chancellor of the Exchequer from 1945 to 1947: 'too much money chasing too few goods'. Friedman himself proclaims that: 'Inflation is always and everywhere a monetary phenomenon in the sense that it is and can be produced only by a more rapid increase in the quantity of money than in output.'

Keynesians, on the other hand, believe that inflation is often caused by non-monetary factors such as wage pressure and import costs, and that relying on monetary policy alone to curb it will entail huge costs in terms of unemployment. 'In the main, control must be . . . over the forces which cause firms and persons to seek loans and not over whether they are given or not the loans', to quote John Kenneth Galbraith.

Monetarists do not deny that sociological factors may be important influences on monetary policy, and through this route, indirectly, on the rate of increase of prices. But they stress that such factors have no direct effect in the long run on prices. Thus if wages rise, and the central bank uses its weapons to prevent any increase in the stock of money, firms will not be able to increase prices, as there will not be sufficient demand; they will have to lay off workers. Wages and unemployment will rise, but, apart from temporary disturbances, prices will remain flat.

But it was not enough to convince people of the role of monetary growth in inflation – they had to believe also that the costs of restricting monetary growth to a non-inflationary rate would not be excessive, or that in any case they had to be paid. This was accomplished by another revolution in economic theory which established that in the long run there is no trade-off between inflation and unemployment. This was a frontal assault on that part of Keynes's legacy that had had the greatest impact on policymaking, especially in Britain and America, the belief that governments could manage demand (mainly by fiscal policy) in order to reduce unemployment.

Now governments were told they did not have the means to do this. Unemployment in the long run was determined by economic forces such as the flexibility of the workforce (including the willingness and ability to learn new skills, to move house, and if necessary to accept lower wages), the efficient functioning of markets in goods and services, the dynamism of the small firms sector, and the general competitiveness of the economy. These were 'real' economic forces as distinct from 'monetary' forces that caused persistent inflation. The rate of unemployment at which forces pushing prices up are exactly balanced by those tending to push prices down was called the 'natural rate' (many Keynesians also accepted this concept). Pumping up the money supply would have zero effect on unemployment in the long run – but if it pushed the rate of unemployment for a time below the natural rate, it would cause accelerating inflation.

Another reason for the growing dominance of monetary policy was that other tools of macroeconomic management had become unusable. Fiscal policy became discredited in the 1970s when it was realized that countries that had tried to use it to manage their economies suffered higher inflation without lowering unemployment. The turning point was the aftermath of the first oil price hike in 1973; countries that adjusted quickly to the shock by restraining demand did better in the end than those that tried to spend their way out of recession. The Bonn Economic Summit in 1978, when Germany was pushed by President Carter into acting as a 'locomotive' for the world economy, was the last gasp of the old fiscal policy school. In the 1980s and since, ballooning budget deficits meant there could be no thought of boosting them still further with the aim of increasing demand.

The quarrels between monetarists and Keynesians that took place in the 1960s and 1970s had died away by the 1990s, though differences in emphasis remain. Keynesians recognized that money has an important effect upon demand, output and inflation but view it only as one influence along with others, such as fiscal policy and exports.

For their part, monetarists acknowledged that factors other than the quantity of money, such as the level and rate of growth of government spending, may influence inflation. Moreover, as monetarists moved into influential positions, and attempted to put their doctrines into practice, the costs and difficulties involved exceeded their expectations, as Keynesians had forecast. They also had to recognize that financial deregulation had increasingly blurred the distinction between money and some other financial assets. Goodhart's Law, which states that when you adopt any particular measure of the money supply as a policy target, its components change so that it becomes unusable for that purpose, seemed to be vindicated. With the relationship between money and income appearing to break down in several countries, the more extreme claims of some monetarists were toned down (though most monetarists had always stressed that the transition to stable prices would be long and painful – all the more so for being delayed too long).

The continuing divide is mainly over the monetarist assumption that, left to itself, the economy will find its own equilibrium with no involuntary unemployment (except that caused by unnecessary state intervention), while Keynesians believe it suffers from so many 'rigidities' in key markets, especially labour markets, that disequilibrium can persist for years. This difference in assumptions underlies monetarists' suspicions of government intervention, and Keynesians' respect for it.

It is reflected in their typical policy stances. Monetarists tend to favour binding policymakers to follow fixed rules – the most famous of which is Friedman's call for a constant money growth-rate rule – whereas Keynesians favour allowing central bankers more discretion to adjust monetary growth to the short-term needs of the economy. Central bankers, though naturally conservative by instinct and training, are also often Keynesian in their insistence on the need for discretion. This is not just because Friedman's rule would seem to put them out of work; as practical policymakers, they are conscious of the fact that the objectives of policy have to be pursued within specific institutional and political settings. However, they are all now monetarists in the broad sense that they believe price stability is the key objective of monetary policy and there is no long-term trade-off between unemployment and inflation.

What is money?

Now that central bankers see their goal as that of delivering price stability, they face the same problems as monetarists had when they first set out to rehabilitate the quantity theory of money. What is money? And how do changes in the growth of the money supply affect the economy? Money is stuff you can use immediately to make purchases. Normally, this includes banknotes, coins, and deposits at banks or other financial institutions which you can draw on simply by using a plastic card or making out a cheque. In some countries travellers' cheques are money because they are generally accepted as means of payment. But if you have to go to a bank and change the travellers' cheques into banknotes before you can make your purchase, they are not money. Cigarettes can be money if they are generally accepted as means of payment. This is the key: money is defined not by what the holder thinks should be accepted (if it were, everybody would have tons of it), but what is in fact generally accepted in the country or area where you wish to make a purchase. In other words, there is no theoretical answer – it is an empirical issue.

Legal tender is what the law of the country states is acceptable as means of payment. Notes issued by the central bank are always legal tender; i.e., people are required by law to accept them. In nearly all countries, moreover, the law gives the central bank the exclusive right to issue banknotes. Historically this was the foundation of central banks' importance. And banknotes are still in most countries a large part of the money supply, that is to say, of the total stock of money in a country. This is especially true in developing countries, where in some cases relatively few people have a bank account.

But, to quote Mervyn King, the Bank of England's economic adviser in 1994: 'Although economic theory has a good deal to say about the role that money plays in the economy, it remains uncomfortably vague about the appropriate definition of money'. Economists and central bankers have conceived many different monetary aggregates, including various 'near money' financial assets. M1 is their attempt to measure statistically the concept of money in a narrow form, cash in circulation plus current deposits at the bank or other financial institutions. M2, M3, M4 and so on are definitions of broader monetary aggregates which include deposits that may be withdrawable only after a certain period of notice. These vary from one country to another, but may include savings deposits, balances at money market mutual funds, securities that are easily cashable, etc.

Movements in these aggregates are used by central banks either as *indicators* of what is happening or will happen to the economy or as *policy targets*. The definitions have to be frequently refined and updated to take account of changes in the financial system. For instance, when building societies (or thrift institutions in America) started offering current accounts with cheque books, or when American money market funds offered 'NOW' accounts (negotiable order of withdrawal) allowing immediate access to cash, then they had to be included in the definition of narrow money, M1. Another problem is that there is no definition of money that bears a fixed and predictable relationship to nominal income, or gross domestic product at current prices. Although economists were always well aware of this, monetarists had thought that changes in the relationship of money to output and prices (the velocity of money) would be fairly predictable; the fact that they turned out to be anything but caused some governments and central banks to abandon the use of monetary aggregates as targets while retaining them among the range of indicators of monetary conditions.

How policy is supposed to work

In principle, monetary policy seems to demand that central bankers pay attention to the balance sheet of the central bank itself. As we shall see, some central bankers deny this, but we feel that most would not disagree. As the present governor of the Bank of Italy, Antonio Fazio, has stated, 'In order to influence the volume, composition and cost of financial transactions, the central bank needs to be able to manage the size and composition of its balance sheet, as regards both assets and liabilities.' On the assets side, you will normally find the following items: gold and foreign currency reserves; investments in government securities and other securities; and loans to commercial banks. On the liabilities side, there will be notes and coin; balances of commercial banks placed with the central bank, and a usually small amount representing the central bank's capital and reserves (accounting practices differ). According to the cardinal principle of all financial accounting, assets must equal liabilities. So when a change in any of the individual assets brings about an increase in total assets, then there must be an increase either in notes and coin or in bankers' balances with the central bank – the two elements that together form the base for all the money in the economy, sometimes called 'central bank money' or 'high-powered money'.

When these liabilities increase, commercial banks will have more cash or larger balances at the central bank, and will be more willing to lend to their customers, possibly at cheaper rates than before. Interest rates will generally be lower. And the total money supply will tend to increase. If a central bank is to control the growth of the money supply in the whole economy, then it must control the growth of its own liabilities. We return to this below.

Changing the money supply

In countries which have a money market, the central bank's main instrument for altering the monetary base is open-market operations. By buying (or selling) securities it can increase (or decrease) the banks' reserves. Because banks keep only a small fraction of total deposits in the form of reserves, the change in the reserves leads potentially to a multiple expansion (or contraction) of total deposits. But first, the banks have to consider whether the central bank's operations have left them with excess reserves or a shortage of reserves. If the central bank intended by its open-market operations merely to offset a contractionary (or expansionary) impulse generated from outside the banking system (e.g. by tax receipts or payments), the banks may find they do not have surplus reserves, and so cannot increase loans and deposits. If, however, they find they have a surplus of reserves or a shortage they will try to expand or reduce their assets accordingly.

Some countries have compulsory reserve requirements, which mandate how much commercial banks should keep at the central bank in the form of reserve balances. Central banks sometimes have discretion to vary these – for instance, to deal with unexpected surges of liquidity in the money markets. This can provide an additional instrument with which to control the supply of money, though it also depends for its effectiveness ultimately on its impact on interest rates.

Shortages of reserves may be relieved by the central banks by means of short-term lending to the banking system (or by buying securities from it). The traditional rule associated with the name of Walter Bagehot is that such lending should be at 'penal' rates. When the central bank wishes to tighten monetary conditions, it will force the banks to borrow from it by deliberately creating a shortage of reserves, and then charge a rate well above going market rates for its loans. This is usually known as the Bank rate or discount rate. It is intended to discourage the banks or money market from borrowing from the central bank which they can only do by reducing their lending.

The central bank will always provide reserves 'at last resort', as failure to do so might cause a breakdown in the clearing system and in any case risk setting off a panic. But if it wished to control its own balance sheet very closely, it would make reserves available only at such high interest rates as to cause a real shock – but hopefully not panic – in the money markets. Some argue that it is impossible for the central bank to operate policy by targeting its balance sheet because of such risks and disadvantages. Other targets, which allow the central bank more discretion, have to be used; but the basic methods by which policy is made effective – notably the determined use of the interest-rate weapon – remain the same.

These three techniques – open-market operations, reserve requirements, and discount-rate lending – form the nucleus of the central bank's armoury. Although it is always difficult to be sure exactly how the money supply will change as a result of the central bank's actions, there can be no doubt of the effectiveness of the instruments when used decisively. Ultimately, the money supply is under the control of the central bank.

From money to demand

How do changes in the money supply affect overall demand in the economy? This is the next stage in what economists call the 'transmission mechanism' of monetary policy – the first stage being the effect of the central bank's changes in interest rates or its open-market operations on the growth of the money supply. What links money with demand?

Interest rates again play the key role. With unchanged demand for money but reduced supply, interest rates will rise. Householders and companies respond to the new level of interest rates by adjusting their real spending and interest plans. The extent to which they cut their spending will depend mainly on the extent of the rise in interest rates and whether they expect interest rates to remain positive in real (inflation-adjusted) terms. Moreover, if the authorities succeed in raising real (expected) interest rates, households will not only feel less wealthy, as the real value of their houses and other assets decline, but also be less willing to borrow.

Effective but not automatic

The effectiveness of monetary policy in curbing inflation has been demonstrated in many countries and at many different times. The most famous example in recent history was the Volcker experiment in 1979–82 (as described in Chapter 7), where the Fed followed a policy of strictly limiting the growth of the money supply irrespective of what happened to interest rates. The high rates that resulted did reduce demand; GNP stagnated, unemployment rose and inflation fell. Indeed, during this episode Volcker experimented with 'brutal' methods of monetary policy that came very close to a direct control of the central bank's balance sheet; and, as we have argued in Chapter I, that episode did more than anything else to bring central bankers back into the middle of economic policymaking.

The lessons of that much-studied episode remain, indeed, controversial. Samuelson and Nordhaus say that although the policy did cut inflation, it did so only at the cost of pushing unemployment up just as much as anti-inflation policies in earlier periods had done. They conclude: 'Money works, but it does not work miracles.'

But was that a fair test? Here we have to introduce another of the keywords of modern monetary policy – credibility. It is argued that

Volcker's experiment lacked full credibility, meaning that people expected it to be abandoned, and that it was not given enough time to prove it could work at acceptable cost. More broadly, economists about that time (the late 1970s) realized that the costs of any anti-inflationary monetary policy would be higher the less people really believed the central bank would persist. Vice versa, if workers and firms believed the policy would be maintained, and would succeed eventually, then they would take account of that in their actions, reduce their wage demands, and moderate their prices. This would allow more output to be produced at any given level or rate of increase of nominal income. Plainly, expectations of economic agents played a key role.

So a search began for ways by which the authorities could have their hands tied. It was hoped that such a ruse might improve credibility. This was one of the strands in economic thinking that started the discussion about the independence of the central bank. If you make the central bank independent, and give it a mandate to pursue price stability, then the government cannot interfere, so policy should have more 'credibility'. And if so, inflation can be reduced at lower costs in terms of unemployment.

Another problem faced by monetarism in action was the variability of the lag between changes in the money stock and prices. In the United States, Friedman's researches suggested that changes in prices tended to follow changes in the money supply by roughly two years. In Britain, research by Andrew Crockett, though open to various interpretations, suggested that changes in money supply led changes in money income by between twelve and fifteen months. In countries that have experienced much more rapid rates of inflation, such as Israel, Brazil, Chile and Argentina, the lag according to Friedman is only a few months. That there is a connection is clear. It is clear that, in the long run, increases in the money supply lead *only* to higher prices and wages, without any long-term effect on real wealth or real wages. But any idea of a mechanical relationship with fixed time-lags had to be abandoned.

The key role of interest rates

In order to influence the money supply, the central bank has to influence (a) the behaviour of commercial banks or (b) the behaviour of companies and individuals outside the banking sector or (c) the behaviour of the government or (d) all three. What do we mean by 'behaviour'? Actions that expand or reduce the stock of money. Lending by commercial banks tends to expand money; but often a bigger influence comes from government borrowing from the banking system, which increases the reserves of the banks (these reserves are part of the monetary base, the other part being cash held by the public). The biggest factor of all in many countries is direct government borrowing from the central bank – monetary financing of the government deficit is often the cause of very rapid inflation.

The techniques at the disposal of the central bank influence mainly the behaviour of the commercial banks and other financial institutions – and through them, the wider economy. However, a central bank can also indirectly influence government policy. Confronted with a large budget deficit, it can offset the expansionary effect that this usually has on the money supply by selling government securities and letting interest rates rise to whatever levels are required. The political unpopularity of such actions, especially at times of recession, may provide a test of strength between central bank and government; but a strong central bank would point out to a government in these circumstances that the inevitable result of its policies will be very high interest rates, and may induce the government to curb the budget deficit.

Central banking instruments rely ultimately on changing the level of interest rates. The higher the level (other things being the same), the less money people hold in their current accounts or in cash, since it becomes increasingly attractive to place it in longer-term forms, such as government savings bonds. High rates also deter borrowers – and lower borrowing means lower deposits. When deposits fall, the banks need to keep lower reserves at the central bank. So by putting up interest rates the central bank can drain reserves out of the system. The stock of money is then reduced by a multiple of the fall in bank reserves. And vice versa in the case of a rise in reserves or a fall in rates.

Threats from the new markets?

The new financial markets, such as the derivative markets, and rapid changes in the financial system pose many problems for policymakers. As the role of the banks in the system is reduced – in America, the banks' share in the total assets of financial intermediaries fell from 37 per cent to 27 per cent between 1980 and 1990 – so the impact of the central banks' techniques for controlling credit flows is blunted. How much weight should be given to monetary targets, and how much central banks should use their discretion rather than follow rigid rules, is much debated.

But the ultimate aim of policy – the control of inflation – can still be achieved, and here again interest rates are the key. By changing short-term interest rates, central banks can influence the cost of borrowing not only from the banks but also directly in the capital markets. As Alan Greenspan has said: 'While this effect may be more indirect, take longer, and require larger movements in rates for a given effect on output, the Federal Reserve and other central banks still have the tools required to implement monetary policy.'

A central bank is a bank

The central bank is a peculiar kind of bank, but a bank none the less. True, it normally has no direct business with members of the public or with non-financial corporations. But it conducts banking business – lending and investing funds on the one hand and issuing monetary liabilities on the other. Where a normal commercial bank will accept deposits from the public (which become its liabilities) the central bank's liabilities are notes and coin and balances from commercial banks. In our view, this aspect of central banking, though often downplayed by central bankers, needs to be discussed in this chapter as it could become important again in the future.

As a bank, a central bank has to be interested in the quality of its assets, mainly foreign reserves and investments in government securities (sometimes loans to the government as well). The role of a central bank as manager of the country's foreign reserves is dealt with in Chapter 11. Investments in government securities have normally been considered riskless, because the state can tax its citizens. However, if a government runs massive budget deficits for a prolonged period, its credit standing will ultimately be damaged. In that case, if it forces the central bank to purchase its securities on an excessive scale, the money supply will expand excessively, the rate of inflation will increase and the standing of the central bank itself will be eroded.

The ECB will look to its balance sheet

This question of the quality of a central bank's assets has in the past been an issue mainly in developing countries, where the credit of the government may be poor; in OECD countries, where the credit of the government is not in question, it has not normally been an issue for monetary policy. However it may become very pertinent if the European

Central Bank (ECB) ever comes about and has to decide what assets it should invest in. Under the Maastricht Treaty, the central bank's executive board is under instruction to draw up a consolidated balance sheet of the European System of Central Banks (ESCB), comprising 'those assets and liabilities of the national central banks that fall within the ESCB' (Article 26.3). Following the practice of America's Federal Reserve, 'A consolidated financial statement of the ESCB shall be published each week' (Article 15.2). Article 18.1 lays down that the ESCB may 'conduct credit operations with credit institutions and other market participants, with lending being based on adequate collateral'.

What is 'adequate collateral'? If the ECB is set up, and is free to decide the composition of its portfolio (the Maastricht Treaty is not explicit on this, but it would be a requirement of true independence), it will need to assess the quality of the securities issued by the governments of member states. How will it decide how much to hold in each individual government's debt? How would Germany respond if the ECB declared that it would only accept securities issued by Italian, French and British governments? An unlikely scenario, perhaps, but clearly, the ECB's decisions on such issues will define the ability of each EU national government to finance its borrowing needs (direct financing by the central bank is forbidden). The point is that, as a bank, a central bank unavoidably takes decisions about lending and investing its assets – decisions of great importance to governments. In this case, the underlying question is: is monetary union feasible without fiscal harmonization – and thus a high degree of political integration as well? We do not believe it is.

In central banking, apparently technical issues often turn out to be politically sensitive. In the early years, when central banks were still establishing their own credit, often in competition with other banks, they were especially anxious to invest only in assets of the highest quality. This concern was reflected in the requirement that banks which borrowed from them 'at last resort' should put up adequate security – and the assets eligible for such central bank lending were carefully defined. The reason for this was of course that if the borrowing bank became bankrupt and defaulted on its loan from the central bank, the latter would still have the security, which it could sell in the market; otherwise the losses would threaten its own credit, and it might in turn have to go begging to the government. As we shall see in later chapters, many central bank governors recently have indeed had to go to their finance ministers to seek budget help to finance large-scale bail-outs of commercial banks under their charge, as they did not have adequate reserves or security of their own. So the central bank's capital and credit are still matters of crucial concern to central bankers. It is no longer enough to assert that, as official institutions, their credit is undisputed. On the contrary, it is tested all the time in the markets.

Their banking judgement is also brought to bear on their choice of assets in which to hold the country's external reserves (see Chapter 11); indeed, this is another aspect of their business where they are becoming more commercially minded again, as their reserve management business becomes more complex with the proliferation of new market techniques.

It has always to be kept in mind that the central bank's decisions have multiple effects on the money supply only because its liabilities (cash or its equivalent) are judged absolutely safe. If a particular central bank's assets became suspect – say, it started investing in property – or its credit was diminished for other reasons, the currency it issues would be undermined. Its currency issue is an extension of its credit. So central bankers as well as commercial bankers are in the business of judging risks and returns. True, central banks have public policy responsibilities which require them to place other objectives – notably the aim of securing price stability – over and above any concern they may have about the bottom line, but many are proud that they do make a profit as well (normally this is handed over to the government).

The burden of the public debt

Before moving to consider monetary policy in practice, we pause for a moment to review briefly one of the most disputed questions in economics: is the public debt a burden on future generations? Nobel prize-winning economists who agree on much else cannot agree on this. We consider it here because of its relevance for monetary policy in the long term. As we have seen, control of the money supply rests crucially on the capacity of the central bank to buy or sell government obligations to the market and thus reduce or expand the reserves of the banking system. Equally, the government has to fund its deficit by selling bonds to cover all or a large part of the deficit. But that may not be the end of the story; as the amount of government debt in the hands of the public grows, will there come a point where they are not willing to accept more at any price?

This may depend on whether they view the tax they have to pay to service existing debt as a burden. The traditional account states that an internal debt, owed by a nation to its own citizens, poses no burden on the future taxpayers who must service the debt, since that does not represent a net claim on current output of the economy; it is merely a transfer of income from taxpayers to those who receive interest on the bonds. On the traditional analysis, an external debt, by contrast, does obviously require interest payments to be paid out to foreigners and so pre-empts a part of the current output of the economy.

However, for many years the Nobel prize-winning economist James Buchanan, an outsider among great American economists, and a few others have been fighting a lone battle against this view. Buchanan maintains that servicing the public debt is a burden on future generations and that it makes no difference whether the debt is owed to foreigners or to 'ourselves'. He fastens on the fact that the current generation of taxpayers experience a reduction in their current income because they have to pay taxes to service debt interest payments. This tax is a burden on them which as far as they are concerned has nothing to do with the fact that at the same time bondholders are receiving interest:

> The person who is faced with a tax bill to finance interest charges will not make any relationship between the saving that his or her parents may or may not have made because the debt was issued earlier. The person faced with such a tax bill will reckon only on the simply observed fact that income which he or she might otherwise use is being taken away in taxes.

In every respect, Buchanan maintains, financing a budget deficit by issuing debt is equivalent to a firm or individual borrowing to finance a deficit. It is tantamount to eating up the accumulated capital of the nation. Visualizing this capital value in terms of an apple orchard, an asset that had been nurtured by generations past, Buchanan declares that 'by financing current public outlay by debt, we are, in effect, chopping up the apple trees for firewood, thereby reducing the yield of the orchard for ever'.

Moreover, Buchanan questions whether future taxpayers can or should be coerced into paying interest on the bonds: why should they pay for benefits that we have used up? Although they may in practice pay taxes to service the debt, this may merely reflect a reluctance to break contracts. Yet governments have often repudiated contracts. Buchanan suggests that default will become increasingly discussed if budget deficits continue.

Other professional economists remain unconvinced. But the latest edition of Samuelson and Nordhaus's *Economics* appears to mark a retreat. Samuelson and Nordhaus now admit that the view that the internal debt poses no burden because 'we owe it to ourselves' is 'oversimplified'. Their restatement is carefully qualified:

> If every citizen owned $10,000 of government bonds and all were equally liable for the taxes to service that debt, it would not make sense to think

of a heavy load of debt that each citizen must carry ... But ... A large
government debt tends to reduce a nation's growth in potential output
because it displaces private capital, increases the inefficiency from taxation,
and forces a nation to service the external portion of the debt.

This debate has a direct bearing on monetary policy. Many observers
think that government debt has been rising too quickly. Even if budget
deficits seem to be quite easy to finance, as they were in 1992–93 during
a bull market in bonds, it is dangerous to let ratios of government debt
to GNP rise too high. As former British Chancellor of the Exchequer,
Lord Lawson, has said, 'debt is deferred taxation'. This sentiment lay
behind the far-reaching provisions in the Maastricht Treaty, ratified in
1993, to enforce budgetary discipline on member countries entering into
the proposed European Monetary Union. High levels of debt cramp
monetary policy. Monetary policymakers are walking along a narrow
ledge where they need strong nerves; a loss of confidence by investors
could make it impossible to finance budget deficits even at very high
real interest rates. Only by curbing government borrowing can monetary
policy recover some freedom of manoeuvre.

A framework for policy

To return to the main theme of this chapter, we mentioned above the
need for monetary policy to be credible. The more that members of the
public understand the policy and what is involved, the lower the costs
incurred in attaining price stability will be in terms of lost output or
higher unemployment. Monetary policy is not a matter of mechanics,
but of changing the incentives facing individuals and enterprises.

The central bank has to earn credibility; a public hardened on many
decades of false promises of stability will not easily be persuaded that this
time they really mean it. But the great battles of the 1980s were not in
vain; in most OECD countries monetary policy has regained some
credibility, despite the growing longer-term threat from budget deficits
and debt.

To retain this, central bankers not only have to follow appropriate
policies but also have to explain them better than they have done. It is
easier for them to do this when they have a clear framework within
which to work.

The discussion earlier in this chapter can be summarized in terms of
such a policy framework. First, a central bank needs a clear statement of
objectives. This is usually now defined as the objective of price stability,

though others are possible (we suggest in Chapter 23 that their mission needs to be broadened, with price stability seen as a precondition of success but not the end of the story). Second, it needs to be able to explain clearly what it will do to reach that objective, and how its actions are related to that objective. Many central banks have an intermediate target such as the rate of growth of a monetary aggregate; or a target for the nominal growth of national output. An intermediate target is used mainly to clarify the relationship between the central bank's day-to-day actions and its ultimate objective. Others, such as the Netherlands Bank, have an exchange-rate rule (a currency board, such as the Hong Kong Monetary Authority, is a central bank with a rigid exchange-rate rule). Third, a central bank needs to be given the tools to do the job. The government has to allow it discretion to raise interest rates to bring the money supply under control and there should be a clear institutional framework laying down who has the final say on monetary policy, and how the governor of the central bank is appointed. Fourth, the government has to keep its borrowing needs under control even in a recession, otherwise it is set on a collision course with the central bank.

Finally, the government and central bank need to recognize the limits to the scope for monetary policy. Even the best and wisest monetary policy cannot be expected to banish cyclical fluctuations in the economy – these are a normal part of economic development and growth. But even within these natural limits, conducting monetary policy successfully depends on the determination of the central bank and the willing cooperation of the public. Giving the central bank greater independence can be helpful if it fits into a wider policy framework that helps to make policy credible. But it would be quite wrong to expect that merely passing a law granting independence will itself make much difference. Credibility has to be earned: will politicians allow the central bank to put up interest rates to whatever level is necessary to bring down bank lending and the money supply?

This is a question that can be addressed better when we look at how monetary policy is conducted in practice; and that is the subject of the next chapter.

9 *Monetary Policy in Practice*

So much for how monetary policy is supposed to work, and some of the challenges it poses to central bankers. How do central banks operate monetary policy in practice? Techniques, objectives and operating procedures vary widely. As we describe the policies of the Federal Reserve and the Bank of Japan elsewhere (Chapters 14 and 16), here we give a brief account of policy techniques in a number of other countries. To begin with, we focus on three big European countries – Germany, Britain and France. To show how the techniques of monetary policy are becoming more similar – notwithstanding the big contrasts that remain – we then go on a whirlwind tour, visiting South Africa, China and the Solomon Islands. The chapter concludes with an overview of recent trends in monetary policies in developing countries.

Europe's anchor

Germans have a well-known, and amply justified, aversion to inflation. This has deep historical roots – even before the experience of hyperinflation followed by depression in the interwar years, the German love of stability and order was proverbial. Germany's money market system also has deep roots and there is a close relationship between the way the money markets work and the monetary policy of the central bank.

Money markets serve the same basic purpose in Germany as elsewhere – namely, to allow banks to adjust their reserve positions. These fluctuate in accordance with the public's demand for cash and with other influences. But the way the markets work differs greatly from country to country. In Germany, banks must by law hold minimum cash reserves (in 1994 they were 5 per cent of sight deposits). These are designed partly to put a brake on credit growth, and partly as an additional instrument for the central bank to keep its grip on the commercial banks. Banks with excess reserves lend these to banks with a shortage, dealing directly with each other rather than through brokers; and there is little trading of short-term money-market instruments such as Treasury bills or commercial bills. This reflects the fact that the German financial system is dominated by banks, with short-term securities playing only a small role.

The monetary policy of the Bundesbank is identified in press reports with the setting of two key interest rates – the discount rate and the Lombard rate. The discount rate represents the lower limit for the rates at which it makes available money for one month and three months. Banks use this as a means of obtaining cheap ('subsidized') discount credit on a permanent basis, up to the limits set by the 'rediscount quotas' decided by the Central Bank Council from time to time. The Lombard rate marks the upper limit, Lombard loans being used exceptionally for meeting peak needs in the money market. (The Bundesbank will always make funds available through Lombard loans if banks need funds and have not been able to raise them at cheaper rates elsewhere.) These rates are set by the Council, which meets every other Thursday. Between these meetings, the management or *directorium* of the central bank tries to keep rates within the corridor set by the Council.

The Bundesbank is required by law 'to regulate the quantity of money in circulation and of credit supplied to the economy with the aim of safeguarding the currency'. It seeks to control money creation and achieve its annual target for growth of the money supply by indirect procedures. It operates both on interest rates and on supply and demand conditions in the money market. First, it may change the interest rate charged for its own lending to the banks. Second, it may change the channels through which it injects or withdraws reserves from the system. In other words, when the banks need to obtain central bank money, the Bundesbank makes funds available at a high interest rate through Lombard loans or at a lower interest rate through the discount rate, or at a rate between these two through repurchase operations. For short-term management of liquidity, the Bundesbank makes extensive use of repurchase agreements, which by 1990 was the dominant influence on short-term interest rates. (Repurchase or 'repo' transactions, where the central bank buys fixed-interest securities from the commercial banks and simultaneously sells them back for forward settlement, provide banks with central bank money for a limited period.)

Like other central banks, the Bundesbank gives 'signals', not 'orders'. It gives signals to the markets by its choice of instrument and by changing the key central bank rates. The Lombard rate, as the rate at which the central bank will always make available 'last resort' funds, has a special role – as the most flexible source of funds, banks will prefer to use Lombard loans if the Lombard rate is close to money-market rates. So the Bundesbank always tries to keep it at a significant margin over

other rates. When rates are falling, markets pay particularly close attention to the discount rate; when rates are rising, to the Lombard rate.
There is normally a gap of about 1.5 per cent between the two rates.
The key short-term indicator is the 'repo' rate, which usually changes a
little every week. Given the role of the D-mark as Europe's anchor
currency, the decisions on its key lending rates are instantly communi-
cated to market traders. And because the D-mark is one of the world's
leading currencies, the interest-rate decisions of the Bundesbank affect
interest rates over a large part of Europe and beyond.

On a week-to-week or even month-to-month basis, the actual growth
of money may diverge quite far from the central bank's targets – which
is why it only sets annual ones. In the short term, an expansion or
contraction in the money supply is usually set in motion by commercial
banks or their customers. Banks may decide to increase their loans and
investments, or customers may take up more of their credit facilities,
without any action on the part of the central bank – and this causes
money creation. But as this process leads to a rise in the notes and coin
in circulation and in the minimum reserves that banks have to keep with
the central bank, then they will need more central bank money. And in
the short run, the central bank is obliged to supply this. Only by its
subsequent decisions on instruments and key interest rates can the
Bundesbank signal whether it wishes this initial expansion of the money
supply to continue or not.

Open-market operations are conducted in a range of securities, including eligible bills, Treasury bills, and bonds listed on the stock exchange.
Although the central bank is not permitted to intervene in the capital
market with the primary aim of financing public-sector borrowing or
supporting the market, the lack of a broad secondary market for
government paper means that the central bank is the 'interest rate leader'
in the securities markets generally.

There has been a reasonably close relationship between monetary
growth and prices in Germany – prices tend to follow movements in the
money supply after a lag of two to three years. When the relationship is
close, obviously there is a strong case for the central bank to set its
monetary policy and interest-rate policy so as to allow only an expansion
of the money supply consistent with price stability. So the Bundesbank,
which was the first central bank to introduce monetary targeting in
1974, remains loyal to this approach. However, occasionally it surprises
the markets by appearing to disregard the signals given by monetary
aggregates. A good example was in May 1994 when it cut its discount
and Lombard rate by 0.5 per cent, despite the fact that the money
supply had been growing at well above its target of 4 to 6 per cent.

The Bundesbank fully agrees with other central banks that sound public finance is essential to the proper conduct of monetary policy. A large borrowing requirement – budget deficit – increases the difficulties and costs of following an anti-inflationary monetary policy. Where the Bundesbank scores is in its unyielding refusal to allow short-term slippage in monetary growth or higher public-sector deficits to lead to a longer-term monetary expansion inconsistent with price stability. When the crunch comes, the whole world can scream at it to reduce interest rates, and it still will not budge.

Frequently accused of being 'rigid' and 'arrogant', criticism reached a climax in 1992–93. As Otmar Issing, its Board member, has stated, 'the criticism voiced in but a single week of September 1992 reveals a mixture of overestimation of the scope of, and the possibilities open to, German monetary policy which sometimes goes beyond the bounds of the farcical'. This was when the British mass media was hurling abuse at the Bundesbank and its president for not helping Britain by reducing German interest rates. These insults, said Issing, showed 'an assessment of its intentions and effects bordering on demonization. The campaign finally reached its sad peak in the popular form of personification with – to put it mildly – unqualified accusations levelled at the Bundesbank president.'

We quote this to show that beneath the apparently tranquil surface of technical money-market operations are potentially emotional and indeed violent clashes of temperament, policy and tradition. Helmut Schlesinger, the Bundesbank president at the centre of this storm, had given newspaper interviews which were widely viewed as extremely indiscreet, to put it no higher. Some of his remarks were interpreted as casting doubt on the ability of sterling to stay in the ERM just when the British government and the Bank of England were throwing everything into the battle for the pound.

Reverting to more technical matters, how efficient are the Bundesbank's monetary techniques? Nobody can dispute its success in attaining its final objective at least relative to other central banks: Germany's average inflation rate of 3.8 per cent from 1971 to 1991 is the lowest in the world (see Appendix). But many experts question whether its actual operating techniques are efficient. Reserve requirements amount to a large tax on banking, without arguably assisting the central bank in conducting market operations. This is because, at the crunch, the central bank will always provide reserves to the banks, as in other countries, so that policy in Germany, as everywhere else, ultimately works through interest rates.

Inflation target in Britain

The objective of monetary policy is defined as that of achieving, delivering and maintaining price stability – not because it is the only aim of economic policy but because it is seen as an essential precondition for the achievement of other aims. It is the contribution that the central bank can make to those wider aims. The framework within which the Bank of England pursues the aim of price stability has changed quite frequently. In the late 1970s and early 1980s, it experimented with various monetary targets, but found them all unsatisfactory. When Britain was in the Exchange Rate Mechanism from 1990 to 1992, the Bank had to deliver monetary conditions that ensured that sterling stayed in the permitted band of fluctuation (in practice, against the D-mark). Even then, monetary policy was not reduced only to an exchange-rate target – there was still some scope for managing interest rates.

When Britain left the ERM in September 1992, the objectives of policy remained unchanged, but the operating framework changed: the operating target was defined as that of holding annual inflation to a range of 1–4 per cent, the first time in Britain that an explicit and precisely defined objective for inflation had been set. The Bank's job was to deliver monetary conditions that would keep inflation within that range. There was no 'intermediate' target, in terms of a definition of the money supply.

Within that framework, the operation of monetary policy falls into two parts: first, assessing performance; second, executing any tactical changes needed. Performance is assessed by looking not only at trends in inflation, but also at more anecdotal evidence from surveys of business opinion, and in particular evidence from the markets and forward indicators of market expectations (such as the yield on securities). The Bank's view of the outlook for inflation is presented in the quarterly *Inflation Report*.

Policy changes are executed through the markets – in practice the Bank will seek through its market operations to push short-term interest rates up or down. It actively intervenes in three markets – the short-term money market, gilt-edged, and foreign exchange market. Many of its operations are concerned with smoothing flows of funds – avoiding the abrupt change in rates that would otherwise take place as a result of payments (e.g. during the tax-paying season) in and out of the banking system. The Bank aims to ensure the money market is 'squared-off' at the end of each day and is not left with an overdraft position at the

Bank. But on a slightly longer-term basis – week to week – the Bank needs to ensure that the market is indeed 'short', which it does by varying the amount of Treasury bills it sells each week. It then signals the direction in which it wants interest rates to move by adjusting the rate at which it will lend money to the market to relieve the shortage. That in turn immediately affects the interbank market rate. Because many other short-term rates are closely linked to the interbank rate, the central bank's signals are quickly transmitted to short-term interest rates throughout the economy. This changes the cost of money to firms, individuals and the government; in the case of an increase in rates, it will reduce profit margins of all firms borrowing money from the bank, make investment more expensive and so in time reduce economic activity.

Tactics in the money market are coordinated with the Bank's operations in the gilt-edged and the forex markets. The primary function of its operations in the gilts market is to cover the government's budget deficit (strictly, the public sector borrowing requirement or PSBR). In 1993–94 that PSBR was about £45 billion, or 7 per cent of GDP; and under the government's 'full-funding' policy the Bank was expected to raise all of it by selling government debt in the government bond market. It was not expected to cover the full amount from day to day – in the short term, it issued Treasury bills to do that. But Treasury bills are so easily converted into cash that they are regarded as 'near money', so it would be inflationary to rely on Treasury bills to finance the budget deficit. Longer-term securities carry a greater risk to the holder (because their price may vary), so are regarded as the least inflationary way of funding the deficit. So long as they are bought by institutions other than the banks, or by individuals, they drain cash from the system. In principle these sales can fully offset the expansionary effect of the budget deficit on the money supply, though, as suggested in Chapter 8, they add to the national debt and thus the burden on future generations. Finally, the Bank's interventions in the foreign-exchange market also have to be taken into account, since buying (or selling) of foreign currencies also injects (or drains) sterling from the banking system.

Like the Bundesbank, the Bank gives 'signals' to the money markets. These, it says, should be as clear as possible; the market can tell where it wants rates to move by the timing of its operations, the choice of instruments it employs, and the amount of intervention. If it wants to resist an incipient rise in rates, it will relieve shortage early in the day – perhaps fully. Or it can make things difficult for the market by delaying assistance until the last opportunity. Or it can simply announce that it will not lend at less than '*x* per cent' – this so-called minimum lending rate (MLR), the successor to the old Bank rate, has not been used by the Bank regularly but can be if necessary.

One very British characteristic of the system is that there are no formal reserve requirements for monetary policy purposes. True, there is a cash ratio deposit of 0.35 per cent of eligible liabilities, but this is used mainly to raise revenue for the Bank and has no monetary significance. The Bank merely insists that the banking system keeps certain 'operational balances' which must be zero or above! It seems at first glance as if the textbook account of the way monetary policy operates – on the fulcrum of a ratio between cash, or 'central bank money', and total deposits, as sketched in Chapter 8 – does not apply to Britain. If banks do not have to keep balances above zero, what is to prevent an infinite expansion of bank lending and deposits? The fact that, in principle, the central bank could still control money by simply issuing fewer banknotes is irrelevant if in practice it supplies as many as people want.

True, banks in practice have to keep some balances at the Bank of England, if only to avoid if possible going into overdraft (when the payments to other banks through the clearing system exceed receipts from other banks, as can happen without warning). However, even that is possible, and the Old Lady doesn't protest. The Bank does not pay much attention to these 'operational balances' either, even as an indicator, and certainly does not target them. In economists' jargon, money in Britain is 'endogenous'; notes and coin are supplied on demand, while 'broad money' is created by the banking system. The focus of policy is on short-term interest rates, which are moved up or down depending on the outlook for inflation.

In practice, monetary policy is determined by two influences – the Bank's forecasts of inflation, and political pressures. When the Bank's forecasts suggest that the rate of inflation will rise above its targets, it will recommend raising interest rates, but its views may not be accepted by the Chancellor. The Bank of England certainly feels it can be trusted to follow a non-inflationary monetary policy, and would like to be given the chance to prove it by being made more independent of the Treasury (in 1993 the Governor was given more discretion in deciding on the timing of interest rate changes, but the ultimate decision lay firmly in the hands of the Chancellor). However, the legacy of Britain's poor long-term record is a heavy burden: Britain comes in at a miserable 55th place in our ranking of countries by price performance (see Appendix). Performance has much improved recently, but it is the long-term haul that counts in the credibility stakes. Many years, perhaps a generation, of first-class, sustained performance will be required to restore credibility fully.

Paris between the *franc fort* and Frankfurt

The French central bank does set targets for monetary growth, and in January 1994 it also quantified its ultimate objective of price stability (an inflation rate of less than 2 per cent). It relies on the tuning of short-term interest rates to achieve the target in terms of money stock (M3) which is set for the calendar year with reference to forecasts for growth and inflation.

The instruments of monetary policy include compulsory, non-interest-bearing reserves of 1 per cent on sight deposits and on passbook accounts, and 0.5 per cent on time accounts of ten days to one year (there are no reserve requirements on longer-term time accounts). If the bank has excess reserves in any given period (usually a month), a portion may be carried over to the following period.

Banks may lose central bank money through withdrawal of banknotes by customers, or payments to the Treasury, or because of sales of foreign currencies by the Bank of France on the exchange market. The budget deficit is not financed by the Bank of France.

The central bank supplies reserves mainly through repurchase tenders, setting both the quantity of reserves provided and the price, namely the interest rate. If the amount supplied is excessive (or inadequate), which may happen as a result either of deliberate intent or of misjudgement, then market interest rates will tend to decline (or rise). The central bank may offset this movement by money-market operations conducted either directly with a bank or through a specialized money-market institution.

Banks that wish to borrow have to deliver a promissory note to the central bank. They must have a sufficient amount of Treasury bills (*bons du Trésor*) or loans to companies of good credit standing. The maturity of the notes is generally twenty to thirty days. There are two key interest rates: the five- to ten-day repurchase rate against Treasury bills and high-quality loans, and the tender rate. The Bank of France determines the spread between them, usually 50 to 100 basis points. Open-market operations as such play a relatively small role, and the central bank does not intervene in the long-term securities market.

The money-market system in France is quite similar to that in Germany or other countries where the interbank market consists of exchanges of bankers' balances at the central bank; all funds are cleared through accounts at the Bank of France. Most of the funds are borrowed or lent 'overnight'. In addition to the interbank market itself, there exists in France a wide money market, open to all agents, where negotiable debt instruments are exchanged, notably Treasury bills.

In practice, so long as the franc and other European currencies were tied together within narrow bands of fluctuation in the ERM, central banks had little discretion in their monetary policies. After the bands were widened in August 1993, they had more room for manoeuvre, at least in theory. However, Germany warned other countries not to take advantage of this to depreciate their currencies by a large amount; also, the French authorities wanted to maintain their *'franc fort'* policy. They did not want to reward so-called 'Anglo-Saxon' speculators who had bet on a big devaluation. So they kept interest rates relatively high, contrary to the advice of many outside observers, who argued that interest rates should be reduced in response to the economic recession. In effect, France continued to shadow the D-mark and to use the D-mark link as an anchor of its monetary policy and price level.

France, and indeed other European countries, have had to steer their monetary policies through a difficult transition period since the days of full dependence under the Bretton Woods fixed-rate system. Then they contracted out their monetary policies to the American central bank. In the 1980s they half contracted out monetary policy to the Bundesbank, so that their policies were 'made in Frankfurt'; but the widening of the fluctuation bands in 1993 despite ten years of stern, stable policies showed how difficult it was to make the peg fully credible (only Austria, the Netherlands and Belgium had fully credible pegged rates). Many economists drew the conclusion that European Monetary Union could be realized only by a 'Big Bang' – a simultaneous leap into a single currency, rather than by a gradual process of convergence.

Banging heads together in Europe

How the European Monetary Institute, set up in Frankfurt in 1994, would tackle these issues remained to be seen. But one of the most important tasks would be to decide how a European central bank, if it came about, would execute monetary policy in the European Union. Hans Tietmeyer, president of the Bundesbank, made clear that he would press hard for the system of minimum reserve requirements to be applied across Europe. The Bank of England argued that this was not necessary, and that it would raise the costs of banks, since, unless the central bank pays market rates of interest, the minimum reserve requirement is equivalent to a tax on banking transactions. In the British view, this would tend to drive banking business to offshore centres and would also encourage the process known as 'disintermediation', where banks lose business to less heavily regulated financial institutions.

The outcome of this debate would plainly have a big impact on the profitability of the banks of different countries. If it were decided to impose a uniform 10 per cent reserve requirement, a large new tax would be imposed on banks from countries that did not have such high requirements, and above all on British-based banks, which had no reserve requirements. If the ECB decided not to have reserve requirements, German banks and others from highly taxed countries would obtain a windfall gain.

Some expected that central banks would compete, on behalf of their financial centres, to keep some key aspects of their business, and this could cause technical difficulties for the transition to a single currency. In particular, French observers were worried that the European interbank market, where banks compete for overnight money to satisfy reserve requirements, would bypass Paris. With monetary union there can only be one price at which banks can obtain central bank money – private banks have to have access to cash at the central bank at the same price throughout the union. This would be set by the council of the new European Central Bank. Large differences in charges and operating procedures of national central banks, such as the types of collateral they accept against advances to banks, would have to be ironed out; the ECB would clarify the procedures to be used by all its subsidiary 'branches'.

This would also have a large impact on the way private banks operate, for at present the assets they hold vary considerably among countries, depending partly on the type of instrument used by the national central bank (for example, Treasury bills in Britain, commercial bills with specified signatures in France). In so far as the assets that banks hold reflect profound differences between national banking systems, with their roots in the habits and customs of the people, rather than mere technical differences, then the attempt to impose a blueprint from the centre could be very costly. This is another example of the difficulty we noted in Chapter 2 of distinguishing between aspects of finance that are in the fast lane and those that move very slowly. Officials and academics tend to view all aspects of finance as being in the fast lane, and also as being amenable to change from above, whereas if they are rooted in the habits of a people, they can be difficult or impossible to change quickly.

If it proves possible to implement standardized procedures, which would be an essential condition for monetary union, it seems likely that one centre would take pride of place as the place where the ECB conducted its market operations and where European short-term interest rates were determined. The examples of other currency areas suggests that one centre quickly attracts the bulk of this business. But which centre would play this role would be decided not so much by competition between central banks but rather by the variety and depth of its money markets.

A study in contrasts – China, the Solomon Islands, South Africa

How does monetary policy work elsewhere in the world? The answer in a nutshell is that, despite continuing differences, more and more countries are adopting the basic features of the techniques and procedures in use in Europe and North America. Indeed, the reform of monetary policy has formed a key component of the economic reform programmes launched by many countries in the past ten to fifteen years. We outline the main features of these monetary reforms later in this chapter. But first, a study in contrasts. To illustrate the wide differences that persist, we visit three countries: the most populous country in the world; a country with one of the smallest populations, far removed from the industrial world; and a country with a robust financial system facing a testing time of political transition. How are the central banks of these three countries using the tools of monetary policy to meet the challenges their countries face?

Beijing blues

Since the opening-up of China to the outside world by Deng Xiaoping in 1979, the Chinese economy has been a miracle in the making. By the mid-1980s it was growing at world-record rates, steadily lifting its billion-plus people out of poverty, and building the basics of a market economy that, sometime in the twenty-first century, will almost certainly be the largest in the world. By the late 1980s, it was clear that China's leaders were still determined to press ahead with economic reforms, and this determination survived the disaster of Tiananmen Square in 1989, when their brutal suppression of the popular revolt brought them international obloquy. The Communist Party remained in place, providing the political infrastructure of government, while the bureaucrats, descendants of the old imperial mandarin class, were allowed to get on with economic reforms.

When one of the authors visited Beijing late in 1993, the reform programme had reached another crucial stage. Inflation was again becoming a threat – and Chinese society has a peculiar horror of inflation as disruptive of Confucian ideals of social stability and order. China's leaders were well aware that the Tiananmen Square disturbances were sparked off by fears of inflation as well as by a revulsion against widespread corruption. Moreover the Chinese have experienced hyper-inflation more recently than the Germans and are not allowed to forget the experience. The very first programme on state-controlled TV which our author watched in Beijing could be understood without knowing the Chinese language – pictures of Central Bank of China banknotes of larger and larger denominations, shot against black-and-white newsclips of the 'heroic' struggle of Mao Tse-tung's forces against the national government in the civil war of 1947–49.

A word on that great inflation. Between 1937 and 1947, wholesale prices increased at least 100,000 per cent and the money supply by 15,000 per cent – principally as a result of increased note issues of the Central Bank of China. The communists did no better in the parts of China they occupied (they entered Beijing in 1949); they set up central banks in North China, Central China and Inner Mongolia. In 1949, prices rose more than 7,000 per cent. When they had established their rule, the communists announced their new central banking policy in 1950–51 in these words: 'Instead of issuing huge quantities of paper money, as we were forced to do previously, we are now collecting taxes in a planned way and the finances of our country thus have a comparatively stable foundation.'

During China's hyperinflation, money lost two of its basic functions – as a store of value and as a unit of account – and was used only as a means of payment. To maintain their savings people used commodities like gold and silver, or consumer goods, or foreign currencies such as the American dollar. To set prices, many shops kept accounts in dollars (using the current exchange rate to set prices in local currency), or used commodity or cost-of-living indexes, calculating prices by multiplying the price of a product in a base year by their current index number. But banknotes continued to be used as means of payment, mainly because most prices were not controlled so the price mechanism could still function despite hyperinflation (carts were used to carry the money about). Although money still functioned in some fashion, the standard of living, especially of poorer people, was drastically reduced as speculative hoarding of goods cut the supply to the market.

The People's Bank of China (originally called the state bank) was set up in 1948 to stabilize the currency. But under the communist economic system it was simply an instrument of the national economic plan; it administered a credit plan, allocating credit to enterprises in accordance with the overall plan, and a cash plan, where currency was issued to enterprises to pay wages. Enterprises were credited or debited with accounting entries when they acquired or sold supplies. Monetary policy had no role. Financial markets and private banking were banned; nor were people allowed to have cheque books, current accounts, or loans. The only form of money was cash.

By the time of our visit in 1993, big changes had already been made. Starting in the early 1980s, commercial banks had been hived off from the monolithic state bank. Many financial markets had been started, including stock-exchanges. The People's Bank (PBC) was acting much more like a central bank in other countries – setting interest rates, controlling the issue of currency, and forecasting the growth of the money supply. With millions of new, privately owned firms driving the economy forward, with the central bank trying to hold interest rates above the rate of inflation, and with money being used to settle payments between enterprises, it started functioning again, for the first time in fifty years, in all three of its basic roles.

In 1993, the country's supreme policymaking bodies, the State Council and Politbureau, assigned a crucial role to the central bank in the struggle to modernize the economy. They looked to the central bank to keep price rises under control – not by old-fashioned methods of price controls but by the indirect methods of using interest rates to control the money supply and monetary demand. They installed a rising political heavyweight, Zhu Rhongyi, as governor with a mandate to push through the changes needed.

Zhu faced a daunting task. The head office in Beijing had not been able to bring the lower-level central banks in the provinces of China under its control; several of them still had in effect independent powers of money creation. So when Deng Xiaoping, supreme leader, visited the southern provinces in 1992 and called for even more rapid economic growth, the provincial governments fell over each other in their rush to start massive infrastructure projects – all financed by credits from their local branch of the central bank. This triggered the sudden worsening of inflationary pressures in 1993–94. This in turn sparked a 'gold rush', as people throughout China sought to buy gold jewellery as an inflation hedge, showing their continuing distrust of paper money.

When we visited the People's Bank, top officials were plainly worried. In a subterranean conference room below the striking modern building that houses the People's Bank headquarters, a short walk from Tiananmen Square, Xiou Gang, director of policy planning, talked frankly of the need for radical measures. The central bank had four immediate tasks: to clarify the goals of monetary policy; to clarify the roles of provincial and lower-level branches; to change its management style; and to get out of direct lending to industry.

Since the setting up of the central bank ten years previously, it had pursued a dual objective: economic development and price stability. In future, it would have only one objective – 'currency stability'. However, this remained 'controversial': 'Some people disagree with this single objective

... but we believe we have to stabilize the currency and the money supply at the level which results from the natural development of the economy.'

Moreover, the rapid increases in the money supply caused by the influence of local governments over provincial branches of the central bank made it essential to redefine the relationship between the branches and the centre of the PBC. 'Decision-making is to be centralized here ... We will have sole right to make policy decisions, and to stop interference by local officials – that is the main priority.'

Xiou Gang indicated that the central bank would probably set up a Monetary Policy Board to advise the governor, including members from various state agencies. Details of the constitution of the central bank were being drafted, after widespread consultation with other central banks; it might have a federal structure as in the United States, though that had not been decided in 1993. A modern system of bank supervision was also being installed, involving the training of thousands of bank supervisors, with the help of a World Bank loan and advice from Price Waterhouse, the large accounting firm where Peter Cooke, formerly of the Bank of England and the BIS bank supervisors' committee, is head of the department on bank supervision. Would it be a copy of the West? 'No, China's financial system will continue to have Chinese characteristics.'

Mrs Wu Xiaoling, deputy director of the Banking and Financial Markets Reform Department, acknowledged that a successful monetary policy required functioning banking and money markets. Starting in 1994, the Ministry of Finance would no longer borrow funds directly from the central bank. The central bank would use open-market operations 'for the first time'. Previously, she said, the government had required institutions and individuals to hold certain amounts of government debt, 'but in future they will voluntarily hold debt because of the interest they receive'. She added: 'If the marketability of government debt improves we will not have to require institutions to have compulsory debt holdings in future.'

Note the 'if': the aspirations of China's top central bankers were still running a long way ahead of actual practice. Nevertheless, given the good track record of the reforms over recent years, it would be very unwise to write off their chances of succeeding. By 1994, there was no significant opposition to the reforms on ideological grounds. The rapid growth in real incomes from 1979 onwards had created a solid basis of political and popular support for the reform programme, which seemed to have become irreversible. The differences among the top leadership were mainly about implementation rather than substance. Deng Xiaoping continued to urge all-out growth whatever the cost in terms of corruption etc. (the families of the top leaders are deeply involved in new business enterprises).

The question was whether the 'monetarist' approach could succeed in covering over the lack of political agreement, especially on the degree of autonomy of different provinces and over the tax system. Central bank officials acknowledged that their real difficulty was in controlling credit creation for unjustified purposes. The central bank had to exert its authority over the provinces. What was clear was that the People's Bank would remain at the centre of China's prime economic and political concerns; the standard of living of nearly a quarter of the world's population depended on it succeeding.

A visit to the Solomon Islands

About 3,000 miles southeast of Beijing and 1,000 miles or so northeast of Australia lie the beautiful Solomon Islands (population 300,000). There you will find another representative of the central banking species. But whereas China's central bank is the largest in the world in terms of staff, employing more than 100,000, the central bank of the Solomon Islands is one of the smallest, with about sixty employees. But, as Tony Hughes, who was governor for ten years to 1993, said in his account of the central bank's work to one of the authors, if you set aside the staff list and balance sheet, and the functions they are expected to perform, there is no significant difference between the largest and smallest central banks: 'Clearly smallness does not mean narrower legal definitions or formal boundaries, or less comprehensive objectives – financial stability, systemic soundness, balanced growth and so forth.'

Like many central banks in former British colonies, the Solomon Islands central bank is one that has evolved from a pre-independence currency board, through being a central bank in name but limited in practice, to become a fully fledged central bank. Commonwealth precedents were used in drafting its statutes with the same basic functions being discharged by all of them, however small. What does make a difference is the smallness of the political system within which such a central bank operates: 'We are performing conventional central banking functions in economies that are often tiny by world standards, only partially monetized, very open to external influences, often making heavy use of foreign aid, lacking in financial and industrial complexity or depth, and where politics is highly personalized.'

In the Solomon Islands, a fair bit of the money supply 'is stashed away in milk tins in villages'. Cash is still the main means of payment. As trade flows can be as big as total domestic output, and the external reserves are not big enough to cushion such external influences on the money supply, orthodox monetary policy is of limited effectiveness. With government accounting for a large proportion of output, its fiscal operations inevitably have a powerful effect on monetary conditions. In these circumstances it is impractical for the central bank to set itself up in opposition to the government. To quote Hughes again, 'The giving of advice to government can be personally hazardous, a bit like bringing news of military reverses to the later Roman emperors.'

Yet given a minimal degree of autonomy, the central bank can still use its influence to improve the conduct of monetary policy. Its priority is to make itself respected in the community. It should hire and fire its own staff (and not be forced to employ relatives of the President or his ministers), make a reasonable profit (in 1991 the central bank of the Solomon Islands made an operating profit of $4.7 million), provide working conditions that attract good people including research staff, and set high standards for efficiency and integrity. It can then develop ways of influencing government policy that rely on persuasion and the good standing of the central bank in the community. Above all, it must convince the government of the need to control state spending and the budget deficit. This is what Courtney Blackman, the highly respected former governor of the central bank of Barbados, had in mind when he said that the task of a central bank governor was to 'grab the nation's feet and plant them firmly on the ground'.

South Africa jumps into the unknown

Chris Stals, the gritty career central banker who heads the South African Reserve Bank, has fought a dour battle to keep the economy going, while holding the lid on inflation, through a succession of crises. Stals has no illusions about the ability of a central bank to carry out an independent monetary policy; his dictum is that 'a central bank is only as independent as the government wants it to be'. Stals's reappointment by incoming President Nelson Mandela in May 1994 was aimed to reassure the markets of the continuity of policy under the new government.

Since South Africa has long had well-developed money and capital markets, the central bank is able to fund the government's borrowing requirement through its operations in these markets; at the short-term end, it manages a weekly tender for Treasury bills, while at the longer end it taps government stock into the market. To promote active two-way trading it trades continuously as a buyer and seller both in bonds and in the bond options market, where it is the dominant player.

The Reserve Bank influences interest rates mainly through its operations in the money markets. Cash reserves are supplied by making overnight loans, secured on the collateral of short-dated government stock; these loans allow the banks to maintain their required cash reserves at the central bank (the basic required reserve is 1.5 per cent of commercial bank liabilities, but this can be varied to deal with exceptional conditions). The central bank determines the interest rate at which it will make such reserves available, and in this way affects the whole structure of interest rates.

Its operations in the short end of the market have to be meshed with those at the long end where the government's budget deficit is funded. If the central bank is having difficulty finding buyers for the government bonds it needs to sell, it will nudge interest rates up at the short end, thus giving a lift to the whole spectrum of rates and tempting buyers back into the bond market.

Money-market operations are guided by targets for the growth of the money supply. The South African Reserve Bank prefers a 'broad money' target, or M3, and it announces this once a year. It believes that if it gives adequate publicity to this target, then enterprises and unions will take this into account in setting prices and wages. If they do so, the unemployment rate associated with any given level of inflation will be reduced.

With the ending of white rule, elections on the basis of full adult suffrage and the adoption of a new constitution, the views of the African National Congress are of course of critical importance for the future of the central bank's monetary policy. By 1994 there was growing evidence that the leaders of the ANC understood that the more they supported and maintained the independence of the central bank, the more they would be able to borrow from the financial and capital markets (and vice versa). As in other countries, a power struggle between markets and government is going on; in South Africa the struggle seems likely to be dramatic.

Trends in other developing countries

From Chile to Malaysia, and from Taiwan to Jordan, central banking has come in from the cold. For the first time, most developing countries see central banks as essential to their economic growth and are putting in place monetary policies designed specifically to provide a stable monetary environment for the economy.

Plainly, it is not feasible to describe how each country uses the techniques of monetary policy. Fortunately, it is not necessary, as there are only a limited number of instruments compatible with market economies, and these have already been described – cash ratios, reserve requirements, and market operations – all of which influence demand through interest rates.

The chequered history of monetary policy in developing countries was reviewed in Chapter 6; here we discuss some recent trends.

Liberalization of financial systems

Central banks have been in the forefront of the movement to open up financial markets and reduce obstacles to financial flows. Throughout the world, developing countries have followed the examples of developed countries in liberalizing their financial systems. That means relaxing or removing administrative controls on interest rates, reducing the role of the central government in deciding who gets bank credit and often relaxing or abolishing exchange controls as well. So the financial systems of most developing countries have been made much more open – with both the new opportunities for international borrowing and the new risks that that brings.

A change was badly needed. The former closed systems, as outlined in Chapter 6, had been highly detrimental to economic development. Monetary policy had been exercised mainly through administrative credit ceilings on loans with handouts to sectors and individuals with political pull. High rates of taxation, widely evaded by people with clout, widespread nationalization and a proliferation of special subsidies all stifled growth. Particularly insidious were the so-called 'development finance institutions', or DFIs, often financed mainly through aid from the international agencies. These proved almost everywhere to be disasters. Much of the money, after swirling around for a time, wound up as flight capital in Swiss and other bank accounts. By the late 1980s, the World Bank realized that virtually all these DFIs were bankrupt, and began suddenly to say that what developing countries needed most were proper central banks and proper money markets.

The new approach recognized that it matters just as much in developing countries as in developed ones for exchange rates and interest rates to be set at broadly the 'right' levels. The good news is that in the 1990s, for the first time, most developing countries appreciate the importance of this. The bad news is that their initial attempts to put this into practice often failed miserably. For many (Argentina, Chile, Uruguay), liberalization initially turned out to be another disaster. As Ron McKinnon, one of the pioneer economists in the field, has stressed, 'successful liberalization is not simply a question of removing all regulations'. Mostly the disasters were due to ballooning budget deficits; macroeconomic stability turned out to be a precondition of successful financial liberalization.

Often the central bank made its own contribution to the mess. It is not just that banking systems were inadequately supervised, but that the central bank was instructed to bail out banks that were in danger of bankruptcy in the newly liberalized environment. The episode demonstrated just how delicate the system of rewards and penalties is in a mature financial system, and how difficult it is to replicate that in a developing country.

In the Philippines, financial liberalization in the early 1980s was accompanied by a rising fiscal deficit and currency devaluation. The stabilization programme launched in 1984 made things worse. Open-market sales of high-yielding Treasury bills pulled funds out of the banking system, but when the banks responded by raising their interest rates to 20 per cent in real terms, the system collapsed. In Latin America, the typical problems included lack of adequate regulation over banking combined with irresponsible lending bred by deposit insurance schemes. In a mirror image of the savings and loans débâcle in the United States, bad debts accumulated rapidly as a result of both outright fraud and undue risk-taking. Unfortunately, a common factor was the expectation that in a crisis of confidence, the central bank would bail out the private bankers. As the British economist Maxwell Fry explained: 'Behind virtually all financial crises that have occurred in the past two decades lies the critical issue of explicit or implicit deposit insurance because it affects the behaviour of both depositors and bankers.'

The fear of banking crashes inhibited the reforms of monetary policy that were seen to be needed. In the early 1990s, many countries in Asia and Latin America were still clearing up the debris left from banking failures. This was being done in a wide variety of ways, but essentially involved restructuring and recapitalizing the banking system. This demonstrated the close connection between the health of the banking system and the capacity to conduct monetary policy.

Bringing capital back home
Reform of monetary policy was designed partly to stem the flight of capital. Many developing countries have suffered for years from the habit of their wealthier residents and corporations of keeping their capital overseas. Capital flight is often attributed to political instability, the fear of expropriation, or to tax policies. But in fact the central bank has often been at least partly to blame. For the only way those who wanted to take their money out of the country could do so at advantageous rates was to change their local currency into dollars or some other hard currency at an exchange rate that made such a deal attractive. Unless the central bank had sold them dollars at such an exchange rate, their demand for dollars would cause their domestic currency to depreciate to such an extent that buying dollars would no longer appear attractive. Thus an improvement in monetary policies can

enable a country to keep the bulk of its capital at home; the central bank again plays a key role.

Improved monetary policies were needed also to encourage efficient systems for channelling savings to borrowers. The ratio of money to national product – a measure of financial development – is much lower in high-inflation countries such as Argentina, Peru, Brazil and Turkey than in relatively low-inflation countries such as Thailand, Malaysia and Singapore. With an underdeveloped banking system, people who need to borrow cannot gain access to savings of others, since these savings are not placed with the banks. Thus the financial system is fragmented; at the extreme it is confined to a number of small localities, cut off from each other, so that new supplies of savings and capital cannot find borrowers or investors.

The reduced role of the banking system in such countries, so damaging to growth, was a direct consequence of bad monetary policies. The reason why governments pursued such policies may have been partly political – to help finance the government's own borrowing by holding down interest rates offered on bank deposits – but was partly due to mistaken ideas inherited from an earlier era that low interest rates stimulate investment. In fact keeping interest rates low means, of course, that banks have to allocate their lending by other criteria – notably by political criteria.

But by the 1990s, the solution to this problem was not only being recognized but put into practice. Governments were allowing central banks to set interest rates above the current rate of inflation. One of the seminal studies of this was by Rüşdü Saracoglu, later governor of the Central Bank of Turkey until he was dismissed by Prime Minister Mrs Tansu Çiller in 1993. Saracoglu and a colleague, Antony Lanyi, showed that countries with positive real interest rates tended to grow much more rapidly than those with negative real interest rates. This finding has been supported by later studies – overturning the former conventional view that interest rates should be kept low 'to stimulate investment'.

Monetary policy in context

Increasingly, developing country governments now want central banks to mobilize savings and allocate credit efficiency. Probably a majority now believe that these aims are most likely to be achieved by policies that rely on market forces and market-related interest rates. This accords with the consensus among economists on how to encourage economic development. Protection for property rights, macroeconomic stability, fiscal discipline, improved legal, accounting and regulatory systems, a fair tax system and a monetary policy that recognizes the key role of the interest rate and the exchange rate in allocating resources – these are the key conditions which international agencies such as the World Bank see as the secrets of success. From China to Venezuela, developing countries are recognizing this. Those that have competent governments can create conditions favourable to growth and are doing so in growing numbers. They have reasonable monetary policies; and they entrust those policies to the care of a competent central bank.

Most of today's central bankers have been in the thick of a financial crisis – or something very close to one. And have come under fire as a result. Yet few, if any, will feel confident of averting another in their working lifetime. Yes, they have taken lessons to heart. But these, they say, may not help them next time round; the markets make the running and are continually taking them by surprise. The central bankers cannot possibly see what lies round the corner.

Submission is dangerously seductive. Is there really no chance of spotting problems before they occur? After all the calamities of the 1980s, was there any excuse for central bankers being caught with their pants down in 1991 over Bank of Credit and Commerce International, which had flagrantly exploited chinks in the armour revealed years before?

In trying to answer such questions in this chapter, we are forced to conclude that central bankers are failing to give the lead they should over the guardianship of the financial system. United and resolute on many fronts, here is one where they show a remarkable degree of disagreement and vacillation. With regulation having assumed a high profile, their reputation is suffering more than they care to admit. And, yes, we are aware that some central banks can protest that they have no formal regulatory or supervisory role. (Incidentally, a typology warning: in theory, regulators set the rules, supervisors monitor them, but in the real world the terms are used almost interchangeably.)

Censoriousness is not arrived at lightly. It is all too easy to savage financial policing for its lapses and to take for granted its successes in keeping money, by and large, a convenient and desirable commodity. Nevertheless, the huge scale of some recent financial scandals suggests it is time to take a hard look at the regulators themselves. Because financial police forces have so many different branches, the buck is continually being passed from one to another. Responsibility rarely comes to rest in one place. It is the absence of a top cop that, in our view, renders most countries' financial regulatory systems inadequate today.

A quarter of a century ago, there was no obvious need for one.

Historically, financial policing relied mainly on restricting market forces. Money could be kept within national boundaries by capital controls. Banks were specialized and could be told how to run their businesses; their interest rates could be fixed and their lending not only rationed but directed into favoured channels. Securities trading in most countries was quite distinct and separately policed. The insurance industry was something else again. Different regulators saw little cause to fraternize with each other at home, let alone with their counterparts abroad.

The barriers were beginning to buckle in earlier years, particularly within banking, but fairly slowly until the free-market philosophy of the 1980s sent them tumbling. Starting with the British removal of capital controls under Margaret Thatcher's leadership in the late 1970s, there was a tremendous opening up of the finance industry almost everywhere. Deregulation, liberalization, despecialization – they are all the same thing – became the order of the day. Competition was holy, restriction sinful. Different financial services became intermingled and financial firms sprawled like huge octopuses across the globe.

Compounding the new problems for regulators, technological innovation and the ingenuity of the so-called rocket scientists bred a new range of financial tools. Known collectively as 'derivatives', they now include not only forward operations such as futures and options, but swaps, swaptions, caps, floors and circuses – a special dictionary is required to understand even half the jargon. So mobile and versatile are the markets in them that lawyers and taxmen can argue for days over when, where and how a transaction took place. Pity, then, the regulator trying to keep track.

The combination of government-led deregulation and market-driven financial innovation has been a powerful force for change. The pace of it was too fast – calamities were inevitable. Arguably the worst of a long string of financial disasters that had their roots in the 1980s were the costly failures in the United States of – by early 1994 – 1,193 savings and loan associations (building societies to the British), with over $417 billion of assets. But at least that was largely a domestic tragedy, without the international repercussions that central bankers have come most to dread. On the other hand, that particular débâcle not only put a brake on financial liberalization in the United States, but also strengthened the resolve everywhere to reregulate.

Not that reregulation is so called; it goes by the name of 'prudential regulation' or 'prudential supervision'. Accepting the current wisdom that markets should be interfered with as little as possible, the new regulatory game focuses on setting standards to try to force the players to behave prudently and not take silly or excessive risks. Since most markets no longer recognize geographical limits, these rules need to be applied internationally to avoid regulatory arbitrage – or 'cherry-picking of the most convenient regulation', as one central banker puts it. But that is much easier said than done.

This is not just because of the amount of head-bashing needed to achieve any worthwhile international agreement. Spawned by differing traditions, cultures, monetary developments and political pressures, financial regulatory and supervisory systems, particularly for banking, differ from country to country in more ways than might be thought conceivable, not least in the formal role the central bank plays. Putting an international topsoil on such uneven ground may flatten some bumps but it will not automatically produce a level playing field.

How the Anglo-Saxons do it

Look no further than the Anglo-Saxon world to see how far apart even the frameworks for banking regulation can be, let alone their content. Reflecting the concern about undue concentration of financial power that has run through its history, the United States opted from early on for a complex system of checks and balances, backed by volumes of detailed legislation. Though to begin with chartering and supervision of banks were entirely in the hands of individual states, currency disorders following the issue of 'greenbacks' to help finance the Civil War led to the creation, by way of the National Bank Act of 1864, of a banking regulator at federal level, the Office of the Comptroller of the Currency. There was more fragmentation, when the Federal Reserve, itself a product of a much later banking crisis, and the Federal Deposit Insurance Corporation were given some supervisory responsibilities.

In sharp contrast, the Bank of England simply took upon itself the job of overseeing British banks as if to the manner born. Like other earlier central banks (such as the Bank of France) which started as commercial banks undertaking special national obligations, it became the bankers' banker during the last century. Holding their cash and bullion reserves, it conceived a duty to keep an eye on its clients and to help the deserving ones in times of trouble – to act as lender of last resort, as the function is called today. The Bank saw nothing unnatural in being both leader and guardian of the flock, pampering it one moment, censoring it the next.

When the Bank was nationalized in 1946, its self-appointed supervisory function attracted no concern whatsoever. Its powers over the commercial banks were so loosely defined in the enabling legislation that Americans could hardly believe their eyes. The then president of the New York Federal Reserve Bank, Allan Sproul, was so 'intrigued' by the 'vague wording' that he sought clarification from his friends in London. Only within the past twenty years, after some nasty mishaps, has British banking control acquired statutory backbone. Even so, while the Bank of England has had to accept, very grudgingly, that it can no longer rule by persuasion alone, it continues to believe its headmasterly wiggings count for quite a lot.

Very different though they are, the Anglo-Saxon arrangements do not span the extremes of supervisory philosophy. Some central banks, notably the mighty German Bundesbank, are given no formal supervisory responsibility at all. The ultimate line of defence, if supervision fails and a crisis develops, is also drawn differently, country by country. Though most central banks are empowered to provide extra liquidity to the markets if a widespread panic is threatened, not all can bail out an individual institution even if failure to so do could have a serious knock-on effect. The Bank of England may use its own discretion (though it is expected these days to consult with the British Treasury first), but the Federal Reserve has to ensure that the institution is suffering only a temporary shortage of cash and is technically solvent, a procedure that takes time and may kill effective action. Among other central banks that work to the book, the Bundesbank cannot feature in a formal way in specific rescue operations, whereas the Bank of Japan can, provided it has the permission of the Ministry of Finance.

Different philosophies, responsibilities, traditions – but common problems. If a central bank has to pick up the pieces from a crash in the end, it needs to minimize the risk of being caught in such a position. As geographical and business barriers fade, how does it do that? What should be its position as lender of last resort towards an international conglomerate that combines banking with commercial business?

These are among the problems still to be addressed. Supervisory policy everywhere has evolved largely over the years in response to crises. Backward-looking, it has responded to yesterday's problems rather than today's, let alone tomorrow's. The worse the crisis, the greater, naturally, the subsequent effort to introduce new procedures and safeguards to prevent a recurrence of its kind. But the impact of a crisis can be lessened by prompt and efficient handling – or vice versa. So the management, as well as the cause, of crises forms an important element in the regulatory story.

Richardson's lifeboat makes waves

A little history, therefore, is needed before the current debate over supervisory philosophy can be joined. In the next few pages, we recall some – a selective few – of the upheavals that colour that debate.

We need go back no further than twenty years, to Britain's so-called secondary banking crisis in 1973–75. Sparked off by the imprudent practices of a few, a whole crop of fringe deposit-takers – which had grown up over the previous fifteen years and, unsupervised by the Bank of England, operated outside the core of long-established banks – looked threatened by a panic withdrawal of confidence. With short-term deposits badly mismatched by long-term mortgage and property lending, they were very vulnerable indeed. Perceived at first as a temporary liquidity (cashflow) crisis, the Bank, still almighty in those days, leaned on the big British commercial banks to bail out their unwelcome competitors and even undertook to put up 10 per cent of the 'lifeboat' from its own funds.

But more than immediate and urgent action was required to get British banking out of danger. The crisis was to drag on, exposing the extreme arbitrariness of the distinction between cashflow problems, which the lifeboat was designed to help, and solvency problems, which it was not. As time went on, the Bank went it alone, without the help of the clearing banks. Altogether, the lifeboat supported twenty-six troubled institutions to varying degrees over several years with loans of some £1.3 billion. In the final reckoning, after arranging mergers and acquiring two troubled firms itself, the Bank of England lost about £100 million, and the clearing banks about half that amount from their lifeboat participation.

Two important consequences of this sorry phase of Britain's financial history were purely domestic, effected through the 1979 Banking Act. First, supervision was put on a legal footing, and the Bank of England's supervisory role over deposit-takers considerably strengthened. Second, a formal deposit insurance scheme was at last introduced in Britain in 1982, funded by levies on the banks. But there were also international ramifications from the British secondary bank crisis.

Though it had been a costly exercise, the Bank of England congratulated itself that it had averted a panic, just as it had done with the merchant bank, Barings, in 1890. Some fringe banks had been allowed to fail, but in an orderly fashion and without causing much disruption in the markets. And certainly without contagion spreading beyond Britain's shores. Rather than being admonished for having let a crisis develop in the first place, the Bank won acclaim for its rescue prowess from other central banks. Gordon Richardson, the lawyer-cum-merchant banker who had been at the Bank's helm for less than a year when he corralled the banks to man the lifeboat, found his authority much enhanced. It seemed not unnatural to his fellows at the Basle meetings that he should mastermind a supervisory clean-up after a disturbance in West Germany, a single failure there that, far from being locally contained, was to lead to profound changes in the conduct of the banking industry throughout the world and to the responsibilities of central bankers towards it.

Herstatt lives on

On 26 June 1974, at around 3.30 p.m. local time, the German authorities abruptly shut down a respected, medium-sized private bank in Cologne, Bankhaus Herstatt, and appointed a liquidator. The Bundesbank immediately ceased clearing for Herstatt's account.

Rather less than twenty years old, Herstatt had done well in attracting over 50,000 customers and sizeable assets. Linked through its owner to an important insurance company, it had extensive dealings with foreign banks, including Chase Manhattan, which acted as its agent in New York. Unfortunately, it also acquired a taste for speculating wildly in the foreign-exchange markets after currencies were floated. Though it tried to conceal its huge losses, the authorities eventually caught up with the situation and found it insolvent. No German bank came to its rescue. Only lawyers could have enjoyed the negotiations between Herstatt and its creditors which took the best part of a year before a settlement was agreed.

The drama in those negotiations arose from the fact that the bank's closure at home came at the beginning of the business day in New York, where Herstatt was due to pay out millions of dollars to complete 'spot' transactions entered into two days earlier and for which it had already received currencies from the counterparties. But as soon as Chase received word of the closure, it decided not to honour payments on orders worth some $620 million from the Herstatt account. Shock waves set off a chain reaction of other payments not being made. The daily clearing of international payments in New York dropped from the usual $60 billion to an average $36 billion in the three days following Herstatt's closure.

The German authorities came out badly from the Herstatt affair; they handled its closure clumsily. Though the Bundesbank apparently played no part in this (the power to close a bank in Germany lies with the Federal Banking Supervisory Office), it nevertheless was charged with negligence for clearing payments due to Herstatt during the few hours that elapsed between the shutdown decision being taken and its implementation. The case against the central bank was unsuccessful, but only after a judgement against it, ordering it to pay damages, had been quashed on appeal. Needless to say, the proud Bundesbank did not take kindly to the much-publicized censure in the first instance and it rankles until this day.

It saw to it that a cooperatively operated deposit insurance fund was created (no scheme was in place at the time of Herstatt). And, as we describe shortly, when another potential banking crisis arose in Germany some nine years later, very different tactics came into play.

But there were much wider after-effects from the Herstatt débâcle. Though it resulted from gambling in the sale of purchases of currencies in the conventional foreign-exchange markets and not from unsound lending of foreign currencies in the offshore and unregulated Euromarket, the latter's vulnerability to a panic reaction was made all too evident. For a few months after Herstatt, smaller and weaker banks had great difficulty in obtaining Eurocurrency deposits, even at premiums above quoted rates. Some banks were unable to obtain funds at all in the interbank market. Some smaller players had to be rescued by their parent banks. But, the question arose, who stood behind the parent in a market squeeze?

At the time of Herstatt, central bankers and their flocks of commercial bankers had a common secret; neither fully understood the workings of the Euromarkets, which had mushroomed so rapidly from tiny beginnings in the early 1950s. But they were clever enough to keep it from each other. So the markets were remarkably reassured by a statement from the central bank governors of the big industrial countries (the 'Group of Ten' plus Switzerland), after one of their regular meetings in Basle on 10 September 1974, that they had had a satisfactory 'exchange of views' about the problem of the lender-of-last-resort in the Euromarkets. All they could announce, however, was that they were satisfied that means were available for the provision of temporary liquidity and would be used if and when necessary. Perhaps the fact that they rarely say anything publicly after their Basle meetings added to the weight of a message which had very little real substance.

International cooperation at last

Still, central bankers knew something more was demanded from them. Fundamental doubts were being raised about banking supervision. Not only Herstatt but also a number of other banks in different countries had failed in 1973 and 1974 or experienced serious losses. Most notably, the United States was witnessing its biggest banking disaster to date.

Long Island's Franklin National Bank had been bought in 1971 by an Italian financier, Michele Sindona, after it had suffered heavy losses. But Sindona was no saintly, white knight. He immediately set about using Franklin for massive foreign-exchange speculation. Like Herstatt, the bank lost heavily. However, he managed to conceal the size of the losses through transfers to other companies he owned. Even so, the bank was clearly insolvent by early 1974. The American authorities, however, were loth to pronounce it so; confidence in American banking had already been jolted the previous autumn by the collapse of the National Bank of San Diego, run by a friend of President Nixon.

Eventually, an expensive rescue was arranged. Franklin was taken over by a group of European banks and renamed the European-American Bank, but only after the Federal Deposit Insurance Corporation had put up $2 billion (though it eventually recouped the sum). Following the collapse of his empire in Europe, with large outstanding debts, including some to the Vatican, the financier was eventually convicted in the United States of fraud and larceny in connection with Franklin's affairs.

But before the full horrors of Franklin had been exposed, central bankers had been shocked enough to recognize the painfully obvious – banking supervision was behind the times. New offshore financial centres were being created, the Eurocurrency market was growing at astonishing speed, cross-border banking was proliferating and multinational banks were springing up, yet banking supervision continued within national boundaries as if there were no tomorrow.

Largely on the initiative of Gordon Richardson, given extra gravitas by his lifeboat experience, central bankers decided in the summer of 1974 that some coordination between banking supervisors was needed. To that end, at the same meeting which brought forth the lender-of-last-resort message, they set up a new committee, with members drawn from the Group of Ten industrialized countries.

The Committee on Banking Regulations and Supervisory Practices, as it was gracelessly named, met for the first time in February 1975 – under the chairmanship of the Bank of England's George Blunden – and meetings have been held regularly since, usually four times a year and nearly always in Basle. Now thankfully renamed the Basle Committee on Banking Supervision, we shall clip its title even further to the Basle Committee in the remainder of this chapter.

The Basle Committee had to build up from nothing. It is difficult now to appreciate how little contact there was twenty or so years ago among banking supervisors in the major countries. Even within the European Community, discussions about how to get closer began only in 1972 and then merely within an informal and autonomous group. So the Basle Committee attached enormous importance to its first aim, which was to reach an understanding among national authorities as to who was responsible for foreign banks operating in their territories. It congratulated itself on achieving this, as it thought, within a year. Endorsed by the central bank governors in December 1975, the agreement (since revised, notably in 1983 and 1992) is known as the Concordat.

From today's perspective, the original Concordat of 1975 looks even weaker than it did at the time. The attempt to draw firm demarcation lines between the responsibilities of the 'host' and 'parent' supervisors (the jargon for the supervisory authorities of the country where the foreign bank is located and the authorities where it has its head office) proved counter-productive; some operations were left in no-man's land, in neither authority. Differences in national legislation and practices also hampered the Concordat's effectiveness from the start. Some countries did not even permit their supervisory authorities to exchange information with their counterparts overseas. German and Swiss banking supervisors were constrained by law in the kinds of information they could demand from their banks about their foreign activities. There were many such weaknesses in the foundation of international banking supervision – and some remain today.

The same was true when an important plank was added in 1978. That year the Basle Committee endorsed the principle that a bank's international business should be monitored on a total or consolidated basis 'as a means of giving practical effect to the principle of parental responsibility'. Saying the obvious, you might think. Not a bit of it. Although banks in several countries -- such as the United States, Canada and the Netherlands -- had for several years been required to submit consolidated accounts for supervisory purposes, not until 1980 was this true in Switzerland, while Britain took until the end of 1981 to fall into line and West Germany considerably longer.

Scandals go on and on

If there were any illusions that the international supervisory net in its early form was impenetrable they were dramatically dispelled when Italy's biggest private banking group, based in Milan, all but went to the wall in 1982. On 18 June of that year, Banco Ambrosiano's president, Roberto Calvi, nicknamed God's banker because of his links with the Vatican, was found hanging under Blackfriars Bridge in London. His bank had debts of $ 1.3 billion that would have wiped out the savings of thousands of depositors. The Bank of Italy immediately organized a lifeboat operation (of around $325 million) to stem the panic withdrawal of deposits and in July it moved in to provide full backing for depositors of the parent bank. But it refused to accept any responsibility for a Luxembourg subsidiary, which was left to default on its loans and deposits. This was to spark off an unedifying spat between Italian and Luxembourg supervisors.

The Ambrosiano group had a very complicated structure. Under the umbrella of a holding company, La Centrale, it held large stakes in important Italian companies, including an insurance company, a publishing group (owners of Italy's largest newspaper, *Il Corriere della Sera*) and two other banks. Abroad it had offshore banks and operations in Luxembourg, under a non-bank holding company, whereby it had managed to collect over $400 million of Euromarket deposits from international banks when its assets were frozen. The Bank of Italy contended, in effect, that the Luxembourg affiliate was not a bank; the Luxembourg authorities insisted it was. Pierre Jaans, the Luxembourg banking commissioner, wrote to the Bank of Italy in August that 'the way in which matters have been handled is not easy to understand'.

The Banco Ambrosiano saga went on and on. After bankruptcy was declared on 26 August 1982, a new bank, Nuovo Banco Ambrosiano, was immediately created to take over the Italian operations. Evidence that there had been fraud on a massive scale took years to sort out, but ultimately resulted in Carlo De Benedetti, chairman of Olivetti, being sentenced on 16 April 1992, along with thirty-two others. Of the more immediate consequences, one was that the Luxembourg authorities obtained guarantees from other Italian banks, whose banking subsidiaries in their country were owned through non-bank holding companies, that they would accept direct responsibility. Another was that the Concordat received a facelift.

By the time of the Ambrosiano collapse, chairmanship of the Basle Committee had passed to Peter Cooke, another Bank of England man, who reacted huffily to the view that the Italian affair had pointed up a glaring deficiency in the Concordat. There might be lessons to be learnt from it, Cooke ceded, but he thought not many because the structure of the Ambrosiano group was 'quite exceptional'. 'It is not replicated, as far as I am aware,' he told a London conference in December 1982, 'among any of the major 500 or so banks in the world which are those principally engaged in international business.' Faced with a disaster, central bankers all too often take refuge in the 'exceptional' notion — they were to do just the same ten years later when BCCI was closed.

Nevertheless, Cooke had to concede a supervisory shortfall when there were non-banking companies within banking groups. The 1983 revised Concordat addressed this issue by laying down that when holding companies' head groups that include separately incorporated banks operating in different countries, the relevant authorities should 'endeavour to coordinate their supervision of these banks'. When a bank is the parent of a group that contains intermediate holding companies, the parent bank should ensure that such holding companies are adequately supervised. If it cannot do that, then the authority supervising the parent should take steps to have such intermediate holding companies closed down.

Cooke thought this last provision was an important addition to the Concordat. Yet Bank of Credit and Commerce International was able to create a structure that allowed it to operate unregulated for years. That was seen as a 'wholly exceptional' case.

Like Banco Ambrosiano, BCCI's highly complex structure — registered in Luxembourg, unclear ownership, biggest business in Britain but shadiest assets parked in the Cayman Islands — might indeed be considered 'exceptional'. But much repetition denies the description. Between these two big banking fiascos were many other scary incidents, on a smaller scale, of evasion of authority through structural ingenuity and the use of offshore centres. One worth recalling is the near-collapse of one of West Germany's most respected private banks just months after the new Concordat had been triumphantly published.

It came to light in November 1983 that Schröder, Münchmeyer, Hengst (SMH) had lent almost one-third of its asset-value, close to DM900 million, to just one company, IBH Holdings, once Europe's largest construction equipment company but by then recession-hit and on the brink of bankruptcy. By the German law that a bank could lend no more than 75 per cent of its capital to any one borrower, SMH's exposure to IBH should have been limited to DM83 million. It had got round the law by lending huge sums through a Luxembourg subsidiary and, to a lesser extent, through a German factoring subsidiary, details of which were not required to be reported to the German authorities.

Determined to avoid the embarrassment of a Herstatt replay and a major disruption in the Euromarkets, the Bundesbank this time moved swiftly behind the scenes. Taking its cue from the Bank of England, it leaned on some twenty German banks to provide financing to keep SMH afloat until a buyer could be found. Three months on, Britain's Lloyds Bank obliged. And two years later, Bonn finally passed legislation requiring consolidation of banking accounts in West Germany.

From this distance of time, it is easy to say central bankers should have tried harder to ensure that nothing remotely like the Ambrosiano and SMH incidents could ever recur. Undoubtedly, the Concordat should have been more radically overhauled in 1983. But changes did go beyond trying to catch oddly structured banks. The revised Concordat was deliberately made more untidy, resorting to overlapping supervisory responsibilities in an effort to plug the holes. One example: host authorities were left still monitoring the liquidity of a foreign bank – on the grounds that this could be subject to local rules – but they had to do so in consultation with the parent authorities, which were given an oversight responsibility. However, it took the BCCI disaster to put some bite into the Concordat. In July 1992, the Basle Committee, by then under the strong leadership of the New York Federal Reserve's Gerald Corrigan, reinforced the Concordat with minimum standards that offered the host supervisors the sanction of sending a foreign bank packing, or preventing one setting up, for non-compliance.

In all fairness, it should be recalled that in designing the original Concordat from nothing the objective was to devise standards acceptable not only to the rich countries, but worldwide wherever finance was played. Cooke worked hard during his time with the Basle Committee to spread the gospel – and, on the face of it, succeeded.

Then, of course, central bankers had a bigger worry in the 1980s than whether another rogue bank was about to spring up. Just as Jaans was writing to the Bank of Italy about Banco Ambrosiano, the Mexican government set financial nerves tingling by announcing that it could not continue to service its debt. Management of the third-world debt crisis and the key part in it played by the Fed's chairman, Paul Volcker, have already been described in Chapter 7. Our concern here is what Volcker powered as an offshoot of his debt-handling – the quest for international convergence of bank capital. Its introduction in the past few years is now hugely influencing banking practices throughout the world; indeed, it almost dictates the way bankers go about their business. The basic idea was simple – all the world's international banks should have at least a minimum amount of capital, related to their overall business, to provide a cushion against loss. It is ironic, therefore, that the plan might never have come about – at least not when it did – but for the strange ways of American politics.

A sop to Congress

The American Congress is never short of big-bank haters. The cry of 'we won't bail out the banks' resounded on Capitol Hill in 1983 when the Reagan administration requested $8.4 billion for an increased contribution to the International Monetary Fund, essential to the overall debt strategy. The only hope of getting congressional approval was to offer a sop – tighter bank regulation. As soon as that was mooted, however, the banks warned that any new American regulations, especially on capital requirements, would place them at a competitive disadvantage to foreign banks, at a time when they could least afford it. This was grist to the mill of the ever-watchful protectionist lobby in the United States.

The upshot was the type of legislatory ragbag which only the United States can produce. Its International Lending Supervision Act of 1983, tagged on to a housing bill, authorized the International Monetary Fund financing, sharpened up bank examinations, increased reserves required against loans, and then called on American regulators not only to require increased levels of bank capital at home but also to encourage other major countries to set about 'strengthening the capital bases of banking institutions involved in international lending'. So was conceived the first common regulation of banks worldwide.

The pregnancy was a painful one, though. When Volcker duly presented the congressional request to his fellow central bankers at a regular Basle meeting in March 1984, it fell very flat indeed. Nor was the Basle Committee enthusiastic; its sights seemed set no higher than devising a matrix to overcome differences in the way countries counted capital, so that its members could realistically compare their standards. Level-pegging capital standards, which Volcker was seeking, didn't seem feasible.

But the matter could not rest. Just two months after Volcker made his bid in Basle, Chicago-based Continental Illinois, America's eighth-largest bank, collapsed. Rumours of the poor quality of its loan portfolio, overweighted in the energy sector, had started a run on deposits that even a $6 billion cash injection from the Federal Reserve did not stem. A federal bail-out followed. And the recriminations.

American regulators were attacked, of course, for letting Continental get into such a mess in the first place. But even more fiercely for acting scared in the aftermath. So frightened were the authorities of possible damage to the interbank market that the Federal Deposit Insurance Corporation stepped in to guarantee not only deposits at Continental of up to

$100,000, as it was legally obliged to do, but all deposits whatever their size.

The small banks' lobby immediately cried foul; a score or more of its brethren had been left to go to the wall that year, with large depositors losing money in the process. Congress was morally indignant, too, protesting that the 'too-big-to-fail' inference was an open invitation to large banks to indulge in recklessness. If ever there was a time in American banking history for a post-crisis, regulatory knee-jerk it was in the summer of 1984.

It took the form, in July that year, of a hike from $5 to $5.50 in the amount of capital American banks were required to hold for every $100 of assets. But, that wasn't enough. Disturbed by the weakness of commercial banks' balance sheets generally, Volcker had come to accept that the Federal Reserve and other American watchdogs were behind the times in judging a bank's capital adequacy. Though they had focused on it for longer than the majority of their overseas counterparts, they used a very crude tool. It took no account of the quality or type of assets – unlike systems developed, each with its own idiosyncrasies, in several other countries, notably Britain (since 1980, as a consequence of the secondary banking crisis), France and Belgium. Nor of one source of Continental's problems, rapidly growing 'off-balance-sheet' business – activities, often fee-based, that do not generally involve booking assets or taking deposits, such as the trading of swaps, options or other derivatives, letters of credit and standby arrangements for loans. Supervisors at the Federal Reserve, in both Washington and New York, began to sharpen their brains.

It took until January 1986, however, before the Fed could announce a new proposal. Hindered by not being the sole regulator in the United States, it had been a tough job to get the others to go along. But, at last, came agreement that in addition to the 5.5 per cent requirement, the capital adequacy of an American bank should also be judged against a measure of its assets that rated their riskiness on a scale rising from nil for cash to 100 per cent for corporate lending, and brought in off-balance-sheet items at 100 per cent. Predictably, American banks protested that this 'risk-weighted' standard amounted to discrimination against them; the proposal would undermine 'the ability of American banks to compete', said the American Bankers Association.

A face-saver for the Old Lady

History might be expected to relate that the Basle Committee then stepped in to appease the grumbling American bankers with a promise of a level playing field – that is to say, equal treatment for all international banks. But it did not work out quite like that. First, Volcker sought a deal with the Bank of England and six months after sounding out its governor, Robin Leigh-Pemberton, managed to effect it. In January 1987, having ironed out technical differences, the two central banks presented – for a three-month consultative period – a common standard for evaluating capital adequacy (though not, it should be recalled, a common level for it).

Some of their fellow central bank governors were not best pleased with Volcker and Leigh-Pemberton, to put it mildly. In the eyes of the European Commission President, Jacques Delors, it was not '*communitaire*'; proposals for a Community capital adequacy regime were by then well advanced and what was Britain doing breaking ranks? But the ringleaders were unrepentant. Volcker, impatient for action, had long believed in spearheading international cooperation. As for Leigh-Pemberton, the kudos to be enjoyed at home from being in cahoots with 'Big Paul' and from the Bank having taught the Fed a thing or two must have been a welcome antidote to renewed attacks on the Bank's wisdom in rescuing a banking–cum–bullion subsidiary of the Johnson Matthey group in late 1984.

Without digressing to recall the Johnson Matthey Bankers affair in detail, it cannot escape mention. Not only did it mark another milestone in British regulatory history – one consequence was that banks in Britain ceased to be classified in two tiers and all became subject to the same set of rules – but, more to the point of our story, to central bankers everywhere it was a disturbing example of the hostility that an individual rescue, however skilfully arranged, can arouse. The weight of City opinion first tilted, then swung quite decisively, towards the view that had Johnson Matthey Bankers been allowed to go bust without any to-do, nothing worse would have happened than turmoil in the London gold market for a day or two; there would not have been the contagion in the foreign-exchange and other related markets that the Bank feared.

So there is a saying in the City: 'Never buy a bank for a pound.' For £1 is the sum the Bank of England paid to acquire the failed institution (after its parent had injected £50 million, half borrowed from commercial banks) to make it technically solvent, before immediately injecting £100 million of its own cash and contributing half of a £150 million indemnity package (the other half coming from City banks and bullion dealers).

This particular rescue probably marked a watershed in the relationship between the Old Lady and the City. 'We may not be so pliant next time,' commented one commercial banker whose arm had been twisted.

One way or another, the Bank came in for a lot of flak, with Sir Kit McMahon, then its deputy governor, who masterminded the ingenious bail-out, receiving his fair share of it. Not a thick-skinned man, his subsequent decision to move to the private sector, to head Midland Bank, was helped by this unhappy episode.

Yet it did not work out badly in the end. Nursed back to life, thanks largely to the efforts of (now Sir) David Walker, then a Bank of England executive director, the bulk of Johnson Matthey Bankers was bought in April 1986 by Australia's largest bank, Westpac, and the Bank recouped nearly three-quarters of its initial £100 million outlay (and more later). But the sell-off did little for the Bank's reputation in this affair, serving rather to renew earlier criticisms. So Volcker's offer three months later of a show of supervisory strength on bank capital must have seemed particularly attractive to the Bank.

Counting capital

That show of strength having been announced, the question was, would other countries follow suit? There was considerable scepticism. The head of a London group of banking analysts spoke for many a banker when he said he had 'zero confidence' in the prospects for full international convergence on bank capital. Yet in less than a year, the Basle Committee made proposals for just that, and six months later, on 15 July 1988, released the now famous Basle Accord. Imperfect certainly, but a big step forward. For, as denoted by the document's formal title, *International Convergence of Capital Measurement and Capital Standards*, a common level as well as a common definition of bank capital had been agreed.

The Accord was no pushover. A hard sell by officials from the Federal Reserve and the Bank of England first captured the Japanese, giving Volcker the satisfaction that his initiative by then encompassed all three of the world's major financial centres. Then the Basle Committee (or the Cooke Committee as it was known in those days) had to struggle to fill out the trilateral pact and resolve wrangles among its wider membership – which had more to do with what would count as a bank's capital than with the risk assessment of its assets, a concept to which all by then were ready to subscribe.

The Basle Accord is aimed at raising the standards of safety and soundness in the world's banking business in a manner consistent with fair competition. (Some will tell you it's really all about curbing the expansion of Japanese banks.) But there is considerable leeway for national regulators to put their own stamp on it. The Accord splits a bank's capital between core (tier 1) capital and supplementary (tier 2) capital. No argument about what goes into the core — shareholders' equity and disclosed reserves. But the second tier of lesser-quality items that can still be legitimately recognized as capital includes a wide range of instruments. And, to some extent, regulators can pick and choose which they will recognize (without ever allowing the secondary tier to exceed the core). The more items allowed, of course, the easier it is for a bank to meet the requirements — which, after a run-in period, were set at 8 per cent of risk-weighted assets (of which at least half had to be core capital) from the end of 1992.

National discretion also comes into play in deciding whether all or just some of a country's banks should be subject to the capital rules. The Accord applies to 'international' banks, without any guiding definition. The Japanese interpret this rather narrowly; at the other end of the spectrum, British and American supervisors apply the rules virtually across the board.

But the greatest scope for diversity arises from the fact that the Basle standards are *minimum* ones. In practice, regulators can be more demanding. The Bank of England, for instance, took a particularly conservative stance from the start, continuing its tradition of individual treatment. In the initial phases of the new rules, a big British clearing bank might have been required to meet an 8.5 per cent ratio, but a smaller bank 12 per cent or even higher. One bank was said to have been penalized with a target of 22 per cent in 1992. That hardly makes for a 'level playing field' with banks from a country where the authorities are content to apply the minimum 8 per cent across the board.

The Basle Committee is continuously trying to refine its capital rules, to iron out anomalies, to close loopholes and to extend their coverage to capture trading and other risks as well as credit risks. The banks respond in age-old fashion; they devise ways to circumvent or minimize the impact of the rules. With the help of lawyers, they can repackage some of their assets into channels that escape or at least reduce the reserves that must be set against them by Basle rules. They can also deliberately direct their new lending to categories ranked low in risk.

Since lending to corporations of all kinds carries a 100 per cent risk, but lending to industrial governments no risk at all, central bankers have been accused of conspiring to encourage banks to purchase government securities and thereby finance government deficits. On the other hand, some critics of the Basle Accord argue that since all business lending ranks equally, banks are tempted to choose riskier corporate clients, who pay over the odds for borrowing, rather than stolid blue-chips. Decide that argument as you may, the capital agreement certainly influences the way clearing banks conduct their business.

Even the philosophy isn't clear

Yet Leigh-Pemberton, when he headed the Bank of England, is on record as saying: 'It is not the task of regulators to prevent financial institutions from making lending mistakes.' If that is so, how *do* they see their task? It is not a silly question. Once the banking industry in a country has been freed, has ceased to be a strategic arm of government economic policy, then the purpose of its supervision is open to dispute. Is it to prevent failures? Or to limit damage to the system? Or to protect depositors?

National cultures colour the answers to these quite basic questions. When Toyoo Gyohten, the highly respected former Vice Minister of Finance for International Affairs in Tokyo, told an international gathering of bank chiefs in the summer of 1992 that, in his view, bank regulation should aim, first, at attaining both stability and efficiency of the market, and, second, at ensuring a fair and practicable risk-sharing among banks, customers and regulators, he was in the vanguard of Japanese opinion. For, as he reminded his audience on that occasion, Japan has behind it a hundred years of banking regulation underscored by two motives: to prevent open competition among banks and to protect them from failure. Given those targets, it was wonderfully successful. Tokyo can boast that throughout all the years of Japan's postwar 'economic miracle' there was not a single bank failure.

Not a boast, however, to impress today's watchdogs in the other two big financial centres, where there is an almost pious belief in the potential sanction of failure to keep markets competitive. When he was the New York Federal Reserve's president, Gerald Corrigan repeatedly warned that no supervisory system can be fail-proof – 'and nor should it be'. And Brian Quinn, the executive director in charge of supervision at the Bank of England at the time of the BCCI closure, has described his job as 'the effort to limit failure'. But any such philosophizing stops well short of defining where the responsibilities of the authorities end and those of the industry and the consumer begin – in short, what is the 'fair' division of risk that Gyohten seeks.

Protection of the individual depositor in the event of a bank failure has not, traditionally, been a high concern of central bankers. The presumption that it is needed because small depositors may be too ignorant to be able to pick the good from the bad among deposit-takers poses a 'moral hazard'. Deposit insurance can but encourage customers to be even less careful in choosing their banks; and the banks, in turn, to be less careful in management of deposits than they might otherwise have been. On the other hand, there is no doubt that a lack of deposit insurance accentuates the sudden withdrawal of funds from a bank at the first sign of trouble, which can lead to the loss of public confidence in the financial system that central bankers so dread.

This last consideration won out as bank failure became a growth business in the 1980s. Most industrial countries now have some deposit insurance scheme, whereas that was true of only a handful in the mid-1970s. After America led the way in 1934, more than a quarter of a century went by before another country – Norway, as it happened – followed suit, in 1961. Even now, there are widely differing perceptions of the purpose and appropriateness of deposit insurance. Some schemes are compulsory, some voluntary. Some schemes are administered officially, as in the United States and Japan, others privately, as in Germany and France. Funding may be entirely from the banking industry, as in the United States and Britain, or entirely from the official sector, as in Spain and Portugal. Or, yet again, provided jointly as in Japan. The British scheme covers only sterling deposits; the German one, at the other end of the spectrum, all deposits in any currency, even those in foreign branches of German banks. Most telling of all, the maximum cover for each depositor ranges enormously – at the time of writing, from £20,000 in Britain to the equivalent of over 200 times that sum in Italy.

So ingrained are some of the differences in European perceptions that attempts to harmonize deposit insurance in the run-up to the Single Market failed completely, though low-level minimum standards were set. Europe also served in those years to demonstrate the lack of consensus on another crucial issue in regulation and supervision, the question of where the central bank should feature in it. Any illusion that, other things being equal, all central banks would choose to play a lead role, was blown away when European central bankers came to draft a statute for the proposed European Central Bank. They agreed it should have an advisory role if the Community legislated supervisory policies, but left it to national central banks and other national authorities to exercise actual supervisory functions. True, the door was left ajar for the 'possibility of designating the European Central Bank as a competent supervisory authority', but that was as far as the Bundesbank was prepared to go towards the Bank of England's way of thinking. And one felt at the time that the skies would have to fall in before 'possibility' translates into actuality.

Where central banks stand

Why do central banks such as the Bundesbank and the Swiss National Bank fight shy of overt supervisory responsibility? The pat answer is because it introduces conflicts of interest, which can endanger monetary policy. They feel that a central bank charged with supervision could be tempted to reduce interest rates, even if there were no macroeconomic grounds for doing so, merely in order to help weak banks. Or not raise interest rates when it should because that could threaten the survival of unhealthy institutions. The Bundesbank has no doubt that taking on bank supervision could create inflationary pressures.

But there is a credible counter-argument that the extra insights gained into the banking industry's operations through direct supervision improve the central bank's assessment of the state of the economy and so help it in running monetary policy. A case can also be made that the dual role enhances its authority with the banks. The debate goes on, unresolved, a matter of opinion. Two investigations in Australia in the 1980s concluded that even though there was potential for conflict in certain circumstances, prudential supervision and monetary policy management need to be coordinated. And, further, coordination can best be achieved by a single institutional framework. On the other hand, at about the same time, a study group reviewing Swiss banking law decided that the interests of creditors required banking to be controlled by an institution legally distinct from that conducting monetary and foreign-exchange policy, though there should be close operational cooperation between the two institutions.

In 1990, Robert Heller, a distinguished banking economist who had served on the Federal Reserve Board in Washington, produced some evidence from the track record during 1980–87 that 'central banks that concentrate all their energy on monetary policy tend to be more successful in achieving the goal of price stability than central banks that have major supervisory responsibility'. But he admitted his examination was limited and that there could be many other explanations of this apparent association, such as the degree of independence of the central bank.

It is surely no coincidence that the larger central banks which enjoy most independence in the execution of monetary policy are the least likely to possess full supervisory responsibilities. Perhaps this might not be so if their monetary autonomy were inviolate, instead of being at the mercy of legislators. But given its propensity to incite political hostility, they will think twice about seeking extra roles in the public domain, which can lead to accusations of being power-hungry. Chairmen at the Federal Reserve spend too much time on the Hill in Washington defending their institution's most precious possession, the right to set monetary policy, to engage in secondary battles. All the same, the Fed managed, rather quietly as occasion arose, to increase its supervisory involvement; in 1991, for instance, it was made responsible for the licensing and oversight of *all* (not just some) foreign banks in the United States – which, incidentally, entailed the New York Federal Reserve Bank finding and training some 200 new bank examiners in 1992–93.

Though it is unlikely to admit it in so many words, a central bank may also be reluctant to take on a no-win job in terms of public relations. No stripes for keeping law and order for most of the time – that is taken for granted. But one mistake, and all hell breaks loose. The public is outraged, the government offers no support, heads may have to roll. A central bank governor can lose his reputation over a single bank failure as easily as falling off a horse – as Robin Leigh-Pemberton found over the BCCI disaster.

While for most of us it is embedded in history, the Herstatt débâcle is as fresh in the minds of the top echelon at the Bundesbank as if it had happened yesterday. It is a constant warning of the public indictment the German central bank would have gone on suffering had it not been able to plead the absence of formal supervisory responsibility. Looking out at Frankfurt's financial centre from their thirteenth-floor offices, the directors easily persuade themselves that it is not their own personal dignity they are afraid of losing, but the Bundesbank's credibility with the public, which they regard as an essential ingredient of their success in fighting inflation. When price stability is not just a priority, but is a unique objective, anything that could weaken it is not even to be considered.

All the same, the Bundesbank sees to it that it is fully cognizant with the state of German banking. Although the Federal Banking Supervisory Office in Berlin reports directly to the Ministry of Economics, it is required by law to operate in a way that supports the Bundesbank's monetary policy, including agreeing with it regulations on bank liquidity. Moreover, not only does the Bundesbank have its own supervision department, but its regional arms, the Land central banks, examine banks for the Supervisory Office.

The Bank of France also manages to eat its cake and have it. It mans the French Banking Commission over which the governor presides, and conducts bank inspections on its behalf. The Federal Banking Commission in Berne is largely independent of the Swiss National Bank but in practice the two cooperate closely. And a similar arrangement holds true in Belgium, where banks have to submit their accounts to both the Banking Commission and the central bank.

With such cosy arrangements, these European central banks are probably getting the best of all possible worlds. While the separate agency may operate much like a central bank department – particularly in the French case – it offers considerable psychological advantages. Inside a central bank, supervision will never have the glossy image reserved for monetary policy. And it can be divisive. When the Bank of England was accused of 'wholly inadequate' regulation of BCCI – by an American congressional committee – the entire central bank came under a cloud, much to the chagrin of its high-flyers who had nothing to do with supervision. At the same time, the public decided the Bank had let BCCI continue trading fraudulently for years because it was too wrapped up in monetary policy, few people knowing that a separate board with outside directors on it advised on supervisory matters.

If central banks with supervisory responsibilities avoid conflicts of interest by erecting 'Chinese walls' between their monetary policy and supervisory functions, any advantages from synergy are surely lost. Yet, ostrich-like, they are reluctant even to air the issue properly. Delivering an important lecture in Washington in September 1990, three years after vacating the Fed chair, Paul Volcker saw a 'compelling case' for central banks to 'have a strong voice and authority in regulatory and supervisory matters'. He went on: 'I would insist that neither monetary policy nor the financial system will be well served if a central bank loses interest in, or influence over, the structure and performance of the financial system.' And when Gerald Corrigan headed the Fed's New York arm from 1985 to 1993, he repeatedly preached that one of the crucial functions of a central bank was oversight of the financial system. But generalities are not good enough. How should 'influence' or 'oversight' be effected? And how can it relate to the 'financial system', rather than just banking, in countries like the United States and Britain, where supervision remains strictly compartmentalized?

A single authority

The securities and insurance industries are now so intertwined with banking – and not only through financial conglomerates – that a botch-up in either of them can quickly threaten the whole payments system. This chapter has given only the merest taste of financial troubles in the horrible 1980s; some of them originated outside the banking sector. A post-mortem on the Wall Street crash of October 1987, orchestrated by Nicholas Brady before he became Treasury Secretary, led to the proposal that the central bank should become the single regulatory overlord of the wider financial system. Yet the Fed chairman at the time, Alan Greenspan, didn't accept the invitation to try to spread his 'influence' or 'oversight' (though later he fiercely opposed the Clinton administration's proposals to divest the Fed of all supervisory responsibilities).

Other big countries have adopted a more unitary vision of supervision. In Japan, banking, securities and insurance are supervised by three separate bureaux, but all within the Ministry of Finance, with the Bank of Japan sharing responsibility for banking. The Bank of Italy stands out as an important central bank responsible for securities firms as well as banks. The German and French supervisory agencies perform a similarly combined duty, while in Denmark, Sweden and Norway all three supervisors have merged into a single authority, though the central bank will not bail out insurance companies.

It is on this mishmash of national arrangements that attempts are being made to superimpose rules for every sort of financial firm or conglomerate doing international business. The European Union has gone furthest along this road, but it is questionable how effective its standardization will be without a supranational supervisor. Bringing in the Americans and Japanese is proving tough, even on a specific issue like common capital standards for securities firms that stand alone and those that are within a banking group.

Yet the markets have moved on, even as regulators hammer out the rules. One well-informed and experienced market commentator, Henry Kaufman, who used to call the shots at the investment house of Salomon Brothers in New York, is exasperated with the failure of regulators to keep up with the globalization of markets. 'One of the most important challenges of the 1990s,' he says, 'is to rectify this untenable situation and put in place an excellent international financial supervisory authority with true accountability.' As Kaufman sees it, the most promising route would be to create an international board of overseers of major international financial institutions and markets, drawn from central banks and other governmental agencies but also including members from the private sector. Ouch. Yet another huge international bureaucracy? Could it really work anyway?

Not unless there is first convergence in national regulatory arrangements. And if greater uniformity in these can be achieved, there is scope for effective international cooperation without – or at least before – resorting to a cumbersome overlord. We think the finger points inexorably in the end to single national regulators for key financial centres. Central banks can't bring this about off their own bats, but they alone, as guardians of the payments system, have the weight of authority to press for it. With that in mind, they should consider very seriously how to put more teeth into the Basle Committee on Banking Supervision.

A Victorian historian, James Anthony Froude, said: 'Experience teaches slow and at the cost of mistakes.' Too many more mistakes by national regulators waiting passively for the next catastrophe, and they may get scalped alive by a public that is coming to expect an awful lot – increasingly high standards of protection yet all the benefits of free markets.

One of the main concerns of all central banks is to secure the safety of their countries' foreign-exchange reserves (and gold, if they have any). But first: why should a country hold any reserves?

This may seem an academic question, since virtually all countries with central banks hold some reserves, and it would be a bold central bank governor who went to his Prime Minister or President and said: 'We don't need any reserves.' Many have had to go to deliver the stark message: 'We have no reserves left', but this has always been seen as an admission of defeat, not a policy objective.

The focus on national reserves of foreign exchange is very much a twentieth-century phenomenon and is closely linked with the attempt to pursue independent national economic and monetary policies. Foreign reserves may be used to cushion the national economy against external shocks like a sudden rise in import prices. They can be protected by various physical controls, such as restrictions on citizens' access to foreign exchange, and some states have attempted by such means to insulate themselves from the world economy.

Indeed, the story of central banks' changing role in the management of their external reserves accurately reflects the changing patterns of twentieth-century history. At first, they were just there; up to 1914 national gold reserves served both as an external reserve and as the base of the banking system. Then there was a split. Nations withdrew from the total integration and openness of the international gold standard, and accumulated foreign-exchange reserves as a means of maintaining a measure of national autonomy. This was the era of exchange restrictions, associated with the Great Depression, fascism and communism. Foreign reserves were to be protected at all costs, even at the cost of punishing a country's own citizens for taking foreign currency out of the country. Then with the fall of communism and the ending of exchange controls, attitudes changed yet again; external reserves were seen just as investments, a source of income to be professionally managed, a national savings account on which the country could draw on a rainy day. Within less than 100 years, the cycle then came full circle, with the reintegration of virtually all countries in a single world economy.

Most central banks kept their balance brilliantly on this political see-saw. After slavishly following the rules of the gold standard game, at a stroke many of them became the willing servants of the all-powerful state, zealously administering exchange controls. Those which fell under communism were destroyed. But there was a silver lining. Through this dark period, even in socialist countries like Sweden, most central bankers kept a feeling for the market system. Indeed, in some countries, they were just about the only institutions representing the liberal, open-market tradition. In 1970, one of the authors described the Bank of England as 'the most powerful repository of a liberal economic philosophy in England today'. That was when most people still believed the future lay with socialism.

Economic theory states that the level of reserves a country needs depends on the degree of flexibility of its exchange rate – i.e., how far it wants its exchange rate to vary from the level that would be set by the free market. With a freely floating exchange rate, an imbalance in the supply and demand for the local currency in the foreign-exchange market will give rise to a movement in the exchange rate, so there is no need for reserves. On the other hand, a totally fixed exchange rate also removes the need for reserves by linking the economy rigidly to that of another economy; at the extreme, one currency and central bank can absorb another, as the West German D-mark and central bank absorbed the former East German Ostmark and central bank, along with its reserves, in 1990.

But in practice the nation-states of the twentieth century typically wanted neither totally fixed nor totally flexible rates. Rather, they wanted to be free to alter exchange rates, but also have the ability to manipulate them – hence the interest, amounting sometimes to an obsession, with their reserves.

Shifts in academic fashions played their part. In the late 1960s and early 1970s, many influential economists advocated floating exchange rates; many had spent years under Bretton Woods arguing the case for greater flexibility. But after the Bretton Woods system broke down, it soon became clear that few governments would let exchange rates float freely, the notable recent exception being the United States during the first Reagan administration of 1979–84. So fashion moved back towards the idea that the exchange rate should be 'managed'; and that in practice requires reserves with which the central bank can intervene in the market. From the mid-1980s, even the United States started intervening again.

Partly because of this fear of free floating, the advent of managed floating rates in the 1970s was indeed followed by a rapid growth in reserves. Brutal external shocks like the oil price hikes during that decade convinced governments and central banks that they needed an extra cushion of reserves. The growth of international financial markets made it easier for those which had access to the markets to borrow to top up their reserves. Countries which did not have access to the markets, which included most developing countries, valued reserves even more highly, and had to make a deliberate effort to build up reserves through a trade or current account surplus.

Reserves and the money supply

Although one of the motives in building up reserves is to enable a country to pursue an independent monetary policy, no amount of reserves can ever provide full independence. For one thing, when intervening in the markets to influence the exchange rate, a central bank will have to consider possible repercussions on the money supply. Under the gold standard, there was a close link between an inflow or outflow of reserves and the money supply. Generally, the central bank would react to a loss of reserves by raising interest rates, thus reducing the demand for credit (though exactly how this worked to make the economy 'adjust' is still discussed). When the external reserve no longer functions as the reserve base of the banking system, there is a less direct link. But intervention to buy or sell foreign exchange against domestic currency will affect domestic monetary conditions, unless it is deliberately offset or – in the jargon – 'sterilized'.

In brief, what tends to happen is this. When the domestic currency is weak, and the central bank is propping up the exchange rate by selling foreign currency from its reserves to banks and other market operators, and buying domestic currency from them, the money supply tends to contract. This is because banks will then hold fewer reserves at the central bank or other domestic assets and more foreign assets. The opposite happens when the domestic currency is in demand, and the central bank is intervening to hold down the exchange rate by selling domestic currency. So operations by central banks in the currency markets have domestic repercussions.

Central banks have had much practice in their efforts to 'sterilize' the effects of such intervention – mainly by offsetting it by open-market operations. Their performance as interveners is considered further in Chapter 13. Even in countries such as Britain and France which have a special account (the Exchange Equalization Account in Britain) to act as a buffer between foreign-exchange intervention and domestic monetary conditions, the insulation is never complete. And in Germany, the potential inflationary impact of the huge intervention by the central bank in selling D-marks was the main reason why it decided to bring down the fixed exchange-rate system in 1973 and the European exchange-rate system twenty years later. This is the mechanism through which the Bundesbank feared Germany would suffer from 'imported inflation'. To quote Otmar Emminger:

> German stabilization policy has repeatedly been undermined by influences originating abroad. In no other major country has imported inflation played such a major role as in the federal republic of Germany.

Why developing countries have reserves

When a country holds external reserves (net of borrowing), they tie up scarce resources, which could be spent on increasing imports. This can be costly, especially for a developing country. The options for doing without reserves altogether – free floating or currency union – are also in principle open to developing countries. However, few have adopted either of these regimes. The free-floating option is not practicable in the absence of financial markets on which the currency is traded. In developing countries, foreign currency needs of importers and banks are often met directly by the central bank, sometimes operating through commercial banks; the exchange rate itself is often set by administrative decision, changing periodically. But while the aim may be to set the exchange rate at precisely that level which will balance receipts and payments of foreign exchange, in practice there is bound to be a net surplus or a net deficit requiring financing.

Though not in widespread use, some countries have adopted a version of the currency board system where the central bank or currency-issuing authority is given no discretion at all with regard to the amount of foreign reserve. (The currency board system is discussed in Chapters 6 and 19.) There the amount of the board's reserve is determined automatically by the demand for the local currency: as traders and others present foreign currency for local notes, or sell local notes for foreign currency, so the currency board's reserve changes. This is still an important model for some of the newer central banks whose main concern is to secure confidence in a new currency. The example of Estonia is discussed further in Chapter 19. Argentina adopted a modified version of the currency board in 1990. By linking the domestic currency rigidly to an external standard of known value, such as the US dollar or D-mark, a domestic currency will immediately gain credibility and acceptability and inflation will be controlled – always assuming that people expect the government to maintain the link.

In practice, a country with a central bank will also have some external reserves (though these may be borrowed), intended to tide it over a shortfall in export receipts or capital outflows. Failure to hold adequate reserves may lead to national ruin if there is a natural disaster, as was indeed the case for some sub-Saharan countries facing extreme drought conditions in 1991–92. They simply did not have any money to buy food and other supplies on world markets, and so became totally dependent on aid. In other instances a shortage of reserves might bring an abrupt halt to development through starving the country of imports when export receipts fall.

Many developing countries still maintain restrictions designed partly at least to conserve precious foreign exchange. Until January 1994 China had three exchange rates. There was an official rate at which tourists were supposed to buy renminbi which they could use while in China for paying hotel bills and making purchases at tourist shops (they were issued with specially printed banknotes called 'Foreign Exchange Certificates') and at which some state agencies could purchase foreign exchange; there was a so-called 'swap' rate where other approved agencies and companies could obtain foreign exchange; and there was the black market rate. In January 1994 the exchange rates were unified; the official rate was abolished, and the 'swap' rate was allowed to move closer to the true market rate. This was widely seen as a step towards convertibility, although China still maintained many restrictions on access to foreign exchange.

The common characteristic of such controls is that they support an overvalued exchange rate. The country is, in a sense, pretending that its currency is worth more than it really is. The currency issued by its central bank is not allowed to find its free market level, so it has to be artificially propped up. Indeed, a depressingly large part of the work actually conducted by many central banks around the world has involved the administration of such controls. Ever since it was founded the IMF has campaigned against the tendency of developing countries to maintain grossly overvalued exchange rates. Indeed, exchange controls, multiple exchange rates and the tendency for developing countries to overvalue the exchange rate have always been anathema to the IMF. One of its founding purposes was to promote the progressive dismantling of controls after the Second World War; we have told that story in Chapters 4 and 5. It had mixed success. But by the 1990s, the examples of countries like those in Asia which have based rapid growth on outward-looking economies and promoted exports with the help of realistic exchange rates were persuading many other developing countries to follow suit. All the same, for many of them full convertibility was still a long way off; in 1994, only about half the world's central banks were issuing currencies that held their own in the markets without restrictions, for current payments as well as controls on capital flows.

How large reserves for the world?

Robert Solomon, author of *The International Monetary System*, perhaps the most widely read book on the subject, acknowledged in 1991 that little attention is paid to international liquidity (the total amount of world reserves of gold and foreign exchange). Although developing countries have had reason to be concerned with their reserves, 'if one were to identify the world's principal economic and financial problems, international liquidity would be far down the list'.

There was more than a touch of wistfulness in that remark. For many years in the 1960s and 1970s Solomon and many others thought that the growth of international liquidity (reserves) should be brought under collective control, or at least that it was an important problem. The idea was that a shortage of world reserves might inhibit the growth of international trade, since countries experiencing a shortage would fight to preserve their reserves even at the cost of reducing imports. But the seemingly endless negotiations and 'crisis meetings' designed to achieve this aim yielded little except for the special drawing right (SDR), the IMF's currency unit, which has never made much impact.

Since the development of the international financial markets, the aggregate amount of world reserves, and their composition, have been determined by the decisions of individual central banks and governments. There is no centralized decision-making or even coordination among countries, although the IMF does keep trends in international liquidity under review. Most central bankers believe there is no alternative to this decentralized system. This is because countries are not prepared to submit their economies to any external discipline other than that imposed by the market. For the same reason, most observers also expect that countries and central banks will remain free to decide for themselves the level and composition of their reserves.

The markets solved one problem but created another. Measured by trade criteria, world reserves appear to be adequate; yet measured by the forces that the private capital market can muster, they are meagre indeed. Since the transition to flexible exchange rates in the 1970s, aggregate monetary reserves, excluding gold, rose from less than $200 billion to $540 billion in 1988 and to $960 billion in 1993. This rise was almost matched by the increase in world trade measured in current dollars. Throughout the period from 1973 to 1992, the volume of world reserves would buy between ten and fourteen weeks of 'world imports'; the equivalent during the Bretton Woods period was only eight weeks. So, contrary to expectations, when freed from the Bretton Woods constraints, countries 'chose' on average to hold larger reserves in relation to imports than they had before.

However, for those countries that hold reserves to influence their exchange rate, the relevant test of adequacy is the amount of reserves in relation to the volume of funds in domestic currency that can quickly flee to another currency. With the liberalization of financial markets and the ending of capital controls bringing diversification of pension funds and other private-sector portfolios during the 1970s and 1980s, the volume of these mobile funds greatly increased. In 1994, it was estimated that the total volume of privately managed investment funds was at least $15 trillion and possibly much more (nobody could be sure of the true figure). Total official reserves including gold (values at market prices) were just over $1.3 trillion. By such tests, the adequacy of reserves has sharply diminished. By 1993, the foreign-exchange markets were turning over $1 trillion *a day*. Reserves no longer provide the cushion they are supposed to.

The most dramatic examples of the use of reserves were in the summers of 1992 and 1993, when the currencies of the ERM came under massive attack in the forex markets. Some DM400 billion was mobilized in 1992 and a smaller amount in 1993 – amounts dwarfing those spent in any previous period. But despite all the money spent, the central banks lost, and the markets won.

The lesson of currency crises of the early 1990s is that international financial integration has overtaken the ability of central banks – either individually or indeed collectively – to defend any exchange rate where there was the slightest doubt of the readiness of the country concerned to subordinate all other objectives of policy to the single objective of maintaining its chosen rate. In other words, the market was demanding that governments dedicate their policy entirely to the achievement of an exchange-rate objective – or forget it (i.e., let it float). Once again, the markets seemed to be narrowing the options open to central banks and government. The freedom they gave with one hand they took away with the other. (Exchange-rate policies are discussed further in Chapter 13.)

Portfolio management in practice

So far we have considered movements of total world reserves. When it comes to individual countries, central banks have to decide priorities among the objectives we have discussed and how to implement them in the specific circumstances with which they are faced. This involves the choice of the currency denomination of investments, the selection of capital and money-market instruments and the development of operational guidelines to govern activity in the markets. About fifty central banks of large and smaller countries are believed to manage their reserves actively.

Central banks attach great importance to maintaining liquidity for at least part of their reserves. Indeed, there is arguably no case for holding reserves in excess of those that may be needed immediately in a crisis or at very short notice. Funds should be readily available for intervention in the currency markets and (for smaller developing countries) for absorbing fluctuations in export receipts, import payments and capital flows. These funds will normally be held in bank deposits with those central banks of the countries whose currencies are held (such as the Federal Reserve Bank of New York), leading commercial banks in the principal financial centres or with the Bank for International Settlements; another part may be held in Treasury bills, certificates of deposit and other very liquid investments.

Holding reserves incurs an opportunity cost – foreign-currency reserves by definition are invested outside the country, and thus involve extending credit to the reserve centre where they are held, whereas they could be spent on goods and services for domestic consumers. Holding reserves in excess of requirements is therefore an expensive luxury. The difficulty is to assess what are a country's 'requirements'.

Some central banks have set up formal procedures for measuring their reserve needs. In practice most central banks are content to accumulate any reserves that may accrue to them in good times. The level of a country's reserves at any time is largely a result of historical accident – the result of the country's recent balance of payments and whether in the course of recent intervention in the markets it has lost or gained foreign exchange. Capital movements swamp movements of funds for current payments (imports and exports and invisibles), and are so large that a few days or weeks of active intervention (buying or selling foreign exchange to influence the exchange rate) will swell or (more frequently) deplete the reserves.

When central banks started diversifying their currency reserves out of dollars in the 1970s with the end of the dollar standard, they were guided to some extent by common sense. If reserves are held mainly to cope with fluctuations in export receipts, their currency composition should clearly bear some relation to the pattern of the country's trade and investment. Where the country had borrowings in foreign currency, that also had to be taken into account. However, the extent of diversification was limited because the dollar remained for all practical purposes the only intervention currency (except within the EMS). Thus even though the volatility of the dollar in the 1970s and 1980s caused central banks to diversify part of their reserves, many kept more than half in dollars.

As the dollar remained the dominant intervention currency, central banks tended to have most liquid reserves in dollars, with longer maturity investments mainly in non-dollar currencies. But by 1992 the share of total foreign exchange reserves in dollars was down to 50 per cent, with the D-mark next at 16 per cent and the yen at about 10 per cent.

Diversification was led by certain developing countries, notably some of the oil-producing countries, and was conducted largely through the Euromarkets – partly to preserve confidentiality but mainly because of the higher yields and greater flexibility. Indeed, given the hostility of the Bundesbank and Bank of Japan to the use of their currencies in official reserves (until the late 1980s, when there were signs of a change), and the restrictions on non-resident investment in, for example, the German domestic market in the early days of currency diversification, the Euromarkets were often the only channel available.

The actual management of foreign reserves is sometimes 'contracted out' by central banks to a leading commercial or investment bank – though usually only a small portion of the total will be managed on a fiduciary basis. Most central banks maintain accounts with the central banks in the reserve centres, as well as with commercial banks and investment banks. Probably a majority of central banks conduct their reserve transactions mainly with foreign commercial banks rather than through other central banks. In the 1980s, competition among commercial banks and investment banks for central banks' business became intense, partly because of the prestige attached and the fee business generated but also because of the incidental benefits, such as the information they gained about the market operations of the central banks, which are big players and can shift exchange rates.

In the early 1990s, some developing countries with substantial reserves were adopting much bolder investment strategies. Some set aside portions of their reserves for higher-risk, higher-return investments. In some countries, up to one-third of their total reserves were believed to be invested in relatively illiquid assets, including investments in equity and real estate – investments that would generally be considered quite unsuitable for a central bank to make. With a rapid increase in portfolio-management skills, and many high-powered advisers eager to sell central banks their services, attitudes towards reserve asset management seemed likely to change rapidly in the closing years of the century.

Gold holds its own

Ever since the days of the gold standard, central banks have held gold in their reserves. Indeed, originally all reserves were in gold, because that was the only form of international payment acceptable in final settlement of international imbalances. Central banks hold about 29,000 tonnes of gold on their own account and another 6,000 tonnes is deposited with official institutions such as the IMF, the European Monetary Institute and the BIS. Including an allowance for countries such as Iraq and Singapore, which do not reveal their gold stocks, and secret gold holdings by institutions such as the Abu Dhabi Investment Authority and the Kuwait Investment Office, total official gold holdings are put at about 36,000 tonnes, about 30 per cent of all the gold that has ever been mined.

In the late 1940s, America had 75 per cent of all the monetary gold in the world. However, as Germany and France moved into large surpluses in the 1960s, both accumulated substantial amounts of gold and the share held by the United States fell. Britain also sold part of its gold during that time. Central banks also were heavy buyers in the market, taking up 44 per cent of the gold on offer between 1948 and 1964. That was when the gold price was held at $35 an ounce, as it was until 1968, when central banks gave up the unequal struggle to keep it at that price (see Chapter 5). As the gold authority, Tim Green, tells the story:

> The Washington Agreement that year created a two-tier market in which central banks were supposedly divorced from the hurly-burly of the market place, but could still turn in official dollars for gold at the Federal Reserve until President Nixon ordered that gold window closed . . .

Since then, there have been only minor shifts of ownership of gold among the central banks and the overall amount of physical gold held by all the central banks together has also been stable, though there was a decline in 1992–93 mainly on sales by Belgium and Holland.

The value of those gold stocks has, however, varied considerably with the market price of gold. This moved from its fixed price of $35 per ounce under Bretton Woods to reach a peak of $850 an ounce in 1980, only to fall back to $320 early in 1993, before rising again to $400 after the much-publicized investment by two world-famous billionaires – George Soros and Jimmy Goldsmith.

By this time, the gold market had become mesmerized by the central banks, for the underlying demand and supply for gold had changed. For the first time, demand from industry, jewellery manufacturers and investors had risen to match annual output of gold from the mines in South Africa, Australia, the United States, Russia and other gold-producing countries. Indeed, most analysts believed that from the early 1990s the market needed a regular supply from the central banks. There had always been sales by some central banks, especially those of gold-producing countries, and occasional significant sales from a few of the larger holders. The question was whether in future these would be enough to bring the market into balance.

The big attraction of gold to central banks is that it has a very good record of keeping its value in the long term. There are a few currencies, notably of late the Japanese yen, that have performed better over a number of years or even a decade or two. But in the long run the price of gold in almost any currency has kept remarkably stable in real terms, that is, in terms of the purchasing power of that currency. The big disadvantage is that it does not pay interest; however, that drawback has been overcome to some extent by the development of a gold loan market in which a growing number of central banks lend out their gold and earn interest on it.

Central banks can control the gold market, because they own so much that they could supply all its needs for a hundred years or more – but only if they actually sell large amounts. They show little sign of doing this. In practice, the big holders like the United States, Germany, France, Switzerland and Italy are 'locked in'; they cannot sell without precipitating a sharp fall in the price. Only smaller central banks have any effective freedom of action. But of these Canada is the only one to have announced and implemented a policy of regular gold sales – and Canada had very little gold left by 1994.

Thus fears among gold-holders that central banks would be sellers on a large scale seemed unfounded. On the contrary, there were signs of increased interest in buying gold on the part of some Asian countries, such as China. Throughout history, gold has followed money. When people become wealthy, they put some of their money into gold. That applies to nations as well as to individuals. The historical record seemed likely to repeat itself in the 1990s as the centre of gravity of the world economy moved to Asia and the Pacific.

Gold has been regarded for many years as the 'last resort' asset of central banks. This is unlikely to change. There is little or no prospect of gold regaining its position at the centre of the international monetary system, at least so long as the central banks keep the lid on inflation. Central banks have ambivalent attitudes to gold. On the one hand, they want to keep what gold reserves they have. On the other, they do not want to bring it back into use as real money. For that would be a reflection on the paper money that they all issue, and might make central banks themselves redundant. Paper money is in competition with gold – in the long run. Central banks want paper money to win. Now that they have greater independence, it has a better chance of doing that than it had.

The politics of reserve management

We have referred in this chapter to central banks 'holding and managing' their country's foreign reserves. The imprecision was deliberate. Their precise role varies considerably, according to legal, constitutional and political conditions. In the United States, reserves are owned by the state, and the central bank manages them as agent of the Treasury. In practice, in most G10 countries, central banks have a wide degree of descretion in day-to-day reserve management, but governments retain control over strategic policy issues.

In particular, governments set exchange-rate policy and thus determine the timing and scale of intervention, i.e., when and how much foreign reserves should be sent, or bought, to influence the exchange rate. Margaret Thatcher asked to see the intervention figures on a daily basis during times of tension in the markets and would let the British Chancellor of the Exchequer know plainly when she thought he was giving wrong instructions to the Bank of England. The Governor of the Bank sometimes requests specific written instructions from the Chancellor on intervention policy.

But here too the role of central bankers is growing. This is all part of the trend towards greater independence. How can they assume real responsibility for price stability if one important influence on monetary policy, notably intervention in the foreign-exchange markets, is outside their control? This is one unresolved issue in the debate on central bank independence, for governments can hardly hand over exchange-rate policy to central banks without handing over much of their general economic policy. This illustrates the difficulty of keeping domestic monetary policy in a watertight compartment.

In conclusion, central banks are getting more active in their reserve management, but are still guided by the principles of security, liquidity and yield – in that order. Reserves have not diminished as a result of flexible exchange rates – just the opposite. And by and large central banks hold on to their gold – the big holders being locked into it. But the former interest in world liquidity – the aggregate of world reserves – has vanished. Reserves have been 'privatized' in the sense that they are managed increasingly with an eye on maximizing overall returns by increasingly independent central banks.

12 *The Safety Net*

As the 1990s opened, many commercial bankers, central bankers and scholars shared a concern about the stability of the banking system, about the risks being run by individual banks and about the costs of providing assurances of security to bank customers. This concern arose partly as a direct result of experience – the scale of banking problems seemed to be growing rather than diminishing over the years – and partly as a result of analysis of the new money markets, especially the markets in so-called 'derivative' products, in which banks actively participated. Nobody could reassure legislatures and governments that the new markets did not increase the risk of a breakdown in the system. So the potential costs of the safety net held under the banking system may have grown to an incalculable extent.

These worries about banking were brought home to people around the world with the closure of BCCI in 1991. Thousands of depositors lost money, and extensive TV coverage dramatized the message that banks were not necessarily 100 per cent safe. In that case central banks themselves closed the bank, as they had evidence that it had been the vehicle for fraud on a massive scale and it had no chance of being kept solvent. In many other cases, however, governments and central banks have in recent years had to prop up banks and entire banking systems, at huge cost to the taxpayer. Were these cost justified? At a time when individuals are expected to make their own provision for many of the risks of daily life – the safety of their goods and property, health hazards and life insurance, for example – should they continue to be protected from the risks attached to putting money in a bank?

But, they protest, money is different and banks shouldn't be allowed to lose it. They don't stop to think that the bank has to do something with the money it receives from depositors; and that every conceivable form of investment or lending carries some risks. The bank bears those risks, and yet it still assures customers that they can always take out a £1 coin or $1 banknote for every £1 or $1 they have deposited. But the bank's investments might have gone bad in the interim: if invested in government securities, the price might have fallen, if in property, the property markets might have collapsed. You might say, if the bank were to keep the whole lot in banknotes in the vaults, then it could be sure of having banknotes to pay out. But then how would the bank earn income to pay for its expenses – staff salaries, strong-rooms, property, cheques, etc? It would have to charge very high fees to its depositors. Moreover it would be very wasteful; while stuck in a bank vault, money is not working, banks are not acting as channels between savers and investors, lenders and borrowers. Part of the point of having a monetary system would be lost. That is why banks have to do something with the money entrusted to them – indeed, they lend or invest it the very day they receive it.

So how does a bank know that it will have the money to pay depositors when they want it? Traditionally, the answer is that banks keep a reserve of capital and liquid assets at the ready. Since the last war, this source of security has been backed up by another: the guarantee of the state. This has not been stated formally, but if depositors ask for their money back when the bank's reserves are exhausted, and its assets are illiquid (i.e. cannot be sold quickly for cash), then the bank can turn to the central bank. In practice, except where the bank concerned is very small, the central bank will then step in with emergency support. True, if the bank has been run imprudently, the central bank may well fire the management, or insist on the bank being merged with another; here we are concerned merely with the fact that the authorities make every attempt to rescue a bank, and are usually willing to inject large sums to keep it afloat.

This role as a 'backstop' of the banking system has for half a century been effective in its main objective of preventing the spread of panic. Yet the cost of providing this safety net is rising and, though it has prevented panic, it has not prevented an erosion of bank solvency and stability. The tension between the public's demand for security and the costs of providing it – a tension felt in many fields besides banking – is the main subject of this chapter.

The calm before the storm

During the period of fixed exchange rates from 1945 to 1971, there were virtually no banking crises. The United States experienced some failures of small banks, but these never triggered any wider problems. Banking was a slow-moving business, kept within rigid confines, and there was little competition at least in terms of interest rates offered on deposits or charged on loans. Moreover, the development of central banks and their assumption of responsibility for the functioning of the banking system had banished fears of bank collapses. These were read about in tales of Victorian fiction; and for those with memories of the Great Depression of the 1930s, the crisis set off by the collapse of the Credit Anstalt of Austria in 1931 and the waves of bank failures in the United States were seen as striking examples of what could happen when there was no adequate lender of last resort.

The work of financial historians seemed to show that the Federal Reserve's failure to act as a lender of last resort to the American banking system contributed to the depth of the Great Depression in the 1930s. Such financial panics were seen as typical symptoms of the early stages of banking evolution, before the emergence of central banks proper. The moral was: the central bank should always be ready to lend. This story has been traced in Chapter 4. What we now see is that the costs of this 'solution' to the problem of banking crises are proving extremely high.

Decisive here has been the change in the role of monetary policy and the banking system. For several years after the war, as we have seen in earlier chapters, money was the obedient servant of the state. The role of monetary policy was to sustain full employment and economic growth. Indeed, in Britain during those postwar years the term 'lender of last resort' was used to refer to fairly routine action taken by the Bank of England to relieve a shortfall of funds in the short-term money markets, rather than to its role in preventing the spread of panic in a banking crisis. The willingness of the central bank to 'lend without stint' in time of financial strain was seen as a way of allowing the commercial banks to hold very low reserves of cash themselves – if necessary, they could always turn to the central bank. This centralization of the system's reserves was thought to represent an efficient use of cash.

Indeed, Richard Sayers, the banking scholar and historian of the Bank of England (covering fifty years to 1944), argued that the central bank's role as lender of last resort should be seen as a means of bringing the commercial banks under its control:

> This duty to act as lender of last resort is highly relevant to central banking control in that it lies at the root of the willingness of the commercial banks to work to a stable cash ratio. If the commercial banks had to provide for the extremities of panic demands for cash, they would feel it necessary to raise their cash ratios as soon as a cloud, however small, appeared on the financial horizon ... If, on the other hand, they are always confident that the central bank will come to the rescue of all well-

conducted institutions in time of stress, they will feel under no compulsion to raise their cash ratios when danger threatens. They will allow their cash ratios to settle down at the lowest level consistent with convenience and respectability.

Other countries were not so fortunate. The low cash ratio of the English banking system was viewed as a state of 'perfection' yet to be attained by less-developed lands where the cash ratio still varied, 'to the embarrassment of the central bank'.

If there had been a banking crisis, everybody assumed the central bank was ready to 'step in'. This was the lesson of history. To quote John Fforde, the later historian of the Bank of England:

> Although there were no examples in the early postwar decades, it must have been presumed that if a clearing bank or a British overseas bank were to encounter serious difficulties, the Bank would be prepared to step in to secure a solution through arranged merger or some other reconstruction.

True, the Bank and other central banks cloaked their real intentions behind a veil of bankerly discretion. They did not openly acknowledge that they had a financial responsibility for the banks – only their historians were allowed to breathe the truth. Indeed, central banks generally don't have much money of their own to inject into insolvent institutions, so that such a claim would have been somewhat presumptuous. They would usually have had to call on government funds, as they still do. They also clung to the theory that they would use their 'lender of last resort' capability only if concern with the troubles of an individual bank were to threaten the stability of the system. But the world believed that central banks – or other state agencies – would intervene whenever any large bank got into trouble.

In the United States, the Federal Deposit Insurance Act passed during the New Deal period, specifically to prevent a recurrence of the problems, provided reassurance to small depositors that they would be protected even if their bank went bust. True, the occasionally wise legislators of the American Congress had prohibited the Federal Reserve from rescuing an individual bank unless it could be proved to be solvent. But of course the central bank was ready to provide emergency liquidity to the system in a panic. But such panics were a thing of the past, or so people thought. It was all a question of confidence. In Japan, the banking system, including at that time the Bank of Japan, was an instrument of the government and plainly had its full support. A panic was unthinkable.

What became clear later was that this tranquillity for nearly thirty years after the end of the Second World War – a period of calm most unusual in the long sweep of banking history – was the by-product of a very special set of circumstances. First, there was an international monetary system worthy of the name. All leading countries were members of the International Monetary Fund and had agreed to abide by its rules – in practice, fixed exchange rates against the dollar and through it to gold. Second, governments in most countries kept their banking systems firmly under control through various direct instructions, prohibitions and regulations; exchange controls were widespread, most European currencies were not even convertible freely (into the dollar or each other) until 1959. Third, the international money markets were underdeveloped and the Eurodollar market had yet to be invented. Fourth, inflation remained at low levels. As interest rates and price levels were relatively stable, domestic banking carried few risks. Of its two main assets, the biggest depreciation of banks' holdings of government securities occurred when the discount rate had to be raised suddenly; and bad debts on loans, although they did occur, were never more than about 1 per cent of the loan book.

So predictable and stable was the business environment that banks did not even have to declare their true profits or follow normal accounting rules on the valuation of their assets and liabilities (they were allowed to follow special rules for disclosure precisely because it was feared that fluctuations in profits, if published, might alarm depositors). In most countries, banking supervision was light and there was no international coordination of central banks' supervisory responsibilities. The very suggestion that a large bank would need to be 'supervised' was considered to be little short of an insult.

How problems have increased

But then came the great change with the ending of fixed rates and the freeing of monetary policy and the banking system. Immediately, banking problems came to the surface again. They have become larger in scale with every business cycle since then. During the secondary banking crisis in Britain (starting December 1973), £1 billion had to be mobilized by the central bank and big commercial banks in the 'lifeboat' to be recycled to fringe banks, many of which were eventually put into liquidation – see Chapter 10. In America, the rescue of the Bank of the Commonwealth of Detroit (worth $1.5 billion) in 1972 was followed in 1980 by the bail-out of the First Pennsylvania Bank of Philadelphia (worth $9.1 billion) and in 1984 by the bail-out of Continental Illinois

National Bank of Chicago (with peak assets of $41 billion). Each of these American bank bail-outs avoided a failure that would at the time have been the largest bank failure in history; all were handled 'behind closed doors', with Congress having no opportunity to take a view. Huge amounts of public money were being spent by bank supervisory authorities at their discretion.

In the 1980s, the rot spread. The banking systems of two superpowers, Japan and the United States, suffered massive losses, first on third-world lending and then on real estate and corporate loans. Those of all Nordic countries except Denmark became insolvent. Spain and Australia suffered severe banking crises. There were systemic bank problems in many developing countries, including Malaysia, the Philippines and Thailand as well as virtually all Latin American countries. How to restructure and recapitalize banking systems became a major concern of international agencies providing assistance to developing countries. Everywhere you looked, large holes were appearing in the fabric of world banking. Everywhere, the central banks were in the thick of the battle.

At this point let us pay a visit to the United States, to see what lessons can be learnt from the biggest banking débâcle so far – the thrift crisis. The stories of this and other banking crises have been told in Chapter 10 from the perspective of the banking supervisor's job; here our concern is with the cost of the safety net.

The frightening case of America's thrift industry

In the United States, by 1993, estimates of the cost to American taxpayers of rescuing the savings and loan associations, equivalent to the British building societies, financing house purchase and other property investments, had risen to a staggering $400 billion, equivalent to about 6 per cent of America's GDP. This disaster cannot be laid at the door of the Federal Reserve, since it was not the industry regulator, but the causes have much in common with other recent banking crises. The chief culprits were deregulation of the industry and the simultaneous expansion of deposit insurance. (This account draws on D. H. Gowland's *Economics of Modern Banking*, published by Edward Elgar.)

Banking is risky; it is also a temptation to gamble. Banks take deposits from the public and use these funds to invest in risky assets. If the risk pays off, the investments do well, and the bank's shareholders reap all the reward. But if the risk does not pay off and the bank fails, losses are shared between the bank's owners and depositors. So the bank's owners have an incentive to take higher risks than the depositors would wish them to take; they will get all the profits, but can spread any losses. The higher the risk, the more the potential profit.

Left entirely to their own devices, depositors have usually developed ways of forcing bankers to look after their money prudently. However, in the United States the government obligingly extended deposit insurance to depositors. This caused depositors to place funds without any regard to the safety or likely behaviour of the bank. So the banks had an incentive and opportuni*y to gamble with their customers' money. Protected by deposit insurance, America's thrifts gambled on a truly heroic scale, pouring depositors' funds into property development and other speculative outlets.

So deposit insurance and deregulation are the chief culprits. However, analysts have identified several other contributory causes of the disaster. Among these are: misleading accountancy practices; inexperienced supervisors (the savings and loan associations had their own regulators) and likewise inexperienced staff; manipulation of the regulators by thrift owners through bribery and political means; and a change in the legal status of some thrifts to limited companies which encouraged excessive risk-taking. The chance of making a fast buck at the expense of Uncle Sam quickly attracted the attention of the criminal fraternity; 'copycat' property lending by the thrifts led to overdevelopment of, for instance, shopping malls and depressed prices; and the decision of regulators to keep insolvent thrifts going rather than close them added to the costs.

The last was a particularly grievous mistake. Owners of insolvent thrifts that were allowed to continue trading had an even greater incentive to take risks than those of solvent institutions. If the gamble succeeded, the owners would reap all the rewards; if it failed, they did not stand to lose any more than they would have done – all of the increased losses being passed on to depositors or their insurers. So many kept on trading and accumulating huge losses whilst under the surveillance of the regulators.

While some of these contributory factors were peculiar to the thrift situation, the last one certainly was not. It raises a crucial question for lenders of last resort: should regulators close banks as soon as signs of trouble appear?

The temptation is to let them go on trading in the hope that they will grow out of their problems. The American authorities succumbed to this temptation with the thrifts. But costs went on piling up. The alternative – immediate closure – is hardly more appetizing: witness how desperately the Bank of England kept hoping for a reconstruction of BCCI with outside money (this time from Abu Dhabi).

Another interesting finding is that, in the thrift crisis, high capital ratios were not sufficient to avert large-scale failure. Statistically, thrifts with high capital-adequacy ratios were no less likely to fail than those with low ones. If regulators were obliged to close down banks as soon as they noticed a sharp decline in capital adequacy, then all the big four British clearing banks would have been closed in the mid-1980s – hardly a practical proposition.

Another lesson that appears at first sight to be obvious is that institutions doing bank-like activities should be supervised by experienced banking regulators. But it is all too easy to call for 'more supervision'; much harder to make sure it is proving cost-effective, or is addressing the crux of the problem.

But surely the biggest lesson is that once you start injecting public money to keep institutions afloat, losses can mount with dismaying speed and reach truly frightening levels very fast indeed. The entire British budget deficit in 1993–94, forecast at over £50 billion, seemed at the time like a lot of money; but start rescuing a few big banks, and £50 billion is just peanuts. That budget deficit can be doubled in just a few months, and the figure go on rising for years.

Economists may say that these are just 'financing' estimates – and it is true that the real economic damage is done when the bad loans are made, not when they are refinanced. There are in fact two distinct kinds of cost involved here. One is the so-called 'economic' cost. If the loans financed ventures that wasted real resources, like building a leisure complex in Miami and then failing to obtain sufficient occupants, there is an immediate economic cost measured by the resources that could have been used for more productive activity. Directors who steal loans made by their friendly bank do not usually ensure the money is invested in a highly productive fashion either. But there is also the financing burden on the budget deficit that comes from paying off depositors who would otherwise have lost their money. Interest on that debt is a burden on present and future taxpayers and therefore is a cost. The thrift débâcle illustrates both kinds of cost and it is misleading to dismiss the financing cost as somehow unimportant.

How safe is the bank?

With that American story as background, what have been the reasons for the relapse into instability in many countries and in the international banking system? The usual reasons given for this are: the deregulation/liberalization of the financial services sector; the greater volatility of interest rates and asset values (bonds, shares, property); the rapid changes in the structure of the sector brought about by new technology; unpredictable monetary policies; and 'moral hazard'.

The international fashion for deregulation was at its peak between 1975 and 1985. It is described elsewhere in this book but generally included abolition of exchange controls; easing or elimination of controls on deposit interest rates and lending rates; easing of controls (if any) or conventions on the demarcation lines between different institutions in the financial sector and new willingness in some countries to allow deposit banks to go into merchant banking activities. The deregulation movement was particularly strong in the United States, Britain, Japan, Scandinavia, Australia and New Zealand – all countries that subsequently experienced severe banking problems.

The new volatility of interest rates and asset prices was a result of deregulation, the policy of monetary targeting and a willingness to let interest rates fluctuate over a much wider range than before. As described in previous chapters, the inflationary experiences of the 1970s persuaded many governments and central banks that they had to focus on bringing the money supply under control and the techniques used required letting interest rates rise to levels unprecedented since the war. The change of policy of the Federal Reserve under Paul Volcker as described in other chapters triggered both the third-world debt crisis and the troubles of the thrift industry described above. Technological changes forced the pace of change. At the lowest level, technology increased the risks of evasion and fraud, tax evasion and money laundering.

Lessons of the débâcle

The question arises whether deregulation has returned banking to an original state of natural savagery and chaos. There is some reason to think it has. What is clear is that the view one takes on this question will colour one's attitude to a whole range of policy issues to do with central banks, governments and the financial markets.

If banks are seen as 'agents' of the bank depositor, lending only to reliable people, how can those depositors control their bankers? How can the bankers control what the borrowers are doing with the bank's money? It is this double uncertainty and lack of information that is the distinctive feature of banking. It is scarcely surprising that some economists conclude that only the state guarantee can give banks any prospect of commercial viability.

In practice, bankers have over the years developed many checks to protect themselves and their depositors – and the central banker's job as bank supervisor is to make sure those checks are in place. To mention just a few. First, they rely on an adequate capital base, i.e., shareholders' funds and reserves. Second, they maintain a large reserve of liquid assets that can quickly be converted into cash if the need arises. Third, the risks attached to borrowing short and lending long can be controlled, for example by ensuring that a sufficient proportion of advances can be called back at short notice. Fourth, modern accountancy and auditing techniques, though far from perfect, do ensure that bank managers can gain a great deal of information about a company's financial situation and prospects. Fifth, bankers generally require borrowers to put up security which the bank can take if the borrower defaults. Sixth, like any other business they can increase their prices and hold down costs; in banking that means charging more to borrowers, paying less to depositors and reducing operating costs. This should have the effect of slowing down the growth of the business but making it more secure.

But are these defences — and others now available through modern financial markets — sufficient? In the past, bankers have also often formed cartels to maintain excess profits and accounting conventions designed to hide their true condition. The cartels normally included fixing prices (deposit rates and bank charges) and sometimes also agreements restricting competition and various forms of market sharing. Such cartels have appeared from time to time throughout the history of banking in virtually all countries. They were especially widespread after the Second World War and may even have contributed to the relative stability of banking in those years. Governments have often taken a benign view of such cartels, especially if they have had recent experience of the chaos that can accompany 'free-for-all' bank competition. Then memories fade and the country is ready for another bout of open competition. For cartels do impose heavy costs on the economy. But recent experience suggests there is something to be said for them: Germany has been virtually trouble free since Herstatt in 1974 partly because it has a cartelized banking system. True, there is intense competition between established banks, but there are high barriers to entry, and banks have long-term relationships with their customers that serve to restrict competition.

Beyond all these mechanisms, bankers traditionally relied heavily on ethical codes — that one should tell the truth, be open, fair and honest in business dealings. Capitalism itself only developed when such an ethical code became accepted generally in business dealings. Legal sanctions and prohibitions are effective only if they are supported by society in general. As suggested in the previous chapter, the central banks' job here is to support and strengthen when needed these ethical and self-regulatory codes (another mechanism is through banking supervision as described in Chapter 10). It is often suggested that these ethical constraints are a thing of the past. We doubt this. But enforcement and interpretation of these codes have obviously become much more difficult in today's anonymous financial markets.

Although deregulation was the trigger for many of these disasters, it should not take all the blame. Indeed, on balance it has been beneficial. It has made financial systems more competitive and efficient. Although it may be very difficult for business owners and managers to see this, it has improved their chances of getting finance from the banks because it has brought to an end the pernicious habit of credit-rationing – allocating available capital to certain preferred categories of borrowers – and forced banks to get closer to their customers. The old paternalism has gone. That is all to the good, so long as the lessons are learnt.

The most important seem to us also to be the most obvious; deposit insurance should be severely restricted and more banks should be allowed to fail when they get into difficulties. Central bankers seem to be moving gingerly towards this. In Britain deposit insurance is restricted to 75 per cent of a deposit, with a maximum payment of £15,000, and is financed by the banks; and the Governor, Eddie George, has spelled out the circumstances in which they may intervene. Stressing that banking authorization itself is not a guarantee against failure or losses by depositors, George also recognized that 'the possibility of failure is necessary to the health of the financial system'. In an address in late 1993, he quoted Bagehot's dictum that 'Any aid to a present bad bank is the surest mode of preventing the establishment of a future good bank'. To show that the Bank does not invariably support a failing bank, he mentioned that there had been nine bank closures in Britain between 1987 and 1993 (a figure that doubtless surprised his audience, most of whom were unaware that any British bank had closed, as those that did were tiddlers). Supporting a bank did not offer management a bed of roses; on the contrary they should 'expect to be penalized'. He recognized that the central bank's support may help the bank and its shareholders but this would be a by-product. The only issues in deciding on support are, first, what effect the failure of the institution would have on the system as a whole and, second, what should be done to protect the system from contagion. 'It is essential that no one – no one – should expect support as a matter of course.'

Disclosing that in the early 1990s the Bank of England had offered support to a number of banks and one institution that had run into 'an

immediate liquidity crisis', he said that this was the first time since 1973/
74 that 'such widespread support' had been given, requiring the Bank of
England to make provisions against losses in its accounts.

The rules applied when considering support are: first, that the Bank of
England will explore every option for a commercial solution before
committing its funds; second, it will try to structure support so that any
losses fall first on shareholders and any benefits accrue to the central
bank; third, it will not in normal circumstances support a bank known
at the time to be insolvent; fourth, it looks for 'a clear exit' – involving
perhaps compulsory restructuring or winding-up; fifth, it tries to keep
the fact that it is providing support secret at the time, in order to
minimize the risk of a wider loss of confidence. Even when the danger is
past, 'It will often be difficult to disclose publicly the details of our
support,' as disclosure could weaken even banks that had succeeded in
dispensing with support. The Bank of England is not required by statute
to produce its accounts for parliament on the same basis as a normal
company; but it does so 'in so far as that is appropriate for a central
bank'.

'Flirting with meltdown'

Although we give central bankers a sporting chance of attaining their
goal of price stability, we give them none whatever of attaining a
nirvana of overall financial stability. In our view banking will remain
much riskier than in the brief interlude of stability from the 1940s to the
1970s. The first reason for this is the effect of the onslaught by the
securities markets on their turf. In order to survive, banks are having to
increase the proportion of high-risk, high-margin business in their
portfolios. The best credits have deserted them. A growing proportion
of bank lending has been going to small businesses, start-ups, and other
higher-margin lending. The question is whether the margins will adequately compensate for the increased risk; they haven't so far. Second,
many big banks will increase their trading and securities-market business,
especially in the derivatives markets. Already some make more money
trading than lending. But trading is risky – after all, that's what made
many countries separate it from banking in the 1930s.

William McDonough, president of the Federal Reserve Bank of New
York, draws a useful distinction between two categories of risk associated
with derivatives. One includes the risk of losses of participants in the
markets caused by factors like the underpricing of credit, or lack of
market liquidity; fraud in the internal reporting of complex derivative

products can be especially hard for management to detect. A second category of risk is that of the market itself – have derivatives increased the susceptibility of the financial system to shocks? There is little publicly available information about the banks' off-balance-sheet activities or the nature of their exposures, and no analysis of the components of their earnings. Central bankers fear that the rapid growth of options, in particular, may increase the instability of the system, because written options are always hedged in a way that requires them to be sold into a falling market. They are also concerned at the fact that trading in derivatives is concentrated in a very few large houses, though no firm is believed to have more than 10 per cent of the market. The liquidity of the market had not by mid-1994 had to face a really stiff test – such as the failure of a large market-maker, though some corporate treasurers and some securities firms suffered large losses on derivatives as rates rose in the first half of that year. There was much concern about the participation in the market of non-banks – subsidiaries of banks and securities firms, as well as corporate treasurers, hedge funds and other unregulated participants.

McDonough's predecessor, Gerry Corrigan, gets the wooden spoon as the gloomiest central banker – present or former. America's banking system had 'flirted with meltdown' and would 'almost certainly' have reached that point but for the central banks: 'Do not forget the period roughly beginning in late 1990 and continuing for some time thereafter when the market-place – as indicated by bond and stock prices – was seriously questioning the very viability of a number of very large US banks.'

In case his audience had not quite got the message, he added: 'I would go a step further and say that for sustained periods over the past decade, the stability of the banking and financial system was, for all practical purposes, dependent on the safety net and/or other forms of governmental, including central bank, presence.'

Corrigan did not have much to offer by way of solution, except for the central banker's routine call for sound policies, and he was perhaps too cavalier with one or two specific ideas for reducing risks and potential costs to the public. One of these is the idea of the 'narrow' bank; 'a gimmick', snorted Corrigan. Maybe, but if the mainstream banking and financial system is to go on 'flirting with meltdown', it's a gimmick waiting its turn (another, free banking, is discussed in Chapter 21). Narrow banks would be required to invest only in high-quality, marketable assets; they would be granted exclusive rights to participate in the payment system and get a deposit guarantee. Depositors who wanted full security would use these banks.

In many countries, the Post Office provides this kind of banking service already.

One day, the traditional banking system may shrink under market pressures until, like an exploded supernova in the cosmos, it resembles a narrow bank – a white dwarf of the financial universe. In the meantime the government can hardly turn a blind eye to turmoil in the rest of the financial system, even if it had set up some 'narrow banks'; and the splitting of the payments mechanism into 'secure' and 'insecure' channels is hardly practicable. Moreover any bank, however 'narrow', will have to invest in some assets, and those will always carry some risk. Yet some central bankers, including Eddie George, are watching the debate on this with interest. So should taxpayers be, if they want to stop footing the bill for endless bank rescues.

Yet the choice, in the end, is stark: either to keep the financial system free, forcing it back on its own defences, and trust these will be sufficient to avert further panic and even bigger mistakes; or to revert to some form of cartelization (or market-sharing, reregulation or other euphemism). Either way, the call on the public purse will have to be restricted. On balance, we still would go for the first option. We would urge central bankers to let more foolish banks fail, and limit deposit insurance, and we would urge the courts to send more fraudulent bankers to prison, *pour encourager les autres*. That way, the disasters of the 1980s and 1990s may be seen as part of an adjustment to new freedom: the children had played with fire and would remember those burnt fingers.

When key currencies were floated in the spring of 1973, after abortive efforts to refix them, many central banks had come to see an attraction in the prospect of having more autonomy to focus policy on national requirements. But before long, excessive volatility in currencies, beyond anything that seemed reasonable, was – as some had predicted – challenging their authority as they found themselves powerless against the strength of the markets. Moreover, as could have been foreseen, tensions built up between central banks and their political masters, who mostly have the say on exchange-rate policy. A central banker instinctively likes the feel of a 'strong' currency, while governments can hanker after a more competitive one that sells exports.

Life was certainly simpler for central banks before 1973. A country's monetary policy was dictated by the linking of its currency to an external standard. When the tie was directly to gold, monetary control was more or less automatic. If a country's domestic wage and prices rose too rapidly, it would run an overseas deficit and so lose gold across the exchanges. This loss would, in turn, cause it to raise interest rates, reduce the country's money supply and consequently also the going level of activity, bringing a strong downward pressure on inflation. For Britons, it was known as stop-go.

The Bretton Woods fixed exchange-rate system worked in much the same way. A country that inflated too fast had to cut demand in order to maintain the external value of its currency within the permitted margins and limit drain on its reserves. Monetary policy, therefore, was guided by the exchange rate. There was some choice about how to make the correction, but if it needed time to work, central banks drummed up temporary credit for their beleaguered brethren. True, sometimes a currency had got so out of line that its parity could not be saved and a new one had to be declared. But, by and large, the currency game was played by the book, monetary policy was assigned to maintaining the currency within its bands and central banks knew what was expected of them. That the price paid for this rigidity by some countries – Britain and Germany particularly, the one suffering deflationary pressures, the other inflationary ones – was much too high was never openly admitted by central bankers at the time.

From today's vantage, it seems none too clever of the United States to have designed a regime that was totally dependent on the dollar being as good as, and convertible into, gold. But to the unchallenged leader of the industrial world fifty years ago it seemed a smart move. General de Gaulle never hesitated to remind the world of the 'exorbitant privilege' enjoyed by America in being able to pay for its overseas deficits in its own currency. On the other hand, the United States not only had to meet untold official demands for gold – since the dollar alone was pegged to gold (while other currencies were pegged to the dollar) – but it was uniquely unable to change its parity against other currencies even in extenuating circumstances. If it declared a change in the gold price in terms of dollars, other countries could simply accept this, keeping their currencies' relationships with the dollar unaltered.

A messy breakdown

Nevertheless, the Bretton Woods system did the world quite proud until the latter half of the 1960s. Then the United States, with a patently overvalued dollar, started to pile up trade deficits and inflate. Its attempts, through capital controls, to stop dollars cascading out of the country simply had the effect of creating the huge offshore Eurodollar market. The Germans howled that they were being flooded with dollars, that their monetary policy was being ruined, that they were being forced to import inflation. America, seeing its gold stock shrink as countries converted their surplus dollars and unable to devalue itself, tried to force Germany to revalue. Under pressure, Germany did oblige in October 1969, after the D-mark had been floated for almost a month. But the revaluation was too little, too late.

As the dollar overhang grew still further, the Germans floated their currency again in May 1971, flouting Bretton Woods rules. This time it brought the curtain – or rather the window – down. On 15 August 1971, President Nixon suspended gold convertibility, a blatantly destructive act.

There was nothing collaborative about the American–German dismantling of the Bretton Woods system; it was essentially aggressive, confrontational. America's postwar assumption of dominance was at last being challenged by Germany's economic muscle and determination to lessen dependence on the dollar. Tensions built up not only between the two governments, but also internally between monetary authorities. The central banks wanted to preserve the status quo, as is their habit. Behind the scenes, a majority at the Bundesbank had favoured earlier revaluation of the D-mark and restrictions on capital imports rather than floating, while Arthur Burns at the Federal Reserve vigorously questioned the wisdom of closing the gold window. But Karl Schiller, the German economics supremo, and the tough-talking Texan at the American Treasury, John Connally, were self-confident, popular ministers who had no need to listen to their central banks.

However, Schiller couldn't dominate the European scene as he would have liked. While the flexibility of floating the D-mark rather than the finality of re-evaluating it appealed to him, he saw an advantage in having fixed rates with his country's closest trading partners. But he failed to persuade the other European Community governments to launch a joint float against the dollar in May 1971. It was nearly two years before Schiller's proposal was adopted, some time after he had resigned from office and handed over to Helmut Schmidt, a proponent of capital controls.

Central bankers were foremost among those wanting to believe that Nixon's move was a temporary measure, that the United States would again resume its convertibility obligation. This was never on the cards, however. There followed eighteen months during which the major governments tried, and failed, to make new pegging arrangements for their currencies – but a renewal of the link to gold was not on the agenda.

A poor repair job

The famous negotiations between the Group of Ten finance ministers and central governors that took place in the precincts of the Smithsonian Institution in Washington on 18 December 1971 were the first ever to aim at adjusting exchange rates on a multilateral basis. The talks went anything but smoothly; indeed, they were decidedly acrimonious. The Europeans, led by the Germans, refused to let the dollar be depreciated by as much as Connally wanted. And they insisted, against his opposition, on an increase in the official price of gold, from $35 to $38 an ounce, although this had no significance for the new currency arrangements since the dollar remained inconvertible.

The Smithsonian deal that was eventually struck introduced, *de facto*, a new dollar standard. The main currencies were pegged to the dollar at central rates (no longer called parities) that represented revaluations varying in size from 8 per cent for sterling, the French franc, the lira and the Swedish krona up to 17 per cent for the Japanese yen. But the pegging was less precise than in the Bretton Woods world, currencies being allowed to move by 2.25 per cent, rather than a mere 1 per cent, each side of the declared rate.

What Nixon hailed as 'the conclusion of the most significant monetary agreement in the history of the world' was a futile exercise. The new dollar standard never had a chance. The American dissatisfaction with their side of the bargain was all too well known; if the dollar could be devalued once, why not again at any time? Moreover, the Americans had made no commitment whatsoever to help defend the Smithsonian structure. The German and Japanese central banks, running their currencies at rates that still undervalued them, faced having to accumulate dollar reserves at a pace the markets judged would so complicate their control of domestic money that they would not tolerate it for long. How right they were.

It is, nevertheless, still worth recalling, briefly, the way the Smithsonian agreement crumbled bit by bit. For it taught dramatically how 'hot money', much less of it then than now, can swoop on one prey after another like a vulture when there are visible pickings to go for. It is a tale that can still make central bankers shudder; and warn off those among them – and there are plenty – who hanker after a return to the 'good old days' of fixed exchange rates.

Pickings can come from either buying a strong currency to force it higher or selling a weak one to depress it further. In the early days of the Smithsonian system, several European currencies and the yen were pushed up close to their official ceilings but central bank intervention contained the pressures. Not so, though, when sterling, still the punters' favourite, came under concerted attack just weeks after Britain stupidly decided, on 23 June 1972, to join its prospective European Community partners in keeping their currencies within a very narrow band, the so-called 'snake'. The pound had to be floated independently, 'for a temporary period', after six days in which the Bank of England spent the equivalent of $2.6 billion defending it. Footloose money then flowed into other European currencies causing some temporary closures of exchange markets. But the next piece of drama was with another weak currency; early in January 1973 Italy resorted to a two-tier exchange system to discourage heavy selling of the lira. It didn't. Italian money flowed across the borders into Switzerland forcing a 'temporary' float of the Swiss franc on 23 January. Then the hot money took off to Tokyo and Frankfurt, despite exchange controls designed to keep it out.

Japanese foreign exchange markets were closed on 10 February, European ones two days later. By then Paul Volcker, as Undersecretary for Monetary Affairs at the American Treasury, had made his legendary, whirlwind visits to Tokyo and European capitals to try to redeem the Smithsonian arrangement. The outcome was the announcement on 12 February of a further devaluation of the dollar by way of a rise in the official price of gold – the price at which the United States would not sell it – to $42.22 an ounce. But the flight from the dollar went on. After closure of European exchange markets for nearly three weeks and several emergency international meetings, the experiment with the dollar standard was over.

A floating honeymoon

The floating of most major currencies against each other in March 1973 was again presented as a temporary expedient – until a new fixed-price regime could be established. Few in power probably believed they could patch up the past. At the American Treasury, George Shultz, a gentler man than his predecessor, would say only that any par value system had to be more flexible than of old. Many Americans, meanwhile, had come to persuade themselves that floating would be an ideal way of preventing renewed overvaluation of the dollar. And the Federal Reserve chairman, Arthur Burns, on returning from the Group of Ten meeting in Paris on 15–16 March 1973 that pronounced the Smithsonian deal dead, reported to his colleagues – disapprovingly – that there had been a dramatic change of attitude in favour of floating.

At that Paris meeting, finance ministers and central bank governors 'reiterated their determination to ensure jointly an orderly exchange rate system' and 'agreed in principle that official intervention in exchange markets may be useful at appropriate times to facilitate the maintenance of orderly conditions'. The Europeans thought they had scored by getting the Americans to concede that intervention could be useful, even if only 'in principle', and felt doubly reassured when Charlie Coombs at the New York Fed was authorized to enlarge the swap network that supports intervention by half as much again, to nearly $18 billion. Nobody foresaw the years of 'benign neglect' of the dollar that lay ahead.

Perhaps the most remarkable feature of the Paris communiqué, hyped up as a new charter for the international monetary system, was the intention expressed 'to seek more complete understanding of the sources and nature of the large capital flows which have recently taken place'. Did ministers and central bankers really want to give the impression they had been taken by surprise by some perverse attack on their currencies? As Erik Hoffmeyer, the perceptive, no-nonsense, tweed-jacketed veteran governor of the Danish central bank put it in his recent recollections: 'Given the many years of disturbing capital flows, such collective ignorance of the consequences of the loss of credibility seems curious.'

Yet in pinpointing capital flows at that Paris meeting, attention was at least being drawn to a factor largely neglected by the academics who were so delighted when floating was adopted in 1973. The market's tendency to overreact to policy shifts and external shocks had not been widely foreseen. As currencies indulged in wild gyrations, faith was soon lost that the markets would always set exchange rates at the right level.

Then the questions

But nobody thought a return to fixed parities as before was possible. The forced move to floating came just six months after a group of international officials (all male incidentally), led by (now Sir) Jeremy Morse from the Bank of England, had begun to design a new world monetary regime that would promise the sort of stability the Bretton Woods system had enjoyed, but without gold at the centre. It had been set up by the International Monetary Fund's Committee of Twenty, so-called because it consisted of finance ministers and central bank governors representing each of the institution's then twenty (now twenty-four) constituencies. Wise, patient and courteous, Morse attempted the impossible, the reconciliation of irreconcilable views. It was clear almost from the start that the exercise was doomed. Agreement on the need for 'stable but adjustable par values' shows just how woolly any consensus language had to be.

Perhaps it was just as well that the oil crisis of 1973 allowed the Morse project an honourable death. When an outline of reform was published in March 1974, leading governments had something much more urgent and tangible to grapple with than esoteric issues like the valuation of the IMF's rum currency, the special drawing right (SDR), or its possible link to development assistance. The plan was put politely on the shelf.

Anyway, by 1974, the top brass at the American Treasury, led by a former bond trader, Bill Simon, were all fervent floaters. In late 1975, it fell to Ed Yeo, then in Volcker's old shoes at the Treasury, to negotiate with his French counterpart, Jacques de Larosière, representing the main protagonist for fixed rates, a form of words acceptable to both that the IMF could adopt as its new legal basis for a floating regime. The outcome was yet more mumbo-jumbo – effective from April 1978 in the IMF's Articles after ratification procedures had dragged on over two years. It bowed to the French only by allowing for a return to a fixed-rate system if there was an 85 per cent majority vote by IMF member countries in favour of it – which gave the United States a veto. Otherwise, the IMF was supposed to exercise 'firm surveillance' over the float, member countries were told to do their best to 'promote a stable system of exchange rates', but at the same time to 'avoid manipulating exchange rates'. These suit-yourself instructions remained on the IMF's statute book.

In practice, it mattered little what the IMF said about key exchange rates. It had no basis for 'firm surveillance' of them and management of the system passed to the Group of Seven leading nations – even if, at times, in desperation they have tried to pass the buck back to the international institution. Of course, any country can act independently to influence its exchange rate, but since, by definition, this is a comparative rate, it cannot determine it unilaterally. Whether management of floating rates takes the form of market intervention by central banks or shifts in policy instruments such as interest rates, cooperation is essential if it is to have any hope of success. So far this has been less than glorious. But how much can reasonably be asked of it?

Political override

It is an illusion that central banks were immensely cooperative in Bretton Woods times. The concept wasn't even tested. Working under strict rules did not require the elements of choice and sacrifice involved in 'cooperation'. Without rules set by their political masters, few central banks, even the more independent ones, have a free hand over intervention policy, though it can be a subject for argument. Floating has exposed the disparities among central banks in both their authority over and their attitudes towards exchange rates that were largely irrelevant before, but which can make them odd bedfellows today.

Among the big central banks, the Bundesbank's legal position on exchange rates is that its task of 'safeguarding the currency' has an external implication; it requires it to try to keep the external value of the D-mark stable as well as its internal value. If that pursuit involves parity changes (as with the Bretton Woods system or the Exchange Rate Mechanism), 'the cooperation of the federal government' is needed, as it puts it. But, as it owns its country's foreign-exchange reserves, it has the means for intervention and the responsibility for policy over the

D-mark's float. In practice, the Bundesbank exercises considerable autonomy on exchange-rate policy.

The German central bank's advice on currency matters usually prevails over the finance ministry's, one notable instance leading to Schiller's resignation in mid-1972 after the Bundesbank successfully opposed his call for a collective European float. And when exchange-rate policy comes up in today's international forums, the Bundesbank president can probably throw his weight about more than any other central bank governor present. His main concern will always be to see that exchange-rate considerations are not given too much weight in monetary policy-making in order to leave the option of an exchange-rate readjustment rather than be subjected to capital inflows. Though he had not yet joined the German central bank, Hans Tietmeyer was talking Bundesbankspeak when he told an international conference in Hamburg in 1988: 'It would be wrong – in my view – to focus too much on exchange rates, even if exchange rates can be of high importance in certain situations. The main focus has, of course, to be on underlying policies.'

As to the power of the Federal Reserve in exchange-rate policy, it can call into play its Act of 1913, which authorizes it to buy and sell in the open market, at home or abroad, bankers' acceptances, bills of exchange and cable transfers. But the American Treasury can also point to later legislation of the 1930s that gives the Secretary responsibility for international monetary policy. For the two agencies to be sending different signals about intervention to the New York Fed, which executes foreign exchange orders for both, would obviously be ridiculous and counter-productive. In his 1992 recollections, Paul Volcker concedes pride of place in exchange-rate and intervention policy to the Treasury, explaining that 'the Federal Reserve would be extremely reluctant to intervene for its own account against the expressed desire of the Treasury'. So while it seems clear that the Bundesbank decides intervention policy in Germany, the Treasury does so in the United States.

That has meant less American intervention in the exchange markets over the past twenty years than the Federal Reserve would have liked. This cannot be blamed – if that is the appropriate word – just on Republican reluctance to interfere in the market-place. Even a Democratic administration in the 1970s watched the dollar slide for over a year from September 1977 before letting the New York Fed have a serious go and giving it the wherewithal to do so. The November 1978 dollar rescue package included innovative plans for America to build up foreign-currency resources by borrowing on private markets abroad – the so-called Carter bonds – as well as augmenting central bank swap lines. But it was a flash in the pan. Shortly afterwards came the Reaganites and American intervention was again on hold until the dollar was once more so out of kilter that America's trading partners were exasperated; but this time the trouble was dollar strength, rather than weakness.

From Plaza to Louvre

Believers in managed exchange rates hail as a huge success the agreement made by the Group of Five finance ministers and central bank governors at New York's Plaza Hotel on 22 September 1985. Quite out of character, they made a public, very positive statement, initiated by the Americans, about exchange rates. The last two sentences of an otherwise platitudinous communiqué read: 'Some further orderly appreciation of the main non-dollar currencies against the dollar is desirable. They [the ministers and governors] stand ready to cooperate more closely to encourage this when it would be helpful.'

That was an unequivocal signal of intention to intervene, and the main central banks did so heavily in the ensuing six weeks – to the extent of $10 billion, with the Federal Reserve and the Bank of Japan accounting for $3 billion apiece. Having shown their hands, they retired at the end of October, their goal of pushing the dollar down 10–12 per cent accomplished. Sam Cross, in charge of the American operation at the New York Fed, was particularly triumphant. Understandably: he had been champing at the bit for eighteen months or more, frustrated by the Reaganite hands-off policy.

But it is not the case that central banks were particularly smart in their post-Plaza effort. We should not forget they were seeking 'further' appreciation of non-dollar currencies. That one word tells all. Foreign-exchange dealers had already decided the dollar had overshot and were selling it. Going with the grain of the market, central banks were guaranteed success. At least in the short term.

Longer term, that extra downward push to the dollar in the autumn of 1985 may have been unhelpful. By the following March, the Bank of Japan was buying dollars. By May, the American Treasury Secretary, Jim Baker, was testifying that there was no need for any further dollar depreciation. By early 1987, concern that the dollar might be in free fall led to the other famous – and more sensational – currency agreement of the past decade.

The agreement, or accord as it tends to be called, at the Louvre in Paris on 22 February 1987 represents the most serious attempt yet made to bring order into floating exchange rates. Finance ministers and governors of six leading nations declared that their currencies were roughly at the right levels – 'within ranges broadly consistent with underlying economic fundamentals'. So they promised 'to cooperate closely to foster stability of exchange rates around current levels'. That public commitment concealed much discussion since the Plaza agreement about reference or target zones, bands within which exchange rates would be constrained by concerted intervention if necessary.

A sort of informal Bretton Woods system, one might say. But a French proposal to set specific figures, made over the dinner table at the Palais du Louvre, went down much less smoothly than the champagne. Most of the diners thought publication of bands would only invite speculation and the Germans were dead against the idea. Nevertheless, although never officially confirmed, the markets guessed right in surmising a broad intention to keep exchange rates within a 5 per cent band around the then going rates of 153 yen and 1.825 D-marks to the dollar. But the margins were to be 'soft', as Volcker put it. Nothing was set in concrete.

This was as well, for despite a lot of intervention, the dollar continued to slide in the weeks after the Louvre declaration and by early April the yen had broken out of its agreed upper range. So much for exchange-rate targetry. The Louvre experiment has never been repeated.

Intervention on trial

Nevertheless, America's conversion to a more interventionist policy from the mid-1980s – the importance of which is pinpointed in Chapter 7 – means that the Louvre concept is still a gleam in the eye of many. Spasmodically, central banks have continued heavy bouts of intervention, particularly in 1987–89 when the dollar went on a roller-coaster ride. But limited success has made it progressively harder for them to win. The more evidence there is of the ineffectiveness of intervention, the more confident punters are that they can beat it. And with the Americans now usually giving a helping hand, they are no longer a convenient scapegoat for earlier failures, such as when in 1977 the big central banks other than the Federal Reserve bought up to $35 billion of dollars without being able to prevent the currency declining.

In hindsight, it may seem that speculators were too faint-hearted in Bretton Woods days. Except in fairly rare periods of crisis other than those centred around the absurdly overvalued pound, the market expectation was that official intervention would do the trick, a straying currency would be brought to heel. Or, if not, that more drastic steps would be taken, even – and this was important – exchange controls if necessary. Speculators had no reason to bet on anything else. So when an exchange rate was at the bottom or the top of its band, they tended to work for the authorities, not against them, making life easy for central banks.

Europe's Exchange Rate Mechanism never enjoyed quite the same respect because realignments were fairly frequent in its early days. Nevertheless, as time went on, the market tended to give the authorities the benefit of the doubt, as it did in the early 1990s when it assumed that, in moving towards the Maastricht Treaty's monetary union, European currencies could and would be kept stable. It was only after the Treaty looked in doubt following the Danish 'No' vote in mid-1992 that speculators picked off one weak currency after another in waves that swamped heavy intervention.

Wise after the event, European central bankers said in early 1993 they were confident that upheavals like those of September 1992 would never happen again. Well, they had to, didn't they? But in blaming the failure of governments to make currency realignments earlier and at one stroke, rather than the rules for their management of the mechanism, they were also admitting their impotence. And inviting the collapse in late July that year which led to 15 per cent margins, margins so wide that to call the system semi-fixed is sparing of the truth. Post-mortems revealed the magnitude of the footloose funds that had shifted from one weak currency to another in the débâcle – an estimated $200–300 billion in the September 1992 episode alone. Official intervention is helpless and wasteful against the strength of such a tide.

Should central banks intervene at all? A special study of its effectiveness, called for by the Americans at the economic summit in Versailles in June 1982 and undertaken by a group of experts under a French Treasury civil servant, Philippe Jurgensen, added little to what anyone might have guessed. The thirty-three-page bland report, completed in January 1983, explained jargon like 'sterilized' intervention (when official purchases or sales of foreign currencies are offset by domestic transactions so as to leave the money supply unchanged). Otherwise, it consisted of obvious statements such as 'closely coordinated action had at times been more effective than intervention by only one central bank because it gave a signal to the market that the authorities were working to the same purpose'. The general thrust was that sterilized intervention could be useful in the short run to smooth erratic fluctuations, but that, whether coordinated or not, by itself it has no lasting effect on exchange rates and is no substitute for necessary changes in economic policies. In short, it supported neither of the extreme camps; it weakened the case for either heavy intervention or none at all.

Private banks operating in the foreign-exchange markets don't pull their punches. Two surveys of their views were sponsored in the 1980s by the Group of Thirty think-tank. The first, masterminded by Dennis Weatherstone in 1980 on his way up to the top of the American blue-chip bank, J. P. Morgan, found considerable dissatisfaction with official intervention. Indeed, many of the European bankers quizzed alleged technical incompetence, accusing central bankers, among other things, of being 'inconsistent', 'unprofessional' and poor at 'reading the markets'. They sometimes intervened, it was claimed, at the wrong moments and in the wrong amounts to achieve their presumed object of stabilization. In short, they made things worse – though it is only fair to add that at least two banks, one in London, the other in continental Europe, singled out the Bank of England for special praise. A follow-up study in 1985 was less critical, but the majority view was that attempts to stabilize exchange rates should be made mainly by harmonizing monetary and fiscal policies. Nothing since has changed that conclusion. Temporarily, foreign-exchange dealers can be influenced by central bank intervention if it signals something new about future policy. Longer-term intervention is perceived as useful only if combined with actual policy changes, not on its own.

With the bag-carriers

The message trips off the tongue lightly. How easy it is for heads of worthy institutions like the IMF and the BIS to preach the merits of harmonization – or convergence, in today's jargon. How easy for heads of state to pay lip-service to it too. Yet even with the carrot of Economic and Monetary Union dangling before them, EC policymakers were unable to prevent their economies from doing just the reverse of converging in 1992.

International cooperation over economic policy is an old concern that has engaged a host of fine minds and engendered a wealth of literature. Our interest here is in the part central bankers play in the process. On the face of it, this is small. Central bank governors, with their aides, attend most of the established forums for discussing international economic policy at ministerial level, such as IMF meetings, but finance or Treasury ministers head the national delegations and call the tune. Willingness to cooperate and accept rules of behaviour in economic and monetary policy is a political decision.

Of course, personalities count and can tilt the balance of power. A long-running, competent central banker can be invaluable to a raw minister. But rarely is such dependence allowed to surface in public. Media-driven as these international events have become, attracting several thousands of press and television correspondents, more time can be spent on tinkering with the phrasing of the communiqué than on debating its substance. And as ministers face the cameras with their minds on re-election at home rather than on whatever may be plaguing the world economy, central bank governors tend to be lost among the bag-carriers.

It wasn't always so. Regular meetings of key finance ministers and central bank governors were first conceived in the early 1960s, when ten industrial countries (the United States, West Germany, France, Britain, Italy, Japan, Canada, the Netherlands, Belgium and Sweden) agreed to stand ready to boost IMF resources. Subsequently, the Group of Ten (joined by Switzerland) continued to meet to discuss international monetary reform, treading somewhat on the toes of the executive directors of the IMF. What might seem surprising today is that central bankers were very much to the fore in these early debates.

But the Group of Ten was soon to be eclipsed by a more exclusive club, not originally open to central bankers. In 1967, the American Treasury Secretary and the British Chancellor of the Exchequer decided it would be a good idea to meet their German, French and Japanese counterparts at Chequers – the British Prime Minister's country residence – for off-the-record talks about international monetary matters and how to hold interest rates down. It was the first sign of American chafing at being swamped by Europeans in the Group of Ten, a feeling immensely exacerbated after the Smithsonian frustrations. With the birth of floating in the spring of 1973, an enlightened American Treasury Secretary, George Shultz, invited the French, German and British finance ministers – Helmut Schmidt, Valéry Giscard d'Estaing and Tony Barber – to an informal meeting in the library of the White House, telling them to bring only one personal adviser each. But the cost of closer consultation between the few was the alienation of the many.

When push comes to shove

Toyoo Gyohten, then with the Japanese finance ministry, recalls how his minister, Kiichi Aichi, jealous at being excluded, manoeuvred an invitation to the next meeting of Shultz's Library Group – as Schmidt dubbed it – to be hosted by Giscard at the Château d'Artigny, near

Tours, in November of the same year. Tragically, Aichi died just before the meeting and his place had to be taken by his deputy.

More to the point of our story, not only did the Japanese worm their way into the château but so, too, did Arthur Burns. Shultz evidently explained that he had brought Burns along because, under American law, the chairman of the Federal Reserve was considered the equal of a cabinet member. But in the book he produced jointly with Paul Volcker in 1992, Gyohten recounts that his co-author told him the real reason was 'that Burns wanted to come and Shultz, who regarded himself as a student of Burns's and revered him, although they disagreed on practically everything, didn't have the heart to say no'. After that there was no keeping other central bank governors away from Group of Five meetings. But maybe some central bankers even today are conscious that they are in the inner policymaking sanctum only because one of their predecessors, a pipe-smoking, professorial, reflective man not short of self-esteem, pushed the door open and barged in.

There was more shoving to come. The annual economic summit at the level of heads of government, which Giscard and Schmidt thought up after they had reached that status, already included Italy at the first 'fireside chat', held at the Château de Rambouillet in November 1975. And Giscard, who had successfully resisted Canada's request for inclusion on that occasion, was unable to prevent President Gerald Ford from inviting Pierre Trudeau to the next summit, in Puerto Rico in June 1976. So, almost from the start, the summits have been seven-nation affairs. Yet, nostalgically, the finance ministers of the Five continued to meet separately and conspiratorially, tantalizing the press, even if – indeed, especially when – there was also a Seven meeting. Until they produced the Plaza agreement in September 1985. Then the Italians and Canadians, resentful at having had no hand in what was voted a success, persuaded the summiteers in Tokyo in 1986 to tell the Group of Five to invite the other two ministers 'whenever the management or the improvement of the international monetary system and related economic policy measures are to be discussed and dealt with'. The message virtually killed off the Five meetings.

Veterans of the international forums have expressed surprise at how much the informality and frankness of discussions were reduced when membership was enlarged from five to seven. Given that the record of recent cooperation is not wildly encouraging, there is a lot to be said for turning the clock back, even for having no more than a triumvirate of American, Japanese and European representation on a steering committee for the world economy (as Gyohten recommended). Paradoxically, there is also a case for enlarging the cast – by involving central banks more closely.

Out in the cold

Central bank governors are not invited to the economic summits; heads of government take along only their finance and foreign ministers. Volcker, for one, says this exclusion never bothered him. But it seems silly to exclude the governors' deputies from the preparatory work of the 'Sherpas'. On technical money matters, on what is feasible and what is not, they should be able to offer more than their Treasury counterparts. This has been accepted in other groups, such as the European Union's Monetary Committee and the thirtysomething-years-old unsexily named Working Party 3 of the Organization for Economic Cooperation and Development in Paris, charged with promoting cooperative management of international payments imbalances.

A forceful case for greater central bank involvement in Group of Seven palavers was made in a 1991 study by a former Canadian finance ministry official, Wendy Dobson. One of those women economists with an international reputation in which her country does a good line, Dobson served as a Sherpa in 1987–89, when she sensed that some central bankers did not feel obliged to accept institutional responsibility for decisions made in their absence. But Dobson failed to point out that this may suit them very nicely. For although central bankers like to taste power, they are extremely wary of being exposed more directly to pressures to coordinate monetary policies which would diminish their independence (assuming they have it) in carrying out their primary aim to contain inflation. Central bankers seem unable to decide where their best interests lie. Letting the arguments go full circle around them is hardly the way to strengthen their credibility.

From time to time, someone in authority tries to stop the merry-go-round. To the French the lack of 'system' is anathema. As boss of the IMF, Michel Camdessus periodically pretended that there was enthusiasm for a wonderfully logical arrangement for exchange rates geared to his institution's currency cocktail, the SDR (special drawing right). Only, of course, to find there wasn't. In February 1988, Edouard Balladur, then France's finance minister, provocatively complained that floating exchange rates had been 'one of the essential causes of the economic disorders of the past fifteen years'. This led to a band of senior officials from the major finance ministries and central banks being told to design improvements. Each country prepared position papers on three issues: economic policy coordination, exchange-rate arrangements and reserve assets. The views were no less conflicting than when Morse had sifted them a decade and a half earlier. There was no consensus on anything. The exercise died quietly in the spring of 1989.

The end of the Reagan/Bush years brought hope in some quarters that the Americans might offer new enlightenment, new diplomacy. But President Clinton's first Treasury Secretary, Lloyd Bentsen, did not go beyond trying to make the IMF take more of the blame for disorderly markets. Another turn of the merry-go-round.

Not many praise the present exchange-rate system. There is a widespread feeling that overshooting and 'misalignment' of exchange rates has damaged international trade and investment. But nobody claims an ideal alternative. A forty-seven-strong private panel convened by Paul Volcker under the auspices of the so-called Bretton Woods Commission did, however, recommend in July 1994 that the major industrial countries should adopt a more formal system for managing exchange rates, focusing on the dollar, yen and D-mark, which might, *in time*, involve 'flexible' exchange-rate bands, meaning the bands should be shifted if they became unrealistic. But a new system was seen as a long-term goal and, meanwhile, in official circles the same questions get asked over and over again. Central bankers don't distinguish themselves in the debate; they seem almost glad to play second fiddle to their finance ministers. On the currency score at least, the irascible German statesmen who called them cowardly types might just have a point.

Where central bankers were failing over exchange rates in the 1990s was in not making their case to the public. By then policy coordination had got a bad name among many of them not only because it had so patently failed (the latest example being the collapse of Europe's exchange-rate system in 1993), but because it threatens the principle of domestic goals and their commitment to price stability. Putting it more succinctly, a senior official of the Bank of Japan told one of the authors in the autumn of 1993: 'Obviously we are against international coordination – it reduces the independence of the central bank.'

Reviled by some, revered by others, its chairman called the man people love to hate, yet at times hailed as a saviour. Why does America's Federal Reserve arouse such extremes of feeling, while its closest counterpart, the Bundesbank, has the German people almost solidly behind it?

The answer lies, in part, in the murkiness of the Federal Reserve's constitutional responsibilities compared with the Bundesbank's clear-cut mandate. More simply, Germans almost unreservedly want what the Bundesbank does, price stability, whereas America's hugely diversified society is more torn if the choice is (misguidedly) seen as between loss of jobs or inflation. Inevitably, too, in the world's leading democracy, there will always be indignant protestors against the nation's monetary policy being in the hands of a quasi-independent body run by officials not popularly elected – even though the Fed is much more accountable to Congress than the Bundesbank is to the Bundestag.

The object of the Federal Reserve Act of 1913 was to provide the United States with safer banking. To that end, it created a system to furnish the country with an 'elastic currency'. Though not defined, it was clear at the time that this meant providing a supply of money that could grow or shrink flexibly with seasonal and cyclical changes in demand, thereby preventing recurrence of the short-term liquidity crises that had wiped out otherwise solvent banks in the early years of the century. According to the Act, the Federal Reserve should conduct its operations 'with a view to accommodating commerce and business'. As additional precautions, it was also told it had a duty to act as a lender of last resort and to establish more effective supervision of banking.

Over the years since then, the Federal Reserve Act, though never completely rewritten, has had many amendments embodied in various legislation. The Banking Act of 1935 was particularly important; it fixed more firmly the responsibilities of the Board of Governors, restructured it into today's form and did likewise with the renamed Federal Open Market Committee, which had been given legal status only two years earlier. It also introduced a broader concept of the Fed's functions in the nation's economic life, which has been elaborated on in several subsequent Acts. Among these, the Employment Act of 1946 required the federal government to utilize all its resources to promote maximum employment and the Federal Reserve was subject to this provision of the law. From the start of his central banking career, Arthur Burns was recommending that the Act be amended to include explicit reference to the objective of general price stability. Eventually, the 1978 Full Employment and Balanced Growth Act – better known as the Humphrey–Hawkins Act – specifically set the Fed the dual targets of full employment and price stability. A mixed blessing, indeed, for a central bank.

Today, the Fed says that it tries to ensure that America's money and credit over the long run is sufficient to encourage growth in the economy in line with its potential and with reasonable price stability. But ask a Board governor which goal comes first, growth or stability, and you may get a different answer depending on which of them you question. Shortly after David Mullins became vice chairman of the Board in July 1991, at the early age of 45, he announced that 'our primary goal is to maximize growth'. Not wishing to be classed as a dove on inflation, however, he added that 'price stability is a means to that growth'. Not the order in which a Bundesbank man would have put it. Nor, indeed, a fellow governor at the time such as Wayne Angell, eager to say that 'over time, there is only one rate of inflation that's acceptable to me, and that's zero'. Healthy as it may be that Fed governors have individual voices, news of division within the Board makes the markets nervous. The chairman works hard to minimize it.

Though a regionalized central bank, the Federal Reserve harbours a more powerful headquarters – at least on paper – than does the Bundesbank, where all monetary policymaking is determined by a single council on which the regionals can outvote the Frankfurt directorate. At the Federal Reserve, in contrast, it is shared between the Washington Board and the Board-cum-regionals, and when the regionals have a say, it is a minority one.

Even with power concentrated at its apex, the Federal Reserve's organization is tantalizingly complex. The main job of the Board of Governors in Washington is to formulate monetary policy, but it also sets two of the implementing instruments, the discount rate and reserve requirements imposed on banks against their deposits. Beyond that, the Board oversees the Fed's regional network and has regulatory duties, which, rather curiously, include protecting consumers against financial skulduggery. But the larger Federal Open Market Committee directs the most important execution of monetary policy on an ongoing basis, through the buying and selling of American government securities. Then, at the bottom of the pyramid, come the dogsbodies, the twelve

Federal Reserve Banks owned by their member banks. Spread around the country, these distribute currency, collect and clear cheques, handle government debt, lend to banks through their discount windows and supervise those banks in their region allotted to the Fed's care under America's somewhat absurdly split supervisory regime.

How independent?

The seven Board members (governors) and, from among them, the chairman and vice chairman, are appointed by the President of the United States, subject to Senate approval. The fourteen-year terms of governors are staggered so that one expires on 31 January in every even-numbered year, regardless of the date on which the governor was sworn into office. The chairman and vice chairman are named for four years only, but can be reappointed if their terms as Board members have not expired. While it is goodbye for anyone who has served a full fourteen-year Board term, someone who has taken up an unexpired term, following a resignation or death, is eligible for reappointment.

This twist in the rules allowed William McChesney (Bill) Martin to hold the chairmanship for close on nineteen years, before he finally had to leave on 31 January 1970. Only one other chairman, Mariner Eccles, has come anywhere near to matching that longevity, serving just over thirteen years until 31 January 1948 – and he, unusually, continued on the Board afterwards for another few years. The others so far have averaged little more than four years apiece, though since 1970 a two-term stewardship – eight years, the same as the Bundesbank offers in the first place – has been the norm, served by Arthur Burns, Paul Volcker and, likely, Alan Greenspan, whose second term ends in March 1996, when he will be seventy. Incidentally, progression is not from within: no chairman so far has won his spurs first as an ordinary Board member or even as vice chairman.

By giving governors long tenure, staggering their terms and decreeing that they can be removed only for 'cause', the possibilities for a US President to pack the Board with his own appointees are, on paper, strictly limited. In practice, however, governors do not serve all that long as a rule; they get old, die or resign to line their pockets. Serving on the Washington Board almost invariably involves financial sacrifice, while pay prospects elsewhere, especially in Wall Street, may be hugely enhanced once you can sell yourself as a Fed insider. The temptation to go after three to five years is often irresistible. One way or another, a two-term President is likely to be able to fill most of the places on the Board with his appointees – as Ronald Reagan discovered.

A second important element making for Federal Reserve independence is more indestructible; the System finances itself with internally generated funds and so is not subject to the power of the congressional purse. The Board of Governors in Washington (a term confusingly used to describe both the whole Fed establishment there as well as the seven-member board) pays its own expenses by levies on the Reserve Banks (the government's General Accounting Office is given sight of its accounts). The Reserve Banks make their money mainly from interest on holdings of government securities. They are profitable concerns. After paying their own and Washington's expenses, as well as the statutory 6 per cent dividend on the Federal Reserve stock that member banks are legally required to hold, plus anything needed to maintain a surplus at each Reserve Bank equal to its paid-in capital, remaining earnings are handed over to the American Treasury. Quite a handy sum for the government. It has acquired about 95 per cent of net earnings since the Fed was established, and in 1993 alone it received $16 billion.

A grip on the regions

When the Federal Reserve System was first organized on twelve regional or district lines, states fought for the honour of housing a Reserve Bank in one of their commercial centres. Lobbying in Washington undoubtedly influenced the eventual selection, though the carve-up had to ensure each district had enough member banks in it to provide a Reserve Bank with a minimum capital of $4 million. Missouri managed to secure two Reserve Banks, one in St Louis, another in Kansas City. The other ten were allocated to New York, Boston, Philadelphia, Cleveland, Richmond, Atlanta, Chicago, Minneapolis, Dallas and San Francisco. Proudly, the new banks over time ensconced themselves in imposing, solid-looking buildings, symbols of a city's strength as a commercial and financial centre. Wounds inflicted in the choice of cities – why for instance, Atlanta rather than New Orleans? – have since been healed a little by the setting up of branches of Reserve Banks in twenty-five other cities.

Until 1980, the Federal Reserve could levy reserve requirements only on its members – that is to say, on nationally chartered banks, which have to belong to the System, and those state-chartered banks that choose to do so. This restriction obviously reduced the effectiveness of this form of credit control, but not disastrously so in the early days;

although only two in five of America's banks were members, they held more than four-fifths of the country's banking deposits. But as the Fed made active use of reserve requirements in the 1960s and 1970s, raising them well above those levied by the states, it rapidly lost membership. Banks decided that benefits from it, such as access to the discount window, did not compensate for the cost of what amounts to a tax on deposits.

The Fed lobbied hard in those years for compulsory, universal membership. It failed to win that. But the Monetary Control Act of 1980 gave it most of what it wanted, the power to impose reserve requirements on all deposit-taking institutions, in return for which all such banks have access to the Fed's services. The question of membership then became largely irrelevant to the functioning of America's banking system. However, ownership of Federal Reserve stock – which cannot be traded – brings closer ties with the local Reserve Bank and a chance, if not of a direct voice in monetary policymaking, of at least influencing the Reserve Bank's president who has one.

Each Reserve Bank has a board of nine outside directors. By law, three represent member banks in the district, while the other six are drawn from industry, commerce, anything other than banking, three selected by the member banks and three by the Washington-based Board of Governors. From its own selection, Washington also designates the board's chairman and vice chairman, so ensuring its grip on the network. But, subject to Washington's final approval, the directors appoint the Reserve Bank's president (chief executive) – on five-year terms that are renewable but subject, unlike those of the governors, to mandatory retirement at sixty-five – and decide his (or her) salary.

One of the oddities of the system is that Reserve Bank presidents may be paid much more generously than the Fed chairman, whose salary is held in line with those of top government officials in Washington. Against Alan Greenspan's $133,600 at the end of 1993, the president of the New York Federal Reserve Bank was drawing $205,000 (while the final pay of his predecessor, Gerry Corrigan, had been $257,500). The salaries of the eleven other presidents ranged from $159,100 to $229,600.

Respectable pay encourages long stays at the Reserve Banks, though there is hopping from one to another. Corrigan had a spell of four and a half years as president of the Minneapolis Fed before returning to the New York Fed to fill the top slot there until the summer of 1993. Robert McTeer at the Dallas bank served his apprenticeship at the Richmond bank under Robert Black, who retired from it at the end of 1992 after being president for nineteen years. Presidents like these, with skills acquired within the System, are important contributors to the making of America's monetary policy, through informal contacts with Washington and their formal participation in meetings of the Federal Open Market Committee.

A collegiate feel

The FOMC is twelve strong, made up of the seven members of the Board of Governors (who, therefore, form a majority), the president of the New York Fed and four of the other Reserve Bank presidents who serve one year on a rotating basis. By tradition – not by statute – the Fed chairman is also chairman of the FOMC and its vice chairman is the New York president. The committee meets eight times a year on a regular schedule and, needless to say, there are frequent telephone consultations between members at other times.

Consultation is, indeed, key to the workings of the Federal Reserve System, although that is not the impression the public gets. Looking from Washington's Constitution Gardens at its headquarters, at the elegant, white limestone building built on classical lines in the 1930s for the agency, it seems strangely cold and aloof. The massive marble eagle, perched on top of the pillared porch, looks down on a well-kept lawn and neat hedges, but the steps below are untrodden, the handsome bronze doors tightly closed. A passer-by could be forgiven for thinking it was some sort of sanctuary, not knowing that the entrance for everyone, from cleaners to governors, is now at the back on C Street where, across the way, an additional massive block has gone up for the Fed's use, named after William McChesney Martin. Here people may be bustling in and out of the older building, though sightseers are not encouraged, but the spacious marbled lobby is cold too, enhancing an image of insularity.

Yet the governors' quarters on the first floor up are not particularly grand. The main waiting room is well furnished, but smallish. So, too, is the ante-room to the chairman's office. And that itself, though spacious enough, is nothing special; even after invasion by information technology, its wall of books and paper-burdened wooden desk suggest that the head of a well-endowed college would feel at home in it. Indeed, there is a collegiate feel about the whole set of rooms for governors, which seems to invite them to indulge their own idiosyncrasies. Unlike executive directors at, say, the Bank of England, they do not oversee departments at the Fed's headquarters. Each is there to make up his or her mind on policy questions, free of management responsibilities. It is convenient if they specialize in different concerns, but even that seems less in evidence than it used to be.

No rulebook is at hand to make life easy for Federal Reserve governors. Six months before he gave up the chairmanship in the summer of 1987, Paul Volcker told Congress that 'we cannot avoid relying upon a large element of judgement in deciding what, considering all the prevailing circumstances, money growth is appropriate'. Being more of a number-cruncher, his successor might shade that view a little, but he also claims there is no automatic pilot. Volcker thought he could judge better than most, but only through keeping in touch with the markets and talking with a few top bankers whose opinions he valued. Informal consultation was his hallmark – or listening might be a better way of putting it.

But Congress also insists on formal pow-wows. The Federal Advisory Council, consisting of twelve members, usually prominent bankers, one each selected by the board of a Reserve Bank from its district, is required by the Federal Reserve Act to meet the Board of Governors at least four times a year. The thirty-strong Consumer Advisory Council must do likewise. And, since 1980, a third advisory council provides information about the thrifts, the equivalent of Britain's building societies. The Fed chairman also confers regularly with the Treasury Secretary, while various Treasury and Fed officials get together at a weekly luncheon. And there are also regular meetings with the Council of Economic Advisers.

Lubricating all this activity is the information and research effort within the Federal Reserve, some of it highly structured, some rather engagingly idiosyncratic. Considering the power it wields, it may seem surprising that the Board of Governors employs no more than 1,600 people. But remember that their policy decisions are executed through the Reserve Banks, which between them employ nearly 25,000 people – just over 4,000 in New York, only 1,200 in Minneapolis, to take the extremes in size. A lot of the Washington staff are doing administrative chores, about a hundred are engaged on bank regulatory and supervisory matters (see below). But work on economic and policy issues gets pride of place, and this is not skimped.

Some 200 economists work at headquarters and perhaps another 250 all told at the Reserve Banks. Young economists come and go, selling themselves as Fed watchers to the private sector after a spell 'inside', Wall Street being a big taker. But some stay the course, and maybe rise to the top. Corrigan was once 'a bright young economist' at the New York Fed, spotted early on by Volcker. The odds are that more than half the presidents of the Reserve Banks at any one time will have worked their way up from the network's economic and research departments, perhaps from one that has acquired a reputation in a particular niche – as the Chicago Fed has in financial markets, for instance, and the St Louis Fed in monetarism gospel.

A palaver that counts

According to some people, the members of the FOMC are the most powerful group of private citizens in America. But they are not deliberately engaging in a conspiracy to subvert the democratic process, as critics may suggest. Nor are they wielding their power lightly or carelessly. Their philosophy may be flawed, their tools defective, but nobody can say that the FOMC takes uninformed decisions. The amount of information it weighs before making a directive is truly awesome.

Among papers circulated to members ahead of an FOMC meeting are three documents known by the colour of their covers. Two present the Washington staff's latest analysis, forecasts and views; the green book covers the domestic economy, while the blue book concentrates on monetary matters, the outcome of what the FOMC had authorized six weeks earlier and policy choices – typically three alternative scenarios – for the immediate future. The beige or tan book (some dispute here about the colour code) gathers together reports from the twelve Reserve Banks on business and financial conditions in their own regions – and this book is made available to the public nearly a fortnight before each FOMC meeting, to the joy of Fed watchers.

Although only five of them can vote at any one time, all twelve regional presidents come to an FOMC meeting, gathering round the thirty-foot long, oval mahogany table in the Washington boardroom. They join the seven governors, Board staff acting as advisers and officers from the New York Fed ready to report on foreign-currency and open-market operations since the previous meeting. Lesser lights – other Board officials and senior research officers from the Reserve Banks – sit round the perimeter of the room.

The meeting typically gets underway with the New York Fed's operational reports – including that on foreign-exchange operations, which also come under the committee's aegis. The committee then starts to discuss the economic situation and to judge the staff forecasts. At this stage, each governor and all twelve presidents air their views. Then it's time to turn to monetary targets and the blue book's alternatives, when again everybody can chip in. Eventually, the chairman will ask the other governors and all twelve presidents for their policy preferences, though he will soon be interested only in an informal tally of voting members' choices. If no clear preference for one approach – his, he hopes – emerges, he will have to throw his weight around, to persuade, coax, bully. Or, perhaps, shade one of the choices.

The formal vote, when it is taken, is on a directive to the domestic trading desk at the New York Federal Reserve — that is to say, to the staff (officers as they are called) who instruct the Fed's traders in the buying aːd selling of Treasury bills and government securities. The document will only be published, along with how the voting went, a few days after the *next* FOMC meeting. After a review of recent economic and monetary developments, the controversial operational instructions come in the final paragraph. This is written in a kind of code, couched in terms of the degree of pressure the FOMC wants to put on banks' reserve positions.

Unhappily, the FOMC has been driven off course more times than is respectable by the deregulation and innovation of the past twenty years. As we have already related, its emphasis in the 1970s was on controlling interest rates, specifically the federal funds rate, the overnight interbank rate at which banks with surplus balances at the Federal Reserve lend them to their brethren in need. However, money growth persistently exceeded its target. Determined to stamp out inflation, Paul Volcker, shortly after taking office in 1979, abruptly led the FOMC to jettison its interest-rate policy and control the money supply directly. It started to target the levels of non-borrowed reserves in the banking system, which then seemed closely linked to growth in a narrowly defined measure of money, M1. It was not long, however, before deregulation played havoc with the reliability of M1. In 1983, the FOMC switched its focus to borrowed reserves, varying the pressure put on the volume of reserves that banks as a group are forced to borrow at the discount window. At the same time, it fell back on judgement, rather than relying on a monetary index, to guide its fine tuning.

That is still, on the face of it, the position today. However, the federal funds rate has, in practice, come back almost to centre stage, although not as a formal target. The market knows that if the FOMC 'seeks to decrease slightly' the existing degree of pressure on reserve positions in the immediate future, the federal funds rate is likely to be nudged down – and vice versa.

The FOMC directive will most probably also indicate that if certain factors, such as signs of inflation, don't behave as expected in the weeks before the next meeting, then 'somewhat' or 'slightly' greater or lesser reserve restraint 'would' or 'might' be acceptable, the choice of words being a subtle key to the degree of concern. In practice, the Fed chairman may be left with considerable flexibility – too much, some would say – in interpreting the directive.

The Desk's choices

The Desk, as it is familiarly called, conducts its open-market operations at the New York Fed with a group of about forty dealers in American government securities, mainly banks and securities houses. A purchase by the Desk adds, of course, to reserves in the banking system, a sale reduces them. But many technical and seasonal factors beyond the Fed's control influence the level of reserves. Staff in both Washington and New York monitor these and help the manager – a woman at the time of writing – formulate her daily plan of operations.

For the Desk's staff, a typical morning includes a call to the Treasury about the balances it keeps at Federal Reserve Banks, which follows a succession of meetings with dealers, discussions with banks, a preliminary sounding of the Washington Board's thoughts, screen-watching to get the market's reaction to some just-released economic data, a final look at reserve estimates and a briefing with the manager. All this before they flank the manager at around 11.15 a.m. when she presents her plan in a telephone conference call that links them with one of the four Reserve Bank presidents outside New York who are serving on the FOMC, as well as with several senior officials at the Washington Fed. After the call, all FOMC members are immediately told what action the Desk expects to take that day. The Fed chairman does not generally sit in on the call, but he is kept fully informed and makes his views known. If things look tricky, he might call a formal telephone meeting of the full FOMC.

The language is market jargon, but the Desk's operations are planned like a military campaign. Decisions have to be taken not only on how much should be added or drained from banking reserves, but which segments of the government securities market to use. The larger part of the Desk's outright purchases or sales typically have been in Treasury bills. But it keeps about half of its $340 billion portfolio in coupon-bearing Treasury notes and bonds. When it sees only a temporary need to provide reserves, it will buy under short-term repurchase agreements (repos), which oblige dealers to buy the securities back at a specified date, one to fifteen business days ahead, at a specified price. Similarly, matched sale-purchase transactions (MSPs) allow the Desk to withdraw reserves temporarily.

The Desk may also make use of orders placed with it to arrange repurchase agreements for foreign central banks which want to invest overnight the dollar balances they keep with the New York Fed. Although these are not open-market transactions but customer-initiated, the Desk can meet these orders from its own account or pass them through to the dealers, depending on how it wants to influence its own portfolio.

Despite all the preparatory drill, open-market operations are flexible and easy to use. The other two tools of American monetary policy are less sharp. However, the Federal Reserve sees them as important supplements. Reserve requirements are now relatively modest and adjusted infrequently. If the Washington Board does decide on a change, it can be assumed that it wants to underline a particular thrust of monetary policy and heighten the public's perception of this.

That is also true to some extent of the discount rate – the interest rate Reserve Banks charge on their loans through their discount windows. When the Federal Reserve Act was drawn up, the rates were expected to differ from one district to another according to local conditions, and so they did originally. Today there is a national rate, give or take a few days if some Reserve Banks are quicker than others in introducing a change. But the original concept explains why it is that a proposal for an adjustment has to come from one of the twelve Reserve Banks, which is then subject to majority approval by the Board of Governors, the vote being always immediately announced. To all intents and purposes, therefore, it is a Washington initiative. Typically the discount rate lags the federal funds rate, but it has a particular importance in the public's eye since it is the only interest rate the Federal Reserve formally admits to controlling. So when it is altered, the Fed is making a particularly strong statement about the direction in which it wants to see short-term rates move.

Minding the store

If the Federal Reserve has coveted powers over domestic monetary policy, its position is that of any other central bank when it comes to external affairs. The dollar's international value is one of the few areas of monetary policy where both law and tradition give America's executive branch higher authority than the Federal Reserve. The Treasury has overall responsibility for the country's international reserves, the Treasury Secretary decides intervention policy in the foreign-exchange market. It is left to the trading desk of the New York Federal Reserve Bank to carry out the policy, but under the direction of the FOMC, which has to act in close cooperation with the Treasury. And the exchange desk's daily afternoon conference call is with Treasury officials as well as Board staff in Washington.

The New York Fed acts in the foreign-exchange market for both the Federal Reserve and the Treasury (specifically, its Exchange Stabilization Fund), almost all transactions being for both accounts on a fifty-fifty basis. Like most central banks, it tries to conceal its presence in the market, though sometimes it wants to make a point and intervenes by dealing directly with commercial banks. More openly than most central banks, it regularly reports its foreign-exchange operations. A quarterly five- or six-page report, presented to Congress by the Treasury and Fed, is made public little more than a month after the end of the three-month period covered.

The dollar is, of course, still the leading international currency, but the New York Fed is relatively new to the foreign-exchange market. It began to operate in it only in 1962, the year it set up the 'swaps' —the network of reciprocal currency credit lines with other leading central banks (see Chapter 18). And during long periods since, America went in for 'benign neglect' of the dollar. Even today, intervention may seem sparse. To give one example, in the three months August–October 1992, which spanned the European currency crisis and sterling's departure on Black Wednesday from Europe's Exchange Rate Mechanism, the New York Fed entered the market on only four days, buying $1.1 billion through the sale of D-marks. In the previous three months, when there was also downward pressure on the dollar, the figure had been as low as $170 million.

But the New York Fed may be carrying out much larger transactions off-market. In May–June 1992, in an unusual transaction carried out so as *not* to influence rates, it bought all of $6 billion against D-marks in spot and forward transactions with the Bundesbank, honouring an agreement between the two central banks not to build up excessive holdings of each other's currencies. The New York Fed also carries out foreign-exchange transactions as an agent for the accounts of foreign central banks – which, of course, are not disclosed.

Most foreign central banks and multilateral organizations hold deposits at the New York Fed – as dollars, securities and/or gold – worth in all over $400 billion. About one-third of the world's official gold stock (some 10,000 tonnes), belonging to about sixty of those institutions, is stacked eighty feet below street level in a vault nearly half the length of a football field. With a little imagination, the fourteen-storey building in Liberty Street – a sham palace-cum-fortress of a Renaissance king, its massive dark stone ornamented by huge wrought-iron lanterns, its windows heavily barred – seems wholly appropriate. The New York Fed does guard treasure.

Throughout the 1980s, management of the open-market account and that of foreign operations came together only at the presidential level of the New York Fed. However, when Sam Cross, who had headed foreign operations for ten years, and Peter Sternlight, who had managed the open-market account for thirteen years, retired within a year of each other, Corrigan, then president, created a new financial markets group in October 1992, under Bill McDonough, a former commercial banker for twenty-two years with First Chicago. The move suggested to some that the New York Fed, if it could have its way, might like more use made of the dollar's exchange rate as an instrument of monetary policy. But that read too much into it, forgetting that Corrigan had merely restored a 1975–79 practice (when Alan Holmes held both titles). When Corrigan resigned and McDonough slipped into his shoes in July 1993, responsibility was once more split and two deputy managers – both women as it happened – were appointed.

As if being the market-operating arm of the Federal Reserve is not enough, the New York Fed also stands out when it comes to supervising banks, since so many of the largest, American and foreign, are huddled in its district. But not all these banks: in a messy system, state-chartered member banks, all bank holding companies and foreign banks operating in the United States come under the Fed's care. But nationally chartered member banks are examined by their chartering agency, the Office of the Comptroller of the Currency, which is an offshoot of the Treasury. And state-chartered non-member banks are examined by state banking departments and the Federal Deposit Insurance Corporation.

While the Washington Board farms out examination of banks in its care to the appropriate Federal Reserve Bank, it engages itself in many regulatory matters, such as the extent to which American commercial banks should be allowed to edge into investment activities, questions of bank acquisitions and vetting of bank mergers. To protect its role as lender of last resort, the Federal Reserve has been inclined to take on more regulatory duties when given the opportunity.

Paul Volcker believed that central banks should be the bank regulators because they are in the best position to know what is going on in the credit markets and have to pick up the pieces if the system fails. Greenspan seemed to have doubts initially and was very content for Corrigan to become the Fed's leading spokesman on regulatory matters, a role greatly increased when Corrigan ran the Basle group of banking supervisors (see Chapter 10). But by his second term of office, Greenspan was adamant that the Fed needed a hands-on supervisory role to do its job properly.

Regulation is only one area, though an important one, where the relative influences of Washington and New York within the Federal Reserve System depend at any one time on the personalities of the bosses. When Volcker took over the New York Fed in August 1975, he felt the pendulum of power had swung too far towards the Washington Board under Arthur Burns and sought to correct that. When he moved to Washington, he didn't noticeably try to stop the pendulum swinging back.

Power and Congress

Volcker and Burns may have dominated the Washington Board more than some, but whoever is serving as Federal Reserve chairman is expected to execute control, such is the aura surrounding the post. From his experience as a governor from 1965 to 1972, Sherman Maisel reckoned that the chairman held about 45 per cent of the total power relative to the other board members, the FOMC, and the research staff. Monetary policy in the United States is so closely associated with the chairman that if he cannot carry the board or FOMC with him the markets are severely shaken. He is the money man the government wants to influence, who will go to the White House alone if the President wishes to discuss Federal Reserve policy. And he is the man on whose shoulders falls the responsibility of preserving the central bank's independence.

The Federal Reserve likes to say it is independent *within* government. Though a creature of Congress, its only formal responsibility to it for a long while was the submission of an annual report. But under the Humphrey–Hawkins Act of 1978, the Fed chairman must now appear twice a year, in July and February, before both Senate and House banking committees to give an account of the central bank's policy and its objectives related to expectations of where the American economy is heading. In July, his report focuses on preliminary targets for money-supply growth in the next year. In February, those targets are finalized. Apart from these highlighted occasions, the chairman and fellow governors spend many hours on the Hill giving testimony on a variety of matters to various congressional committees.

The relationship with Congress is an uneasy one. There are always congressmen who, like the economist Milton Friedman, want to strip the Federal Reserve of its independence. Wright Patman of Texas, a liberal Democrat, waged war on it for nearly fifty years in the House. After the new building on Constitution Avenue had been completed, Patman mischievously suggested that, since it was an independent department, the Federal Reserve should be subject to local property taxes. It gave lawyers quite a lot of work before the Fed escaped that threat.

No chairman of the Federal Reserve worked harder at justifying its degree of independence than Arthur Burns. Characteristically, in his last address to the National Press Club as chairman, in January 1978, he reminded his audience of the special status of the Federal Reserve and why this can 'make an enormous difference to the future of our country'. This is how he put it:

> Throughout the ages, national governments have had a chronic tendency to engage in activities that outstrip the taxes they are willing or able to collect – a practice that was facilitated in earlier times by clipping precious coins and in modern times by excessive printing of paper money and coercion of central banks. To afford a measure of protection against such political abuses, the authors of the Federal Reserve Act provided for an independent central bank, and their action – while at times questioned – has been confirmed time and again by the Congress. In other words, substantial independence in exercising power over money creation is not something that Federal Reserve officials have arrogated unto themselves, nor is it something that others have conferred because of a belief that central bankers have unique insight that sets them apart from other people. Rather, the ability of the Federal Reserve to act with some independence from the executive branch, and also with immunity from transient congressional pressures, was deliberately established and has been deliberately maintained by the Congress in the interest of protecting the integrity of our money.

Burns would still have been able to make that speech today. Congress has not altered the rules. But proposals are made almost continuously to rein in the Federal Reserve, perhaps by enlarging the size of the board, shortening the term of its members, removing the Reserve Bank presidents from the FOMC, having the President select them (a running issue in 1994), enabling the President to remove Board members, making the term of chairman coincide with that of the President or having the system subject to congressional appropriations.

The fact that none has succeeded prompts the cynical thought that perhaps the Federal Reserve conducts its policy in such a way as to protect its independence. Is it a 'prisoner of its independence', as someone has suggested? The channels of influence from the Executive and the Congress to the Federal Reserve are many and complex. It is hard to determine them. But it is easy to accept that Federal Reserve policy is not insensitive to Presidential influence, particularly at a time when the chairman is seeking re-election.

Political pressures and paranoia

Personal elements in the context of 'independence' are particularly relevant in the Fed's case because of the shortness of the chairman's term. Bill Martin, who thought synchronizing that term with the President's would be wrong because the nation needed continuity in its money management at a time of political upheaval, nevertheless believed that if a Fed chairman found difficulty working with a new President, he should resign – say, a year into the new administration's time. That he himself never felt the need to do so in nearly nineteen years can be interpreted variously, but maybe implies give-and-take on both sides.

Martin's successor, Arthur Burns, appointed by President Richard Nixon from early 1970, enjoyed a reputation in Washington as a stern but eloquent sermonizer against inflation – he was a Columbia University economics professor and one of the world's leading economic historians. The trouble was he never managed to quash inflation during his two terms in office, so laying himself open to criticism. An ugly accusation that in 1972, at the request of the White House, he deliberately let the money supply rip and pumped up the economy to help Nixon to his landslide reelection was vigorously denied not only by himself but also by his fellow governors, who simply thought Burns had made some 'honest' mistakes. Still, the smell of political collusion lingered.

When the Fed was thought over-generous with money growth in late 1976 and early 1977, tittle-tattlers said Burns was trying to ingratiate himself with President Carter in order to secure a third term of office. Though he didn't get it (he was, after all, seventy-three when the appointment came up in early 1978), Wall Street's summing-up when he departed was that Burns had been extremely accommodating to both Presidents Nixon and Carter.

Temptation, therefore, for any Fed chairman in love with his job – or intoxicated by its power, some might say less kindly. But surely even more for a President to make political loyalty the requirement above anything else when choosing a Fed chairman? Well, no. Not if he wants a confident Wall Street and the markets behind him. As Carter discovered after picking Bill Miller to succeed Burns.

A former corporate chief executive (of Textron), neither an economist nor a banker (though he had served as an outside director of the Boston

Fed), Miller could certainly be relied on to cooperate with the Carter administration. But he didn't understand technical monetary matters. He had to learn the vocabulary, then bring a lot of highly experienced and opinionated fellow Board members along with him. He also had the bad luck to serve at a time when Keynesian economic management was in tatters but the monetarists had not yet established a new orthodoxy. Valiantly, Miller did campaign against tax cuts. But, all the time, Wall Street was critical, its analysts complaining about the Fed's softness, its subservience to the Oval Office – and the markets reacting accordingly. Although not directly responsible for Miller's transfer after only seventeen months to the Treasury, where Carter thought his loyalty would be even more valuable, Wall Street had made its point. For the past decade and a half, the Fed has had strongly professional leadership, first from Paul Volcker, then Alan Greenspan, described in 1994 by his British counterpart as 'unquestionably one of the outstanding central bankers of our generation'. Miller will surely be the last non-pro Fed chairman for a long time.

Still, the game of catching out the chairman 'politicizing' the Fed goes on. In the spring of 1991, *The Economist* and a veteran Wall Street Fed-watcher, David Jones, were among those openly complaining that Greenspan, known as a keen Republican, was being too cosy with the White House. Such accusations are not always fair; sometimes the fault is poor communications. But perceptions can mould expectations, and they, in turn, drive the financial markets. So a wise Fed chairman will accept that he is always liable to be suspected of caving in to political pressures and do his best to dispel unreasonable doubts.

But the Fed's toughest struggles are with Congress, and very tricky these can be. By today's standards – which, admittedly, may change – the Fed is old-fashioned in both its short-term chairmanship and its fuzzy, two-pronged objective. Volcker, when in office, apparently considered pushing for a change in the law to have price stability made the single, clear goal, but drew back, afraid that Congress, if it granted it, might demand so much in return that it could be worse than a zero-sum game. Subsequently, a bill introduced in 1989 by a Democrat, Stephen Neal of North Carolina, one of the Fed's best friends in Congress at the time, would have required the Fed to eliminate inflation over five years, but failed to get through Congress.

As can be seen, the Fed remains something of an oddball among the growing band of independent central banks.

History can be an institution's worst enemy. Can it make sense, in today's free-flowing money world, for the central banks of the four largest powers in Western Europe to be so very different one from another, not only in legal respects, but in organization, responsibilities and operating procedures? Of course not. But each of these central banks is bound by its own traditions and customs. None is free of the past.

Compare their size. The Bank of England, the oldest and snootiest, employs around 4,500 people. The German Bundesbank has not just half as many again, as might seem appropriate, but *four times* that number. In between, the Bank of Italy weighs in with 9,400 while – surprisingly – the Bank of France is almost as big an employer as the Bundesbank, with nearly 18,000 staff.

In part at least, the huge difference in size between Britain's central bank and the Bundesbank is readily explained. One is highly centralized, the other a federal institution, decentralized, regionally structured. The Bank of England is thinly represented in the provinces – just five branches and four small intelligence-gathering agencies employing between them fewer than 300 people. In contrast, the Bundesbank's main office in Frankfurt is backed up by the Land central banks (Landeszentralbanken) – nine of them, after a reorganization in 1992 that cut the number down from what had been eleven and would have been sixteen after Germany's reunification had it not been agreed that five of the regional offices should cover two or three Länder. Each has branch offices in provincial cities; that of North Rhein–Westphalia alone has fifty, twice as many as all the Federal Reserve Banks muster throughout the United States. With some 200 branch offices in all, the Bundesbank spreads its presence thickly across Germany. And swells its payroll.

Less well known – at least internationally – is that the other two big European central banks also have regional networks that account for a lot of jobs. But theirs are purely branch networks, which don't have the power-sharing glamour of the Bundesbank's or the Federal Reserve's.

In the Bank of Italy's case, a law of 1894 has 'obliged' it to have a branch in each of the country's ninety-five provinces, although a recent modification offers some flexibility. With two additional branches in Rome, one in Milan, and one in Naples, the central bank has ninety-nine branches in all. Of these, fourteen have elevated status. Not only do they coordinate activities regionally – notably the supervision of local banks, distribution of banknotes and management of clearing operations – but they also provide headquarters with valuable reports on local economic and financial conditions. Though it may seem an unduly fussy system – with only about 4,000 people at head office and the other 5,400 or so in the branch offices – it can be defended on the cynical grounds that the Bank of Italy is one of the few things that work in a politically unstable country and that a banking system often described as 'totally medieval' cannot be controlled at arm's length.

It may seem harder to find a rationale for the Bank of France's *succursales*, which are peppered over the whole countryside. These are a relic from the days when it was primarily a commercial bank. While other central banks with similar origins, including the British and Italian ones, dropped or slashed their services to private customers, the Bank of France insisted for a long while that it benefited from keeping its counters open to business and individuals. Today, as in Italy, the French central bank is required by law to have a branch in each of the country's 100 or so departments. But it has many more. André de Lattre recalls that when he was appointed a deputy governor in 1966, the number of branches had remained at 260 for nearly forty years, and the Bank of France was still the largest commercial bank in Corsica. However, by then, the central bank had concluded that it needed to be more selective. Plans to close forty branches were drawn up, only to be scotched by the government in the face of the 1968 labour unrest. The French trade unions successfully countered later attempts at pruning until determined efforts by two recent governors, Michel Camdessus and Jacques de Larosière, trimmed the number of branches to 212 by 1992. Still an astonishing coverage. Still providing some odd services – for instance, local representatives of the central bank may arbitrate in disputes between commercial banks and their customers. The main functions of the branches today, however, are said to be twofold: acting as banker to the state, including receiving tax payments; and monitoring local economic conditions, assessing business creditworthiness, and so on.

No end of variety

If regionalism, or lack of it, is the biggest influence on the relative sizes of the four main European central banks, their differing involvement in banking supervision possibly runs it a close second. That the Bank of England employs fewer staff than the Bank of Italy on this activity – only some 350 in 1992 even after an expansion in the 1980s – is not surprising. Both have sole responsibility for banking supervision in their countries, but while the Old Lady relies on outside audits and statistical returns from the banks, the Bank of Italy makes its own on-site examinations.

Odder, you may think, that the Old Lady is outstaffed on supervision by both the Bundesbank and the Bank of France, neither of which has any formal responsibility for it whatsoever. But here is an area where all is not what it seems (see Chapter 10). In Germany the Land central banks inspect and examine banks for the separate Federal Banking Supervisory Office, and a department at headquarters in Frankfurt has a substantial watching brief. France goes in for camouflage too. Not only does its central bank governor chair the 'separate' supervisory agency, the Banking Commission, but the Bank of France staffs its secretariat and conducts on-site inspections of the banks for it.

At least you would expect like thinking over the management of a country's financial lifeline, its payments system, the clearing of cheques and interbank settlements. But no. Astonishingly, the Bank of England has no specific responsibilities for these arrangements, and the large-scale payment system in Britain, called CHAPS (clearing house automated payment system), is owned and run by member banks. The other three central banks do have legal obligations but interpret them rather differently. Characteristically, the Bundesbank, which has only to ensure that banking arrangements are made to handle domestic and international payment arrangements, runs Germany's giro network itself. Until twenty-odd years ago, the Bank of France had only a broad remit to oversee the banking system, but then a law of January 1973 gave it the job of administering interbank payments, a duty it fulfilled until recently entirely through credit transfer on its own books. Now a new national system handles large interbank settlements exclusively on telecommunications links, but the central bank still regards oversight of the payments system as one of its core functions. Typically, the Italian payments system has been governed over the years by a series of obtuse decrees, but recently the Bank of Italy has done much to foster closer integration and modernization among different types of operators. It has broad authority. A law of May 1926 made it solely responsible for managing both banks' and securities houses' clearing systems, while a banking law, *testo unico*, that came into force on 1 January 1994 states that 'the Bank of Italy promotes the smooth functioning of the payment system. In this respect, it may promulgate regulations aiming to ensure safe and efficient net and gross settlement systems.' This still allows it to sub-contract some day-to-day running – which it does for a modernized interbank payment system introduced in 1989.

Such richness of variations – and there are many more – might suggest these central banks view their duties very differently. Not so. Not in essence, anyway. Evolving in response to expanding economies, dramatic revolutions in financial markets and the spread of technology, their aims have inevitably become much more alike. Each sees its primary goal today as running a monetary policy that achieves price stability. They all accept they cannot hope to do this successfully from an ivory tower. Whatever they may, or may not, be charged to do, they have to be on the ground floor, trying to keep up with financial markets and watchful for inefficiencies in payment systems. Even though not statutorily obliged to do so, the Bank of England has (even if belatedly) had to concern itself with the adequacy of British payment systems; indeed, it was a driving force behind recent improvements in the British clearing of large payments. No surer sign of the times than that Robin Leigh-Pemberton saw this involvement as one of the most important developments in his ten-year governorship to mid-1993.

Yet the institutional frameworks of these central banks had changed remarkably little when the 1990s began. The Bank of England, in particular, had long been disdainful of the need for legislation, kidding itself it could do the necessary off its own bat. Pushed, kicking and screaming, into a more formalized mould, it still takes delight in a charter more flexible than most. More surprisingly, even at the law-driven Bundesbank, which has seen over twenty amendments to its launch Act of 1957, it took thirty-five years to bring the first substantive alteration to its structure. And that came only because five new Länder had to be embraced after reunification.

Breaking free

The Bundesbank, pleased with its status, is also remarkably confident of its technical competence when it comes to the nitty–gritty of choosing the instruments for executing monetary policy. It is the least active of the four European central banks on a daily basis; it relies heavily on weekly tenders for reversible security transactions with banks – repurchase agreements ('repos') – and on levying minimum reserve requirements on the banks that, although progressively reduced since 1980, are still regarded as an indispensable instrument of German monetary policy. In sharpest contrast, the Bank of England favours fine tuning, operating very low – virtually negligible – reserve requirements but active daily intervention in London's short-term money markets. However, after sterling was forced out of the Exchange Rate Mechanism and London money markets became more volatile, the Bank resorted to some rough tuning in addition to its normal procedure, offering repos directly to the banking sector every two weeks, at first experimentally and then formally from January 1994. So the Bundesbank and the Bank of England have therefore drawn nearer to each other in their operating techniques. If ever a single set of techniques has to be adopted for a Europe-wide monetary policy, the two could still be set on a collision course, but the confrontation promises to be less hostile than when the Maastricht Treaty was drawn up. No prizes for guessing which will win. Anyway, the Bank of England – and several other European central banks – will be prepared to pay that price for the bonus promised from European monetary union.

That bonus is 'independence'. This is not a question of ownership, which has become largely irrelevant. Nobody fusses because the Bank of Italy's shareholders are banks and insurance companies, while the other three central banks are fully state owned. Independence revolves around the freedom to determine monetary policy, seemingly out of reach for most European central banks until the Maastricht Treaty for European economic and monetary union suddenly made it a real possibility – and for one, the Bank of France, a reality by the end of 1993.

Only the Bundesbank of the four big European central banks was anywhere near satisfied with its degree of independence at the time of designing the Maastricht Treaty. The Bank of England is an outright agent of the government, though less ostensibly than the Bank of France had been up to then. Threadneedle Street is given its instructions from Whitehall – it has been dubbed the East End branch of the West End Treasury – in such gentlemanly fashion that the majority of the British public is probably unaware of its subservience. Or was until Maastricht came along. (The Treasury has never needed to bring the Bank to heel by invoking the powers of enforcement written into the Bank of England Act.) In the face of fashionable pressures to concede much more, the British government in 1993 gave the Bank the right to publish its thoughts on inflation in a quarterly report without submitting it in advance to the Treasury's scrutiny, and also the right to decide the exact timing of a change in interest rates once the Chancellor of the Exchequer has decided on one.

More substantial was the decision in April 1994 of the Chancellor of the Exchequer, Kenneth Clarke, to publish in future, with a six weeks' gap, the minutes of his monthly monetary meetings with the Governor of the Bank of England (which, incidentally, are not just *à deux*: each has a small supporting team, the Bank's including the Deputy Governor and its chief economist). This has given the British central bank independence of voice though not of action. The Governor's immediate reaction to this innovation was none too enthusiastic. Putting the Bank's advice to its political masters on public record could lead to less robust arguments. It has been given a unique chance to build up credibility – but a reputation can be lost more quickly than it can be gained.

More often than not, the Bank of Italy has been mistakenly regarded in the past as one of the least independent of central banks. In reality, it has long enjoyed an autonomy over intervention in both domestic and foreign-exchange markets. What's more, a succession of weak coalition governments allowed it in practice to set the discount rate most of the time. Intriguingly, in order to demonstrate Italy's enthusiasm for EMU, that *de facto* authority was legalized in January 1992.

While largely symbolic domestically, that Italian legislation marks an important milestone in central banking history. For the first time, a major central bank had asserted itself and won an independent position, unlike the Bundesbank – and America's Federal Reserve – which had it presented on a plate from the outset. The Bank of Italy has since distanced itself from the government in other ways. Its obligation to provide monetary financing for the Treasury's needs (to help fund the country's huge budget deficits), suspended *de facto* since 1990, was legally abolished in November 1993, thus meeting the requirements of the Maastricht Treaty. At the same time, it was also given the power to set the level of commercial banks' minimum reserves. But the Bank of Italy had still some way to go. What all European central banks are striving for is a mandate as definite as the Bundesbank's.

The Deutsche Bundesbank Act lays down that the functions of the German central bank are two-fold. First, to regulate the quantity of money in circulation and of credit supplied to the economy, using the monetary powers conferred on it by the Act, 'with the aim of safeguarding the currency'. Second, to provide for the execution by banks of domestic and external payments. True, without prejudice to the performance of its functions, the Bundesbank is also required to support the general economic policy of the federal government. But then comes the let-out: 'In exercising the powers confirmed on it by this Act, it is independent of instructions from the federal government.'

On the face of it, the Bank of France now has a very similar mandate. By a new Act of December 1993, it has to 'formulate and implement monetary policy with the aim of ensuring price stability' and it is free of government instructions in so doing. But the proviso that it carries out these duties 'within the framework of the government's overall economic policy' leaves room for some scepticism as to whether the French government really has relinquished its long-held grasp on the central bank.

None escapes politicization

Even with a mandate that unambiguously precludes interference, a government may be able to influence decisions at a central bank if its own supporters hold key positions there. And, *de jure* or *de facto*, the top brass at all four big European central banks are chosen by their governments. None, therefore, escapes politicization. And perhaps least of all the Bundesbank. Although the German federal government appoints only the top executives at the Frankfurt headquarters – the directorate – who are outnumbered on the principal decision-making body, the Central Bank Council, by its other members, the presidents of the Land central banks, some of the latter will have strong political links.

The formalities are that the president of the Bundesbank (the more popular name of governor is not used in Germany), the vice president and the five other members of the directorate are nominated by the federal government. After 'consultation' with the Central Bank Council – whose majority view has been ignored on occasion – they are appointed by the federal Chancellor. (The statutes provide for a board of up to ten members but at the same time prohibit the federal government from handling a majority of appointments to the Central Bank Council.) Like their counterparts at the Federal Reserve Board, they cannot be dismissed other than for unlawful wrongdoing.

Presidents of the nine Land central banks are appointed in much the same way except that nominations are made by the Bundesrat, the upper house of the German parliament which represents the Länder, and the names have to be proposed in the first place by the Land government concerned. Council members are usually appointed for eight years to make nominations independent of electoral cycles. Second terms are possible. The seven members of the directorate are supposed to have 'special professional qualifications', while politics comes more openly into play in selecting regional members. But hands-on political influence does not go far down the Land central banks; their vice presidents and other directors (members of the managing boards) are selected by the Central Bank Council and appointed by the Bundesbank's president.

There are few restraints on the government's hold on top appointments at the other three big European banks. Under the new system at the Bank of France, the governor and two deputy governors – the top trio – are appointed by the government on six-year terms, renewable once but subject to retirement at sixty-five. All three serve on the key body, the Monetary Policy Council, along with six other members, also chosen by the government – from a list of 'persons of recognized standing and professional experience in monetary, financial and economic matters' who give up any job they may have to serve a nine-year term. The first appointees in 1994 came from a wide spectrum of backgrounds – industry, insurance, journalism, academia, financial regulation and politics; the youngest at forty-one was Michel Sapin, a finance minister for eleven months in the former socialist government and a strong defender of the franc. The nine members of the Monetary Policy Council also have to regroup as the central bank's administrative body, the Conseil Général, with a tenth member traditionally decided by the staff – a slot once filled by Jacques Delors.

The governor of the Bank of Italy has an indefinite term of office and there is no tradition he should step down after a suitable period. He is chosen by the bank's High Council, but subject to government approval – and the government has turned down nominations not to its liking. The same procedure goes for the other three members of the top management team, the director general (the governor's deputy) and two deputy director generals. The High Council consists of the governor, who chairs it, and thirteen other members, chosen on a regional basis by the shareholder banks for terms of three (renewable) years, who must not have active political roles. The Council meets routinely once a month to consider general administrative matters; the Italian Treasury can send a representative who can speak but not vote.

The British go in for shorter terms. The governor and deputy governor of the Bank of England hold office for five years, but can be reappointed. Alongside them, four other executive directors, together with twelve outsiders, serve on the Court, as the managing body is quaintly called, for four-year terms, staggered so that four finish – they are renewable – at the end of February each year. All are appointed by the Crown. In practice, power of appointment lies with the Prime Minister, who confers with the Chancellor of the Exchequer and generally acts on his recommendation. When the governor's job is up for grabs, the Chancellor will probably sound out some of the directors and it is customary, although not obligatory, to consult the political opposition if a general election is in sight, say no more than a year away. The government has no power to dismiss either the governors or other directors. Nor to fix their pay. (Incidentally, not even their worst enemies can say the outside directors on the Court are there for the money: for their weekly attendance, they receive a princely £500 a year, unchanged since set in the 1946 Charter.)

National images

So what sort of figures do governments choose to head these prestigious central banks? Arguably, there will always be a temptation to install a loyal servant, a party faithful, if the central bank has leeway to act on its own or even a penchant for awkwardness. In practice, however, any government will hesitate to be moved by such considerations – although Margaret Thatcher was accused of so doing when she picked Robin Leigh-Pemberton to head the Bank of England in 1983. In the public's eye, the governor symbolizes the central bank and his credibility is all-important. Politicking in making the choice has to be subtle, aimed at finding someone the markets will respect but who is sympathetic to the government's ideology.

The Bank of France, which in the past was notoriously subject to political pressure, is likely to be headed by an eminent and highly professional figure, but one from the public sector, used to taking orders from political masters. In succession, three governors, today's Jean-Claude Trichet and his two predecessors, Jacques de Larosière and Michel Camdessus, had earlier risen from the élite rank of *inspecteur des finances* to top the civil service side of the French Treasury (the latter two also neatly interchanging the plum job at the International Monetary Fund). Even before the recent move to independence, when it carried strictly limited powers, governorship of the Bank of France was seen as a prestigious post and successive governments kept it that way.

The image of Italy's governor is of a dedicated professional, a student of economics combining learning and intellectual thought with a capacity to stand up to politicians. Since tenures can be long, however, the post tends to be identified with its incumbent. Such was the case with Carlo Azeglio Ciampi, who had fourteen years behind him as governor before becoming Prime Minister in 1993. After university and war service, he joined the central bank in 1946 at the age of twenty-six, was heading the highly respected research department by 1970 and before the decade was out had scaled the heights by way of two intermediary stops. Both his successor and predecessor were of similar mould, insiders who worked their way up, so a pattern seems to be developing. Antonio Fazio, appointed in May 1993 at the age of fifty-six, had already spent nearly thirty years within the Bank of Italy, notably on the research side as chief economist, and had written extensively on topics ranging from monetary theory and policy to the problems of economic growth and unemployment. He too looked set for a long reign. But Paolo Baffi, who preceded Ciampi, fell victim to a trumped-up charge against the Bank of Italy's top management over its handling of the affairs of Banco Ambrosiano, and resigned in 1979 after what he was later to describe as 'my five years in the firing-line'.

Before Baffi was someone much more difficult to pigeon-hole. Guido Carli, the most famous name in the Bank of Italy's postwar history, served only a year in the bank before starting his fifteen years as governor in 1960 at the age of forty-six. Briefly foreign trade minister before joining the bank, he had earlier held several public sector posts. He had also been on the world monetary stage ever since serving on the first board of directors of the International Monetary Fund in 1947, and it was the international side of central banking that really caught his fancy. A man who for two pins might have become an actor rather than a central banker, he retained a sense of the dramatic. In his darkened room in the Palazzo Koch in Rome's via Nazionale, the artificial light focused on this slender, angular-featured man sitting in front of a painting of San Sebastian, from whose pierced breast red paint spattered in horribly realistic fashion. Could it have been this setting that inspired Arthur Burns to talk of the anguish of central banking?

Intense in conversation, Carli's eyes would flash when he spoke of the potential dangers of the unregulated Eurodollar market, a subject he brought up time and again in international circles. At home he was the country's economics maestro, the miracle man. A mystique, close to reverence, surrounded the Bank of Italy under Carli. Introducing him when he gave the annual lecture sponsored by the Per Jacobsson Foundation in Basle in June 1976, Marcus Wallenberg, a Swedish private banker, said: 'He is well known in the whole world for his vision, his knowledge, and his warm friendships, and he is a man of the world, not only of one country.' On the same occasion, Milton Gilbert, one year into retirement from the Bank for International Settlements, commented: 'It is an axiom of central banking that a central bank must maintain a certain independence from the government, but under Governor Carli it was said in Italy that the government must retain a certain independence from the central bank.'

Tributes such as that to a central bank governor are not earned easily. But they may come more readily in a country where weak government gives the solidity of the central bank a special premium than in Britain with its relatively stable political system. Evaluation of Bank of England governors since Montagu Norman is made difficult because of ambivalence about what the job entails. The notion that the Old Lady can be both the City of London's watchdog and its champion, always ready to spring to its defence, to battle for it against Whitehall, may seem stupid today. Yet it lingers on. The present governor, Eddie George, appointed from July 1993, is an insider who has learnt the tricks of the business the patient way. As also was Leslie O'Brien, at the top from 1966 to 1973. But the more usual choice these past fifty years has been a merchant banker – the likes of Barings' Rowley Cromer (1961–66) and Schroders' Gordon Richardson (1973–83) – who may have served on the Court as an outside director, but otherwise came new to the business. Walter Bagehot, if alive today, might well question the logic of such selection, so scathing was he of the amateurish direction of the privately run Bank of England compared with that of its counterpart across the Channel. 'The Bank of France keeps the final banking reserve,' he wrote in 1873, 'but the state does not trust such a function to a board of merchants, named by shareholders.'

So ingrained, however, was the concept that the Bank of England Governor should, for the most part, come from an élite investment banking house, that it was a shock when Margaret Thatcher in 1983 appointed Robin Leigh-Pemberton from a commercial bank. But perhaps the more questionable element in that selection at the time was whether he rated as a banker of any kind, having served at National Westminster Bank only as an outside director and then non-executive chairman before being given the City's highest office. In the event, though policy analysis and presentation were not his strong points, he confounded his critics by putting up a good show on European money and running a *sotto voce* campaign for independence.

Top Bundesbankers

Perhaps rather surprisingly, in the land that rules by the book, the identikit of the Bundesbank president is also fuzzy. The finance ministry has provided two of the last three presidents, but earlier appointees don't fit into that pattern. The legendary Karl Blessing, the first president after Bank deutscher Länder was transformed into the Bundesbank, serving from 1958 until 1969, had an early career in the Reichsbank, joining its directorate under Hjalmar Schacht in the late 1930s, before being removed by Hitler. But it was from corporate Germany, from the chairmanship of the German subsidiary of Unilever, that he was eventually plucked to head the Bundesbank.

Blessing's successor, Karl Klasen, who takes the story of the presidency to 1977, began a career with Deutsche Bank in the 1930s and was a board member there when he departed for the Bundesbank. But he had also made a splash in central-banking circles as a young Social Democrat president of the Hamburg Land central bank between 1948 and 1952. After Klasen's retirement came a well-earned two-and-a-half-year stint for an insider, Otmar Emminger, who had served faithfully as vice president under Klasen. A man whose courteous, schoolmasterly manner – he would painstakingly correct a journalist for slovenliness of thought – belied a brilliant mind and awesome grasp of all aspects of his craft, Emminger was succeeded by his deputy of two years' standing, Karl Otto Pöhl, a larger-than-life figure with a background and style of operation very different from those of his predecessors. What Emminger and Pöhl shared, however, was an outstanding virtuosity of speech, in English as well as German; both could discourse at length, on the spot, about any monetary topic.

A sports reporter, then an economics journalist, Pöhl, a Social Democrat, had gone into government service in 1970. Karl Schiller, the economics minister, invited him into his department, a step that led to him serving as principal economic adviser to Chancellor Willy Brandt. Three years later, in 1973, he moved to the finance ministry, then under Helmut Schmidt, where, until 1977, he was State Secretary (most senior civil servant) for Monetary Affairs. It was Schmidt who, as Chancellor, appointed Pöhl top dog at the Bundesbank after he had served a two-year apprenticeship in the second slot. Not for nothing had the poor boy from Hanover worked his way through college and obtained the requisite 'special professional qualifications', in his case, the equivalent of a master's degree in economics at the prestigious University of Göttingen.

Cocky, seemingly self-assured yet probably a touch insecure, Pöhl assiduously cultivated an international image, dismaying his more stuffy colleagues with the frankness and frequency of his chats with the foreign press corps at gatherings such as the annual jamborees of the International Monetary Fund and the monthly meetings of the Bank for International Settlements in Basle. With those he trusted not to finger him he could be immensely indiscreet, showing no hesitation in pouring scorn on some of his fellow central bankers. But he was a staunch ally of those who impressed him. His pragmatic approach to monetarism appealed in particular to Paul Volcker and the links between the two were probably the strongest since Montagu Norman and Benjamin Strong cultivated such ties.

With a formidable reputation abroad and respected at home, Pöhl gave Chancellor Helmut Kohl little choice but to give him a second term of office from the beginning of 1988, even though he had the wrong political colour. Pöhl, never long on modesty, was nevertheless tickled and took the reappointment as a great tribute to his skills. Who could have foreseen then that, less than halfway through that second term, in May 1991, Pöhl would stand down, retire from the limelight? By that very unusual move, by his voluntary relinquishment of the trappings of central banking, Pöhl assured himself a place in world financial history more securely than all his years in office could promise. Yet with much to make him disgruntled, he could readily persuade himself that, at sixty-one, it was time to launch himself into the private sector if he was ever going to do so.

Age itself is no obvious handicap at the Bundesbank. Pöhl's three immediate predecessors left the presidency only a year or two short of seventy. As did his successor, Helmut Schlesinger, his deputy who served a stop-gap two-year term at the top from August 1991. As with Emminger fourteen years earlier, Schlesinger's appointment was a gesture of respect for a long-serving Bundesbanker, in his case as the high priest of economics within the central bank. Portrayed by the British press as a villain in the autumn of 1992, when he resisted foreign demands for German interest-rate cuts – which he considered impertinent – he suffered a personal assault from Norman Lamont, then British Chancellor, as sterling was forced to leave the European Exchange Rate Mechanism. Schlesinger was an austere hardliner on inflation if ever there was one. He plainly demonstrated the Bundesbank's strength when it refused to go on supporting the pound and, later, the franc, so bringing the ERM crashing down. But he was considered politically naïve.

That is not an accusation ever likely to be hurled at Hans Tietmeyer, for whom Schlesinger kept the seat warm. This tough Westphalian Christian Democrat, who took over in September 1993, when he had just turned sixty-two, had been, like Pöhl, top official on the international side of the finance ministry before he joined the Bundesbank directorate, which he did at the beginning of 1990. But he had entered public service much earlier than Pöhl – in 1962 – and had spent twenty years at the economics ministry, at one time heading its division in charge of European Common Market affairs, at another running domestic economic policy. And from 1982 he became Chancellor Kohl's 'Sherpa', charged with West German preparations for world economic summits. All of which means that the Bundesbank is now headed by a soft-spoken intellectual, who is a tough negotiator, and a hawk on inflation, but a pragmatist who thinks in terms of international cooperation, preferably in a very small group, rather than formal coordination. Perhaps most important of all for the evolution of central banking over the rest of this decade, Tietmeyer is highly regarded by his fellow central bankers around the world.

The other members of the Bundesbank directorate, apart from the president and vice president, will be as mixed a bunch as Federal Reserve governors. But the politics of choice is more complicated than in America. Coalition partners in the Bonn government have to be satisfied, a balance has to be struck in political affiliations. A further consideration is that these executive directors are in charge of specific activities at the central bank. So a former state finance minister might oversee banking and credit, a professor from a respected university could be responsible for macroeconomic issues, and a former public-sector banker might look after notes and coins.

Presidents of the German regional central banks, who make up the rest of the Council, also come from a variety of backgrounds. They will almost certainly include a professor or two, probably a technocrat with a long career behind him at the Bundesbank's headquarters and a former state politician. Occasionally a businessman will take the inevitable cut in salary. Occasionally, too, their numbers will include a former Bonn official – such as Horst Schulmann. State Secretary at the finance ministry just before Tietmeyer, after having been Chancellor Helmut Schmidt's 'Sherpa' for economic summits in 1978–82, and subsequently head of the Institute of International Finance in Washington, Schulmann was elected president of the important Hesse state central bank, with Frankfurt in its domain, at the beginning of 1993.

Power and pay

Schulmann and his fellow presidents taste power much more than directors of some of the other big European central banks. It must feel important to sit at the long table in the grand Court Room of the Bank of England, but the non-executive directors of the Bank – mostly captains of British commerce and finance – are not dealing with sensitive policy matters, nor being given special inside knowledge. Though they may offer the Bank's management valuable advice on a wide range of matters, questions of interest rates and foreign-exchange policy are dealt with between the governor and the Chancellor of the Exchequer, supported by their closest advisers. Internally, the Bank's affairs are discussed in inner cabinets, the most senior and important of which is known as the Committee of Treasury.

Until the Maastricht Treaty threw a spotlight on it, the Bank of England could keep its lack of independence out of the public eye and nurse its pride. Not for it the indignity of visible government interference that even the Bundesbank has to endure. No member of parliament or civil servant can sit on the Court, whereas members of the German federal government can attend meetings of the Central Bank Council and even propose motions. Moreover, although these intruders cannot vote, they can have any decision they don't like deferred for up to two weeks. French politicians don't have that power, but the Prime Minister and the Minister of Economic Affairs can attend meetings of the Monetary Policy Council and, although they cannot vote, they may submit proposals for consideration.

No comparison of the main European central banks can neglect the sensitive subjects of accountability and pay. All have to produce audited financial accounts. But not necessarily justification of their policies and behaviour. Surprisingly, the Bundesbank enjoys its freedom with minimal scrutiny. There is no obligation to give any account of itself to the German parliament or to print reports of its meetings. The only constraint is the duty to support overall government policy if that does not conflict with the commitment to price stability.

Elsewhere, the governors give evidence to parliamentary committees, although the practice is relatively new at Westminster and the enquiries there are usually about supervisory and City affairs. In the new French system, the governor has to address an annual report to the President and to parliament, and the accounts of the Bank of France are subject to scrutiny by the finance committees of both the National Assembly and the Senate.

Oddly, autonomy deserts the Bundesbank when it comes to pay. Large numbers of its staff are rated as civil servants, though perhaps with a modest pay top-up. Salaries of the top brass are settled by the Council but, like those at the Bank of France, are subject to government approval. The other two central banks have the most freedom to pay as they like – in the Bank of England's case to the ceaseless irritation of the poorer Whitehall mandarins and the occasional embarrassment of a governor who may waive a part of his emolument.

Which of the four governors comes dearest? Nobody knows for sure, because the continentals, particularly the Bundesbank, are cagey and only in Britain has the figure been displayed for all to see in the annual accounts. But, on best estimates, the Bundesbank pays DM600,000 (around $400,000) plus, and the Bank of Italy about the same – or even more. As someone commented, the Italian governor can probably justify this, given his workload in shifting the mountain of Italian debt.

The least-known of the world's major central banks is one of the most successful. Judged by the objective that central bankers nowadays set themselves, the attainment of price stability, the Bank of Japan is consistently near the top in the world ranking. Admittedly, a good average performance has been punctuated by short periods of rapid inflation, but these have been brought quickly under control.

Moreover, the key instrument for achieving this control over prices has been monetary policy. While Japan's fiscal policy has been volatile, determined by haggling among politicians about tax rates and public spending, monetary policy has been under the control of experts. Throughout Japan's postwar history, monetary policy has been directed to specific long-term goals – rapid economic growth in the 1950s and 1960s, low inflation in the 1970s and 1980s, together with a strong yen policy, which keeps down import costs.

The Bank of Japan's role in policymaking has been enhanced also by the liberalization and deregulation of Japan's financial system. In the first three decades after the Second World War, interest rates and the flow of credit in Japan were closely controlled by the authorities – in practice, by the Ministry of Finance, with the central bank playing a dependent role. It was called, somewhat scornfully, 'the Nihonbashi branch of the Ministry of Finance' – a reference to the area of Tokyo where the central bank's offices are. But as interest rates were freed, the money markets developed rapidly and international influences came to play a larger part in Japan's financial markets, the scope for direct controls was severely curtailed, and more reliance had to be placed on indirect methods of control, notably through open-market operations. These factors, described more fully below, served to push the Bank of Japan to the forefront of monetary policymaking. Successive governors of the bank were quick to seize this opportunity to demonstrate that the central bank is nothing like as dependent on government as its formal structure would suggest. By the 1990s, Japan's monetary policy was publicly identified as that of the Bank of Japan under Governor Mieno.

There are other reasons for paying particular attention to the Bank of

Japan. As the biggest international creditor country, Japan has a huge influence on global financial conditions. When the authorities tighten monetary policy in Japan, Japanese banks slow their international lending and international interest rates tend to rise. When Japan relaxes domestic policy, its banks become readier to lend overseas as well as at home, and interest rates tend to fall. The fates of thousands of manufacturing plants, construction projects and other enterprises in the United States, Europe and the developing world are determined by decisions taken by bankers and businessmen in Tokyo, Osaka and the other main centres of Japanese commerce. The Bank of Japan and the Japanese Ministry of Finance have a big influence on the environment in which those decisions are taken.

The sheer scale of Japan's financial involvement in the outside world – through both its direct investment and bank lending – also gives it growing political clout. No head of government or finance minister is unaware of this. Many of them have already made their pilgrimages to Tokyo, the new Mecca of international finance, pleading for aid, loans or simply for Japan's blessing of their policies. This growing dependency is most apparent in the developing countries of Asia, especially in the Philippines, Indonesia, Thailand, and increasingly in the Indian sub-continent as well. Japan has overtaken the United States as the leading source of new foreign investment in these countries – and in many of them it already owns the largest stock of foreign investment. So governments have to take account of the wishes of Japanese investors and lenders. And Japanese banks in turn take account of the attitude of the Japanese authorities.

After taking a back seat for decades, Japan is making its voice heard in all the international financial institutions. Increasingly, Japanese officials occupy senior staff posts in them – it will surely not be long before one of them is appointed managing director of the IMF. Japan's IMF quotas and voting rights have been enlarged to reflect its economic weight. And increasingly Japan wants a bigger say in determining the policies followed by these institutions – and the rules of the game in international monetary relations generally.

The following sections describe the responsibilities of the Bank of Japan for monetary policy and how it has carried them out; lessons of the bubble economy; banking rescues and supervision; how the central bank is run; and relations with the Ministry of Finance. It concludes with an assessment of its performance.

Delivering stable prices

Japan's phenomenal rate of growth in 1950–73 was financed partly by internal profits, which companies ploughed back into investments, and partly by bank borrowing. Most companies were chronically dependent on their banks for finance; and the banks were chronically 'over-lent' to the industrial sector. Through government controls, bank depositors received artificially low rates of interest, and these were passed on to industry in the form of cheap loans. The banking system was seen as an instrument of national economic policy designed above all to secure rapid economic growth. It would not be accurate to say that a liberal supply of low-cost finance caused the Japanese economic miracle – plenty of countries have tried that illusory route to prosperity and all have failed. No, the Japanese miracle was caused by high levels of education, technological capacity, superb traditional skills, social discipline and the thriftiness of the Japanese people, allied to an intensely competitive spirit and a ruthless determination to succeed. The banking system merely adapted itself to these conditions; but by efficiently mobilizing the rapidly growing stream of savings, it certainly oiled the wheels of Japan's record-breaking burst of growth.

Every so often, the economy hurtled off the tracks. Overexpansion sucked in imports, the balance of payments dived into the red, and the brakes had to be slammed on; this happened in the mid-1950s and again in the 1960s. The government invariably responded by tightening monetary policy; in those days, that meant asking banks to cut back their loans to industry. As industry was wholly dependent on bank finance, this had an immediate and pervasive effect on economic activity. A brief Japanese-style recession (growth at 5 per cent rather than 10 per cent a year) would curb imports and boost exports, putting the balance of payments back into the black and so allowing a resumption of rapid growth.

The oil shock of 1972–73 changed all that. The long-term rate of growth was halved, as industrial economies everywhere adjusted to the burden of higher oil prices. Japan itself faced a mammoth increase in oil bills. Like some other industrial countries, it initially tried to bluff its way out of the problem, and Japanese banks borrowed massively on international Euromarkets – the first of several such bouts of borrowing and lending which were to have such a disruptive effect on international money markets in the next two decades. But then the bluff was called: the markets grew reluctant to lend Japanese banks more money, except at penalty rates (involving shameful loss of face). Moreover the expansion of the domestic economy was clearly getting out of control: by 1975 the money supply was growing at 20 per cent a year. This was the Tanaka era – named after Kakuei Tanaka, Prime Minister from 1972 to 1974, who was subsequently arrested on corruption charges and served four years in prison, and whose acolytes controlled every aspect of policy-making in Japan.

In the mid-1970s Japan clamped down on domestic demand – again using monetary policy. But the traditional methods by which credit squeezes were imposed were now being sharply criticized inside Japan. These relied heavily on instructions from the finance ministry to the banks about how they should allocate loans and how much credit, overall, they should allow. As in other countries, such direct controls over credit were grossly inefficient, as they limited banks' freedom to compete; moreover, their effectiveness was slowly undermined as companies tapped other sources of finance. Gradually, such direct control on lending, called 'window guidance' in Japan, was supplemented and eventually replaced by market-oriented policies, such as open-market operations, aimed at controlling the growth of the money supply and/or interest rates. Japan started its flirtation with monetarism.

If the money supply was to be controlled, it had to be measured and the desirable rate of growth determined. Japan began publishing 'forecasts' for the money supply in 1978, four years after the Bundesbank started to announce 'targets' (see Chapter 15). Observers suspect that the Japanese authorities opted for the different terminology because they could not risk the loss of face involved in not meeting specific targets – although in the event the Bank of Japan proved much better at hitting its goals than most other central banks. (Cheekily, the Bank of England even boasted about its lack of success in hitting targets for the money supply, implying this showed up faults in the monetarist approach rather than any defects in the Bank's execution of policy.)

Before the mid-1970s, there was no consensus in Japan on whether the money supply mattered or not. As in other countries, policymakers were influenced first by the experience of rampant inflation in the 1970s and second by the new monetarist economics associated with the Chicago school. Later, in the 1980s, they took note of the attempts of President Reagan and Mrs Thatcher to put their versions of monetarism into practice. So the Bank of Japan also mimicked a monetarist position. But like other central banks, it probably never believed in it.

Curbing money-supply growth did prove effective in eradicating inflation, and the Bank of Japan has continued to monitor it over the medium term as a check on inflationary tendencies. But, as in other countries, far-reaching changes in the money markets in the 1980s made it difficult to define the money supply as individuals and corporations shifted their assets among the different instruments in search of the best terms and conditions. As long as this process of deregulation continued – and even by the mid-1990s it was not fully complete – so would large-scale 'portfolio shifts', making the interpretation of money-supply changes difficult.

Although liberalization of financial markets in Japan made it difficult to implement monetary policy, it gave the central bank potentially much more influence over the economy. Before liberalization, the government could only change specific interest rates by official guidance, with limited effects on the economy. After liberalization, interest rates on all financial instruments moved in response to changes in the central bank's interest-rate policy. Interest rates on bank deposits came into a market-determined relationship with interest rates on government bonds, Post Office accounts and certificates of deposits. At the same time, the banks came to depend on interest-bearing deposits for their own funding. So when interest rates rose, they had to charge borrowers more, whereas in the 1950s and 1960s these were separately controlled by the Ministry of Finance and interbank agreements. With interest rates free to move, the volume of bank lending fell more quickly when interest rates were increased, and rose more quickly when interest rates were cut. This gave monetary policy more leverage on the economy.

The whole approach to policymaking changed. As inflation was brought to low levels in the 1990s, the focus of monetary policy switched to market interest rates. Here the increased efficiency of financial markets, flowing from liberalization, was a great help to monetary policymakers. The objective of policy – price stability – remained unchanged but the Bank of Japan paid increased attention to market interest rates as indicators of whether it should tighten or relax policy. It started to mention market interest rates when policy changes were announced. The first time it did this was in May 1989; in raising the discount rate, it referred to 'rising market interest rates' as reflecting strong economic growth and changes in prices and exchange rates. In fact, that discount rate increase was a signal that the central bank had decided to bring the unsustainable boom to a halt.

The exchange rate of the yen, above all against the dollar, became another key influence on monetary policy. At certain times the Bank of Japan came close to having an exchange-rate target. The cuts of the discount rate in 1986 and 1987 followed the Plaza agreement of 1985 (see Chapter 13) – and in mid-1993 the soaring value of the yen (to below 100 to the dollar) also encouraged a relaxation of monetary policy.

Under Governor Mieno, the Bank of Japan specifically took into account the impact of its policy not only on exchange rates but also on international financial markets and the world economy – a perhaps overdue recognition of the weight of that impact. Previously, the Japanese authorities had appeared indifferent to these considerations.

Monetary policy in practice

So much for the formulation of Japanese monetary policy. How does it work in practice? The Bank of Japan influences interest rates and monetary conditions through its operations in the money markets, its official discount rate and public policy explanations by the governor, who in 1992 made fifty speeches and thirty-two appearances before the Diet – making him probably the most prolific public speaker among governors of the major central banks. It has been very anxious to establish and maintain the credibility of its policy in the money markets. This was a feature of the money-market reforms of 1988, when the Bank of Japan reasserted its authority.

Authority, but not dictatorship. The Bank of Japan can no more dictate the level of interest rates than any other central bank. It can nudge them up or down, using a variety of techniques, mainly: lending to banks at the discount rate, purchases of commercial bills at rates set in the interbank bill market, sales of short-term government bills and purchases of government bonds from financial institutions. Each of these operations either (in the case of sales of securities) drains reserves from the banking system, or (in the case of purchases) injects reserves into the system. To affect market rates, the central bank must be in touch with the market at all times, and come to terms with it. Like many other central banks, the Bank of Japan now does this by focusing on very short-term rates, allowing longer-term rates to be determined in the markets. Its influence over longer-term rates is indirect – achieved mainly by the market's expectation that it will continue to limit the supply of reserves to the banking system and thus maintain the purchasing power of the yen over the long term. In central banking, success turns crucially on credibility – on achieving success and convincing the market that it can continue to do so.

Finally, what about 'window guidance'? Its original purpose – controlling the granting of credit by banks – ended in 1982, but until 1990 the authorities still used a modified form to give banks information about expected total credit demand in the following quarter. That residual function as a signal and channel of information was then officially discontinued. The central bank still, however, knows exactly what each commercial bank plans to lend and makes clear its preferred policy. How much this may in certain circumstances amount to a form of official guidance is anybody's guess. As a finance ministry official once told one of the authors: 'Foreigners will never be able to understand our system, but the effort is appreciated.'

After the bubble economy

At the outset of this chapter, we called the Bank of Japan one of the most successful central banks. This judgement was based on Japan's superb long-term record of attaining price stability at least as convention- ally measured by the consumer price index. On the other hand, the 1980s 'bubble economy' witnessed wild stock-market and property speculation. If it is part of a central bank's job to forestall such excesses, the Bank of Japan fell down badly. And there is a strong case for arguing it has to be part of a central bank's task – just look what havoc the property and stock-market boom-and-bust wrought in Japan's bank- ing system. By 1993, it was estimated that the big Japanese banks had bad loans of $500 billion (50 trillion yen), which would make the losses about the same as those of American thrifts, but larger as a proportion of Japan's GNP. It would take the banks the rest of the decade to work these off their balance sheets.

However, central bank officials acknowledged in 1993 that they were still analysing what lessons to draw from the excesses of the bubble economy. The easy answer is that monetary policy was too lax, fuelling the inflation of property and stock prices. But the most acute officials, people like Masaki Shirakawa, director of the planning department, were not satisfied with such answers: they saw the real problem as being due more to the tendency for commercial banks to make more risky, high-margin investments and loans in an effort to keep their profits up when they were losing business to securities markets. Some felt there had been a lasting decline in the stability of banking systems, and that such boom-to-bust cycles would recur.

Another lesson was that definitions of price stability had to be refined. A new approach pioneered by the Bank of Japan, one which may be taken up by other central banks in future, was to construct a new index of prices of services – which, much more than prices in the goods sector, are determined by wage costs. Published on a quarterly basis since 1993, the services prices index came to be seen as a leading indicator of inflation. During the stock-market boom, it rose sharply – by about 6 per cent a year – even though the retail price index was up only modestly. Because of the amazing capacity of Japanese manufacturers to absorb wage increases, the retail price index had become a poor indicator of inflationary pressures.

Whatever the long-term lessons to be drawn, there is no doubt that the central bank was determined to avoid even a hint of a relapse into permissive monetary policies. This explained the much-criticized stance taken by 'strong man' governor Yasushi Mieno in sticking to a deflationary monetary policy, leading in 1992–93 to a rapid appreciation of the yen, increasingly tight credit conditions and deepening economic recession. In early 1993 there were even months in which the money supply was actually falling – a decline that Bank of Japan officials attributed to a stagnant economy but which many outside observers saw as anti-inflationary overkill. But, apart from a small discount rate cut (see below), Mieno stood his ground – giving the lie to the view that the central bank is merely a creature of the finance ministry. The underlying message was: if monetary policy was, as Mieno fervently believed, an art rather than a science, it should be entrusted to central bankers, not politicians.

Rescuing the banking system

The Bank of Japan plays a part in banking supervision along with the Ministry of Finance. Though the ministry is represented on the key Basle Committee on Banking Supervision (see Chapter 10), it was the Bank of Japan that spearheaded Japan's input to the 1993 requirements for banks active in the derivatives markets – the so-called new 'superbanks'. Like most central banks, it has an ambivalent attitude to bank supervision – recognizing the need for the central bank to be closely involved and well informed, but dreading the political brickbats that come the way of bank supervisors.

There is a parallel here with monetary policy. Because the central bank is the only organ of government in direct daily contact with the money markets, and with the major participants in those markets, deregulation brought it new power. In a situation where only the central bank knows what is technically feasible, and what instruments can be used to achieve a desired objective – whether in the field of monetary policy or banking supervision – governments have to defer. This is true for all central banks with free money markets, but particularly true of Japan, where the contrast between the old controlled system and the new liberalized system is particularly sharp.

So the long-term picture is clear: the Bank of Japan was being pushed to the front line. But could it survive the political heat? The first test came with the bad news of 1990–92. The massive bad debts accumulated as a result of the collapse of property values, coupled with the erosion of banks' capital in the wake of the share price collapse, constituted the most severe domestic challenge to the monetary authorities since the first oil shock twenty years before. The foreign and domestic press was full of stories about the collapse of Japan's banks. The authorities' constantly repeated reassurances that 'the basic health and soundness of the Japanese banking system' was 'not in doubt' carried little credibility beside reports of escalating losses on bad loans by all the big banks. Then came a succession of financial scandals which brought into disrepute some of the great names of Japanese banking.

The public looked for someone to blame. Had the Bank of Japan fallen down on its job? How could confidence be restored? By late 1992, with the Nikkei share index languishing at 15,000 (compared with its peak of 36,000), recession deepening and foreign criticism of Japanese policy rising to a crescendo under the new protectionist American President, Bill Clinton, the pressure on Mieno to relax policy was intense. He blinked. In February 1993 the discount rate was cut to 2.5 per cent, equalling the lowest ever level, and the ten-year government bond yield fell to 3.9 per cent, an historic low. The Bank of Japan stoutly denied that it cut the rate as a panic measure to rescue the banks – rather, the move was aimed to stimulate the real economy. But nobody denied that a useful side-effect was to ease the pressure on the banks by lowering the costs of bidding for deposits; the measure was comparable in its motives to the easing of Fed policy in 1991–92 (see Chapter 14).

The Bank of Japan was also involved in prolonged talks among the commercial banks on ways of relieving the burden of their bad and doubtful loans. Eventually the banks, led by Mitsubishi Bank, set up the Co-operative Credit Purchasing Company to provide a secondary market for bad loans. The banks sell their bad loans to the agency at a price assessed by an independent committee; if a particular loan was valued at, say, 60 yen in every 100 yen nominal value, and the bank sold the loan to the agency, then it can record a loss of 40 – and the bank can write off that loss on its books. The main benefit anticipated from this scheme is the tax savings to the selling bank. Though officially it is up to the tax authorities to decide the extent of the concession, banks expect that in such a case 40 yen would be tax-deductible from profits – this is the channel through which public funds will be injected into the banking system.

This experience seemed likely to lead to tighter supervision, and the authorities were expected to make a major effort to monitor the activities of banks and securities firms in the new 'derivative' markets. But this may not be enough. The underlying problem was how to exert greater discipline not only on bankers but on corporate managers and households.

The Bank of Japan needs to ensure not only that it monitors the banks under its care more carefully, but that they monitor the activities of their corporate clients. The biggest weapon at its disposal would be to leave open the possibility of a bank being allowed to fail.

There has been no bank failure in Japan since the Second World War. This has long been one of the proudest boasts of the Bank of Japan. But is it a hollow claim? Possibly. In the long term, a belief in banking immortality seems to engender corporate immorality. If your bank will always be bailed out, why not gamble with the bank's money – there is no market discipline on the bank, or on its customers, to refrain from gambling. So what held the system together for so long? Analysts had resort to psycho-sociological theories, attributing self-discipline to various features of Japanese culture, such as the senses of 'shame' and 'duty'. The bubble economy of the late 1980s signalled the breakdown of that culture. At least, the excesses suggested that such mechanisms were not strong enough to counter systematic incentives to corporate greed, folly and corruption.

How to protect the public purse from the cost of bailing out bad banks? Central bankers around the world who face this question are conscious of the need to protect government budgets from the huge potential costs involved in supporting banks in trouble. One way to limit costs is to let banks fail (see Chapter 21 for a further discussion). Even the Japanese authorities, probably the world's most conservative in this respect, started hinting in the early 1990s at the possibility of bank failures. As we have seen, other central banks started letting banks fail – and proclaiming that no bank could expect rescue.

How stable is the system?

Continued sources of weakness are the Japanese love of gambling, which could again drive stock prices to unimagined heights (what price the Nikkei at 100,000 by the year 2000?), the unpredictable results of investment banks entering commercial banking and vice versa, even if only through subsidiaries, political pressure to maintain the safety net of the Bank of Japan for each and every bank throughout the country, and the erosion of traditional restraints on companies, households and the bankers themselves. The ongoing Westernization of Japanese culture also breeds a gangster mentality which the authorities seem ill equipped to deal with (as in Britain, the traditional approach to supervision in Japan assumes trust and good faith on all sides).

Against these forces, the Japanese system has sources of stability missing in some other systems. Central to this is the key position – neglected by many foreign observers – of the Post Office Bank. This institution has offices in every town and village of the country, offers a wide variety of financial services, is close to the people (a woman whose husband dies will receive the life assurance proceeds in cash, delivered by a delegation, even before the funeral takes place) and enjoys total trust – in contrast to the reputation of commercial banks which, despite Japan's unblemished record, are not totally trusted. The Post Office Bank has 20 per cent of all personal bank deposits, is guaranteed by the state, and is a pillar of stability in a somewhat flawed financial system.

Other forces promoting stability have already been alluded to: the determination of the Bank of Japan to pursue consistent money policies, its interest in tightening supervisory standards, the shock of the 1990–92 stock-market crash in encouraging prudent behaviour, and the effects of the 1991–94 recession on corporate financial policies. Beneath it all is the continued dynamism of the real economy. On a long-term perspective, a period of financial exuberance and excess was perhaps natural at a time when the Japanese were newly aware of their awesome financial strength and facing up to the opportunity this afforded them for peaceful economic leadership unprecedented in world history.

Inside the bank

The headquarters of Japan's central bank are functional. The visitor is directed to a somewhat grim, boxlike structure in Nihonbashi and after a rigorous identity check, skirting the innumerable black limousines from which ushers in white gloves whisk top bankers into the central bank for confidential briefings, enters the reception area. There the first sight will probably be that of a uniformed messenger (either sex) trotting past with a look of total dedication to the job in hand. That's Japan for you.

The offices of governors and executive directors are comfortable but not lavish; these are, after all, public servants, though of a rather princely type. Though certainly more pleasant than the repellent 'rabbit-hutches' which the mighty Ministry of Finance officials occupy in Kasumigaseki, they are a far cry from the supremely spacious elegance of the presidential suites of some of Japan's big commercial and investment banks – the salon of the president of Fuji Bank down the road, for instance.

How does the institution function? How are top appointments decided? Though there are some similarities to both Federal Reserve and Bundesbank procedures, there are distinctive differences. For one thing, regionalization plays no apparent role in the structure, although quite senior central bank officials serve time in local branches. The formal picture is as follows. The supreme policymaking body under the Bank of Japan Law (amended 1949) is the Policy Board of seven members: the governor (five-year term, renewable, with voting rights), four other voting members (four-year terms), each with experience in either City banking, regional banking, commerce or industry or agriculture; and two representatives (without voting rights) from ministries – one from the Ministry of Finance and the other from the Economic Planning Agency. The governor normally serves as chairman. Policy Board members cannot be dismissed against their will.

The management and staff of the Bank of Japan implement policy in accordance with the general guidelines laid down by the Policy Board. The governor, senior deputy governor (five-year term), the deputy governor for international relations (four-year term) and executive directors (four-year term) constitute the membership of the executive committee, or *marutaku*, where the key decisions are made.

The governor and senior deputy governor are appointed by the cabinet. The deputy governor for international relations and the executive directors are appointed by the finance ministry from persons recommended by the governor.

Decisions by the Policy Board are based on members' opinions representing various sectors of the economy as well as the government and the Bank of Japan. The governor usually presents his proposals, as drafted by various departments of the central bank, then discussed and finalized at meetings of the executive committee. As a member of both key committees, he is a crucial link between the two bodies. Executive directors and senior officials also frequently report to the Policy Board, which normally meets twice a week. The *marutaku* meets every business day except Wednesday. In the central bank's money-market operations, the broad direction of policy is decided by the Policy Board, which also sets the interest-rate margins within which intervention is to take place; the detailed *modus operandi*, including the choice of instruments and the actual intervention rates, is delegated to the credit and market management department, which undertakes market operations.

Outsiders sometimes say that the Bank of Japan's governor does not dominate the policymaking board in the same way as his counterpart in

Washington tends to do. But they overlook the extent to which he will have already helped formulate proposals in the *marutaku* before they reach the Policy Board. Of course some governors are stronger than others, as is the case everywhere. Yasushi Mieno, who took over in late 1989 at the age of sixty-five, has been a particularly redoubtable fighter for his institution and has won more autonomy for it than any of his recent predecessors. But then, he has had no divided loyalty; his whole career has been in the Bank of Japan.

By contrast, Satashi Sumita, who preceded Mieno for a single term from late 1984, retiring at the age of seventy-three, reached the post of vice minister at the finance ministry in the early 1970s before running Japan's Export-Import Bank for six years and getting the deputy governorship at the central bank. He will be remembered best by the outside world for notable speeches in favour of internationalization of the yen. Before him was a Bank of Japan man, Haruo Maekawa – the tendency has been to alternate appointees from within and men with a finance ministry background.

As to relations with the government, again foreigners cannot hope to understand – but 'the effort is appreciated'. First, monetary policy: this is decided upon and implemented by the Bank of Japan but not 'in a vacuum' – it takes into account the government's overall macroeconomic policy. Second, the position in law: under Article 42 of the Bank of Japan Law, one of the legal responsibilities of the Ministry of Finance is to supervise the Bank of Japan, and Article 43 gives the ministry full power to 'order the bank to undertake any necessary business' (by 1994, the central bank was lobbying to have the law changed to give it more independence). Third, the central bank's shareholders; in a most unusual set-up for a central bank, the government holds 55 per cent of the shares and 45 per cent is held in the private sector. Fourth, central bank financing of the government; the Finance Law prohibits the Bank of Japan from underwriting government bonds or extending loans to the government; but the bank may underwrite short-term financing bills. The central bank may also underwrite on maturity the refinancing of government bonds that have been bought from the private sector – so-called red bonds that played such a large role in its operations from 1973 to 1988.

A heavy hitter of high finance

Central bankers are ambassadors for their countries' financial policies. In the Bank of Japan, a key figure here is the deputy governor for international relations; typically, this is not an official title, but one sometimes accorded to a senior executive director who can speak English and communicate with foreigners. The directors who have this title have become leading spokesmen for Japan in international diplomacy: such figures as Masaru Hayami, who masterminded the response to the first oil shock in 1972–74, later moving into the private sector as chairman of Nissho-Iwai, the huge *sogososha* or trading company; Shijuro Ogata, a key figure in the currency shuttle-diplomacy of the later 1970s and in the negotiations over the BIS capital adequacy guidelines, which were aimed partly at curbing the expansion of Japanese banks overseas; and Mikio Wakatsuki, who held the post for several years to 1993, at a time when Japanese banks were under attack for cutting their international lending despite a new surge in Japan's chronic current-account surplus. After Wakatsuki–san retired, the title was not given to another director, for none was yet considered of sufficient seniority.

These are the men who have had to deal with the international financial frictions that have been the inevitable counterpart to Japan's trading success. When Japan has been accused of rigging the market in currencies – engineering to push the yen down too far in the mid-1980s, for instance – these are the people who explain, conciliate and calm their counterparts abroad. And feed back foreign views to the staff of the Bank of Japan and the bureaucrats of Kasumigaseki (the offices of the finance ministry). As a consequence of their constant travelling, participation in countless high-level meetings and their ability to listen they are among the most well-informed group of people on international finance anywhere.

They have generally kept a low profile, but their influence is set to increase further along with Japan's voice and voting strength in the principal international institutions. The agenda for Japan in the 1990s in the Bretton Woods institutions is clear-cut: to gain more say in the policies of these institutions, in deciding which countries get support, the conditions attached to loans and credits, and how conditionality is worked out in practice. It could soon have a veto power over some aspects of the institutions' operations. It will push for more lending to Asian countries, possibly at the expense of Latin America.

At home, we expect that the bureaucrats will, after the turf-fights, accord a larger role for the Bank of Japan. As we have described in this chapter, 1980s deregulation changed the approach to monetary policy-making. In the future the breaking down of barriers between the hitherto fragmented structure of Japan's financial institutions will have an equally powerful impact on the regulatory and policymaking framework. Already the demarcation lines between city banks, regional banks, long-term credit banks, trust banks and especially between bank and securities firms are eroding. In these conditions the Bank of Japan will be a crucial intermediary between the commercial markets and the bureaucrats who really run Japan.

There is no hard and fast distinction between large and small central banks. But it is obvious to anyone who has attended, say, the annual meetings of the IMF and World Bank that such a distinction exists. If, when the governor of a central bank calls a press conference, the room is full of international journalists, then it is a 'large' central bank; if only a few people show, mostly from the local press, it is 'small'.

By this test the central banks we have focused on so far in this book are large – their actions and policies are of interest to a wide range of reporters and commentators. On this count, everybody agrees that the Federal Reserve is number one, followed by the Bundesbank and the Bank of Japan. The Bank of England still probably comes fourth, partly because the City of London is the world's largest international financial centre but also because of the history and continuing influence of the Bank of England in the international institutions. These include the BIS, headed by a former Bank of England man, Andrew Crockett, the IMF, where the personal assistant to the managing director is, by tradition, always a Bank of England official (Crockett himself was personal assistant to Johannes Witteveen when the latter was managing director of the Fund in the 1970s), and the World Bank. The Banque de France is a large central bank for many reasons – the unparalleled skills of French financial diplomacy, France's special position in international finance, its close links to Francophone countries in the third world and the size of the French economy. The Banca d'Italia also counts, as the most impor-tant institution in Italy, and as the provider of so many talented individuals who have played a role in international monetary affairs. Canada squeezes in with the big boys as its head of government participates in the annual economic summits. These are the 'big seven' at present. Let us call them the 'large' central banks. All the others are 'smaller'.

In terms of populations represented, however, there is no comparison. What the smaller central banks do is far more important to more people than what the big boys do. The seven 'big' central banks come from industrial countries with a total population of fewer than 700 million, a mere 12 per cent of the world's population. The 'smaller' central banks come from countries which together make up more than 80 per cent of the world's population. Moreover, there are forty-one 'rich' countries which do not have a seat at the top table. Any informed commentator would accord considerable importance to the views of governors of central banks of countries such as Saudi Arabia, Taiwan, Switzerland, New Zealand, Mexico, Denmark or Sweden. For one reason or another, the central bank of each of these countries has come to prominence at some time in the past twenty years.

It would be quite absurd therefore to focus this book exclusively on the central banks of the Group of Seven industrial countries; nor have we done so. We have already discussed central banking in developing countries (Chapter 6), monetary policy in China, the Solomon Islands and South Africa (Chapter 9), and supervision, reserve management and last resort lending in Chapters 10, 11 and 12 – much of it as applicable to smaller as to larger central banks. Later, in Chapter 19, we turn to the 'new' banks of the former Soviet Union. In this chapter we look more generally at the rapidly changing environment within which central banks other than those of the Group of Seven conduct their business, and the people who run them.

No leverage

Smaller countries have to accept that the big countries call the shots in international policymaking. They have little leverage on the outside world by financial, economic or political means. Their economies are generally too small to matter much in the general scheme, their interest-rate policies can be ignored by other countries, and they have only a minor influence in the international bodies where economic policies are discussed and hammered out.

On the other hand, for the people living in a country and the firms doing business there, the policy of their nation's central bank and monetary authorities matters more than that of other countries. Who cares a hoot for international policymaking, whatever that means (which is precious little)? For China, it is the People's Bank of China's policies that are important; for the Malaysians, those of Bank Negara; for Australians, those of the Reserve Bank of Australia. True, when a country pegs its currency to that of another, it has to follow the monetary policy of that other country; that is why much of this chapter inevitably is about the options for exchange-rate management – which option you choose determines the scope for your monetary policy. But that is a policy decision. Governments and central banks can strike out on their own, and increasing numbers have done so.

The key change came more than twenty years ago with the advent of flexible exchange rates. Ever since then, countries have had a choice of exchange-rate regimes – fixed or flexible. Any country with a central bank could have its own currency and, in principle, enjoy a degree of monetary independence. In Chapter 1, we noted that central banks of the big countries 'came in from the cold' during the 1980s as governments looked to them to deliver price stability. Fair enough; but the event that set the ball rolling occurred earlier – the end of Bretton Woods. And for all the smaller central banks, that was the more important change, for they could now become the guardians of their national currencies. They had slipped their anchors.

In central banking also, small can be beautiful. It means you do not generally have to pay much attention to the effect of your actions on the outside world. You are too small or too far away for what you do to worry anybody very much. By contrast, big countries are bound to be criticized, often bitterly, for what they do because it affects others, often in ways they do not like. A small central bank does not need to concern itself about that – though there can be exceptions. If a country suddenly finds itself with great financial power (Saudi Arabia, Taiwan) or large debts (Mexico, Brazil), it will draw the attention of big countries. A small central bank has to accept the world as it is – its small size means it cannot change its environment in the way a large country might seek to do. It cannot start laying down the law, or lecturing and bullying others. It has to adjust. This puts a premium on flexibility and speed of response to changing circumstances. This is where the central banks of East Asia and Southeast Asia have performed particularly well.

Juvenile currencies

Central banks issue currencies; that is, in the modern jargon, their core business. Recently it has been a hotly contested field. In the thirty-odd years to 1993, the number of smaller central banks rose from 66 to 160, adding nearly a hundred currencies to the world's total. By the 1990s, a multitude of juvenile currencies were jostling for their place in the sun, all seeking the elixir of acceptance, of being actually used by people and traders, not out of fear or force but voluntarily. These new currencies had entered a world of intense currency competition; for although governments may pass laws making a currency legal tender within a country's borders, what really counts, as every central banker knows, is the degree of acceptance a currency finds in the wide world outside, beyond the writ of the local government. The central banker sends his currency issue forth into the world, to sink or swim in the deep pools of world commerce, far from the shores of home.

In smaller countries, traders often use foreign currencies in their invoicing exports and settlement of imports more than do traders in a large economy like the United States. This means they get paid in foreign currencies for more of their exports and have to pay in foreign currencies for a higher proportion of imports than do traders in large countries. This in turn makes them more vulnerable to changes in the value of those currencies. Some smaller economies are still dependent on a narrow range of exports. So the government and central bank have to be particularly careful to retain international competitiveness for their exports. These influences constrain the actions of smaller central banks; they have no room to make mistakes.

Small size is not necessarily a handicap – small countries can grow as fast if not faster. But it is not necessarily a help either. The fastest-growing economy in the world in the ten years to 1993 was a giant – China roaring away at 10 per cent a year. It was followed by medium-sized economies, South Korea, Thailand and Taiwan. The city states, Hong Kong and Singapore, grew at only about 6 per cent annually, but from a much higher starting point in terms of their standards of living (by the 1990s these countries had reached about the same standard of living as Britain, but were growing twice as fast). Economists generally agree that growth rates are influenced more by a nation's policies than by its size or natural resources.

Exchange-rate options

Economists also agree that any country, large or small, can take control of its own monetary destiny. The big issue is how to ensure monetary stability. One way is to tell its central bank to control the supply of money and let its exchange rate find its own level on the markets, either by floating or some other flexible exchange-rate regime. The validity of this method has been proved in countries as diverse as New Zealand, Taiwan and Chile. The alternative is to fix the exchange rate to a stable currency; popular currencies for this role are the D-mark, yen and the dollar. If the central bank then mistakenly pumps up the money supply relative to that of its 'anchor currency' country, the fixed exchange rate will collapse, and with it the anti-inflationary strategy.

There is no hard and fast way of telling which system is better. It depends on the circumstances in the country and the openness of its economy. The biggest distinction, a matter which arouses passionate political debates, is that in the first case, where the central bank controls money supply, the country is, or at least appears to be, 'independent' of other countries' policies. In the second case, where the exchange rate is fixed, the country has in effect 'contracted out' its monetary policy to that of the anchor country; it simply plays 'follow-my–leader'.

To manage their exchange rates without appearing to be in thrall to another country, many smaller countries use an external benchmark such as a currency 'basket' or the SDR (special drawing right) rather than a particular national currency. This enables a central bank to keep the external value of its currency constant in terms of an average of the values of its main trading partners. However, one or other of the 'big three' international currencies usually bulks large in the composition of the 'basket' or average. For instance, the Nordic countries have experimented with such 'baskets' but the D-mark invariably has a large weight; in practice, their exchange-rate policy has often come down to 'tracking the D-mark'. For a small central bank, it is difficult to escape the pull of the large economies and their currencies.

The Asian compromise

As governments have relaxed exchange controls, freed interest rates and opened up their financial systems, international influences on their policies grow. Asian countries provide a striking example. Traditionally part of the dollar area, these countries held the bulk of their reserves in dollars and looked to the dollar as their reference currency when fixing or managing their exchange rates. So New York interest rates had a widespread influence throughout the region (except in communist countries such as China which totally sealed their borders). The chairman of the Federal Reserve was then more important than their local central bank governor – in fact, he was their central banker in most respects. This fitted in with the fact that America was their main market and it was not irrelevant that the United States was the dominant military power in the region also. The Pacific was America's ocean.

The dynamic growth of Japan made no difference to this arrangement for many years, partly because the Japanese did not want the yen to become an international currency and had pretty effective exchange controls of their own. 'Hands off the yen' was their motto. But after the coming of exchange-rate flexibility in the 1970s, things gradually began to change. Under the pressure of market forces, the needs of the Japanese economy for a better financial system, and American pressure to liberalize, a great change took place. Japan opened up. At the same time, the Japanese market was becoming more important to many countries than the American market; so they needed to hold balances in yen to pay for imports; and they increasingly left some of their proceeds of export sales to Japan in yen accounts. They had no qualms about this, despite the rather low yen interest rates, as the yen has been expected to appreciate against other currencies.

So the central banks of Asia have pulled two ways, the new interest in joining the yen area tugging against their traditional ties to the dollar. Does this mean they are becoming 'dominated' by Japan's monetary policy? Is the governor of the Bank of Japan their central banker now?

Although by 1993 no country pegged its currency to the yen, there were also no longer any countries in Asia, apart from Hong Kong, that pegged to the dollar. The Americans indeed discouraged these countries from fixing to the dollar, because that policy tended to make their exports more and more competitive in the American market, causing outcries among American producers. Most of the countries therefore managed their exchange rates using a 'basket' of currencies; though few made the composition of the basket public, in many cases the yen was believed to have a large role. Moreover, there was evidence that Japanese interest rates were having a pervasive and increasing influence on other countries of the region. One study by an American economist, Jeffrey Frankel, found that 'Tokyo appears to have recently acquired a dominant influence over interest rates in Singapore and Taiwan'. He added that the yen 'also has important and increasing effects on interest rates elsewhere in the Pacific, though its overall influence is as yet no greater than that of New York'.

The influence of the yen and thus of the Bank of Japan on other Asian central banks clearly increased further in the next few years. However, they did not wish to give up their ties to the dollar; the American capital market remained unrivalled both as a haven for surplus funds – no other market in the world could match it – and as a source of borrowing as required. The dollar remained in many ways uniquely well suited to play a key currency role. So these smaller central banks increasingly adopted various forms of flexible exchange rates, where the rate is managed with reference to a basket of currencies. In practice, this gave them a considerable degree of autonomy in monetary policy. Although countries like Taiwan, South Korea, Singapore, Thailand, the Philippines and Indonesia found the inconveniences of free floating too great to allow them the luxury of a fully independent monetary policy, they were not entirely dominated by any outside currency.

A case study from Europe

Countries that are 'small' in broad economic terms may align themselves with big currencies and central banks voluntarily – but only when it is in their interests to do so. In modern conditions this would happen not because the dominant country insists on it, but rather as a natural evolution.

Admittedly, such a relationship may carry political implications. For example, over time the relationship could be formalized, as was Britain's relationship with countries of the overseas sterling area after the Second World War. That amounted to a bargain whereby Britain offered access to its capital markets in return for these countries banking their reserves in London; exchange controls existed between the sterling area and non-sterling countries. Such currency arrangements can in turn harden into economic and trading blocs. But there is nothing inevitable about it. In the 1990s there was no sign that the countries that had linked themselves to the D-mark area had any intention of developing such economic and political links with the country of their 'anchor' currencies – although the formation of the European Monetary System could be viewed in that light. What is clear is that they had given up full independence of monetary policy. But the breakdown of the Exchange Rate Mechanism in 1993 proved that such a peg only lasts so long as it suits all parties.

A large industrial economy like that of Britain can also be small in some respects. The British debate on exchange-rate and monetary policy from 1985 to 1990 between Nigel Lawson, Chancellor of the Exchequer from 1983 to 1989, and Margaret Thatcher, then Prime Minister (both since ennobled), aroused much passion. Why? Because it was felt to be a debate about whether Britain was in this respect a big country or a small one, independent or dependent; about whether it had the political capacity to take its destiny in its hands, or whether it should hold on to the Bundesbank's coat-tails. The arguments used on both sides illustrate both the political and financial aspects of a problem facing many countries.

Lawson argued that British monetary policy was becoming 'difficult to conduct' and even more 'difficult' for the public and the markets to understand. At the time monetary policy was focused on the control of the money supply – the first of the two ways of controlling inflation. But with financial liberalization, different measures of money were giving different signals. Moreover, large fluctuations in the pound's exchange rate – against both the dollar and the D-mark – were upsetting the economy (in February 1985 the pound briefly touched a record low of $1.04, but bounced back to $1.90 in 1987). In his 1985 budget speech Lawson argued that 'significant movements in the exchange rate, whatever their cause, can have a short-term impact on the general price level and on inflation expectations'. Moreover, this process 'can acquire a momentum of its own' making sound domestic policies harder to implement: 'Benign neglect is not an option.'

In his subsequent memoirs, Lawson wrote:

> New arguments, I reminded her [Margaret Thatcher] were now being put forward in favour of the ERM. The financial markets were having difficulty understanding the government's position so far as the exchange rate was concerned, and the ERM would provide clearer rules of the game. Moreover, as there was now substantial support for ERM membership within the Conservative Party in the House of Commons, it would be helpful in future arguments about spending and borrowing if our backbenchers in effect faced a discipline of their own choice . . . It would help domestically, as £M3 was becoming increasingly suspect as a monetary indicator.

Discipline, credibility and the facts of life as seen from the Treasury were the key arguments. But the Prime Minister's instincts were against surrendering British monetary policy to German bankers: 'I could think of no particular reason to allow British monetary policy to be determined by the German Bundesbank rather than the British Treasury, unless we had no confidence in our own ability to control inflation.'

With the help of Sir Alan Walters, her personal economic adviser, Margaret Thatcher also spotted what, in her view, was a central weakness: membership of the ERM could make sterling even more vulnerable to speculative attack. It might become expensive to defend a fixed rate: 'I also doubted whether the public would welcome what might turn out to be the huge cost of defending sterling within the ERM.'

In the event, however, the pressure of events caused Britain to join, in 1990, and the reason Thatcher allowed this move is significant; it was to help get interest rates down. When she could see the tactical advantage from hitching the pound to the D-mark, using the Bundesbank's market credibility, she agreed to the move even against her instincts. Her misgivings were proved correct when Britain came out two years later, after having suffered the 'huge cost' she had feared (estimated at between £3 billion and £4 billion net).

This debate neatly sums up the benefits and costs of joining a club run by a dominant member, as viewed by the politicians directly involved in the decisions. A patriotic English Prime Minister who hadn't a good word to say about Germany nevertheless agreed to link the pound to the D-mark because the advantages seemed to outweigh the costs. Central bankers and policymakers the world over have faced similar dilemmas.

Smaller banks in Eastern Europe

Among the central banks whose room for manoeuvre has been closely circumscribed by the policies of other central banks and other governments are the former communist states of Central and Eastern Europe. When the civil war in Yugoslavia comes to an end, a further two or three countries can also be expected to join the list. There were functioning central banks in Croatia, Slovenia and Macedonia – all of which took steps to stabilize their currencies in 1993–94. Even during the war, a central bank continued to function in the capital of the Serb-led Yugoslavia, Belgrade, serving in effect as the central monetary institution for Serbia (a territory not recognized internationally as a sovereign state).

The efforts of the authorities in Belgrade to keep the dinar acceptable currency inside Serb-led Yugoslavia provide another illustration of the limits of monetary independence. The economy of Serbia and Montenegro – all that remained from former Yugoslavia – was in 1992–94 crippled by sanctions and inflation was reported at 1 million per cent in the single month of December 1993, making it one of history's few examples of true hyperinflation, usually defined as prices rising at more than 50 per cent a month. In autumn 1993 the government took fifteen zeros off the banknotes in a bid to keep the currency in circulation; then in January 1994 it introduced a new currency, the 'super dinar', claiming it would be 'fully convertible' and backed by DM500 million in hard currency and gold (the new dinar was worth 13 million old dinars). But there were reports that the new currency was not being accepted and that D-marks had become in effect the only acceptable notes and coin. This in turn would mean that the government would be unable to fund its deficit by printing money.

In Central and Eastern Europe, smaller central banks are being advised by the IMF and several Western central banks. The International Monetary Fund has advised Romania and Poland on the creation of independent central banks. In Poland the job security of the president is protected by statute. He or she can be removed only 'for personal misbehaviour', and the president in 1993, a capable lawyer and politician named Mrs Gronkiewicz-Waltz, claimed that the legal obligation to promote the stability of the currency gave her 'considerable independence': 'I have already survived two Prime Ministers and three governments,' she said. When they ask for central bank assistance, if she thinks it will be inflationary, 'I simply tell them, I cannot break the law.'

In practice, several countries have pegged their exchange rates to the D-mark or given it a large weight in their exchange-rate policies. So they have given up domestic policy independence. They considered it more important to have a credible 'anchor', to help them achieve and maintain reasonable price stability than to use their room to follow an independent policy. So it was a sign of maturity that they were willing to accept the D-mark link – and interesting that Germany helped them with credits and advice, a marked contrast to previous Bundesbank resistance to the D-mark becoming a reserve currency.

Yes, Mr Governor

All governors are equal. That is one of the unwritten rules of the central bankers' code. And rightly so – for reasons we have stated, in each sovereign state, the fate of the currency is in the hands of the central bank or government of that country, not of the United States or Germany. That is why it makes little sense to talk of a world inflation rate – the rate of increase in prices varies from one country to another depending on its monetary policy. Increasingly, that policy is identified with the governor of the central bank. He or she has to formulate, explain, defend and implement it.

Not surprisingly, there is growing interest in how these top central bankers should be trained and appointed, and how much job security they should enjoy. Most central bank governors are not career central bankers but rather public figures from politics, private banking or the universities/research institutes. As we pointed out in Chapter 1, governors of the larger central banks also have until recently rarely been career central bankers. But this appears to be changing – the recent crop of top appointments in Europe were virtually all career central bankers and the smaller central banks seem to be following suit. Central banking is becoming a profession where you can reach the top – if you have political skills as well.

In developing countries, the appointments are usually made by the President or monarch of the country, sometimes by the head of government or Minister of Finance. However, as more countries change the statutes of their central bank, the method of appointing people to the top job is also being changed. In Chile, for example, the appointment has to be confirmed by the senate; in Venezuela, by a two-thirds majority in the senate; in Malaysia and Thailand, the governor is appointed by the monarch on the recommendation of the government. In Nordic countries central banks are answerable to parliament; in Sweden the governor is appointed by the Board members, who in turn are appointed by parliament. But being creatures of parliament is no guarantee of independence; most of the central banks of the former Soviet Union are creatures of parliament without having any independence.

The most frequent term of office is five years, with very few appointed for less than three years or for more than six years. Quite a few are appointed for indefinite terms, though sometimes that means they can be sacked easily (as in Brazil, where few governors serve more than one year), and sometimes it means that they have a high degree of job security, as in the case of Denmark, where Erik Hoffmeyer was governor from 1965 to 1994, a record of central banking longevity surpassed only by his colleague Johannes Nordal of Iceland, governor from the foundation of the central bank in 1961 to his retirement in 1993.

A crowded agenda

In truth, statutory rules and formal provisions tell one little about the real position of the governor of a central bank, though they can express a government's desire to be seen to be granting autonomy to its central bank – at least for a time. The more powerful forces operating on smaller central banks everywhere were those coming from the international money and capital markets, and from growing currency competition.

Most of these countries were borrowers – actual or potential. Like finance directors of publicly quoted companies, their central bank governors had to be able to tell a good story to international investors, to woo the big institutions, to put on a good show. Thus when Lebanon came back to the Eurobond markets with a $300 million issue in 1994, the governor of the central bank led the delegation to London to drum up support. He had to put forward a compelling argument, of the growing chances of a peace treaty with Syria, the opportunities for investors to help make Beirut once again a leading international financial centre of the Mediterranean. Governor Riad Salame (appointed for six years by the Council of Ministers) knew he was in competition with other sovereign borrowers with much higher credit ratings, so he would have to concede a larger margin over the US Treasury bill rate to get his loan. To impress institutions he had to show that the central bank knew what was going on and had a grip on the economy and banking system.

Lebanon is a special case. But central bankers are equally important in helping to preserve market access for countries in less dramatic circumstances – countries such as Algeria, Colombia, Hungary, India, Indonesia, Korea, Pakistan, Thailand, Turkey and Malaya. Some of the countries had maintained access to the capital markets through the debt crisis, but several had faced difficulties and had to make considerable efforts to avoid rescheduling. Their central bankers had to be on hand to explain what was happening, to polish the personal contacts that count for so much in the markets and negotiate acceptable programmes with the IMF and World Bank where needed.

Some smaller central banks were by the early 1990s so successful that they faced the opposite problem – coping with an incoming surge of capital in search of high returns in 'emerging markets'. They had to decide whether the inflow was sustainable, or whether it would again bring short-term pleasure at the cost of long-term pain. Some, like Chile, faced what the World Bank described as an 'avalanche' of foreign funds. Could they rely on the reflux of flight capital staying at home? Or on improved risk assessment making for a longer-term commitment by foreign investors? More especially, could they rely on consistency of policy by their own government? To many observers, the 1990s showed all the signs of another unsustainable boom in private investment in developing countries. But on this occasion the signs were that the losers would be the investors rather than the developing countries. The good central banks were advising their governments how to keep the risk firmly on the shoulders of the foreign investor – and how to prevent the inflow disrupting domestic monetary conditions. Quite an agenda.

The curved glass doors shut behind you. Those ahead stay closed. You are encapsulated. Are 'they' rechecking your credentials? Do 'they' suspect you of really coming from a finance ministry, sneaking in under guise? Though it may be seconds rather than minutes before the security guard relents, you step into the foyer of the central bankers' bank with relief bordering on gratitude.

This mode of entering – and leaving – the Bank for International Settlements in Basle lacks the old-fashioned courtliness offered by some of its owners – by the functionaries at the Bank of Italy in Rome's via Nazionale or the pink-coated ushers at the Bank of England in Threadneedle Street. Instead, it is non-fussy, efficient and labour-saving – the image of itself which the BIS now actively encourages.

The doyen of multilateral institutions also became less self-effacing when it commissioned the building that has been its home since 1977. Nearly seventy metres high (twelve metres less than originally planned after the locals protested), the cylindrical tower block dominates the landscape. Nobody coming to Basle can miss it, whereas probably few even of its citizens noticed the bank's discreet sign on its previous office near the Bahnhofplatz, squeezed between a pastry shop and a jeweller. Inside, the décor has gone upmarket, distinctly less spartan. But it is not designed to awe. The office of a recent chief executive (or general manager in BIS-speak) was even enlivened by blown-up colour photographs of his handsome family, which took up an entire wall. There is flesh and blood behind the austere exterior.

Yet the mystique about the BIS will not go away as long as top central bankers huddle there every month (or, more precisely, ten times a year), choosing a provincial Swiss town far from the political pressures of any national capital, and saying as little as possible about what they are up to. They meet behind doors closed not only, as goes without saying, to prying journalists, but to anyone not of their fraternity.

In 1966, when the institution had been running for thirty-six years, the financial journalist Fred Hirsch wrote that 'a Treasury official has yet to set foot in the BIS'. The very next year, one did. Unwanted, unwelcome, the American Treasury Undersecretary, Fred Deming, attended the meeting of the so-called 'gold pool', much to the undisguised resentment of the European governors who were members of it. Today a few Treasury or finance ministry officials do go through those glass doors – legitimately – perhaps to attend a special committee on banking supervision, when this is their ministry's responsibility in their country. But it is still true that none of their ilk is ever invited to the main Basle meetings. No wonder that a British Treasury mandarin who never got his nose inside described the BIS as 'a Holy-Roman-Empire kind of place for central bankers to meet'.

The BIS, though, is not just a central bankers' club. It is a bank, taking deposits and doing some lending, but with customers restricted to central banks and international institutions. It has a sizeable research department and harbours committees monitoring various monetary issues. It also has a large databank that feeds central banks and provides, in particular, a snapshot of the Euromarkets. Yet, despite an impressive worklist, there is no doubt that it is as a talking shop that the BIS is most valued.

Peculiar origins

In a private conversation, so we cannot name him, a leading American central banker pronounced: 'The BIS as an institution is nothing; it is a focus for central bankers to meet.' It was not intended as a derogatory remark; he wanted no change, would not have it otherwise. European central bankers have in the past got most from the institution itself but even they, while rating the BIS highly, invariably add 'within its limits'. The qualification is a reminder that, despite radical changes in structure and functions, the BIS remains true to its peculiar origins in many ways.

Peculiar? Yes, because although German reparation problems provided the rationale for establishing a new institution and that was what it was supposed to be about, its founders had something they thought much more exciting in their sights. Since central banks were to play a key role in carrying out the reparation agreement, it was not unnatural that it should be their creature, that they should put up the capital – though governments had to be persuaded. Having won that victory, the more visionary central bankers like Montagu Norman looked beyond the immediate task. Article 3 of the BIS statutes, unchanged to this day, reads:

The objects of the bank are: to promote the cooperation of central banks and to provide additional facilities for international financial operations; and to act as trustee or agent in regard to international financial settlements entrusted to it under agreements with the parties concerned.

Norman's dream had come true. An organization had been created whose role, above all, was to serve as a focal point for cooperation among central banks. No matter, then, that reparation payments were suspended from 1 July 1931, little more than a year after the BIS opened its doors opposite Basle's railway station on 17 May 1930. True, the widespread abandonment of the gold-exchange standard, the preservation of which had been one of the founding members' aims, was a severe blow. But at least the goal of 'cooperation' could still be pursued.

Or so central bankers naïvely believed. In practice, there was little to show for their efforts in the 1930s. The BIS did inaugurate the fire-drill which it was to employ extensively some thirty years later. In response to cries for help, and using some of its own limited resources, it combined with a number of its member central banks to make short-term advances to central banks in countries worst hit by flight capital after the 1931 crisis – Austria, Germany, Hungary, Poland and Yugoslavia. But only on a very modest, hopelessly inadequate, scale. There was no concept of the full extent of the economic crisis.

Chivvied by Norman, central bankers continued to assemble in Basle, exchange opinions, blame the politicians and go home. In its 1932 annual report, the BIS lectured that exchange control 'forces trade into a kind of straitjacket'. Nobody listened. As to its banking business, that languished as foreign-currency deposits were switched into gold or withdrawn altogether as the crisis deepened. The BIS looked back on a sorry first decade. And the Second World War, of course, did nothing for it; it more or less closed shop.

Notice to close

So it could not have come as a bolt from the blue that when the International Monetary Fund was conceived at Bretton Woods in 1944, at a conference dominated by delegates from finance ministries, an American-inspired decision was taken to demolish the BIS. The long-serving American Treasury Secretary, Henry Morgenthau, a Jew of German antecedents, disliked his country having a part – even the dormant one it was at the time – in an essentially European institution that Germany had helped to create. Moreover, Americans felt that the BIS had been pro-German in its operations. Hardly surprising, then, that Harry Dexter White, the chief American negotiator at Bretton Woods, saw no major role for it once the IMF was established.

In the event, the decision to axe was never carried out. Ironically, it was an American initiative that came to the rescue. The war over, European central bankers started meeting again in Basle from the end of 1946, hoping against hope for a stay of execution. Quite unexpectedly, the BIS got a break; Marshall aid to Europe gave it a vital job. It was soon apparent that restoration of currency convertibility in Europe would take longer than expected and that, to get the full benefits from Marshall aid, some multilateral clearing arrangements for payments would be essential to open up regional trade, then restricted by quotas and bilateral pacts. The BIS acted as that clearing agent in 1948–50 for the first intra-European payments agreements. It had made itself visibly useful.

By 1950 its dissolution was a dead issue, as the American Treasury formally admitted. But the Americans saw no use for the institution themselves. The Federal Reserve had never picked up the BIS shares initially allotted to it – and still hasn't, as discussed later in this chapter. The Bank of Japan had been thrown out at the end of the war. So it was as a European body that the BIS went on, until 1958, to manage the European Payments Union, judged one of the most successful initiatives in postwar monetary history. From that success it was a natural evolution for it to perform functions for the European Community even though (perhaps because) it isn't located in a member country. But before it expanded its European connections, the financial world had changed again. The Fed had come to Basle and the BIS was on the world stage.

Nannying the dollar . . .

When European countries began to make their currencies convertible in 1958, the Bretton Woods exchange-rate standard had its first chance to show its mettle. By the autumn of 1960, seemingly to everyone's surprise, it was exposing its main weakness – its vulnerability to the open-ended commitment of the United States, as banker for the system, to convert dollars into gold at $35 an ounce. Of America's payments deficits in the three years 1958–60, totalling $11.2 billion, over 40 per cent had to be financed by selling gold to foreign central banks.

Suspicions that the young Jack Kennedy, virtually unknown in financial circles, might renege on the commitment if he got to the White House fanned a flare-up in the gold price in the private market to $40 in October 1960. European central bankers meeting in Basle were worried men. They felt that Federal Reserve participation in their monthly meetings had now become essential. With the blessing of the Fed chairman, then William McChesney (Bill) Martin, and the American Treasury, Charlie Coombs, not long in charge of the New York Fed's foreign exchange department, attended the December 1960 meeting of the BIS. The Americans had come on board.

In his memoirs, written immediately after his retirement fifteen years and many, many trips to Basle later, Coombs is unstinting in his praise of BIS weekends. They were, he wrote, 'what the French would call *sérieux*'. A touch of guilt that he enjoyed them so much? At his first appearance, he was charmed by being invited to the governors' dinner – 'a great privilege' – and 'impressed by the sheer competence and personal distinction of the men who had reached the top of their profession'. Among them were Karl Blessing of the Bundesbank, Marius Holtrop of the Netherlands Bank, Lord Cobbold of the Bank of England, Guido Carli of the Bank of Italy, Baron Ansiaux of the Belgian National Bank and Per Asbrink of Sweden's Riksbank, all names to conjure with in their own country at the time. Apart from Cobbold, they were to stay in office throughout most, if not all, of the crisis-prone 1960s.

The gold market was calmed when Kennedy, on taking office, made his famous personal pledge to maintain the $35 gold price, in an address to Congress on 6 February 1961 – even if it meant the United States having to borrow from the International Monetary Fund. The respite lasted no more than a few weeks however. After the 5 per cent upvaluation of the German mark on 4 March, speculators began to gamble not only on a devaluation of sterling but also on an upvaluation of the Swiss franc, bringing another threat to America's gold stock if the Swiss followed their usual practice of converting any surplus dollars. At the next Basle meeting, however, the Swiss did the decent thing and offered Britain a three-month credit of $310 million, which was soon enlarged to $900 million by contributions from six other European central banks. 'At one stroke,' Coombs recalled, 'European central bank cooperation had not only saved sterling but also had protected the dollar against heavy gold drains.'

A quick response to an emergency and comforting reassurance to Bretton Woods disciples. But central banks were left in no doubt that new defences for the dollar must be built. One way they did so, involving the BIS, allowed the United States to depart from its usual passive practice and intervene in the foreign-exchange markets to steady the dollar.

To that end, the New York Federal Reserve initiated a formal network of 'swap lines' – standby arrangements with other leading central banks so as to provide it with foreign currencies for intervention. In the first swap on 1 March 1962, it arranged to pay $50 million into the Bank of France's account in New York against payment of the equivalent amount in French francs by the Bank of France into the New York Fed's account in Paris. As Coombs was to point out, those two central banks had produced out of the air an extra $100 million of international reserves. But as the transaction was reversible at the same rate of exchange in three months – unless renewed – the money then disappeared.

Dubbed 'monetary incest' by a British journalist, this cross-crediting caught on as a means for defending not only the dollar but other currencies too. The New York Fed built up a network of bilateral credit lines with other central banks, which either party could activate, and also with the BIS. The swaps survived the breakdown of the Bretton Woods system. Today, the New York Fed has facilities totalling $30.1 billion with fourteen central banks and the BIS. The largest is for $6 billion with the Bundesbank, followed by $5 billion with the Bank of Japan and $4 billion with the Swiss National Bank, while with the BIS Swiss francs can be obtained against dollars up to $600 million and against other authorized European currencies up to $1.25 billion.

A second defence effort of the 1960s has long been forgotten. Meeting in Basle in November 1961, the central banks of Belgium, Britain, France, Germany, Italy, the Netherlands, Switzerland and the United States formed a gold pool or syndicate to help stabilize the price in the London gold market within tiny limits around the $35 parity. Hush-hush (though soon leaked to the press), no written rules, just a gentlemen's agreement to have a pool of $270 million worth of gold available for open-market operations by the Bank of England. The BIS's job, apart from attending gold pool meetings, which took place alongside the regular monthly ones in Basle, was to provide all the statistics it could lay its hands on about gold demand and supply.

The pool worked well for a few years, but was breaking down by the summer of 1967 against the background of a Middle East war and sterling speculation. When the Bank of France withdrew from it in July 1967, the Federal Reserve took up its share and the American Treasury had the cheek to send someone to a Basle meeting, as we noted earlier, just after sterling's devaluation in November that year really rocked the boat. A meeting of pool members in March 1968 at the Federal Reserve in Washington, called by Bill Martin, was its last. The London gold price was left to find its own level. And the BIS lost a job.

. . . and sterling too

But its role in the sterling saga went on. And because it colours BIS attitudes today, we are backtracking to where we left that story, in the spring of 1961. The Basle credits offered then so quickly to the Bank of England were regarded as a major breakthrough in postwar international finance. But they were only short term. Eating humble pie, the British turned to the IMF, obtained a $2 billion standby credit from it in August that year and immediately drew three-quarters of it in order to pay back the Basle debts and to boost their dwindling reserves with what was left over. It was the kind of money juggling at which Britain became adroit over the following fifteen years.

The reluctance to admit that sterling was overvalued, that it was far too vulnerable to serve as a world reserve asset second only to the dollar, may now seem amazing. Britain not only had a weak trading account in the 1960s but had to live with a constant fear that sterling-area countries, which banked in London, would encash their sterling balances, demanding dollars or whatever whenever the pound looked threatened. But the Bank of England was certainly not being advised by fellow central banks to face up to the inevitable. 'Success' to them in the sterling drama was withstanding the attacks. No fewer than eleven credit arrangements were made in Basle in the 1960s to 'beat the speculators' over sterling and a further two in 1976–77. The sums involved on each occasion ranged from $250 million to over $5 billion.

In the heyday of currency rescues, it was thought important to impress the markets with the solidarity of central banks when the talking stopped and the money was rounded up in last-minute scrambles, often in less than twenty-four hours. Most of the Group of Ten central banks were contributors to each package, quite frequently also the Austrian National Bank. Occasionally, there would be a drop-out. The November 1964 rescue nearly went ahead without the Bank of France, as President de Gaulle became louder in his criticism of sterling's role as a reserve currency. And the next one actually did. When the Bank of England called for $925 million of new short-term credits in September 1965, the French central bank passed.

However, if the Basle creditors' club lost one member for a while, it had by then gained an important new one. The BIS committed $250 million in its own name to the November 1964 support for Britain, more than any individual central bank other than the New York Fed and the Bundesbank. It has joined most Basle rescues ever since. In particular, it spearheaded the so-called Basle Group Arrangements of

1966 and 1968, which were something new. They were longer-term credits and, for the first time, central banks attached conditions to their loans.

Those new arrangements were the outcrop of teamwork master-minded by the BIS's chief economist at the time. He was a small, energetic American, with a sarcastic wit, who, after working at the forerunner of the OECD in Paris, came to the BIS in 1960 and stayed in the post of economic adviser, as it is officially called, for fourteen years. A gold bug if ever there was one, Milton Gilbert thought the dollar could be rescued from its misery just by raising the monetary price of gold. Events did not turn out as he would have wished. Not soft spoken, he badmouthed the negotiations in the mid-1960s to create a new international reserve asset, the SDR (special drawing right). 'I'll believe in SDRs,' he said, 'when my wife asks me for an SDR bracelet.' But Gilbert was such a relentless and astute researcher that he was elected to chair a group of central bank officials charged in late-1965 with solving the problem of the sterling balances. It included Charlie Coombs from the New York Fed, Otmar Emminger from the Bundes-bank, Rinaldo Ossola from the Bank of Italy and Bernard Clappier from the Bank of France – a distinguished bunch.

Gilbert's small team didn't take long to conclude that if exchange markets knew assistance was at hand to protect Britain's reserves from fluctuations in overseas holdings of sterling balances, 'there is a good chance that not much of it would have to be used'. But it took six months and much quibbling at successive BIS meetings before agree-ment was finalized in June 1966 to provide Britain with a conditional $1 billion credit package – the amount the Gilbert report had sug-gested. Under the collaborative arrangement, Britain was offered credit facilities by nine central banks and also – a particularly impressive commitment – the BIS itself contributed $75 million of its own funds. The money was originally available for nine months, but the arrange-ment was renewed for a year in March 1967 and likewise again in March 1968. In a typical compromise to ensure life was not made too easy for it, the Bank of England's use of the new credit was limited to no more than 50 per cent of reserve losses attributable to conversion of sterling balances.

The 1966 Basle deal marked a turning point in central bank cooper-ation. It had become visibly politicized. Though there was considerable sympathy, except in France, for Britain's problems arising from the heavy sterling liabilities it had incurred, largely as a result of its borrow-ing during the Second World War, this was a highly sensitive issue. Which is why it took so long to stitch up the deal. The French central bank governor made it clear his institution could not participate in any shoring-up of sterling's prestige, though it did in the end offer $90 million of credit unilaterally on its own terms. The Americans, too, had to find a roundabout way of contributing.

Still, the die had been cast. Strings were tied even tighter around the second Basle group arrangement, worth $2 billion, in September 1968, which was renewed at intervals until September 1973. The Bank of England was forced to offer sterling-area countries dollar guarantees on 90 per cent of their official sterling holdings in return for undertakings to limit their conversions.

To the extent it was intended to shore up the sterling area, all this was in vain, of course, as many observers foresaw at the time. A final Basle arrangement was concluded in 1977 to help wind down the sterling balances and let sterling fade away as a reserve currency, which is what France wanted – and was in Britain's interest too.

There is always banking

By then the BIS had established itself as a lead coordinator in times of crisis and central banks have ever since been reluctant to do anything collectively unless it holds their hands. But in a floating-currency world and with capital markets now able to mobilize huge amounts of private money at the drop of a hat, the BIS's role as a shock-absorber on a multilateral basis has all but gone (although, with no publicity it does provide short-term credit bilaterally to central banks in an emergency). True, it could be asked to lend to the IMF again, as it did in 1981–84. True, too, it may still provide bridging finance to third-world countries, usually linked to subsequent IMF programmes. But whereas that was an important role during the Latin American debt crisis (see Chapter 7), the BIS set up only one such multilateral operation in each of the financial years 1991/92 and 1992/93 to tide things over for the National Bank of Romania until it got a loan from the European Community.

In contrast, BIS services for the European Community grew apace over some thirty years. It 'hosted' a permanent secretariat in Basle for the Committee of EC Central Bank Governors which had access to the bank's information and data systems. It acted as agent for the European Monetary Cooperation Fund, which was set up when the currency 'snake' was created in 1973 and then had much larger responsibilities under the more sophisticated European Monetary System. It carried out various transactions connected with running the EMS and kept all the Fund's complicated accounts, which reflect, among other things, the swaps whereby EC central banks deposited 20 per cent of their gold and dollar reserves with the Fund in exchange for European currency units (Ecus). And, since October 1986, the BIS has also taken on the agency job for the private Ecu clearing and settlement system, in which nearly fifty banks take part.

Now, however, the European Monetary Institute has been set up in Frankfurt and the BIS has lost many, if not all, of these Community-related jobs and the fees from them. It can no longer boast of being the meeting-place for EC central bank governors, and their secretariat has departed. If the Maastricht Treaty on economic and monetary union runs its course, the BIS will lose some of its banking customers too. With a single European currency, EC central banks would no longer need to keep short-term money at the ready to prop up their individual currencies. Just how much of its bread-and-butter it stands to lose on this score, however, is a closely held secret.

Some eighty to eighty-five central banks from around the world have currency deposits with the BIS these days. From a tiny amount handled at the end of the last war, the sum rose to about $40 billion by the mid-1980s and further to just over $100 billion at the time of writing. With even the newer central banks getting cleverer at managing their money themselves and in very competitive markets, the BIS has done well in recent years to attract a fairly steady proportion, around 10 per cent, of a growing volume of world currency reserves.

It does so by paying its depositors a little more than they would get from American Treasury bills. But it can get away with giving them a little less than a commercial bank would because it offers more liquidity, is very strongly capitalized and guarantees a total blanket of secrecy on whose funds it holds. Needless to say, it is conservative in how it employs the money – remember it is acting not as a fund manager but as a principal; the deposit represents a claim on the BIS. Working on no more than a three-month horizon, most of the money goes into the interbank market, the BIS taking neither maturity nor foreign-exchange risk and spreading its custom by dealing with about 200 banks, or into short-term negotiable paper such as Treasury bills. More recently, however, the BIS has also developed special investment instruments to give central banks extra liquidity, including the 'FIXBIS', its own brand of certificate of deposit.

In managing its own funds, some $4 billion, a little more daringly, the BIS experiments with a few fund managers to get a yardstick for its own performance. It also holds gold both on its own account and for central banks under various arrangements. The BIS also intervenes in the foreign-exchange markets either on behalf of central banks which don't want to reveal their hand or on its own account. And it offers central banks assistance in managing their reserves, providing tailor-made portfolio management schemes.

For all that it prides itself on its professionalism, having an eye to the bottom line and keeping up with technology in its dealing rooms, the BIS manages to infuse mystique even into its banking business, on which it depends for most of its income. Its accounts are expressed in Swiss gold francs, an esoteric unit representing just over 0.29 grammes of fine gold. When the bank was set up, its paper gold was equivalent to Swiss francs, which was dandy. No longer. True, a unit now roughly equals two dollars, so an approximate conversion is easy. But it is a tiresome idiosyncrasy.

A voteless power

Another peculiarity about the institution is that America's central bank has continued its oddball status in it while increasingly influencing decisions made in Basle. Patience is needed to understand how and why. The covenant setting up the BIS was signed by the governments of Germany, Belgium, Britain, France, Italy and Japan on the one hand and the Swiss Confederation on the other, the latter granting the new institution exemption from Swiss taxation. Not being a signatory to the Treaty of Versailles, the United States deemed it inappropriate to participate – that, anyway, was the formal e cuse. The founder members subscribing the capital were the central b nks of those five European countries (neutral Switzerland was not inv lved), Japan and an American banking group – J. P. Morgan, National Bank of New York (now Citibank) and First National Bank of Chicago – acting in the absence of the Federal Reserve.

The three American banks were not – and are not – the only private shareholders in the bank. The Belgians and French central banks exercised the right to arrange for public subscriptions to their share allocations, though for only half the amounts. Today, some 16 per cent of the issued share capital is in the hands of private shareholders. They get their whack of profits but no right to attend the annual meetings and their voting power is transferred to their country's central bank. So the BIS is quick to point out that individuals cannot influence the conduct of its affairs in any way.

As with most rules, however, there are exceptions. If a central bank is not in a position to exercise its voting rights (however that may be interpreted), BIS directors may appoint another institution from the same country to do so. And, in America's case, a commercial bank, Citibank, is so empowered.

Since the Federal Reserve has never exercised its privilege, as a founder member, to sit on the board of directors, this is now exclusively European, Japan having been forced out after the Second World War – though long back in the fold as an ordinary member. The central bank governors of Belgium, Britain, France, Germany and Italy are *ex officio* board members and each appoints another member of his nationality, not necessarily, but almost invariably, a colleague or his retired predecessor. The rules allow nine more governors but, for most of the bank's history, only three – from the Netherlands, Sweden and Switzerland – have served. So there is a thirteen-member board today representing eight European central banks.

Though much wider, membership of the bank – confined to central banks with voting power at the Annual General Meetings – is still predominantly European. Many are in the club through the initial public subscriptions. Five more became members in 1950 when the BIS called in shares originally taken up by the founder central banks over and above their quotas, and reissued them to the central banks of Iceland, Ireland, Portugal, Spain and Turkey.

Then the chance to bring in some non-Europeans arose when the bank's authorized capital was trebled in 1969. Existing shareholders holding 200,000 shares between them were offered the same again on a one-for-one basis, but took up little more than a third, only 73,125. The other 200,000 were reserved for additional central banks 'deemed to make a substantial contribution to international monetary cooperation and to the bank's activities'. The central banks of Australia, Canada, Japan and South Africa were judged subsequently to fit the bill and took up the special tranche of shares between them.

So, counting in the Federal Reserve, just five of today's thirty-three members are non-Europeans. But in voting strength they are nearly a match for the Europeans. The latter include ten 'central banks' (their nearest equivalent) from Eastern Europe (excluding the former Soviet Union), an oddity that, until the demise of communism, added another flavour of mystery to the BIS in public eyes, once its origin as a reparations bank had been forgotten. Apart from the Bank of Hungary, however, the East Europeans have been regular attenders at Basle meetings only in the past few years as ties with the West have strengthened.

Why is the Federal Reserve content with observer status? Two reasons. First, it avoids the sort of political interference that Congress likes to exercise over American voting in other multilateral institutions such as the IMF and World Bank. Second, very shortly after the Fed came to have any interest in the BIS in the early 1960s, the regular monthly meetings ceased to be centred around the discussions of board members and switched to those of the governors – and their officials – of the Group of Ten countries. And in that group, niceties of BIS membership are totally irrelevant; the Bank of Canada and the Bank of Japan have been active in the Group of Ten from its start but did not even join – or rejoin – the BIS until 1970. While the Group of Ten (actually twelve nowadays) has been upstaged by 'the Seven' on the world economic stage, it remains the conclave for central bankers on their own patch.

The BIS's board meetings, held every second Tuesday morning of the month other than July and August, are likely to last fifteen minutes, thirty at most; the general manager reports on the institution's banking business and that is usually all there is to it. It is what has gone before this meeting and what is to follow that counts. A Basle monthly gathering is not the cosy affair some may imagine. True, it starts with informal dinners on Sunday evening for smallish groups (the governors meet on their own), which are looked upon as especially valuable. But Monday, which sees the meeting of the Group of Ten governors, finishes with a formal dinner attended by perhaps a hundred people, giving governors and officials of member central banks outside the charmed inner circles a chance to feel important – the seating plan is arranged diplomatically. Tuesday – after the board meeting – used to see the gathering of EC governors but with that no longer on the schedule, there is more opportunity for countless informal one-to-one meetings on the sidelines, before everyone departs on Tuesday afternoon. Nothing may have been decided, but for opinion-swapping in a diversity of forums, for determining what will fly and what will not, the arrangements are wonderfully convenient and economical of time. But much less so for the Europeans than they used to be; five of the Group of Ten and six of the board members are European Union members who now have to hold their own meetings in Frankfurt.

The BIS plays down the consequences of losing about 10 per cent of its activity when its European limb was amputated. This will push the institution, it says, into becoming more global – and, anyway, it is already playing a greater part in Group of Seven and Group of Ten affairs. What it refused to contemplate was that the Basle monthly gatherings could become less attractive and influential now that European bankers conduct their joint efforts elsewhere. But there was no denying that the Basle game of musical chairs had been much diminished.

The romance is over

Over sixty years old, the BIS has made its name in fire-brigade operations. Keeping a good public image could be more difficult in future. As central banking gets increasingly technical, as the prudential security of international banking becomes more complex than ever before, new problems are being thrown up all the time, few of which are readily solvable. A mixture of central bankers' interests and its own initiatives has been driving the BIS deeper into technical research. It harbours important longstanding committees set up by the Group of Ten governors, such as that of the Basle supervisors (see Chapter 10) and a Eurocurrency one that tracks international banking and capital-market developments, meeting about four times a year under the general manager's chairmanship. Among newer committees operating in 1993, one was reviewing cross-border payments, while there were working groups studying such dry subjects as computers and databank systems. Little of this is the stuff of headlines.

Nor has the BIS a monopoly among the international agencies of central-banking intelligence. The OECD comes close to duplicating some of it, while the IMF has a department devoted to central-banking issues and training. Some feel the BIS could have responded more directly to the needs of Eastern Europe and the former Soviet Union instead of confining itself to coordinating, with the IMF, the technical assistance and training offered to the region by Western central banks, together with arranging for donors and recipients to get together for discussions. But this is the kind of role the BIS feels it fills most comfortably.

It is, indeed, a modest institution, lean by the standards of others of its kind. Even after steady expansion since the late 1980s, it supports no more than 450 people, of whom only some fifty are employed on research, including twenty or so pukka economists. Bearing that in mind, it is something of a miracle that its annual report is such a valuable document, particularly since its conclusions have become more outspoken over time. (Signed by the general manager, the report is not subject to Board approval.) Though salaries may be generous – queries about their scale are regarded as cheeky, but they are said to be 'competitive' – keeping staff between the ages of thirty and forty-five in Basle is not easy. The so-called Philadelphia of Switzerland is not everyone's idea of heaven, however dreamy the views across to the Black Forest on a clear day, and middle management at the BIS is poorish.

But successive generations at the BIS have had the challenge of keeping up the formidable reputation of the annual reports established by the Swedish economist, Per Jacobsson, who ran the bank's research efforts for its first twenty-five years before moving to Washington in 1956 to head the IMF. In her biography of him, his daughter Erin says that PJ, as he was known to Americans, 'always gave his best ideas to the BIS and the annual report'. She also provides the key to his personality in this one sentence, which refers to his first days in Basle and takes phrases from his diary: 'Generally incapable of doing anything moderately, PJ at thirty-seven was further stimulated by being where he had always wanted to be, namely in "exclusive circles" at "the centre of the action."'

Though Jacobsson was indefatigable in pursuit of 'people of influence', he didn't necessarily kowtow to them and he loved arguments. While orthodox in his economic thinking in many ways – he was all for the discipline of the gold standard, for instance – his postwar blueprint for a monetary policy that would use interest rates to counter inflation, at a time when cheap money was the rage, showed he could take a stand, and a good one, against the consensus. His worst error, made at the IMF, was to oppose strongly the German revaluation in 1961.

Fifty years ago, when financial expertise was sparse and immature, it was much easier for international officials like Jacobsson to make waves than it is today. Still, personalities matter more at the BIS than at other multilateral organizations since it has neither a detailed mandate that governs its every turn nor the power that comes from lending to governments, which is forbidden. Presidents are elected by the board from among its members – and inevitably come from one of the smaller countries because of the workload and time involved. They used to be long-stayers and made their mark on the bank. Marius Holtrop held the post for eight years up to 1967 and then it passed to his successor at the Dutch central bank, Jelle Zijlstra, for the next fourteen years. Today, the post rotates every three years and much more depends on the character of the chief executive.

Who is he – never yet a she – likely to be? Gunther Schleiminger, appointed in 1981, differed from his predecessors in several ways. For a start, he wasn't French, as all five general managers up to then had been. He was also the first to have climbed up through the ranks – or at least from two rungs down the ladder. After serving in the OECD and the Bundesbank, Schleiminger went to the BIS in the first place as secretary general in 1975, a year before Alexandre Lamfalussy, who was to succeed him in the top slot from May 1985 until end-1993, arrived as economic adviser.

Hungarian born but now a Belgian national, Lamfalussy had previously gone from economist to chairman at Banque de Bruxelles. So he had dirtied his hands in commercial banking as well as earned a standing in the economics profession that kept a chair at the University of Louvain in Belgium open for him. This unusual combination of qualifications in its chief stood the BIS in good stead at a time when the complexity of the financial world increased almost beyond belief.

The BIS has become more technically efficient – and, for better or worse, more structured, more organized. It had no dealing room, for instance, when Lamfalussy took over; now a substantial one supports a very efficient wholesale money market for central banks, with its own internal controls. Heavy investment in information systems has bumped up employment in this area to seventy from a mere sixteen in 1985. The BIS's databases on banking business and financial markets even capture some off-balance-sheet items and are offered on-line to member central banks. Another sign of the times is the spawning of technical committees that meet at the BIS – eighty-seven such meetings in 1992 involved an average of twenty participants at each, more than three times as much activity as six years earlier. All these meetings need secretarial back-up and usually some input from the BIS's own researchers.

So the BIS grew apace under Lamfalussy by almost any indicator – even profits. (Its net operating surplus rose from $138 million in 1985 to $315 million in 1993.) But what about the institution's importance as a mouthpiece for central banks on the world economic stage?

One big contribution in this respect in recent years has been to help central banks formulate their case for independence. Its ongoing responsibility is to justify that new role in society; it cannot with any conscience avoid upholding this when things go wrong, when economies do badly, when central bank independence is resented.

A second challenge for the BIS comes from the loss of European Community activities. It plans to respond by becoming a more global central banking institution but it can only realistically do so if it discards its bizarre shareholding structure and the European monopoly of the board. In short, the BIS needs to be reborn. And renamed?

So its new boss in 1994 was handed a splendid chance to be a mover and shaker. Taking over when Lamfalussy, who had been due to retire at mid-year, was appointed the first president of the European Monetary Institute from the beginning of the year, Andrew Crockett, at the age of fifty, became the first British head of the BIS. His ability and experience should ensure that the integrity and generally high standard of BIS economic counselling is continued. A Cambridge economist who subsequently took an MA in international economic adminstration at Yale, he joined the Bank of England, working on economic research and then in the cashier's department before being seconded to the IMF as personal assistant to its managing director in 1972. Captivated by the international civil servant's life in Washington, he subsequently joined the Fund's staff, eventually overlording its *World Economic Outlook*, before rejoining the Bank of England as its international executive director in March 1989. But Crockett's vision will have to extend beyond macroeconomic crystal-gazing.

Though the BIS may need new direction, this does not mean it has to shed all its wraps. It has grown in influence along with the rising powers of the central bankers who gather there every month. It is indeed a secretive club, but so long as its member central banks are properly accountable the secretiveness is probably on balance benign.

The New Central Banks of the Former Soviet Union

Communism attempted to subordinate bankers, and everything to do with money, to the needs of society – as defined by the 'leaders of the proletariat', the Communist Party. Karl Marx's vision of a society responding to people's needs rather than their cash-buying power – their real worth rather than their class – held enormous appeal, not only to the working class of nineteenth-century Europe but also to intellectuals, economists, and a large number of thoughtful middle-class people. The dream of an egalitarian, classless society was one response to the experience of industrialization then transforming every aspect of life; either one could 'retreat' to a conservatism rooted in nostalgia for a vanishing agricultural and hierarchical society, as so many poets and novelists did, or one could dream of creating a better society in the future, based on need rather than greed.

In neither the conservative nor socialist visions of society did bankers – still less central bankers – loom large. But whereas conservatives tolerated their existence as part of the rather sordid, but necessary, monetary dimension of society, socialists wanted to root them out, expel them, and make sure they never acquired a grip over society again. In Marx's view, the traditional monetary system had given people the dangerous illusion that they were in control of their destiny:

> In the credit system, of which banking is the most complete expression, the illusion is created that the might of the alien, material power has been broken, the state of self-estrangement abolished and man reinstated in his human relationship to man ... But this abolition of estrangement, this return of man to himself and thus to other men, is only an illusion. It is self-estrangement, dehumanization, all the more infamous and extreme because its element is no longer a commodity, metal or paper, but the moral existence, the social existence, the very heart of man, and because under the appearance of mutual trust between men it is really the greatest distrust and a total estrangement ... We should reflect on the immorality implicit in the evaluation of a man in terms of money, such as we find in the credit system.

According to Marx, the monetary system supported the rule of the bourgeoisie; the foundation of the Bank of England in 1694 was the 'first legitimation' of the 'rule of the financial bourgeoisie'. Marx spurned the quantity theory of money as first adumbrated by Hume. It was 'absurd' to believe 'that commodities enter into the process of circulation without a price and money enters without a value'. Commodities have value because of the labour it takes to produce them.

To end man's state of alienation, and give due respect to the dignity of his labour, the system had to be brought under the control of the workers: the market, which had given rise to such injustice, had to be stamped out; the means of production had to be brought into public ownership; prices controlled; and banks had to be made servants of the proletariat. Property and money had to be abolished and a massive programme of public education launched to prevent a regression to 'bourgeois' possessive habits.

All European countries were affected by these ideas. In France, Britain and the Nordic countries they influenced economic policies into the 1960s. In Eastern Europe, Soviet Union, Southeast Asia, China, North Korea, Cuba and socialist developing countries they were carried to fanatical extremes. With the communist takeovers of many states in the forty years to 1958, old-established banks and central banks, where they had existed, were abolished, their owners and managers executed or driven abroad, and subservient managers installed. Money changed its whole meaning; even in Western Europe, where less virulent forms of socialism prevailed, people lost sight of its true function. It was driven into a corner, to be seen as the 'small change' of society – just pocket money, to give to workers at the end of the day or the week to enable them to purchase things that the national planners had decreed should be produced. Money's central function, which (as Marx recognized) is to help to coordinate the actions and preferences of innumerable economic agents, through the market mechanism, was deliberately eliminated.

Another thirty-odd years on from 1958, the challenge to the new states rising from the debris of Marx's dream has been to refashion society's coordinating mechanism – to replace planning by new work-horses, money and markets. Some have made big strides down the track; others have hardly got off the starting blocks. What is clear is that a new generation of central bankers has been born. In 1990–93 no fewer than twenty-five central banks were established or subject to such radical changes in their statutory and economic functions that they were in effect newly born. Moreover, the dramatic transformation in former communist countries was echoed by a more moderately paced but none the less profound evolution in the industrial countries. In many of these countries also central banks were being reformed; and this gave their leaders a new confidence. During the 1990s, pioneers from these old banks spread out from the heartlands in Western Europe and North America, like old-time missionaries, teaching, inculcating, indoctrinating the newly liberated peoples to the east. Thousands of bright young people were sent to 'training camps' to sit at the feet of delegates from the great central banks of the world, to pick up the arcane arts and mysteries of their profession and so bring the magic of the market to their backward lands. There wasn't a socialist in sight.

This process had a special poignancy for many of these older banks, which had come to that stage in life when they had begun calmly to contemplate their own eventual demise. Central bankers in the European Community spent an inordinate amount of time and energy during the late 1980s discussing when and how they might gracefully expire. They were a little vague about the date, but in 1993 they even entered into a solemn suicide pact called the Maastricht Treaty which called on them all to lie down by 1999. In the East, by contrast, many new central banks were being born or reborn. The life cycle of a central bank seems to be tied to that of its nation-state.

If there is a natural cycle of this kind, this chapter is about their birth (or rebirth, where central banks had existed before the communist takeover), and their infancy. When is a country or state ready to have a central bank? What conditions are needed to allow it to do its work? How does it get going? What does it do?

Among the sixteen successor states of the former Soviet Union, a wide variety of approaches developed in the 1990s. Nearly all were having a go at creating their own currency in place of the Russian rouble. This was not surprising: the Russian rouble was one of the worst currencies on earth. Why should anybody want it, least of all a new country trying to rid itself of the past? The first country successfully to launch its own currency was Estonia. The other Baltic States, Latvia and Lithuania, followed suit. Others, such as the Ukraine, broke from the rouble only to plunge into even worse inflation and instability than if they had remained in the rouble area. Of the countries closely tied to Russia, such as Belarus and Tadjikistan, most supplemented the use of the rouble by issuing their own coupons, and in 1993 nearly all of these announced their intention of issuing separate currencies.

Making payments

What were the main issues raised in designing modern central banking systems for the region? The most urgent was to make it possible for banks to perform their most basic service of all – as a depository where people could keep their money, withdraw it on demand and transfer it to others by written or other authorized form of instruction. Banks did not provide these services in the Soviet Union. They usually needed notice of withdrawal of cash; they could not be used to make payments; cheques did not exist. Individuals used cash for making purchases, keeping surplus funds in a so-called 'savings bank'. Enterprises accounted for their supplies and sales through credit transfers, if authorized by the production plan. These took place through the Gosbank, the people's bank, and inter-republic payments were coordinated by a so-called central bank (each of the republics had one of these accounting institutions). But the payments systems remained not so much underdeveloped as non-existent, for ideological reasons.

Installing a payments system was a top priority of governments everywhere, for, without its active use, the effective value of the money in making purchases from vendors a long distance away is much reduced – and with it, the effective scope for commerce. Another key feature of the whole area was the lack of money and capital markets, which previously had of course been prohibited. This meant that it was impossible to regulate the money supply by open-market operations – the whole idea was anathema. Instead of controlling the supply of cash, inflation was ruthlessly suppressed by price controls.

By 1994, some republics (such as Moldova) had made some progress at this level. Rudimentary payment systems were operating, allowing enterprises to make and receive payments from other enterprises (individuals still relied on cash). These payment systems were in some cases run by the new commercial banks, in others by the central banks. Western advisers also noted a growing public recognition of the role of a central bank and growing awareness of the connection between monetary expansion and inflation. What was lacking was the political will to use the central banks responsibly. In most republics budget deficits were out of control and the central banks financed them. Central banks remained answerable to local parliaments, dominated by vested interests. To quote Victor Yuschenko, Ukraine's central bank governor in 1994, from an article by John Lloyd in the *Financial Times*: 'The central bank and the new commercial banks are in a very tough position. They have to act as champions of change in an environment where most of the government and the large state sector are resisting or slowing such change.'

With that background, we review the experience with the establishment of central banks (or re-establishment, in those cases where central banks had existed before the Soviet takeover). At question is whether they really were central banks in anything but name, and what benefits they were bringing to their countries.

Russia's hopes and handicaps

The unstable and inflationary policies of the Russian central bank in 1990–93 provided the worst possible conditions for establishing a market economy not only in Russia itself but also in neighbouring countries closely linked to Russia.

When on 3 October 1993, Boris Yeltsin, President of Russia, decided to use military force to crush the rebellion of the so-called parliamentarians, who had locked themselves into the White House, one of his first actions was to seal off the central bank with a tank cordon. The next thing his aide Yegor Gaidar did was to ask the central bank for large emergency reserves of rouble banknotes – a request that the central bank reportedly refused. These actions symbolized the key role that the central bank, then headed by former Soviet Union banker Viktor Gerashchenko, had come to play in the power struggle in Moscow. For the central bank had become a tool of parliament, in opposition to the government and the reformers. Whether the crushing of the rebellion would be followed by a purge of the central bank was not immediately clear; but by early 1994, following the strong showing of the extreme nationalist right in the elections it was clear that the reformers were on the retreat. There had been no change at the top of the central bank; and no progress towards establishing sound monetary conditions.

Reformers showed little appreciation of the need to have the right people in charge of the central bank. Georgy Matiukhin, who became head of the central bank in 1991, appeared to be a genuine reformer, and one who also understood the old system, but he was an academic rather than a practising banker. He had to battle with powerful interests inside Russia – notably the politicians representing big state organizations and the members of the former *nomenklatura*, who eventually secured his resignation. These were the very early days, under President Gorbachev, when *glasnost* (the removal of censorship and the freeing of many political prisoners, and the shocking rediscovery by Russians of their own bloodstained history under communist rule) was being supplemented by *perestroika*, the effort to reform the economy. But the Party leadership, including Mikhail Gorbachev, could not accept the central role that had to be given in a market system to the institution of private property. Even many of the reformers baulked at that hurdle.

Western advisers for their part failed initially to understand the special difficulties facing reformers in the monetary field. A few words of background are necessary on that.

Money in the former Soviet Union took two rather distinct forms: first, banknotes, used to pay wages; second, credits extended by the Gosbank (central bank) and by its 'central bank' branches in the republics to industrial enterprises, credits which firms could use to pay for goods bought from other firms or states. With inflation suppressed by price controls, underlying inflationary pressures – which eventually burst into the open when prices were liberalized in January 1992 – could be caused either by an increase in the supply of cash or by an increase in credits extended to enterprises. Increases in the supply of either type of money were caused mainly by demands from the central or regional governments, to finance their budget deficits, and those of large enterprises.

These two types of money circulated side by side, without meeting. In the absence of financial markets, and of interest rates responding to supply and demand (these were fixed by government decree), there was no market mechanism for ensuring they were even moving in the same direction. Thus enterprise credits could be increasing fast, allowing state enterprises to continue producing and purchasing supplies and selling their products to other enterprises – all on credits created just by entering more rows of noughts on to company ledgers – while the supply of banknotes was restricted. With a constant stock of banknotes, if enterprises did not have enough money to pay workers (or, after price liberalization, enough to increase their pay sufficiently to keep up with rising prices), consumer purchases had to fall. And this is what actually happened.

A further complication was that roubles served as the currency in circulation throughout the former Soviet Union. Traditionally, when a central bank of a republic or regions needed more rouble notes, it ordered them from the Gosbank and they were supplied on demand. Remember that money was part of the evil bourgeois society which communism had superseded. Credits allowed planning targets to be fulfilled; actual cash was needed to pay workers, but only as tokens in response to their 'real needs'. So banknotes were supplied on demand; but after the 'shock therapy' of price liberalization, the printing presses fell behind the need for banknotes. The central bank's biggest task in this period was ensuring the distribution of sufficient notes to enterprises and other republics, where they were carried by air and in convoys of trucks. But the supply of notes was extremely erratic, causing massive problems throughout the former Soviet Union.

Georgy Matiukhin was often confronted by Western demands to

'reduce the supply of money'. But he pointed angrily to the need to integrate these two circuits: the supply of banknotes had to be increased and central bank credits reduced. Without this, he maintained, unscheduled arrears of debt would build up between enterprises because of their inability to sell enough goods at the right prices to ultimate consumers. His attitude aroused consternation among Western economists and bankers, many of whom joined in the demands for his resignation.

Viktor Gerashchenko, who had already served as head of the old Gosbank in 1986–90, made an astonishing return as central bank president in July 1992, just before the attempted coup which, though it failed, reduced Gorbachev's prestige so greatly as to bring about his resignation at the end of 1992 (that coup itself was, according to Matiukhin, triggered by the army's desperate need for cash to pay the soldiers). Although President Yeltsin, who came to power as a result of his heroic defence of parliament against the generals who were holding President Gorbachev at his house in the Crimea, appointed a government of reformers headed by Yegor Gaidar, he acquiesced in parliament's demands that Gerashchenko should stay at the central bank.

The latter greatly expanded the supply of both types of money, in response to demands from enterprises and regional governments. 'Monetary policy has to be tough, but not so tough as to strangle the economy,' said Gerashchenko at a press conference in 1992. This attitude brought the central bank into continuous conflict with the government, which was trying to get the money supply under control. Gerashchenko does not believe that inflation can be caused by an increase in the money supply.

The currency issue and reserves of banks increased by over thirteen times in 1992; the accompanying increase in the money supply brought about an equivalent increase in prices, after a lag of about three months. The share of cash in the money supply increased relative to bank deposits – one of the classic symptoms of hyperinflation. Even though there was little reason to hold roubles, there was even less reason to keep money in the bank (though interest rates offered to savers by banks were increased, they were far below the rates of inflation). Moreover the price explosion following the ending of most price controls in January 1992 meant that the real value of bank deposits fell dramatically – a large proportion of the savings of most Russian citizens was wiped out in a few months by the rise in prices.

Geraschenko, a jolly figure who gloried in being called 'the worst central banker in the world', fuelled inflation at annual rates of over 2,000 per cent in 1992–93. The exchange rate with the dollar slumped.

Progress in laying down the infrastructure of a market economy was agonizingly slow. About a quarter of the 250,000 state and municipal-owned enterprises had been privatized by 1993, but most of these were small firms. Little progress was made in defining private property rights in land; farming was still basically done on the old collectivized system. Few of the promises to the IMF about fiscal and monetary policy during this time were honoured. Access to foreign bank loans was cut off while Russia, which had assumed the debt of the Soviet Union, negotiated with its foreign bank creditors. Capital flight accelerated; holding dollars either in notes or in bank accounts abroad was the only way Russians could make any savings. Between 1989 and 1993, total output of the Russian economy fell by more than one-third; it fell another 25 per cent in early 1994.

With output slumping, savings decimated by the inflation following 'price liberalization', corruption rife, and some getting rich quickly by stashing money abroad, it was not surprising that the reform programme got a bad name. By 1994, many observers were predicting civil unrest. The October 1993 crisis, when Yeltsin survived only by ordering the army to bombard the parliament which he had defended little more than a year earlier, and the gains of extreme nationalists in the parliamentary election, caused many political leaders in the West (such as Senator Bob Dole, the leader of the Republicans in the American Senate) to conclude that the emphasis of the reforms should be changed. Had the West got the priorities wrong? Should institution-building have come before price liberalization?

Everybody agreed that the political capacity to implement reforms was pitifully weak. The problem was not one of designing an economic programme or a central bank, but of overcoming the legacy of Russian history – a task which would have been easier to accomplish if Western advisers had spent more time understanding how history conditioned the present.

An easier start for the Balts

As the most European parts of the former Soviet Union, the Baltic republics were expected to make more rapid progress towards establishing a market economy. Estonia started its reform programme in 1992, at a time when output was falling rapidly as a result of the disruption of exports to Russia (real domestic output fell by nearly half in 1990–92) and when prices were soaring after the ending of price controls (they rose 1,000 per cent in 1992). A centrepiece of the reform was the introduction of a new currency, the kroon, on 20 June 1992, replacing the rouble as legal tender. Estonia then became the first country to leave the rouble zone.

The kroon was fully backed by gold and hard currencies, and the exchange rate was fixed to the D-mark. The kroon notes and reserves issued by the Bank of Estonia became its liabilities – if presented with kroon, it was legally obliged to give the holder D-marks at a fixed rate of exchange. It could only be sure of doing this by having assets equal to the value of the kroon it issued. It secured the required capital by a stroke of luck; its predecessor had placed over eleven tons of gold in banks abroad prior to the Soviet takeover in 1940. On 25 March 1992, the central bank received the 4.8 tons of gold it had placed with the Bank of England with a market value of about DM80 million in 1992; this was considered adequate to back the initial currency issue. Later, other gold was recovered from Sweden, the United States and the Bank for International Settlements.

The Estonian authorities decided to use the central bank as a currency board (see Chapter 6), under which the supply of banknotes adjusts automatically to demand. When demand for local Estonian banknotes increases, they can only be issued by the board in exchange for foreign currency at the predetermined rate; the assets of the board – gold and D-marks – have to rise. So interest rates have to increase to induce an inflow of cash by holders (of both local and foreign currency) to take advantage of higher rates payable on local bank deposits; high rates also reduce borrowing and deposits by local residents in kroon.

The advantages of this system are that it is easy to create (so long as the country has the required initial capital of foreign reserves or gold) and to operate. Also it enables the central bank to earn income on its assets; as it does not pay interest on the banknotes it issues, it makes a profit (called seigniorage). (This is the basic reason why central banking should be a profitable business.) From the public point of view, however, the biggest advantage of the currency board arrangement is that the possibility of inflationary government financing is excluded.

The currency reform in Estonia was a success. Many people wanted the new notes and, as they presented D-marks and other foreign currencies to the Bank of Estonia, so its reserves grew – to more than required to 'back' the local banknotes. But the key to lasting success of the reform will be the political will to allow interest rates to rise to whatever level is necessary to maintain the fixed rate between the D-mark and the kroon. One immediate threat came from the poor state of the banking system. As in all former Soviet republics, the commercial banking system started life bankrupt, with massive loans to enterprises that could not survive in a market economy. Several commercial banks had to be closed and there were inevitable calls for the Bank of Estonia to rescue some of them, by creating money without the backing of additional foreign reserves.

To protect the reserves being used in any such way, the Bank of Estonia was divided into two – the Issue Department and the Banking Department. The Issue Department represented the currency board; as liabilities, it had all kroon banknotes and bankers' deposits with the Bank of Estonia, and as assets the foreign exchange and gold necessary to back them. The Banking Department held, as its assets, surplus foreign exchange and gold, and any kroon-denominated loans to the banking system; on the liabilities side it had a notional sum called its 'capital'. Thus 150 years after Peel's Banking Act split the Bank of England, a central bank in the Gulf of Finland was adopting very similar rules – with similar intent, to preserve price stability.

Under such arrangements, the rules have to be followed strictly. The Bank of Estonia cannot interfere in the setting of interest rates by commercial banks, it cannot lend to them except in emergency and, even then, it can lend only funds derived from the external reserves held in the Banking Department; nothing must be allowed to undermine the commitment that the domestic currency is fully backed. Siim Kallas, governor of the central bank, attributes the success of the reform to the fact that 'money is seen not just as money, but as a crucial national symbol'.

This currency reform enabled Estonia to break away immediately from the malign influence exerted by the unstable supply of rouble banknotes and chaotic monetary conditions in Russia itself. In one bound, Estonia was free. It had tied itself to the West, and specifically to the symbol of monetary stability, the D-mark. It wanted the kroon to be seen to be as stable as the D-mark. Why did it not just get a lot of D-mark notes from Germany and make them legal tender in Estonia? That is more or less what it did do, except that the notes declared themselves to be 'Bank of Estonia – Kroon'. But first it would have had to pay for the D-mark notes somehow. Second, it could not have regulated the conversion of old Russian roubles held by Estonian citizens into D-marks (individuals were permitted to convert up to 1,500 roubles at the standard rate of 10 roubles per kroon, but amounts above that at a penal rate of 50 roubles per kroon). For such an operation, it is necessary to have an official institution.

The Bank of Estonia also moved quickly to improve the payments mechanism; under the old system, as in other countries of the Soviet bloc, bank customers often had to wait for weeks until they could withdraw money at commercial banks. By 1993, delays in access to bank deposits and in clearing payments had been reduced to two days – faster than in many West European countries.

Having gained much-needed credibility by the way it introduced its currency, Estonia could probably get away with a devaluation, if required to adjust the external value of its currency to continuing domestic inflation – so long as this was understood to be part of the transition rather than the beginning of a spiral of inflation and depreciation. Finland, which has given considerable moral and economic support to Estonia during the transition (the peoples are related by language and culture), has itself run the gauntlet of many devaluations in recent years even while modernizing its economy and financial system. It would cause no surprise if Estonia were to follow in the Finns' footsteps. The big problem for Estonia is the continuing inflation caused by large capital inflows.

The Latvians watched the Estonian experiment like hawks. The Bank of Latvia was established even before the country achieved independence in September 1991, and by mid-1992 had already introduced a transitional currency – the Latvian rouble – which gave Latvia some independence from inflationary Russian monetary policies. Like Estonia, Latvia also had some gold tucked away with foreign central banks – left abroad when the Soviets took over the country in 1940 – and the availability of this reserve helped establish the credibility of their policies. Again, this showed the role that gold can still play for transitional economies in building confidence in the domestic currency and financial system.

The Latvian rouble was floated in July 1992 and initially appreciated against the dollar as well as against the inflationary Russian rouble. However, wages in dollar terms remained very low; it was calculated by the IMF that in 1993 the average wage in state enterprises in Latvia remained below $50 per month (less than £10 per week), about the same as in Romania and Bulgaria but less than a third of the levels in Czechoslovakia and Poland, where wages were put at $169 a month (about £25 per week). In 1994 the independent Bank of Latvia had become one of central banking's success stories.

The Lithuanians also made a good start to financial reform. The Bank of Lithuania, re-established in February 1990, was in September 1992 given power to set interest rates and foreign-exchange reserves and to manage issues of government securities. In March 1992 coupons, or *talonai*, were issued to supplement Russian rouble notes and in September roubles ceased to be legal tender, the intention being to establish the litas as the national currency. However, after a bad inflation during 1993 the political climate changed and the central bank was transformed into a currency board, as in Estonia. At the time of writing, it was still too soon to judge whether the experiment would succeed.

Loads of Western advice

The process of financial reform for the new republics started really only at the beginning of 1992, when most of them became independent. All joined the International Monetary Fund and World Bank in 1992–93, and the Group of Seven major countries asked the Fund to coordinate technical assistance for the former Soviet Union countries in cooperation with the G7 and other central banks. Assistance was offered in specific areas, such as banking supervision, accounting, monetary research, public debt management, organization and methods and new currency issue. Twenty-four central banks provided assistance in one or more of these areas to fifteen countries – first in diagnosing the major problems, then in providing experts to visit the country. In addition, large-scale training programmes for central bankers are offered by a number of central banks, the IMF Institute in Washington, and a special training school, the Joint Vienna Institute, set up with the support of the Austrian government and central bank, but sponsored by six international institutions, including the Bank for International Settlements.

In general, legislation framing the constitution and mandate of a modern central bank was designed and passed by legislatures in most of these countries in 1992–93. The problems lay rather with the implementation of the legislation. In addition, foreign-exchange reserves were usually still managed by a different agency under closer political control. Another feature of the evolving system was the proliferation of new commercial banks in many countries – banks that often had only a tenuous link with the local economy but were often designed rather to make profits on exchanging foreign currencies and money-market dealing. Most of the central banks established their independence of the government of the day, but were still dependent on parliament – often dominated by representatives of the old *nomenklatura*, the power élite from the days of the Soviet Union. The laws frequently stated that 'no credits should be granted by the central bank to governments – except where authorized by the parliament'. But, as in Russia, the word 'parliament' did not refer to an institution like that familiar in mature democracies. In fact it appeared in 1993 that parliaments dominated the central bank in all these countries.

Nevertheless, as mentioned above, progress in installing modern systems of accounting and payments clearing and improving financial and economic data-collection had been made. Most of the republics were moving towards establishing conditions for greater autonomy in monetary policy, by leaving the rouble area. This involved treating the Russian rouble as a foreign currency – a revolutionary break with the past. This process was spurred by the abrupt decision of the Russian central bank to demonetize 'old' pre-1993 roubles, which had two big effects: first, many republics made bilateral agreements with Russia to guide their monetary relations; second, more countries accelerated their plans to introduce their own currencies even while planning for a currency union with Russia. Some of the republics were too closely tied to Russia to avoid monetary integration in the long term but needed at all costs to insulate themselves from the inflation in Russia in the shorter term. Conversely, Russia itself wanted to protect itself from the effects of credit expansion by other republics. Its ability to do this depended on the exact terms of the bilateral agreements setting ceilings on the credit limits granted by the Russian central bank to others.

Other 'European' states of the former Soviet Union

These states followed contrasting policies. Belarus introduced a national currency. However, the central banks' autonomy remained limited, and Belarus came under strong pressure to enter into a monetary union with Russia – pressure that many viewed as signalling a new era of economic imperialism.

Until 1993, Moldova and Armenia remained members of the rouble area with monetary conditions determined by the Russian central bank. However, Moldova then declared its intention of introducing a separate currency. By 1994 Western experts were full of praise for the rapid progress being made by the Moldovan central bank.

Ukraine introduced a new currency by converting all Russian roubles, including deposits, into karbovanets (the Ukrainian word for the rouble) but this rapidly depreciated even against the rouble due to overissue. The budget continued to be financed by the central bank (the National Bank of Ukraine), meaning it had no control over the money supply. Inflation rose to 4,000 per cent a year.

Georgia left the rouble area in 1993, thus establishing conditions in which it could follow an independent policy; previously it had suffered from the highly erratic supply of banknotes from the Russian central bank. However, in practice, the National Bank of Georgia continued to finance the budget deficit of the republic, and hyperinflation quickly made the currency virtually worthless.

'Central Asian' states

Azerbaijan introduced its own currency – the manat – to circulate alongside the rouble. Kazakhstan was by 1993 ready to introduce its own currency, but the President wished to preserve the monetary union with Russia for political reasons. Turkmenistan also was preparing to introduce a separate currency. Tadjikistan and Uzbekistan had both signed framework agreements with Russia looking towards the formation of a 'new' rouble area. These were countries where 'conservative' forces favouring the continuation of the former power élite and close ties with Russia remained in control of the state. Yet by mid-1994 it was very doubtful whether the new rouble zone would get off the ground.

A hollow shell

In these newly independent countries, the fate of the currency and central banking arrangements would clearly be determined by the outcome of the local power struggle. In many cases, this was as in Russia between the conservatives, who often dominated parliaments, and proponents of reform installed in key positions in the ministries and governments – reformers whose views were more in accord with those of the International Monetary Fund. To obtain finance from the Fund or other sources, the countries had to commit themselves to carrying through a reform programme aiming to establish a market economy. But as many of these countries were rent by civil strife and complex divisions on ethnic and religious lines, and as so few had had any historical experience of either democracy or capitalism, nobody was expecting miracles.

How successful have the old-established Western central banks been in their missionary aims to pass on the torch to a new generation, to extend the frontiers of their domain? The territory of the former Soviet Union proved to be stony ground, but offered a huge potential payoff. If Russia and the other republics could be brought within the market system, a bridge would have been built across the Eurasian landmass to the massive continental-size economy of Japan and the newly dynamic economies of the Chinese language area – an area of rapid growth extending south to the second generation NICs (newly industrialized countries), such as Thailand and Malaysia. Moreover, the central bankers would have enlarged their potential collective influence on the development of the global economy.

If the experience of the first few years after independence showed the potential it also defined the limits to the role that central banks can play. Above all, it showed that there was little they could do in the absence of a constitution – in the broad sense of a general consensus on the rules to be followed by the principal institutions of a society, that is to say, the President, parliament and the main political and business interests. Western advisers can help to install the technical capacity to pursue a monetary policy – a central bank, currency arrangements, a banking supervisory system – but implementation requires the political capacity and will to breathe life into the technical arrangements.

Thus the main lesson from the last few years of monetary experiments is that while a society needs a reliable and preferably stable money, the converse is also true. For money to fulfil its proper role, it needs a market economy and preferably a commercial banking sector able to allocate credit to borrowers and provide basic banking services to customers. It is no good creating a hollow shell, a mere legal entity called 'The Central Bank of Ruritania', appointing a president to run it, getting a firm of printers in England or Germany to run off some Ruritanian banknotes and then expect Ruritania to have a functioning money.

Yet the former USSR governments (and their Western advisers) focused on developing the institutional apparatus of central banks – training, accounting, clearing of payments, bank supervision, etc. – before the basic foundations of a market economy were put in place. This was not only a question of installing a Western legal system protecting 'property rights', but also of assigning actual property claims to specific individuals. Who owns this particular field? Where are its boundaries? Who owns this book? What are the rights of authors? What is a mortgage, or a loan secured on collateral property? Can banks seize a person's assets if he or she defaults on a loan agreement?

In most of the former Soviet Union, the answer to such questions was 'don't know'. In the West, too few grasped the central importance of such issues. Discussion of this subject came under the heading of 'privatization'. But the process of putting large state-owned enterprises into private hands, though important, is not the main point. The key is that individual people have to know exactly where they stand in terms of what they own and what the procedures are to let them sell and buy particular bits of property – including their skills – in a free market. Very few people even in the West really understood how profound a change this would be, partly because of all the propaganda coming from countries like Sweden on the case for 'a middle way' between socialism and capitalism, involving greater competition but not private ownership. This was always a mirage – Sweden itself had a developed welfare state but its economy was almost wholly capitalist and everybody knew exactly what they owned.

Having said that, it was understandable that Western agencies should provide what help they could with the technical aspects – and on that front much progress was being made. This was true especially of improving settlement procedures, establishing the basic legal framework for a functioning central bank, and laying conditions for the growth of commercial banks and financial markets.

The collapse of empires has provided fertile ground for central banks. In fact, a large majority owe their existence to the dissolution of empires – of the Spanish empire in the nineteenth century, of the Austro-Hungarian empire in the First World War, of the French and British ones in the Second World War, and then of the Russian empire in the 1990s. Each wave has been marked by its particular characteristics; what was special about the 'class of 1990' was that so many central banks came into being at a time when central bank independence was newly fashionable. If only the countries can get their acts together politically and cease their internal feuding, the voice of the central bankers in office over this vast region of the world will indeed become a force to reckon with. What would Karl Marx have thought about that?

Nearly a century and a half ago, John Stuart Mill declared that 'a party of order or stability, and a party of progress or reform, are both necessary elements of a healthy state of political life'. Today we need to ask whether the same principle applies to financial life, where markets thrive on instability, but central banks have made stability their god. Surely this cannot make for a sustainable, healthy state of affairs?

Central bankers seize every opportunity to tell you that stability of prices is their main objective in life, the ultimate aim of monetary policy. But in the next breath they stress their part in preserving, indeed enhancing, the stability of the banking and financial system, a role that is, in fact, the older of the two.

We have reminded readers in earlier chapters that central banks first emerged as privately owned commercial banks – and later non-competitive institutions – given a quasi-regulatory responsibility for the financial system and special privileges, such as an exclusive right of note issue, perhaps limited to a local area to begin with, in return for granting government assistance in raising finance. The first clearly distinctive role was as 'the government's banker', and this brought with it some supervisory responsibilities. The consensus on price stability is relatively recent.

While it is this focus that provides central banks with some scholarly support for independence, it does not bring them closer to the public, it does not give them a human face. Whether or not M3 is a reliable indicator in the pursuit of monetary policy is hardly the stuff of chat shows. The older role has much more to do with how central banks are perceived in the community. And also, less obviously, with how they are having to adapt their organization and staffing. This chapter explores these latter developments and what is behind them – largely from the point of view of leading central banks which are in the vanguard of change.

Ultimately, the orderliness – a word we prefer to stability – of a country's financial markets is regarded as the central bank's responsibility because it is the intermediary between the state and the markets. It has the money, the wherewithal to pick up the pieces as lender of last resort. But the emphasis is on 'last resort'. Financial institutions, so the argument goes, must share responsibility, backed up usually by deposit insurance, and form the first line of defence. But if that breaks? How strong is the backstop? What keeps central bankers awake at night is the prospect that traditional 'last resort' assistance – channelling liquidity through the banking system – may be irrelevant to tomorrow's breakdowns, which may occur in any one of the myriad links in a hugely complex financial system no longer dominated by straightforward banking.

Gluttons for punishment

Central bankers must have known that removal of control and barriers would store up trouble for them. But they were all for it. This can be explained in virtuous terms; more choice for investors makes for more competitive and efficient markets. And if only because money markets are the channel through which monetary policy impacts on the real economy, central banks have a special interest in seeing they are efficient. But their sponsorship of liberalization – which usually requires governmental action – also demonstrates that, like the best of old-fashioned nannies, they want their charges to be good but also to excel in the world, to do better than their playmates. Strong international competition has made central banks nationalistic, keen promoters of their own financial centres.

In detail, a central bank's relationship with the markets differs from country to country, coloured by history and national culture, influenced by differing institutional, legal and political commitments. Perhaps not surprisingly, since governments part with power reluctantly, the more independence a central bank has on monetary policy, the less likely it is to be able to control markets directly. Two illustrations bear this out. First, the Bank of England, which has little monetary policy independence, lords it in sole command over London's gilt-edged market, but the more independent Federal Reserve is barely a minor regulator of the largest market in government securities in the world, the bond market in the United States. Second, the independent Bundesbank is not allowed to impose ceilings on bank lending to the private sector, nor to fix interest rates in credit and securities markets, while the dependent Bank of Spain has wide powers to constrain the domestic banking business. (Not, incidentally, that the big central banks look for such powers; Arthur Burns had a point when he said that selective controls were bad news to him, because then 'it's the Fed that is setting the priorities for society'.)

Such differences used to influence the execution of a nation's monetary policy more than they do today. With direct controls out of fashion and markets liberalized, at least in the large industrialized countries, operating techniques have converged to some degree. Relying less on discount lending to banks, the majority of big central banks now use either interbank or open-market transactions to fine tune the supply of reserves to their banking systems. But not in exactly the same way. Some – including the Federal Reserve, Bundesbank and the Bank of France – rely more on securities repurchase agreements (repos) than do, say, the Bank of Japan or the Bank of England, which mostly purchase and sell securities outright. Individuality is still preserved.

There are, of course, plenty of other reasons why a central bank may be in the markets on any one day. It may be selling government paper to finance government overspending. Or parking the government's surplus cash. Or placing securities for a public-sector borrower. In the foreign-exchange markets, it could be intervening to influence the exchange rate or doing a currency swap as manager of the nation's currency reserves. And it may be handling a substantial volume of foreign-exchange transactions on behalf of other central banks or, more occasionally, for a multilateral institution like the World Bank.

In financial markets, someone once said, credibility in monetary policy takes years to gain but minutes to lose. A central bank, therefore, cannot afford to be seen as other than streetwise, not even for a minute. Moreover, it needs to keep up with techniques not only for its own operational success, but even more importantly so as 'to have its finger on the pulse for lender of last resort functions', as one central banker has put it. Trouble is that it may not be actually finding the pulse.

This is not because central banks are inept market technicians. While their strategy has often come to grief (as on Black Wednesday), by and large the big central banks put up a respectable showing in their day-to-day dealings in traditional markets. They have the ability to attract market skills and they can demand a high standard. The Federal Reserve in New York, the biggest operator among them, says it has no trouble getting good traders; they come usually through its research department. But what happens when traditional trading gives way to off-exchange business?

Central banks for their own purposes are not big players in the new instruments created to manage risk that are in themselves creating new risks – the so-called derivatives. As a reminder, this umbrella term takes in standardized futures and options traded on organized exchanges such as the Chicago Board of Trade, London's LIFFE and the Paris MATIF. But it also covers a bewildering variety of privately negotiated, over-the-counter, customized forward and swap contracts offered by banks and securities firms to corporations, institutional investors, financial institutions and even governments, which might want, for example, to manage oil price risk. So extensive has this business become that the transmission channels of a nation's monetary policy and the authorities' capacity to stop an incipient crisis turning into meltdown are now hostage to fast-evolving financial innovation. But central banks are being very slow to face up to the new challenges. They are also divided in their attitudes to the new wizardry – the Bundesbank defensive, even hostile, the Bank of England interested, even to some extent supportive, with the Fed somewhere in between.

After reviewing the huge expansion in banks' use of derivatives, some twenty-odd experts from the Group of Ten central banks concluded early in 1992 that their employers needed 'to develop further their understanding of the nature of financial activities' and 'place high priority on continued monitoring and analysis of developments in wholesale markets'. Translated, their message was that central bankers must get off their high horses, grovel when they don't understand what financial rocket-scientists are up to, be prepared to learn and keep continuous contact with market players. Central banks did listen, and they do have their derivatives-watchers. But the message has not been taken sufficiently to heart.

If, as seems evident, a central bank needs technical expertise about market instruments and market mechanisms, not just on its trading floors but in the upper reaches of its hierarchy, this raises interesting questions about what is needed to make a good central banker. What indeed? Let's examine some evidence about the species.

A breed apart

A few years ago, an American journalist, William Neikirk, wrote: 'Central bankers are a breed apart from the rest of humanity . . . They are aloof, secretive, frugal, independent, public-spirited, responsible and judgemental.' But are these characteristics inherent or acquired? The answer is probably a bit of both; central banking may curb natural spirits, but these are unlikely to have been wild in the first place. Those attracted to it are mostly inclined to the centre politically, instinctively against extremes in any form, *laisser-faire* addicts.

Forgetting about qualifications for the moment, compare the career choices for anyone set on playing a part in a nation's economic and financial life. Politics and central banking offer some stark contrasts – a life of instability, rough-and-tumble but under the limelight compared with one of job security and prestigious trappings played out mostly in the shadows. The next choice is harder, but even conservatives (with a small 'c') can value scope for individuality and originality, which is perhaps where central banking scores over the more sprawling civil service – not to mention also in its usually better pay.

As this book has already described, no two central banks are alike and there is no set pattern for making senior appointments at them. There are more political posts at the top of the two major independent central banks, the Washington Federal Reserve and Germany's Bundesbank, than there are at, say, the Bank of England, which, because it has no mandate to decide monetary policy, can choose all its own executives other than the top two. One consequence is that Bank of England recruits can look sky-high more hopefully than many of their foreign colleagues, though their rise may still be blocked by outsiders brought in at executive level, even though they are not political appointees.

A model for so many of its newer brethren, the Bank of England's efforts to update its staffing concepts in the past twenty years or so are of special interest. Outwardly nothing has changed; the Old Lady is still regarded as fuddy-duddy, a little wimpish with its attendants in pink coats while those at the Federal Reserve wear guns at the hip. But the days have gone when the men who ran the Bank were expected above all to have social background in common with the City's merchant bankers – schooled at Eton or Harrow, classics or history read at Oxford or Cambridge, followed perhaps by a spell with one of the crack army regiments. True, the Bank still turns first to Oxbridge for its graduate intake, but economics, mathematics, business studies, these are the disciplines now sought. As the City has opened up to every nationality and the old boy network, though still a factor, counts for less than bottom-line performance, Threadneedle Street has had to spawn its own technocrats and specialists. Its present boss, Eddie George, didn't go to the 'right' school, but was bright enough to read economics (the first Governor of the Bank of England to do so) at Cambridge. Unusually – though we think this will become less true from now on – the Governor is a career man who has spent his entire working life at the Bank (with spells abroad on special assignments), winning the City's respect by astuteness and professional competence.

Applied economists

While it may breed arrogance at an early age, the Bank of England's training of its high-flyers has much going for it. Typically, he (or often she nowadays) will join the Bank straight from, let's say, Oxford, having graduated in PPE (philosophy, politics and economics), spend five years in the economics research department, followed by three years in one of the operational departments, then perhaps two years seconded to Washington as personal assistant to the International Monetary Fund's managing director or on special assignment at the Bank for International Settlements in Basle, followed by a short spell back in London as secretary to a special task force or with some quasi-government body like the Monopolies and Mergers Commission before landing in gilt-edged and money markets or foreign exchange, lined up to become a division head. When Michael Foot, at the age of forty-six in the summer of 1993, switched from headship of the European division to that of the banking supervision division (under executive director Brian Quinn), he had already had eleven jobs in and out of the Bank. If variety really is the spice of life, then that at the Bank of England is very spicy indeed.

Most central banks start graduate entrants in their economic research and statistical department, into which they pour an impressive amount of resources. So much importance is attached to its work these days and so influential has it become internally that it is often headed by a distinguished economist, brought in as an executive director. The Bank of England, for instance, in 1990 appointed Mervyn King from the London School of Economics, an engagingly unpretentious man in his early forties who had made a name with his writings on finance, taxation and corporate behaviour, while the Bundesbank's department is in the charge of Otmar Issing, who built up a considerable reputation while holding a chair of economics at Würzburg University from 1973 to 1990. The Federal Reserve relies on staffers for departmental work, but brings in some professional economists as governors in Washington, Bob Heller and Jerry Jordan being two examples of late. And not only at the Bank of England are youngish central bankers given a chance to develop international expertise. Even the Bundesbank, hardly the most outward-looking of central banks, has introduced a special staff-training scheme of international scope, recognizing that its middle and upper ranks will increasingly have international duties.

Another welcome development is that there is more movement in and out of a central bank than there used to be, a healthier two-way exchange with the private sector – and, to a lesser extent, with the finance ministry. Also, there is more curiosity about how other central banks operate; those in the European Union even run a staff-exchange scheme.

Central bankers like to call themselves learned. The Bundesbank in particular takes pride in the preponderance of professors and holders of doctoral economics degrees on its boards, many carrying both titles. The Bank of Italy is also keen on academics. Alliance with the economics profession is now very strong. Most of the governors of the rich countries and the large third-world ones have studied economics formally (the notable exception at the time of writing was Mieno in Japan, who had a degree in law instead). This makes them a prey to denigrators, who express growing scepticism about what economists do. But, provided central bankers share some of that scepticism, economics is probably the best first discipline for them and gives them a common jargon in which to communicate with each other. Moreover, to give them their due, if you ask them for their job description, they will stress that they practise *practical* economics, *practical* monetarism.

Better PR matters too

Of course, a successful central banker needs more than academic excellence. Critical intelligence is essential, as is good judgement. Financial markets need quick and flexible reactions; there won't be time to resort to mathematical models if a crisis blows up. He must also be able to communicate with a conscious regard for the interests of the community. An open democratic society has the right to demand a broad degree of public understanding of what central banks do and how they do it. One consequence of their having come in from the cold in the past decade or so is that they receive much more media attention than before. And not always respectful attention. To meet criticism, central banks are being forced to work in less isolation than before, to strengthen contacts not only with government and politicians, but also with private banks, businesses and economists. With greater independence, they will have to be able to explain what they do even to the man in the street.

This is awkward. Scholarly central bankers can be as autocratic in their way as the urbane grandees of the past who often gloried in having no professional qualifications or even competence for the job – and just as disdainful of PR-speak. But the newer generation is having to accept the need to acquire some political skills, to be publicity conscious. The identikit may be getting a face at last.

Take just one encouraging indication. In the early 1990s, the older central bankers preached, with missionary zeal, the merits of price stability as if it were the be-all and end-all of economic policy. They seemed oblivious of the indignation of the general public, certainly in Europe and particularly in Britain, which saw unemployment as far and away the most important issue. But the more down-to-earth Eddie George is less careless. Listen to him on the eve of his elevation to the governorship. 'Monetary policy,' George said, 'is ultimately about growth, about output and about jobs. But there are no short cuts.' He might have elaborated further rather than signing off with: 'Growth – beyond the very short term – can only come through stability, by which I mean achieving and maintaining price stability.' Nevertheless, he was on the right track, and his deputy, Rupert Pennant-Rea, on transferring from the editor's chair at *The Economist*, declared a particular interest in how the Bank presents itself. As we noted in Chapter 2, now even central bankers have to market their services.

However good public relations may become though, talking will not bring markets to heel. True, it may help to persuade them that some prudential care in their management is in their own interest, but they will continue to push their risk-take beyond the boundary with which central banks feel remotely comfortable. Central banks never were complete masters of the markets, at least not since these have been deserving of that name, as recurrent financial crises have borne witness. And central banks are still doing more than simply act as referees; they are setting some rules of play. Nevertheless, they increasingly behave like servants, rather than masters, of the markets.

The limits to control

It is important to distinguish between two quite different manifestations of liberalization that have changed the face of finance and given central banks new challenges. One is the enormous growth in the sheer volume of funds that can be switched from one asset to another and across the exchanges at the drop of a hat – or, rather, by a blip on a screen. The other is the ever-widening range of fancy financial products, engineered in a continuous search for higher yields, lower funding costs and tools to manage risk.

On the first score, the new scale of mobile funds has certainly left central banks the losers if it comes to a pitched battle in the currency markets, as it did in the European Exchange Rate Mechanism in September 1992 and July–August 1993. The sums poured in by the

Bank of England (or on its behalf) in the first episode and likewise by the Bank of France in the second were horrifyingly large in relation to their own (or rather the nation's) resources, but not to those of private speculators. Governments can try to reimpose capital controls, but the ability of central banks alone to maintain 'orderly' currency markets is now very limited. If speculators are of like mind in a worldwide market with a daily turnover of nearly £1,000 billion, they can make their forecasts of currency movements self-fulfilling, regardless of how central banks act.

The Swedish central bank governor, Bengt Dennis, said as much when he addressed the 1993 annual meeting of the Bank for International Settlements as its president. His most telling comment was: 'We must recognize that a new financial environment has emerged; policymakers will increasingly have to take market expectations into account in the formulation and execution of policies.' It was a long-overdue swansong for central banks as major movers in the currency markets. In what seemed no little despair, Dennis added that 'the unprecedented increase in capital mobility has made it more difficult to operate any type of exchange-rate regime'. Another central banker used to say he felt 'naked' in front of the big guns of the market.

At least central banks understand foreign-exchange markets, which are deep, traditional and, for the most part, transparent. New fears about systemic breakdown are reserved for the second development just mentioned, the activity in financial derivatives, still modest in relation to foreign exchange (or bonds or equities, for that matter) but growing rapidly. To head off any clampdown by the authorities, a number of users of this new wizardry, under the guidance of Dennis Weatherstone, chairman of the American bank, J. P. Morgan, came up with a shopping list in July 1993 to improve its safety. One item on it was the need for legislators and regulators to work with market participants to improve legal and regulatory uncertainties. Another was that they should provide guidance on accounting and reporting. Hardly earth-shattering. In fact, rather suspect if it leads central banks into a minuet with bankers or a game of musical chairs. For on past form, the central banks will be the ones still dancing when the music stops.

Buckle under

True, central banks and other regulators, while not interfering directly with the deregulated markets, have not stood idly by; they have imposed some restraints on players. As we have described in Chapter 10, the Basle Committee on Banking Supervision, without any statutory basis, has, rather remarkably, been able to levy what amounts to a new tax on international banking business through its risk-based capital requirements. And by extending these requirements to capture some trading as well as counter-party risks, the Committee has made a stab – no more and far from perfect – at demanding good management from users of the new financial instruments.

But it is not good enough for central banks to say they cannot hope to understand all the new financial products, only to ensure that the users do. Nor should they whinge about innovation – their concept of stability must embrace it. All right, the markets set the pace and it will be a scramble to keep two strides behind. And that may seem undignified. But scramble central banks should do.

Markets have been made much more powerful relative to the authorities as a result of liberalization, particularly in smaller countries. We see dangers in this – of central bankers being in thrall to the markets, of molly-coddling them, and of being forced to adjust their policies to the perceived needs of the bankers; even the mighty Federal Reserve was in 1992–93 widely thought to be following a monetary policy designed to boost the profits of America's banks. And the central banks' interventions – as on Black Wednesday – have sometimes brought great windfall gains to market participants. But there could be compensation for central banks, indeed potentially great reward. The more successful they are in keeping up with the markets – while minimizing the costs involved – the greater will be their authority vis-à-vis finance ministers. Relegation to second mate in international forums, even for those enjoying so-called independence, has always riled. In superior market intelligence lies their chance of come-uppance.

A nose for the ingenuity of markets, a sense of the gambler's instinct, an interrogative curiosity, a love of computer technology – these are not natural talents of the high priests of economics in central banks. Indeed, they may secretly despise them. But they are essential alongside their own. Central banks could be in danger of becoming too predominantly seats of learning; a better balance is needed. Here other big central banks might take a leaf out of the Federal Reserve's book.

Responsibility for protecting America's financial system is given kudos by being in the hands of the New York Fed, 200 miles away from the holy of holies where monetary policy is decided. When Gerry Corrigan stepped down from the presidency, it seemed entirely appropriate that his successor, Bill McDonough, should have been a former commercial banker, brought into central banking only eighteen months earlier. This is a central banking arm that really does give priority to familiarity with the markets, to hobnobbing with private bankers and securities dealers, worrying about payment and settlement systems. Its motto could well be an old English proverb: 'Many things are lost for want of asking.' Although geographical separation makes no sense for most countries, the high ranking accorded to the New York president in the Fed's hierarchy could be replicated elsewhere.

Central banks will need to keep reshaping themselves in response to the new problems that will arise as financial markets grow ever wider and more diverse. New rules may be needed to cover risk, but they must not smother innovation.

There is no turning back the clock. The concept of controlling one market by itself will become ever more archaic. But, although it may not seem obvious as of this moment, we are hopeful, given the right attitudes, that the answer to the question posed at the start of this chapter is 'Yes': old and tired markets do nobody any good; change and movement are what they feed on, not stability. But they need a healthy and balanced diet. It is up to central banks to see they get it.

We are not suggesting this is easy. There is no ready-made measure to guide central banks in managing markets, no counterpart to the inflation index as the yardstick of monetary policy. An absence of crises does not signal success if it is at the cost of stagnant markets. Equally, market innovation should not be pursued at the cost of recurrent crises. Central bank staff must make their own judgements and be prepared to justify them publicly. They need to be held individually accountable – just as private bankers should be at risk personally. Too tough? There is too much at stake for molly-coddling.

The core business of central banks has changed several times in their history. At the start it was mainly to provide finance for governments. During the late nineteenth and early twentieth centuries their main job was to act as backstop to the banking system and maintain convertibility into gold, and long-term price stability was guaranteed by the gold standard. The destructive potential of central banks was unleashed with the abandonment of the gold standard. In several societies they became engines of hyperinflation. In virtually all countries they became subordinate to governments; their core business was to finance welfare and warfare. Then from the 1970s their core business was seen increasingly as providing price stability. It is on the back of this consensus that central banks are claiming the need for independence. But they also lay great stress on the second and more traditional justification for their existence, their role in providing discipline and a safety net for the banking system.

Central banks have been gaining in influence and independence at a time when, ironically, economists have been once again debating whether they are really necessary at all. Although such questioning may seem rather surprising at this late stage in our story, there are several reasons why it is appropriate. Central banks are insulated from market forces in that the compensation and career prospects of their staff do not depend on their ability to deliver and sell a service or product in competition with other producers. So it is difficult to measure their performance or to find out if they are 'producing' the right things. They do not conduct market research to find out what their customers want; who would they survey anyway? True, some offer a performance evaluation in terms of their own goals by setting targets for money-supply growth and inflation. As we shall see towards the end of this chapter, they may become more commercially minded in future. But at present there is no telling how cost-effective they are.

They also have a large degree of administrative autonomy. Central banks are usually masters of their own operating budgets. The appurtenances of a senior central banker's life are of the highest order – first-class travel, excellent pay (with some notable exceptions) and working conditions, a high degree of job security (though not as fully guaranteed as it was), genteel company, an opportunity to exercise intellectual faculties on problems of public interest and importance. With all those advantages, there is no reason why they should also enjoy the warm glow of being perceived as acting in the public interest unless they really are doing so.

Central banks do not come cheap. The total staff and other operating costs of EU central banks were estimated to be in the region of $5 billion in 1994. This makes it all the more important to review the arguments put forward by those who say that central banks are unnecessary. Some economists go further. Some maintain that just by existing central banks do more harm than good. They constitute a constant source of temptation to governments to finance their spending programmes by printing money, or to pump up the economy before elections, and a constant source of temptation to bankers to lend unwisely on the assumption they will be bailed out. Is it enough merely to put barriers in the way of such monetary financing and bail-outs under the banner of independence? Why not go the whole hog and abolish them? Or push them back into the private sector where many of them started?

To jump ahead to our conclusions. First, societies have managed without central banks in the past and central bankers need to be reminded of this. Second, economists who say we can do without central banks in future have not yet made out a convincing enough case, but their arguments are being listened to with respect, rather than simply dismissed as cranky. Several of the greatest economists have either been sceptics or outright opponents of central banking. These include Adam Smith, Walter Bagehot, Friedrich von Hayek and Milton Friedman. The wider the areas of policy in which the central banks exert an influence, the more they can expect such criticism to grow. Third, there are reasons to expect central banks to behave more like competitive enterprises in the future; and the main force pushing them out into this brave new world will be currency competition.

Yes, Minister

A case can be made in favour of doing away with central banks and letting a government department, such as the Ministry of Finance, implement monetary policy. It is arguable that in Britain's case, for instance, there would be gains in such an arrangement over the present one. For while the Bank of England is constitutionally no more than a government agency, there is nevertheless considerable ambivalence about who is responsible for the practical implementation of Britain's monetary policy. If a minister were clearly in charge, at least somebody could be held responsible. The absence of clarity may well itself have contributed to the frequency of crises and disasters that have befallen British monetary policy and even to the country's mediocre ranking in the medium-term performance tables (only 55th in the ranking of countries according to their performance in the price-stability stakes; see Appendix).

When after the Second World War governments decided that institutions like the Bank of England and the Bank of France should no longer remain in private hands, nobody (so far as we are aware) considered establishing them as government departments. This could have been because the idea of a politician running a bank seemed too way-out. Or because there was a bad smell about a government department being in control of a domestic money market on the basis of the financial needs of a national Treasury. In practice, sheer inertia carried the day.

This is how the Bank of England's historian, John Fforde, sums up the way Norman's creation was brought under public ownership while doing little to change it: 'Virtually nobody questioned whether the central monetary institution of the UK, as it had mainly evolved over the preceding quarter-century, was in practice the best obtainable, fully fit for pouring into a statutory mould at the start of a brave new postwar world. Almost everyone just assumed it was.' A cynical comment from a British Treasury official at the time is even more telling: 'The more the permitted independence on inessentials, the easier will it be for the Bank to maintain its intimate relations with other parts of the financial system and with City interests.' So the Old Lady was encouraged to deceive, to pretend to authority it does not have, abetted by Whitehall which, for the most part, behaved courteously in public to its servant.

No, Minister

As Paul Volcker recently pointed out, the real reason why central banks have been separated institutionally is that governments have wanted markets and public to have confidence in the promises and commitments of the institution that issues the national currency and operates in the markets on behalf of the public interest. Those characteristics can be developed only within the framework of an institution that has a degree of functional independence from the government of the day. It is interesting that all countries maintained the façade of a separate central bank, even though in nearly all cases until recently policy was actually determined by ministers.

This justification for central banks also legitimizes their supervision of the banking system. Clearly, a central bank needs to have a good idea of the strengths and weaknesses of the banking system at a given time if it is to be able to judge the likely impact of its decisions on monetary policy. If the banking system is weak, it may not be possible to tighten credit without causing widespread disruption in the financial markets. The best way to ensure the banking system is strong enough to act as a channel for the 'macroeconomic' regulation of credit by the central bank is for the latter to exercise continual 'microeconomic' supervision over the banks. Again, the central bank is needed for both functions.

The two main justifications for the existence of central banks – to reduce the frequency and severity of banking crises and to regulate the flow of credit – are closely interrelated and bound up with the problem of information in banking. Banking is a business where customers cannot easily distinguish between good practice and bad; where there is an inbuilt tendency for overexpansion leading to both bank crises and longer-term fluctuations in credit and the money supply; where the failure of a bank can inflict severe damage on third parties; where the failure of an individual bank can quickly lead to a widening crisis of confidence in the banking system; and where self-regulation by insiders or 'clubs' is inherently difficult and the outcome uncertain.

That may appear to add up to an unanswerable case for central banks. Or does it? Perhaps the strongest criticism of central banks is based not on theory but on practical observation: that they have failed in practice to fulfil the stabilizing function expected of them. The key argument for the very existence of central banks has to be the tendency for banking systems to veer out of control and to inflict severe damage on other firms and the economy generally. Central banks are supposed to be the stabilizers of the system.

Yet recent years have witnessed boom-to-bust cycles ending in severe bank crises in many countries with well-established central banks: all the Nordic countries, Australia the United States, Spain and about ten other countries, quite apart from the disastrous situation in many developing countries. In many countries the largest banks in the system became insolvent. The losses made by big banks in the past twenty years dwarf those made in the previous two centuries since the development of Western commercial banking – and of central banking. Similarly, most countries have suffered wide fluctuations in credit and monetary growth over the medium term – notably the United Kingdom, Japan and the United States. There can be no assurance that this twenty-year period of instability is to be a prelude to greater stability – or whether it heralds even greater turmoil in the future. Whether the theoretical case for central banks is accepted or not, the practical problems facing central banks in managing their credit systems have clearly not been resolved.

Free banking can work

Critics point to historical examples where 'free banking' has in practice regulated the supply of credit without any need for central control of reserves. 'Free banking' refers to a system where privately owned banks issue their own banknotes; these notes circulate freely in competition with those of other banks, and where there is no central control of reserves, no central bank. Recipe for chaos? Not a bit of it, say the advocates of free banking. Where banks compete to put their notes into circulation, the supply of money may adapt naturally to the demand for it. History has witnessed many examples of such private competition to supply the means of payment, starting in China in about AD 1000. As we have seen in Chapter 3, Sweden's central bank started as a private note-issuing institution in 1656.

A recent survey put together by economists Kevin Dowd and Kurt Schuler identified about sixty historical cases of free banking, lasting from a few years to over a century, and in most parts of the world. Such systems showed no tendency towards monopoly, and 'government notes never drove free banks' notes out of circulation, except where punitive taxes or outright prohibition hindered competition'. In Scotland there were twenty-nine issuing banks in 1826 and nineteen at the end of the free-banking era in 1845. Clearing houses were used as vehicles for cooperation among banks, but 'attempts to use them to form cartels were largely unsuccessful'. Free-banking systems were not unstable: 'Overissues were usually disciplined by the banks' clearing systems which provided a rapid and effective reflux mechanism to return excess notes and deposits to their users'; and in the absence of a lender of last resort or government deposit insurance, banks had to be careful in their lending policies.

Such critics argue that banking *per se* need not be unstable but that the special characteristics of deposit banking do make banks vulnerable to panics, crises and uncontrolled credit cycles. As one of the greatest critics of central banking, Vera Smith, argued in her classic study, *The Rationale of Central Banking*, 'it seems not improbable that the tendencies to misdirection are magnified by the form of the system, and in particular that part of it which entrusts the determination of the volume of credit to a single authority, between which and the government there exist reciprocal incentives to paternalism'. Smith added that, 'it is not unlikely that the bolstering up of banking systems by their governments is a factor which makes for instability'.

Historically such banks have pledged to convert the notes they issue into some other acceptable asset – nearly always into gold. Modern theorists have speculated about the possibility of substituting some other asset in place of gold, such as a share in the market value of all stocks and shares in an economy. Money-market mutual funds, pioneered in the United States in the 1980s, offer a chequing service against 'deposits' the value of which can fluctuate – so customers are not guaranteed $100 for every $100 they invested. But this again is not a good test of the theory that 'free banking' would do without either a central bank or convertibility into gold because the certificates of deposit in which the money funds invest are themselves issued by banks which themselves, people assume, are backed by the central bank. The corollary is that even most theorists of free banking acknowledge that given present markets and political reality, central banks are necessary, at least for any country that wants to follow an independent monetary policy.

In the grip of powerful forces

Moving out of the study and into the real world, in the 1990s central banks are once again being challenged by radical changes in their environment – changes that are raising with new force old questions about their *raison d'être*. One of these is the shrinking of the banking system; another is the growth of currency competition. These are two strands in the evolution of modern financial systems that have woven their way through many chapters of this book; it is now time to pull them together and consider their joint impact on the world of the central banker. It could be devastating.

The arguments for and against central banking discussed in this chapter are mainly about the risks of the banking system, and whether private, commercial banking is inherently unstable. Nobody denies that lending or investing money is risky or that somebody has to be ready to take those risks which are an integral part of the way a free market functions. The debate has been rather about whether a central institution is needed as a backstop, safety net, and regulator of the boom-and-bust credit cycle that tends to be thrown up by a deposit banking system. But now it seems that this type of banking may be about to disappear.

It is already shrinking fast. Throughout Europe and America, big commercial banks are closing branches and reducing staff numbers. This process is expected to accelerate in the rest of the 1990s. As people switch to telephone banking, credit and debit cards and as companies increasingly use electronic means of payment, the way the money stock is measured also has to be redefined. So central bankers can no longer give pat answers to the question: what is money?

More important, the way in which the risks of economic enterprise and unexpected shocks are distributed is also changing. Big companies have always looked primarily to the securities markets for risk capital – raising equity and fixed-interest loans by issuing their paper to investors. In the 1980s not only did big business further cut back its use of bank loans, but the practice of 'securitizing' loans was extended to a large number of other areas, such as mortgages, traditionally supplied mainly by credits from banks or other financial institutions. Banks responded to this at least partly by moving into higher-risk lending, such as lending for new businesses, and property development – a gamble to maintain their profits which landed many with unprecedented losses. The central banks were forced to help them out, but that did not solve the longer-term problem of the declining share of deposit banking business. Banks earned more and more of their income by advice and services other than lending; by the mid-1990s many banks were making more money from such activities, and by trading in the burgeoning securities markets, than they did by taking deposits and making loans. Indeed, some decided to move out of such traditional activities completely.

Central bankers were quick to broaden their concern with stability to include the risks involved in the new securities markets. It would be unfair to suggest this was because they saw a threat to their existence from the shrinking of the commercial banks. As we suggested in Chapter 1, the new markets discovered they needed nannying. But what is the public interest? As we have noted at several points, the powers of a central bank to create cash can be abused as much by the private sector as by the public sector. Just because the markets like to have a central bank around is absolutely no reason in itself why society should support one. If the new markets distribute risks to those best able to bear them, why should public money be called on? Public money simply puts the costs of those risks back on to the taxpayer, whereas they should be borne by the market participants and those who use them. Deposit banking was thought to be so risky as to need a central bank because banks issued nominal claims of fixed amounts to depositors who could not know the true value of the assets those claims indirectly financed, so there was a chronic tendency to boom-and-bust cycle. But with securities markets, all one needs arguably is a good market regulator – an industry body with teeth to ensure fair play. This is another illustration of the maxim that 'to the extent markets work, there is less need for the state'.

Moreover, monetary policy is undermined. As we have seen, the new uncertainties and difficulties have already led many central banks to abandon the targeting of monetary aggregates and instead target the level of prices directly. But even that does not provide a clearly defined target. Readers will have noticed that we have been somewhat ambivalent about the meaning of the glib phrase – now on every central banker's lips – 'price stability'. How exactly is it to be defined, operationally? As Robin Leigh-Pemberton replied when challenged by *Central Banking* as to why he did not have a contract like his counterpart Don Brash of New Zealand to attain a precisely defined target:

> Clearly the governor of the Reserve Bank of New Zealand has been ready to put himself on the spot and I suppose any central bank governor who is worth his salt should say, 'I too am ready to put myself on the spot'. But it's the position of the spot which is the important thing . . .

He added that even the New Zealand contract recognized that external forces may throw the governor off course. We discuss this problem further in Chapter 23.

Thus by the mid-1990s central bankers found the ground slipping under their feet. They could no longer supply easy answers to three key questions: What is money? What is a bank? What is inflation? Yet the answers to those questions defined not only their traditional role but the role they thought they had all now agreed to pursue.

Currency competition

With this new vagueness about their objectives, and uncertainty about their methods, what in practice was becoming more and more important to them was another very direct and immediate indicator of what the market thought of them – the external valuation of their currencies as indicated by the rate of exchange. With the removal of exchange controls, currencies entered directly into competition with each other. They were still issued by central banks with a monopoly of issuing high-powered money – bank reserves – denominated in the national currency, but there was less and less compulsion on anybody actually to use a given currency. Taxes still had to be paid in national currency, but that could be obtained the instant before remitting funds to the tax authorities; and it was useful to have a national currency for small change – taxi fares and local shopping. But with trade taking up to one half of GNP, more and more people maintained bank accounts in foreign currencies – even to save up for the annual family holiday. Survey evidence showed that 40 per cent of firms exporting goods and services from Britain had bank accounts in one or more foreign currencies – sometimes with a bank overseas, though more often with a British bank.

For big capital-market transactions also there was competition between currencies to be used to denominate bonds, equities and derivative products (strictly speaking, the competition was among the products or instruments themselves, but their currency denomination was an important aspect of their attractiveness or otherwise to investors). The number of currencies used to denominate such transactions, and trading in them, was much larger in the 1990s than ten years before; although the markets were still dominated by the big three – dollar, D-mark and yen – many other currencies were also familiar in the markets. Underlying this was an astonishing rise in the number of fully fledged currencies. The number of fully convertible currencies (that is, countries with Article 8 status in the International Monetary Fund) rose from only ten in 1960, to thirty-five in 1970, fifty-two in 1980, sixty-eight in 1990 and eighty-three in March 1994. A fully fledged central bank should be defined as one that issues a fully convertible currency, since only then does the country concerned promise to pursue sound economic policies that will obviate the need to use restrictions on the making of payments and transfers for current international transactions. In other words, only then does a currency stand on its own legs (though controls on capital movements may be applied, under IMF rules, these also were increasingly being abandoned by convertible-currency countries).

Thus central banks are beginning to behave more like privately owned firms without actually being privatized. To maximize their 'shareholder value' they will tend to increase the value of their core product – their currency. Certainly, central banks will see their destiny as determined increasingly by the fortunes of their currency as it engages in competition with others in the world market for goods, services and capital. This will put enormous pressure on them to make that currency as attractive to investors as possible. Investors rather than borrowers will be in the driving seat. As big borrowers, governments will have to cut their coat according to their cloth. They will look to their central banks to follow monetary policies that allow the country to borrow on the best terms available; and to avoid being penalized by investors they will make their currencies as hard as possible. And if eventually the central banks themselves were privatized, and governments threw the last of their family silver to the markets, then the governors and their staff could doubtless stage a management buyout (assuming their product was indeed valued highly by the markets) and transform themselves into shareholders of profit-seeking central banks.

How much would they be worth? So long as they have a monopoly of currency issue, their market value is likely to be very large indeed. A central bank required to maintain price stability, with a constant money stock, earning interest of 5 per cent annually on its assets (securities used as backing for the currency issue and banks' reserve balances) and liabilities of about 25 per cent of GNP would have a present market value of 23 per cent of its country's GNP, according to estimates by Maxwell Fry in a paper published by the IMF. This is because of the seigniorage; it spends very little on the notes it issues (annual costs are generally less than 1 per cent of the face value of notes issued), but earns interest at the current market rate on its claims (which for the purpose of this illustration are assumed to be claims on the private sector of the economy – such as commercial bills).

The main reason for the enormous potential profitability of monopolistic central banks is the rate of interest they may earn on their assets, and the main effect of withdrawing their monopoly would be to lower this. With free banking, excess profits would be eliminated by competition. Central banks would not exist and commercial banks would merely provide notes as an additional service, making profits no higher than those required to keep enough note-issuing institutions in business to satisfy the demand. With competition among currencies internationally, but with each maintaining its domestic monopoly, the erosion of profitability will depend mainly on the effect on the demand for the currency and on the interest rate. International financial integration is proceeding rapidly but is very far from complete; and as noted elsewhere, people are generally reluctant to change their longstanding currency habits. So national central banks have in effect a protected home market, and continue to earn monopoly profits (normally transferred to the government, of course). But the international market is wide open to competition; certain currencies such as the D-mark and yen are being held more and more widely, while the domain of others such as the French franc and pound has shrunk.

The big danger in such a world is of course that of competitive appreciation achieved by excessive domestic deflation – offering international investors assets denominated in a currency that markets expect to rise in value in terms of domestic purchasing power as well as against other currencies. To some observers, the behaviour of the Bank of Japan and the Bundesbank looked as if these central banks had adopted such a policy. If so, the big danger for the world economy in future will be deflation rather than inflation.

This chapter has examined three crucial questions. Does a commercial banking system by nature require a central institution to protect and promote the public interest? Does a market economy by nature require a central institution to carry out monetary policy? Does such an institution, if necessary, have to form part of the public sector? The answer seems to be in each case, 'No'. But they are there; they are not going away in the near future; so they need to be helped to do their job as well as possible (for our suggestions, see Chapter 23). And none more so than those involved in planning Europe's new central banking system.

Accept that politics and emotion are inexorably entwined with economics. It still seems bizarre that something as important as a supranational central bank, running a single currency and a single monetary policy for the whole European Community, should have been designed without any serious official debate as to whether such a creature was desirable. Yet suddenly it seemed there was no time to lose.

The ball started to roll at the Community summit in Hanover in June 1988. The President of the European Commission, Jacques Delors, was determined that member states should not forget that in approving the first significant revision to the Treaty of Rome – the Single European Act – they had confirmed 'the objective of progressive realization of economic and monetary union'. Badgered by him relentlessly, the twelve leaders set up a committee under his chairmanship to 'study and propose concrete stages' leading to such a union. No messing about with ifs or buts. No taking forever; the committee was asked to report to the Madrid summit a year hence.

It did better than that. It reported by April 1989, astonishingly quickly. And Delors achieved what he had set his heart on, a unanimous report (except for a minority view, not strongly pushed, that a European Reserve Fund should be set up at an early stage as a transitional step). Though its recommendations ranged beyond what had been expected, the committee had kept strictly to its remit; its thirty-eight-page report told governments how, assuming they actually wanted EMU, they should set about achieving it.

The Delors Committee was not an official one in the conventional sense; the twelve EC central governors who sat on it did so in their personal capacities. (Which, incidentally, allowed the Bank of England's Robin Leigh-Pemberton (now Lord Kingsdown) courageously to sign a report he knew would outrage the then British Prime Minister, Margaret Thatcher, to whom he owed his job.) Nevertheless, its findings were accepted by the EC government heads as defining a 'process' designed to lead to EMU. And although worked over, elaborated and refined, the three-stage procedures for arriving at a European single currency spelt out in what is known popularly as the Maastricht Treaty are essentially those recommended by the Delors Committee.

What went in, what did not

Just why EC leaders stuffed that committee with central bank governors, so that its report inevitably had a monetary bias, is not clear. But apart from Delors and another Commission man, there were only three non-governors on it; and one of these was of their ilk, their very own banker, Alexandre Lamfalussy, then head of the Bank for International Settlements. (The other two were a former Spanish finance minister, Miguel Boyer, and a Danish academic, Niels Thygesen.) The fascination of the Delors document, therefore, is that it shows how far seasoned central bankers feel they can push their luck, the political constraints that they accept as inevitable and the limits to their own consensus as to what their business is about. Though strictly a European view, it helped to bring central-banking issues into the public domain in countries as far flung as New Zealand and Chile. Indeed, it has had an enormous impact on the conduct of central banking worldwide.

Just as revealing as what went into the Delors report is what did not. The price of unanimity was omission or the papering over of points of disagreement with an indulgent dose of ambiguity. Conspicuously absent, for instance, were any guidelines as to how a common European monetary policy would be implemented in practice, what tools would be used and how responsibility for its execution would divide between national central banks and a central monetary institution. Even broader and less technical matters were left up in the air. While the Delors team believed monetary union had to be accompanied by a degree of economic union, the provisions made for this were imprecise, reflecting no clear consensus as to how essential it was or how extensive it should be.

On this last score, however, the Bundesbank's Karl Otto Pöhl seemed in no doubt. In the longest of ten written papers submitted to the committee by its members, he argued that any attempt to fix exchange rates and, finally, introduce a European currency 'would be doomed to failure so long as a minimum of policy-shaping and decision-making in the field of economic and fiscal policy does not take place at Community level'. And his 'minimum' was a large measure; he was asking governments to surrender much of their national tax, budget and wages policies. Moreover, as he made clear in statements at the time, while admitting that 'complete political union is not absolutely necessary' for monetary union, he believed the loss of national sovereignty in economic and monetary policy associated with it 'would probably be bearable only in the context of extremely close and irrevocable political integration'.

Yet not long afterwards, by then out of office, Pöhl was to change his mind dramatically. He saw the currency crisis that dealt a body blow to the European Exchange Rate Mechanism in September 1992 as 'a chance for, rather than an end of, the integration process'. Tear up the Maastricht Treaty, he advised. Replace it with one strictly limited to allowing a hard-currency core of Europe to go ahead and fix parities. A new central bank serving these countries could be set up, he said, without political union, so long as its main priority was price stability. Linking the two, Pöhl conceded, had been 'a big mistake'.

Would Pöhl have admitted that if still running the Bundesbank? Almost certainly not. At least not publicly. Bundesbankers still see nothing but loss in swapping the D-mark for a foreign currency, in diminishing their own powers. Their instinct is to put every obstacle they decently can to block such an eventuality. Outside their confines, however, broader considerations prevail. If not in so many words, Pöhl was telling the world by the autumn of 1992 that Europe was in disarray, its governments weak, federalism no longer on the agenda, the people dissatisfied with Maastricht, East Germany's experience a glaring example of the pain that comes from an unrealistic exchange rate. Yet at the same time he knew Germany needed to reassure its partners that it was not about to drift eastwards.

Others have changed their attitudes towards EMU for less reason than Pöhl. Future generations of researchers who sift through the column-miles of newspaper clippings, the countless speeches, books, lectures, parliamentary reports and statesmen's rhetoric about EMU will be lucky to keep their sanity. For the dry evidence will not distil the swings in mood that governed the course of the Maastricht Treaty. Searching in vain for consistency in the debates, they will do well to remember the words of the philosopher Bertrand Russell: 'There is no arguing with a mood, it can be changed by some fortunate event, or by a change in our bodily condition, but it can never be changed by argument.'

The lure of independence

However, central bankers largely isolated themselves from the maelstrom of speculation and counter-speculation over ratification of the Maastricht Treaty. Behind the scenes, they got cracking on laying the foundation for monetary union, as if time were running out, as if it might come about at the earliest conceived, in 1997, though increasingly that looked out of the question. Some had much to gain from this gambit, for one of the prerequisites for the union is that national central banks must have independent status. By early in 1993, moves to meet this provision were underway in several Community countries. By the end of that year, the unthinkable had happened; the French government had ceded monetary policymaking (on paper at least) to the Bank of France.

Could that explain why EC central bank governors came close to committing hara-kiri, putting their names so willingly to a scheme that handed over key responsibilities to a central body and cut down their own institutions to potential nonentities? Did they suspect they could rely on its completion being pushed further and further into the future, yet see in it a powerful ploy to gain autonomy? Such Machiavellian ideas could well have been at the back of Leigh-Pemberton's mind, whose appetite for independence knew no bounds. But for others independence of another kind was paramount.

One of the main thrusts behind the pursuit of EMU in the late 1980s was jealousy. Many Europeans, but particularly the French, quite bitterly resented the dominance of West Germany in economic affairs and especially that of the Bundesbank in setting monetary policy within Western Europe. The Exchange Rate Mechanism had become in practice a D-mark bloc, its members (which did not include Britain at the time) dancing to the tune of the German central bank. To the likes of the Danish central banker, Erik Hoffmeyer, who served on the Delors Committee, it was better to have a voice, even if only one among twelve, in the setting of a common European monetary policy than have the Bundesbank alone speak for everybody.

A strong mandate

Just because the Bundesbank had become so dominant, it was widely thought that it was only through its insistence that price stability was made the primary, or only, aim of the proposed new central banking system and that so much emphasis was put on independence from political interference. Wrong. After the worldwide runaway inflation of the 1970s, these two principles were very much the prevailing *Zeitgeist* in central-banking circles. However, knowledge that the Bundesbank would reject anything less undoubtedly played a part in the politicians' acceptance, with remarkably few changes, of the statutes that EC central bankers developed from the Delors outline. With only two differences of note, the version accepted for ratification at the European summit in the Dutch town of Maastricht on 10 December 1991 keeps closely to the governors' draft.

This means that the Maastricht text is long on the mandate, independence and constitutional structure of the proposed European System of Central Banks, about which there seems to have been little to argue about. Modelled on the Bundesbank, the new European Central Bank (ECB) would have an executive board – president, vice president and four others – and a governing council which adds the governors of the national central banks in countries that have moved to the final stage of economic and monetary union. The council would formulate policy, the executive board implement it and give necessary instructions to the participating national central banks. These national central banks would be the only shareholders in the ECB and their capital shares would reflect their countries' relative economic strengths. Certain formal decisions, such as those involving capital subscriptions or transfer of foreign reserves to the ECB, would involve weighted voting, but most only a simple majority with the president able to cast a tie-breaking vote.

Choosing personnel would be tricky, as with any international body, and a tedious process. The ECB's board members – needless to say, EC nationals – would be selected 'from among persons of recognized standing and professional experience in monetary or banking matters' by 'common accord' of the participating governments, on the recommendation of the Council of Ministers after it had consulted with the European Parliament and the ECB's governing council. Whew! They would serve single eight-year terms (after some variation at the start-up to enable membership to rotate thereafter). Under another provision, the term of a national central bank governor could not be less than five years and reappointment was not ruled out.

The fuzzy areas

The Maastricht Treaty lays down that the new central banking system will have maintenance of price stability as its primary objective. Neither the ECB nor a national central bank is to take instructions from governments or the Commission in carrying out the duties entrusted to them by the Treaty. The insulation from interference looks total, especially when the ECB's directors would have no incentive to pander to politicians since they cannot be reappointed. But all is not quite what it seems. First, the new central-banking system is told in effect that it must pay attention to growth and employment whenever it can do so without endangering price stability – which invites disputes if nothing more. Second, and more controversial, its powers are limited when it comes to exchange-rate policy and here governments did have their say in finalizing the treaty.

In their own recommendations, the governors were of one mind in conceding the right of governments to choose the foreign exchange *regime* but of two minds about exchange rate *policy*, the day-to-day management of currencies, some thinking that here decisions should be subject to the ECB's consent. That minority view, needless to say, was not firmed up in the Maastricht Treaty; the convolutions of Article 109 – it went through many drafts – cannot disguise the fact that in certain circumstances the ECB might be directed by the Council of Ministers to intervene in foreign-exchange markets even when this would be inconsistent with maintaining price stability.

True, this was not inevitable. Before concluding any formal arrangements for the new European currency unit vis-à-vis non-Community currencies – like, say, the Bretton Woods binding arrangements – the Council of Ministers must consult with the ECB 'in an endeavour to reach a consensus'. But, provided it could act unanimously, the Council could force its choice on the ECB however much the latter might protest. In the absence of such a system – i.e., in a floating world – the ECB looks more secure; the Council, acting by a qualified majority, could formulate 'general orientations' for exchange-rate policy only if these were compatible with price stability. But who would judge whether they were? The Treaty doesn't say. Though EC central bankers don't like it highlighted, the ECB's much-acclaimed autonomy in managing the money supply – which, of course, is affected by foreign-exchange intervention – could be circumscribed by Article 109.

If there was some excuse for the obfuscation of Article 109 – exchange-rate policy was always going to be a problem – there was none for that of the two paragraphs about supervision in the ECB's statute, where again governments meddled. It is faintly ridiculous that the EC governors could not get their act together on this, each extraordinarily hidebound by his particular national heritage. Their original draft stopped short of giving the ECB direct supervisory powers but left the way open for these to be granted – in response, one suspects, to Leigh-Pemberton's belief that this would be essential if pan-European banks develop as a result of the Single Market Act. However, the French and German governments strongly opposed even a hint of such an involvement for the ECB. Result: the gobbledegook of Article 25. This declares that the Council of Ministers, armed with the European Parliament's approval, may invite the ECB to carry out 'specific tasks concerning policies relating to the prudential supervision of credit institutions with the exception of insurance undertakings'.

Accountability in question

Even if its role in exchange-rate and supervisory matters will be less than many governors would have liked, the ECB, if it ever comes about, promises to be a powerful creature. The public would need to be assured that it is fully accountable for its actions. Would it be? Quarterly reports would be required and the ECB president would have to present an annual report to the European Council, Commission and Parliament, which may debate the report. Moreover, he and other members of the board could be hauled before committees of the European Parliament. However, the Parliament would not have the ultimate sanction possessed by American and German legislatures, which is that they can amend the laws defining the duties and behaviour of their central banks, even abolish them altogether. The European statutes can be changed only by amendment to the Treaty, which requires ratification by every EC country – or EU country, as one must say post-Maastricht.

So inadequate accountability of a European Central Bank may be a worry of the future. If it comes about. Despite the optimism of Brussels officials, the damage done to Maastricht when the European Exchange Rate Mechanism started to disintegrate from the autumn of 1992 and then virtually collapsed in the summer of 1993, after central banks had intervened on unprecedented scales to hold it together, was irreparable. The effective suspension of the ERM in August 1993 merely confirmed how premature all these ambitious plans for an early monetary union had been.

The treaty laid down that the site of the ECB and its forerunner, the European Monetary Institute (EMI), should be chosen by the end of 1992. It was not. It was only after the Treaty was finally ratified and just three days before it became effective on 1 November 1993 that EC leaders agreed – the British and French very reluctantly indeed – to let the Germans have their way. But what had Frankfurt won? By then, the EMI, due to open its doors on 1 January 1994, was envisaged as little more than a somewhat strengthened version of the Basle-based Committee of EC Central Bank Governors.

All will not be lost

Yet Maastricht is important to our story. And, yes, we do mean the Treaty, rather than the Delors report, which, as we have already indicated, prodded many countries into reconsidering their central banks' constitutions. For as long as the Treaty survives, however irrelevant it may seem to Europe's most pressing problems – its widening, its weak economic growth, its high unemployment – there remains the possibility that some countries in the European Union may keep to the Maastricht track, come near to satisfying the so-called convergence tests and proceed to monetary union. But this would be possible only if a lot of preparatory work had been done. The Bank of England's present supremo, Eddie George, much less committed to EMU than his predecessor who signed the Delors report, was not just being a Jeremiah when he warned that the Maastricht timetable was ambitious.

But even without early moves to EMU, the EMI possesses plenty of potential for improving the art of central banking in Europe. In the care of ex-BIS Alexandre Lamfalussy, it promised to relish intellectual challenges. It has the job of preparing for the conduct of a single monetary policy. It began with the benefit from preparatory work put in hand after EC governors decided the issues involved were so complex and would require so much time to resolve that they had better tackle them without delay. As soon as the first stage of EMU started on 1 July 1990, they began to strengthen their back-up in Basle, adding an economic unit to the secretariat there. And various sub-committees, composed of central bank officials, have been busy on EMU matters from the word go, one even considering the design of a future single currency. All this activity was rebased at the EMI in Frankfurt.

Much effort has gone into trying to standardize national definitions of money supply. For the first time, critical comparisons are being made of the way European central banks conduct monetary policy, with a view to establishing some rules for the European Central Bank – a fascinating exercise that, as yet, has raised more questions than answers. Should the ECB set a broad money target for the eventual single-currency area? Should it be able to levy uniform reserve requirements on commercial banks? Would national central banks have a part in conducting monetary policy?

The Bundesbank would want a European central banking system to stick to monetary targets as the principal guide and to make active use of reserve requirements. The Bank of England thinks it is expecting a lot to imagine that targets could play a dominant role in the determination of

ECB policy for some time to come and argues for looking instead at a crop of indicators, including forecasts of inflation, and relying principally on open-market operations to influence short-term interest rates. On the question of where national central banks would come in, the Bank of France has been the loudest in favour of them being involved as much as possible – perhaps intervening in the money markets in amounts prescribed by the ECB. An earlier notion, however, that one of them would be the equivalent of the New York Federal Reserve Bank in the American system seems to have bitten the dust.

And if the European system does not come about? It can be no bad thing that there have been some extremely interesting debates about monetary policy and that central banking knowledge will have been much extended. But will that have been all? We think not.

As we argue in this book, global competition and technological advances are ironing out many of the differences in financial marketplaces that allowed central banks to be idiosyncratic. Whatever the fate of Maastricht, the Single Market Act will accelerate that process in Europe. Central banks, perforce, will also become more of a muchness in Europe. The EMI's work will not be wasted.

23 *A New Mandate*

While the designing of the proposed European Central Bank enormously advanced interest in the role of central banks everywhere, and the case for their independence, it did not produce an ideal prototype for a future generation of central banks. Such a prototype should have a more specific mandate for a commitment to achieving financial stability, with the degree of accountability that a democratic political society in our view requires. In this final chapter we draw together the essential threads from our research and distil our own conclusions as to how best to reconcile the principles of democracy with the concept of a monetary policy that is independent of government.

Our starting point is that nothing should be taken for granted about central banks. The large ones, created at various times to deal with financial worlds very different from today's, are an oddly assorted bunch. Many national idiosyncrasies persist that may no longer have a place, though as we have noted in Chapter 2, these may have deeper roots than many people assume. Leaving aside the collective efforts of European central bankers made brave by numbers, pressures for constitutional change have come mainly from without rather than within. Arrogant and self-confident though they may appear, central bankers are in reality uneasy under the spotlight newly directed at them; most of them are decently aware of the limitations of their craft. The more seasoned the hand, the greater the caution about their apparent triumph. Most notably, the world's leading central bank has not dared to seek an updated mandate even though one is needed; the Federal Reserve still doesn't feel confident enough to invite a full-blown congressional debate about its status, afraid that in the end it might lose more than it gained.

But imagine that the Fed – or any other big central bank – did promote a public and parliamentary debate that started from very basic considerations. How would we like to see it go? That a country needs an institution whose main task is the execution of monetary policy seems self-evident. In whatever way that policy is technically operated, it is a continuous process, requiring constant professional attention, rigorous monitoring. The institution may take on other duties, but these should not conflict with, or distract from, its main purpose.

Less obvious is what monetary policy should have in its sights. To those who have only just begun to take an interest in these affairs, it may come as a surprise that there is any argument, any dissent from the widely held view today that price stability should be the principal, if not the only, goal of monetary policy. But this doctrine – to which we strongly subscribe – is relatively new and, we should warn, could be overturned. It will falter if monetary policy fails to deliver low inflation. It will also be questioned if the world economy performs badly in other respects over the next few years, particularly if unemployment remains unacceptably high.

Those are tomorrow's fears and problems. Today, we are glad to say, economic policymakers agree that high inflation is, in the long run, bad for growth, jobs and productivity. They also agree that it is a monetary phenomenon that can be prevented only by strict control of money growth and credit.

Trial by jury

Given that monetary policy is now virtually the only effective economic tool available and that its goal is price stability, it becomes much easier to argue that it is in a class of its own. And also that, because of the immediacy and transparency of its effects, it is particularly prey to the temptations of politicians to manipulate it in the interests of getting themselves re-elected. The case for taking it away from the control of the government of the day seems considerably strengthened.

On the other hand, some of these arguments can be stood on their head. Just because monetary policy is playing a much bigger role than it did, and fiscal policy a smaller one, politicians are giving away more when they cede it into other hands. So the contention that it should not operate outside parliamentary control cannot be laughed out of court.

A jury might decide that the case rested on whether it can be proved that the higher the degree of independence of a central bank, the lower the rate of inflation it can deliver as a rule. There are at least three problems in arriving at any such judgement. First, comparatively few countries have as yet opted for an independent central bank, even fewer have had one running for any length of time, so evidence is limited. Second, while what evidence there is does suggest a correlation between independence and price stability, it is not overwhelmingly conclusive. For instance, New Zealand, which granted its central bank independence in 1990 (see below), achieved a low inflation rate in 1992–93, but neighbouring Australia, with a controlled central bank, did just as well. Last, a jury, in seeking proof that transferring responsibility to the central bank makes for a more successful monetary policy, would be doing a poor job if it did not factor the terms of independence into the equation.

In a democratic society there is no place, in our view, for a central bank that is entirely free to form its own policies. It must be given a mandate by society, either direct by the legislature or in the constitution. Central bankers are not the obverse of politicians; those at the top can be equally concerned with their reappointment and tempted, with that in mind, to curry favour with their governments. They, too, can make mistakes, take wrong decisions, lack professionalism – there are always plenty of critics who say they are inept and misuse their office. The public needs reassurance that if the nation's money is in the charge of non-elected managers, they are working to ends that society approves. If for no other reason than that, the mandate needs to be specific. More so than the Federal Reserve's, which is ambiguous. More so, we believe, even than the Bundesbank's or the European Central Bank's; rather than just 'price stability' as the objective of an anti-inflation policy, we see virtue in a no-nonsense, numerical inflation target. Such visibility enhances the credibility of monetary policy with the public, since it can monitor progress.

Lovers of privatization will say at this juncture that if a precise job description can be worked out, why not hive off monetary policy to the private sector? However, we have made our reservations about that solution in Chapter 21, and we do see our ideal central bank taking on some other tasks appropriate only for a public-sector organization. But without going the whole hog, central bankers should take a leaf out of the way other large service organizations are putting accountability into practice. This has two elements: first, a clear mandate; second, means by which citizens can hold organizations accountable.

How New Zealand does it

On the first point, the New Zealand 'model' is certainly an imaginative compromise. It has three special features. First, the price-stability target for a specified period is agreed between the finance minister and the central bank governor, so, in practice, it is decided by the government. Second, there is an override that allows the government to substitute a new target, but only if the change is done very openly, with a full explanation given to both parliament and the public. Third – and perhaps the most controversial part of the deal – the governor's job is put on the line; if he fails to discharge his duties properly (i.e., if the Reserve Bank does not deliver the target inflation rate), he may be dismissed by the finance minister before his term expires, an embarrassing, even humiliating, penalty.

Perhaps the success so far of the New Zealand experiment – at this stage it is no more than that – owes something to the unusual character of its guinea-pig. Before being appointed governor of the Reserve Bank in 1988, when he was in his late forties, Don Brash had not only soared from being a young World Banker to running one of his country's biggest banks, Trust Bank (after taking the Kiwifruit Authority under his wing at one point on the way), but also – and this is really rare among central bankers – he had been an active politician. His political sense doubtless helped him enthuse about what he calls the 'elegant constitutional structure' of the Reserve Bank Act of 1989, which came into force in February 1990. One year on, Brash said in an interview: 'The model the Bank is working under has much to commend it and I would quite happily recommend it to any country wishing to improve its monetary discipline.'

Brash's first assignment was to achieve a 'stable' level of prices in New Zealand by the year ending December 1993, this being defined as an annual rise in the consumer price index of between 0 and 2 per cent (inflation had been running at 9 per cent when he took the governorship). So well did he succeed that before the test period had expired, he was reappointed for another five years from September 1993, instructed to continue to keep the inflation rate at no more than 2 per cent.

The New Zealand 'model' is built around the view that in a democratic society the elected government should ultimately be free to determine the goals of economic policy. The central bank presents the finance ministers with a policy statement, signed by the governor, at least every six months – or more frequently if the minister requests it – which goes to parliament and is published. The statement must not only review monetary policy in the preceding six months, but also specify what policies will be adopted, and why, to achieve the target ahead. These statements are considered as important as budget ones in New Zealand.

The New Zealand system has many fans. However, other countries may decide it could not be transplanted easily in its entirety. For instance, a British parliamentary committee (Treasury and Civil Service Committee) recommended in late 1993 that the Bank of England should be mandated 'to achieve and maintain stability in the general level of prices' as its primary objective, adopting the New Zealand policy of government-agreed, publicly stated targets, with room for override. But, not unexpectedly, it favoured the Bank, if given more autonomy, being accountable to parliament, rather than government as in New Zealand. We have more to say about this below.

To include financial stability

We believe central banks should divest themselves of direct banking supervisory duties. We have argued strongly in the course of this book that a central bank needs to be plugged into the market-place and to have a division keeping up with, and advising on, regulatory practices. But we think supervision of individual financial institutions is better hived off. Central banks which conduct banking supervision argue that for good people to be attracted, supervision must carry the aura of central banking. This view seems to us questionable. Organized on its own, supervision has a chance to build up a solid reputation, whereas within a central bank it will always suffer from being second or third best to monetary policymaking.

At the same time, so long as the central bank has the unique power to create high-powered money, or central bank reserves, it will and must play a crucial role in the financial system. Monetary policy does not operate in a vacuum, but through banks and markets. Moreover, some of the most severe problems in modern banking arise from moral hazard – notably the incentive offered to banks to behave irresponsibly because they expect to be bailed out by the central bank or government (it matters not which for this purpose). The central bank must be deeply involved in questions about bank rescues, and the terms and conditions thereof. In short, central bankers have to continue to be concerned with general financial stability.

No need for a boss

Debates about a central bank's accountability for monetary policy tend to revolve about how formal lines of answerability can be established and whether these should be to parliament or the executive. Though the answer may have to take constitutional frameworks into account, many feel that the public will be better served and the credibility of independence enhanced if a central bank reports directly to parliament, as the

Federal Reserve does, and there are several ways by which such reporting can be formalized. However, we recognize that parliament may often be as big a threat to monetary stability as the government, since delegates want their pet projects financed.

What matters more are the provisions, if any, whereby the judgements of the central bank may be overridden or set aside. We believe there should be no such provisions. Though we recognize that in times of acute national emergency, as in wartime, the central bank's obligations doubt-less would have to be suspended, there is a strong case for leaving that to the judgements of the people at the time. Just as Sir Robert Peel made no provision for suspension of convertibility in the 1844 Act, thereby making it easier in practice to suspend convertibility without damaging credibility, so we would favour giving the central bank a mandate with no 'ifs and 'buts'. There are, however, other issues at stake.

The basis for a central bank's answerability is increasingly seen to be whether or not it is delivering low inflation, perhaps defined as a target range. Allowance for any inflation at all suggests failure to attain its objective of price 'stability'. Should excuses be allowed? As already mentioned in Chapter 21, there can be some dispute over the most appropriate indicator of price levels. Moreover, measures such as America's consumer price index may overstate 'actual' inflation by a full percentage point. So at present, price stability tends to translate into an inflation rate of 0 to 2 per cent. As this book goes to press, economists in several countries are searching for better measures of prices, not just as indicators but also as targets for policy. One idea that goes back in modern form at least to Keynes is to use a basket of commodities and other real assets as a guide to interest-rate policy. Some analysts believe that the Federal Reserve under Alan Greenspan has indeed recently followed such a 'price rule'. With the decline of confidence in the targeting of monetary aggregates, we expect other central banks to adopt such price rules.

Thus in time, as more reliable concepts of price stability are developed and as the industrialized world experiences long-term economic growth built on a low-inflation foundation, so that people learn to like and want money that keeps its value (or nearly so), so stricter standards should prevail. It would then be seen as immoral, as Keynes declared, to defraud a person of his or her money through inflation. Would it then be possible for a High Street bank, when accepting a deposit, to promise to pay back the full amount, worth in purchasing power as much as when it was put in? It would be if central bankers attain what they are now promising.

Making bankers keep their promises

The crucial change now taking place is that central bankers say they will in future make it possible for commercial bankers to promise to pay back the full amount of our money. The full amount means it should be worth in purchasing power as much as when we put it in. This is indeed a moral issue. As citizens, we do not want to gamble in our long-term contracts; society is an enduring institution in which contracts should be able to be made for many years in monetary terms. Money should indeed be a store of value; yet, as shown in the Appendix, even the mighty D-mark is now worth less than 50 per cent of what it was in 1971. This is wrong. It is wrong that one man should become a millionaire just because he happened to buy his house on a mortgage when still young while his brother, who lived in rented accommodation, remains a pauper. Critics who complain that monetary policies which cause unemployment are immoral should recognize that it is also immoral to defraud a person of his or her money through inflation.

If society could get back to this concept of money, another promise comes in. If the depositor enters into a contract with the bank, so does the bank enter into a contract with individuals or enterprises who borrow from it; the borrower promises to repay the full amount with interest on the agreed terms and conditions. The banker here is acting essentially as the agent of the depositor. It is in the interests of all depositors, indeed of all members of society, that banks should rigorously enforce monetary contracts, and be assisted to do so by the courts. Depositors also should be able rigorously to enforce their implicit contract with their bankers; as they cannot do this through the courts, they rely on trust. In effect, depositors rely on the central bank to follow policies that allow the private banks to fulfil this contract and that means preventing undue monetary expansion.

In the absence of gold convertibility, there is no institution other than the central bank which can perform that task. That is what is really meant by the glib phrase, 'price stability'. It is even worth considering whether this contract should be made formal and statutory. Could central bankers be liable in law for keeping their promises, just as other businesses are becoming liable for the quality of products and services? If airlines or chemical companies pollute the environment, how much more damaging is the economic pollution caused by depreciating money?

But central banks will point out rightly that they can only undertake such an obligation – a new gold standard – if their service standard can be clearly defined – which brings us back to the problem of defining their mandate. To do that it is first necessary to consider what their real contribution to society is and how it is made.

Money's many faces

In preceding chapters we have encountered several contrasting views on what money is, why society should care about it, and what central banks should do about it. Your views on the nature of money will go far to determine what view you take of the central banker's job. You can view it as entirely a matter for the state or the government – money in the old-fashioned sense of a coin or note with the monarch's likeness stamped on it. In the next stage, you develop a kind of money which is accepted because somebody trustworthy has vouchsafed that it is good – these people were originally often goldsmiths and became bankers. Florentine merchants caused scandals when in the sixteenth century they went to France and set up business with only a desk and an inkstand and made fortunes simply by adding their names to a bill or piece of paper; today, commercial banks that issue deposit liabilities and prestigious investment banks like Merrill Lynch and Goldman Sachs that bring new borrowers to markets are all doing much the same thing as those Florentines did.

Another view, corresponding to a further historical stage of development, would have us regard money as part of nature, a thing over and above kings and queens, parliaments or central banks. The gold standard was something to which everybody had to adjust, at whatever cost to their personal convenience; at least you knew where you were. Then there is money as an instrument of policy, something to be manipulated to any ends that politicians choose, subject to the appropriate procedures being observed. Thus a totalitarian state may try to abolish money, or use it only for wars, while a democratic state may try to use it to achieve full employment, or price stability; whatever the procedures to be observed (notably the need to obtain parliamentary approval in a democracy), money is here viewed as malleable, flexible, and is thus unpredictable. In Chapter 21 we discussed another important aspect of the developing role of currencies – as competitors in the fluid world-capital markets. Finally, there is money as the property of the community, to be passed on to future generations in as good a shape as we found it, a part of the environment to be protected from corruption, a language. Keynes himself likened money to a dictionary. Unhappily he claimed – tongue in cheek? – that states could rewrite the dictionary at will. We like the analogy, but point out that states cannot rewrite dictionaries, as shown by the failure of the many attempts by communist countries to do just that.

The language of money

We favour the last interpretation – money as part of our inheritance, like language. Just as we should cherish our language, so should we safeguard our money – it is collective property, a good that once destroyed takes generations to rebuild, an asset not to be abused under the pretext of helping some social groups, but not to be abused by the rich and powerful either. The gold standard was in some ways a great advance in that it did protect money from abuse. But it was also a cruel standard, requiring abrupt changes especially among poorer people and developing countries on the periphery of the system. It was aristocracy's way of controlling central banking; but broke down under the impact of democracy. The twentieth century has not found a suitable successor. It has, however, learnt that in a democratic age governments cannot be entrusted with society's money. So experiments are being made with new kinds of rules that will protect the monetary order; we return to this below. But first a few words on this perhaps unfamiliar concept of money.

This alternative theory of money views it as a natural growth, the product of custom, law and contractual obligations. This concept goes back to the German sociologist Simmel and has recently been revived by Herbert Frankel of Oxford University:

> The debate about the future of money is not about inflation or deflation, fixed or flexible exchange rates, gold or paper standards; it is about the kind of society in which money is to operate.

On this view, money is itself a fruit of civilization because its functioning depends on trust, not on centralized decisions or on force. Trust in money depends above all on controlling the power of the state. Hence the reason so many countries joined the English gold standard in the nineteenth century was not because of the strategic or military power of England, but because of the strength of its social institutions. People came to believe that, in monetary affairs, the state would be subject to these institutions and rules, with the result that the monetary standard would be maintained. Frankel argues that the great spurt of savings and investment in the nineteenth century was a direct result of people's new faith that their property was safe – that the economic power of the monarchy and of parliament had been fettered. This concept of money runs contrary to the very idea that its value is due to its being accepted by the state and so can be varied at will by the state. From this angle, the debate about the independence of central banks is really a debate about restoring money to society, to the public.

Frankel's thesis has recently been developed by one of the brightest central bankers of the younger generation – Andrew Sheng, deputy governor of the Hong Kong Monetary Authority and formerly with Bank Negara Malaysia (Malaysia's central bank). How is it, asks Sheng, that with all our modern knowledge of monetary management and bank supervision, banking systems remain so fragile? To answer this, Sheng points out that the financial system is a complex of interlocking contracts between various parties, such as the government, banks, households, companies and foreigners. In making monetary contracts, parties rely on the standard in which all their agreements are expressed to be stable and incontrovertible. When governments inflate away their obligations, they shake the whole foundation of banking and destroy its main benefit to society, which is to introduce certainty in a world of uncertainty. The attempt by the public sector to extract gains for itself from the public good of money leads inexorably to similar behaviour by the private sector; rocked by the inflation tax, borrowers try to obtain special terms, or have their debt forgiven; banks and securities companies gain private benefits from the safety net offered by central banks. Public and private sector behaviour influenced by moral hazard (the temptation to self-interested parties to appropriate a public good for themselves) systematically weakens the financial system.

Sheng's views on the need to see banking as offering a public good – and the absolute need for the central bank to protect this contribution to society at all costs – reflect his experience of the bankruptcies of banking systems in many developing countries. These have done serious damage to employment and growth prospects in countries affected, leading sometimes to the bankruptcy of the state as well, so that the state cannot rescue a banking system because its own credit has been destroyed. It can print increasingly worthless money, but it cannot inject new capital unless it has some 'last resort' savings of its own – such as a reserve of foreign currency or gold.

Comparable processes have been at work in Eastern European countries and in the West also. Under communist regimes there was no pretence at a contractual system serving citizens; the state decided who should get credit. Those with political clout obtained cash and put it in their pockets. But in the West credit controls, bank rescues, inflation, subsidies, debt renegotiation and debt forgiveness all have much the same effect: sectional interests making gains for themselves courtesy of central banks. An implication of this view is that the primary task of central banks should be to protect the monetary order of society.

If they adopted this perspective, central banks might avoid repeating some of the mistakes that they have made in the past. For instance, they would not even try to iron out normal fluctuations in the business cycle by manipulating interest rates. This mandate would also require them to give more weight than they seem to give at present to the longer-term effects of their actions – e.g. in a bank bail-out – in creating 'moral hazard', undermining financial discipline throughout the economy. Central bankers would look more to the possible long-term effects of their interventions in the markets. They would insist on narrowing the range of institutions covered by the safety net. At present there is a trend to widen rather than narrow the range of institutions implicitly eligible for support – securities houses and merchant banks are next in line. All these private interests want direct or contingent access to public funds – arguing of course that that is in the public interest. We would encourage central bankers to say 'No' more often.

If central banks are to be responsible to society for achieving price stability and protecting the monetary order, that mandate should presumably be enshrined in the constitution – the basic rules of political activity. And this is the concept enshrined in the Maastricht Treaty. But in many countries putting the mandate in the constitution would require a degree of social consensus that, we acknowledge, does not at present exist. The mid-twentieth-century view of money as something to be manipulated for this or that purpose dies hard, though in the end it will be seen as a diversion. However, while that view continues to have many adherents, the danger is that 'accountability' can easily be used to smuggle in political control over the central bank by the back door.

Centralized states like Britain and France, and especially those without a written constitution, have great difficulties in putting any body beyond the reach of parliament. The debate on central bank independence raises questions about whether such traditional constitutional arrangements are compatible with contemporary market realities. The Maastricht Treaty prohibits central banks from taking instructions from any outside body. It can be predicted that the new 'European Constitution' being drafted as this book goes to press will enshrine the independence of the European Central Bank and member countries will have to accept it. Quite apart from Maastricht, the financial markets seem to be demanding something similar. If it turned out, for example, that countries which made their central banks fully autonomous, with no provision for an override, found they could borrow at 2 per cent or so less than other countries, how many would resist? (Significantly, real short-term interest rates in the twelve months to March 1994 fell in France and in Spain, which had made their central banks independent during the year, but rose in Britain.)

Extending their domain

So much for theory and constitution-drafting. What about practical politics? As they acquire a broader mandate and nurture a broader base of political support, central bankers will press outwards the boundaries of their domain. This is how we think it will happen.

They are already finding out that to do the job that society seems to have asked them to do means giving monetary policy priority over broader economic policy. Next, they will need control over exchange-rate policy – to prevent monetary policy objectives being undermined. Indeed, if some German economists have their way, the Bundesbank will make this a condition of joining a European monetary union. Then they will start pushing for wider reforms.

In December 1993 the governor of the Bank of Japan, the redoubtable Yasushi Mieno, calmly asked the Japanese government to reform Japan's taxation, legal, and accounting systems. He also called for far-reaching deregulation of the economic system in order to help the commercial banks write off their bad debts. It was the responsibility of the government, he said, 'to remove all obstacles in their way'. He openly challenged Japan's once-powerful finance ministry, which had been trying despairingly to keep hold of its grip over the country's financial system, to move over. Deregulation was code for giving independence to the central bank, and for handing over wide areas of economic policy to it.

Japanese companies also had to complete the adjustment of their stocks and their balance sheets after the collapse of the 'bubble economy' in the late 1980s: 'Unless the economy goes through these adjustments, it cannot proceed to the next stage,' said Mieno. At a time when Japan was experiencing a serious economic slowdown, Mieno was in effect appealing over the heads of the politicians to business and public opinion. This was an example of the new breed of central bankers in action. In our view, they will often be justified in urging governments to implement reforms. If money is to be protected from sectional interests, it needs champions. And those champions need to have the skills to sell their ideology to the general public.

Challenges and cunning

This is for the future. Central banks' immediate task in the mid-1990s is to provide price stability – without overdoing it and plunging the world into depression. Any notion that this is a straightforward task, even with freedom from political interference, and even if central bank governors are personally held to certain standards of service, should have been dispelled by reading earlier chapters of this book. Monetary policy has to be transmitted, and as financial markets get ever more innovative the channels of transmission become harder to identify and catalogue. This has important implications for both the delivery of monetary policy and the lender-of-last resort function of central banks.

Speaking in the summer of 1993, the Federal Reserve's then vice chairman, David Mullins, called the development and growth of financial derivatives 'one of the most dramatic success stories in modern economic history'. At the same time, while he thought it important not to overstate the risks derivatives might pose to the financial system as a whole, he saw them as something central bankers have to worry about. Moreover, he and his colleagues were beginning to voice an additional concern – the ways in which the expanded use of derivatives by a wide variety of end-users has altered the channels of influence of monetary policy. 'This important topic,' said Bill McDonough a few weeks into the presidency of the New York Fed, 'has just begun to get the attention it deserves.'

We mention derivatives in the closing pages of this book because they are the trendiest example of a financial innovation that is pervasive and recognizes no national frontiers. Other varieties will doubtless follow. This underscores the need for central banks to be united in purpose and to cooperate fully if the financial system is to function efficiently and smoothly. Has strengthening of international banking since the 1980s lowered the probability of systemic meltdown – a global financial crisis? Probably it has. At the same time, however, compared with then, the cost to the financial system and the world economy, were such a global breakdown to occur, gets ever larger as different markets are linked and as they embrace a wide range of non-financial as well as financial firms.

So central banking needs to attract bright people who will respond, both intellectually and with neat footwork, to the enormous challenges of the future. What should their CVs indicate about them beyond their academic qualifications, expertise and experience? Central bankers take a mischievous delight in not providing an answer, in seeing themselves as impossible to stereotype. As one volunteered, 'central banking is a unique profession demanding a variety of attributes and defying any categorization'. Really? When pressed, central bankers make play of the need for 'flexibility' to adapt to a changing environment – an implicit acknowledgement that market innovation is leading them a dance and they have a devil of a time just following the footsteps.

We hope central banks will become less nationalistic and recruit from each other. Why should not a Federal Reserve staffer be eligible for a senior post at the Bundesbank, say, or the Bank of England? Not that we recommend a closed bureaucracy, even an international one; there must always be room for the brilliant outsider with the right experience who is willing to accept a call to public service. What we can confidently say is that top central bankers of the future will need a lot of technical expertise. Increasingly, they will be called on to monitor and even manage some of the most incalculable, complex and potentially catastrophic risks of the global financial markets that knit together the world economy. It is no world for the amateur.

Appendix: Annualized Twenty-year Inflation Rates

Country	Rate % *	Rank	1991 value of monetary unit (1971 = 100)
Germany	3.8	1	47.88
Czechoslovakia	4.0	2	45.49
Switzerland	4.1	3	44.41
People's Republic of China	4.3	4	42.84[a]
Panama	4.3	5	42.71
Malta	4.5	6	41.83
Netherlands	4.7	7	40.11
Malaysia	4.7	8	40.05
Singapore	4.7	9	39.93
Austria	4.8	10	39.04
Japan	5.3	11	35.60
Luxembourg	5.4	12	34.70
Niger	5.8	13	32.11
Saudi Arabia	5.9	14	31.92
Belgium	5.9	15	31.85
Burkina Faso	6.1	16	30.47[a]
United States	6.3	17	29.70
Cyprus	6.4	18	28.96
Bahamas	6.6	19	27.78
Netherlands Antilles	6.6	20	27.65
Bahrain	6.8	21	26.76
Togo	6.9	22	26.49[a]
Canada	7.1	23	25.27
Liberia	7.2	24	24.89[b]
Tunisia	7.2	25	24.72
Thailand	7.3	26	24.39
Papua New Guinea	7.4	27	24.11
Senegal	7.6	28	22.95
Denmark	7.7	29	22.80
Congo	7.8	30	22.37[b]
France	7.8	31	22.17

Norway	7.9	32	22.00
Morocco	8.1	33	21.09
Sweden	8.5	34	19.55
Ethiopia	8.5	35	19.45
Gabon	8.7	36	18.84[a]
St Lucia	8.8	37	18.68
Côte d'Ivoire	8.8	38	18.65[c]
Mauritania	8.8	39	18.55[e]
Finland	8.8	40	18.40
India	8.9	41	18.30
Seychelles	8.9	42	18.28
Haiti	8.9	43	18.07
Fiji	9.0	44	17.74
Algeria	9.1	45	17.61[a]
Australia	9.1	46	17.53
Cameroon	9.3	47	16.85[b]
Rwanda	9.4	48	16.63
Honduras	9.4	49	16.62
Jordan	9.4	50	16.48
Dominica	9.5	51	16.19[a]
Pakistan	9.6	52	15.90
Nepal	9.7	53	15.60
Barbados	9.8	54	15.35
United Kingdom	9.9	55	15.23
Central African Republic	9.9	56	15.22[b]
Burundi	9.9	57	15.15
Ireland	10.3	58	14.00
Suriname	10.6	59	13.45[d]
Solomon Islands	10.7	60	13.09
Sri Lanka	10.9	61	12.55
Korea	11.0	62	12.46
New Zealand	11.2	63	12.03
Western Samoa	11.4	64	11.50
Mauritius	11.7	65	11.01
Zimbabwe	11.7	66	10.95
Kenya	11.8	67	10.73
Italy	11.9	68	10.49
Spain	12.0	69	10.35
Trinidad and Tobago	12.1	70	10.24
Swaziland	12.1	71	10.11[a]
Myanmar (Burma)	12.5	72	9.51

Indonesia	13.0	73	8.71
South Africa	13.1	74	8.55
Madagascar	13.4	74	8.10[a]
Guatemala	13.6	76	7.78
Guyana	13.7	77	7.61[c]
Egypt	13.9	78	7.40
The Gambia	14.1	79	7.19
Philippines	14.2	80	7.06
Bangladesh	15.3	81	5.78
El Salvador	15.5	82	5.59
Syrian Arab Republic	16.1	83	5.05
Iran	16.1	84	5.03
Venezuela	17.1	85	4.24
Greece	17.5	86	3.99
Portugal	17.9	87	3.73
Nigeria	18.1	88	3.62
Paraguay	18.3	89	3.44
Jamaica	18.6	90	3.32
Costa Rica	19.3	91	2.94
Dominican Republic	19.6	92	2.78
Tanzania	22.2	93	1.83
Colombia	23.4	94	1.48
Sudan	24.6	95	1.24[b]
Somalia	24.9	96	1.17[c]
Ecuador	25.9	97	1.00
Zambia	30.9	98	0.46
Iceland	33.0	99	0.33
Poland	37.6	100	0.17
Mexico	39.9	101	0.12
Turkey	40.9	102	0.11
Sierra Leone	41.7	103	0.09
Ghana	42.3	104	0.09
Uruguay	69.0	105	0.00
Yugoslavia	76.0	106	0.00
Zaire	76.4	107	0.00
Brazil	162.2	108	0.00

*Long-term inflation rates, annualized to a constant rate. The annualized rate expresses the observed change in the purchasing power of the monetary unit over the period as a constant annual rate. This is a more accurate indicator of long-term inflation than the arithmetic mean of annual inflation rates.

[a]1970–90 [b]1969–89 [c]1968–88 [d]1967–87 [e]1966–86

Select Bibliography

Bagehot, Walter, 'Lombard Street' [1873] and other economic essays [1848–1877], in Vols. IX, X and XI. The Collected Works, London: *The Economist*, 1978.

Bank for International Settlements, Annual Reports. Various years.

Eight Central Banks. London: Allen & Unwin, 1963.

The BIS 1930–1980. Basle; BIS, 1980.

Bank of Italy, *The Bank of Italy: Portrait of an Institution*. Rome, 1991.

The Bank of Italy: 100 Years, 1893–1993 (Foreword by Antonio Fazio). Rome: Edizioni Dell'Elefante, 1994.

Banque de France, *La Banque de France: son histoire, son organisation, son rôle*. Paris, 1991.

Organisation et fonctions de quelques grandes banques centrales. Paris, 1992.

Beckhart, Benjamin Haggott, *Federal Reserve System*. New York: American Institute of Banking/Columbia University Press, 1972.

Bordo, Michael D. and Eichengreen, Barry (eds.), *A Retrospective on the Bretton Woods System*, Chicago: NBER/University of Chicago Press, 1993.

Buchanan, James M., *Essays on Political Economy*. Honolulu: University of Hawaii Press, 1989.

Burns, Arthur F., *Reflections of an Economic Policy Maker*. Washington, DC: American Enterprise Institute, 1978.

The Anguish of Central Banking (Per Jacobsson Lecture). Washington, DC: The Per Jacobsson Foundation, 1979.

Capie, Forrest H. (ed.), *Major Inflations in History*. Aldershot: Edward Elgar, 1991.

Capie, F. H. and Wood, G. E., 'Central Banks and Inflation: An Historical Perspective', *Central Banking*, Vol. 2, Nos. 2 and 3, 1991.

Cecco, Marcello de, and Giovannini, Alberto (eds.), *A European Central Bank?* Cambridge: Cambridge University Press, 1989.

Clapham, Sir John, *The Bank of England, 1694–1797*, 2 vols. Cambridge: Cambridge University Press, 1944.

Collins, M. (ed.), *Central Banking in History*. Aldershot: Edward Elgar, 1993.

Coombs, Charles, *The Arena of International Finance*. New York: Wiley, 1976.

Crabbe, Leland, *The International Gold Standard and US Monetary Policy from*

World War I to the New Deal. Washington, DC: Federal Reserve Bulletin, June 1989.

Dale, Richard, *Banking Supervision Around The World.* New York: Group of Thirty, 1982.

Davis, E. P., *Debt, Financial Fragility and Systemic Risk.* Oxford: Clarendon Press, 1992.

Deane, Marjorie and Pringle, Robert, *Economic Cooperation from the Inside.* New York: Group of Thirty, 1984.

De Boissieu, L. (ed.), *Banking in France.* London and New York: Routledge, 1990.

De Kock, M. H., *Central Banking.* New York: St Martins Press, 1974.

Dobson, Wendy, *Economic Policy Coordination: Requiem or Prologue?* Washington, DC: Institute for International Economics, 1991.

Dowd, Kevin, *Private Money: The Path to Monetary Stability.* London: Institute of Economic Affairs, 1988.

(ed.), *The Experience of Free Banking.* London and New York: Routledge, 1992.

Deutsche Bundesbank, *The Deutsche Bundesbank: Its Monetary Policy, Instruments and Functions,* 3rd edn. Frankfurt: Special Series No. 7, 1989.

Dykes, Sayre Ellen and Whitehouse, Michael A., *The Establishment and Evolution of the Federal Reserve Board, 1913–23.* Washington, DC: Federal Reserve Bulletin, April 1989.

Eichengreen, Barry, *Elusive Stability: Essays in the History of International Finance, 1913–1939.* Cambridge: Cambridge University Press, 1990.

Fazio, Antonio, 'Role and Independence of Central Banks', in Downes, Patrick and Vaez-Zadeh, Reza (eds.), *The Evolving Role of Central Banks.* Washington, DC: IMF, 1991.

Federal Reserve Bank of New York, Annual Reports.

Quarterly Review, Special 75th Anniversary Issue, 1989.

Federal Reserve Board of Governors, *The Federal Reserve System: Purposes and Functions,* 7th edn. Washington, DC: 1984.

Fforde, John, *The Bank of England and Public Policy 1941–1958.* Cambridge: Cambridge University Press, 1992.

Frankel, Jeffrey A., 'Is a Yen Bloc Forming in Pacific Asia?', in O'Brien, Richard (ed.), *Finance and the International Economy: 5,* The Amex Bank Review Prize Essays. Oxford: Oxford University Press, 1991.

Frankel, S. Herbert, *Money: Two Philosophies. The Conflict of Trust and Authority.* Oxford: Blackwell, 1977.

Friedman, Milton, 'The Role of Monetary Policy', *American Economic Review,* Vol. J8, 1968.

A Program for Monetary Stability. New York: Fordham University Press, 1959.

Friedman, Milton and Friedman, Rose, *Free to Change.* London: Secker and Warburg, 1980.

Fry, Maxwell, *Money, Interest and Banking in Economic Development*. Baltimore: Johns Hopkins University Press, 1988.
   Financial Repression and Economic Growth. The Birmingham Business School, International Finance Group, 1993.
   The Fiscal Abuse of Central Banks. IMF Working Paper. Washington, DC: IMF, 1993.

Funabashi, Yoichi, *Managing the Dollar: from the Plaza to the Louvre*. Washington, DC: Institute for International Economics, 1988.

Galbraith, John Kenneth, *Money: Whence It Came, Where It Went*. London: André Deutsch, 1975.

George, Eddie, 'The Pursuit of Financial Stability', *Central Banking*, Vol. 4, No. 3, 1993/4.

Goodhart, Charles, *The Evolution of Central Banks*. Cambridge, MA: MIT Press, 1988.

Gowland, D. H., *Economics of Modern Banking*. London: Edward Elgar, (forthcoming).

Green, Timothy, *The World of Gold*. London: Rosendale Press, 1993.

Guth, Wilfried (Moderator), *Economic Policy Coordination*. Washington, DC: IMF, 1988.

Hayek, F. A. von, *Denationalisation of Money*. London: Institute of Economic Affairs, 1976.

Hennessy, Elizabeth, *A Domestic History of The Bank of England, 1930–1960*. Cambridge: Cambridge University Press, 1992.

Henry, J. A., and Siepmann, H. A., *The First Hundred Years of the Standard Bank*. Oxford: Oxford University Press, 1963.

Hirsch, Fred, *Money International*. London: Allen Lane, 1967.

Hoffmeyer, Erik, *The International Monetary System: An Essay in Interpretation*. Amsterdam: Elsevier, 1992.

Hughes, A. V., 'Central Banking at the Small End', *Central Banking*, Vol. 3, No. 1, 1992.

Hume, David, 'Of Public Credit'; 'Of The Balance of Trade' [1741–52], in *Essays: Moral, Political and Literary*. Oxford: Oxford University Press, 1963.

Issing, Otmar, *Central Bank Independence and Monetary Stability*, London: Institute of Economic Affairs, Occasional Paper 89, 1993.

Jacobsson, Erin E., *A Life for Sound Money*. Oxford: Clarendon Press, 1979.

Joslin, David, *A Century of Banking in Latin America*. Oxford: Oxford University Press, 1963.

Kennedy, Ellen, *The Bundesbank: Germany's Central Bank in the International Monetary System*. London: Royal Institute of International Affairs/Pinter Publishers, 1991.

Kettl, Donald F., *Leadership at the Fed*. New Haven, CT, and London: Yale University Press, 1986.

Keynes, J. M., 'A Tract On Monetary Reform' [1923], *The Collected Writings*, Vol. IV. London: Macmillan, 1973.

'A Treatise on Money' [1930], in *The Collected Writings*, Vols., V and VI. London: Macmillan, 1973.

'The General Theory of Employment, Interest and Money' [1936], in *The Collected Writings*, Vol. VII. London: Macmillan, 1973.

Kindleberger, Charles R., *A Financial History of Western Europe*. London: Allen & Unwin, 1984.

Lawson, Nigel, *The View from No. 11*. London: Bantam Press, 1992.

Marsh, David, *The Bundesbank*. London: Heinemann, 1992.

Marx, Karl, *Capital: A Critique of Political Economy* (translated by Ben Fowkes). Harmondsworth: Penguin, 1976.

Meek, Paul (ed.), *Central Bank Views on Monetary Targeting*. New York: Federal Reserve Bank of New York, 1983.

Mendelsohn, M. S. and Pringle, Robert, *How Central Banks Manage Their Reserves*. New York: Group of Thirty, 1982.

Meulendyke, Ann-Marie, *US Monetary Policy and Financial Markets*. New York: Federal Reserve Bank of New York, 1989.

Morgan, E. Victor, *The Theory and Practice of Central Banking, 1797–1913*. Cambridge: Cambridge University Press, 1943.

Nevin, Edward, *Capital Funds in Underdeveloped Countries*. London: Macmillan, 1961.

Nölling, Wilhelm, *Monetary Policy in Europe After Maastricht*. German edition, Berlin: Verlag Ullstein GmbH, 1993, English translation, London: Macmillan, 1993.

O'Brien, Richard, *Global Financial Integration: The End of Geography*. London: Royal Institute of International Affairs/Pinter Publishers, 1992.

Parkin, M. and King, D., *Economics*. Reading, MA: Addison-Wesley, 1992.

Pecchioli, R. M., *Prudential Supervision in Banking*. Paris: OECD, 1987.

Polak, Jacques J., *Financial Policies and Development*. Paris: OECD, 1989.

Pringle, Robert, 'Financial Markets versus Governments', in Banuri, Tariq and Schor, Juliet B. (eds.), *Financial Openness and National Autonomy*. Oxford: Clarendon Press, 1992.

Banking in Britain. London: Charles Knight and Co., 1973.

The Changing Monetary Role of Gold. London: World Gold Council, 1993.

Radcliffe Committee (Committee on the Working of the Monetary System) Report. London: HMSO, Cmnd 827, 1959.

Ricardo, David, *On The Principles of Political Economy and Taxation*, (ed. P. Sraffa). Cambridge: Cambridge University Press, 1953.

Roll, Eric *et al.*, *Independent and Accountable: A New Mandate for the Bank of England*. A Report of an Independent Panel. London: Centre for Economic Policy Research, 1993.

Salin, Pascal, *La Vérité sur la monnaie*. Paris: Editions Odile Jacob, 1990.

Samuelson, Paul A. and Nordhaus, William D., *Economics*, 14th edn. New York: McGraw-Hill, 1992.

Sayers, R.S., *Modern Banking* [1938]. 3rd edn, Oxford: Clarendon Press, 1951.

Central Banking after Bagehot. Oxford: Clarendon Press, 1956.

The Bank of England, 1891–1944. 3 vols. Cambridge: Cambridge University Press, 1976.

Schuijer, Jan (ed.), *Banks Under Stress*. Paris: OECD, 1992.

Schwartz, Anna J., *Do Currency Boards Have a Future?* London: Institute of Economic Affairs, 1992.

Skanland, Hermod, *The Central Bank and Political Authorities in Some Industrial Countries*. Norges Banks Skrift Series, 1984.

Solomon, Robert, *The International Monetary System 1945–1981*. New York: Harper & Row, 1982.

'Changing Perspectives on the International Monetary System', in Frenkel, Jacob and Goldstein, Morris (eds.), *International Financial Policy: Essays in Honour of Jacques J. Polak*. Washington: IMF, 1991.

Smith, Adam, *The Wealth of Nations* [1776]. Harmondsworth: Penguin, 1993.

Smith, Vera L., *The Rationale of Central Banking* [1936]. Indianapolis: Liberty Press, 1990.

Skidelsky, Robert, *John Maynard Keynes: The Economist as Saviour*. London: Macmillan, 1992.

Sundararajan, V. and Balina, J. T. (eds), *Banking Crises: Cases and Issues*. Washington, DC: IMF, 1991.

Treasury and Civil Service Committee, *The Role of the Bank of England*, 2 vols. London: HMSO, 1993.

Volcker, Paul A., *The Triumph of Central Banking?* (Per Jacobsson Lecture). Washington, DC: The Per Jacobsson Foundation, 1990.

Volcker, Paul A. and Gyohten, Toyoo, *Changing Fortunes*. New York: Times Books, 1992.

Volcker, Paul A., Mancera, M. and Godeaux, J. *Perspectives on the Role of a Central Bank: People's Bank of China*. Washington, DC: IMF, 1991.

Wallich, Henry C., *Monetary Policy and Practice*. Lexington, Ma.: Lexington Books, 1982.

Weatherstone, Dennis *et al.*, *The Foreign Exchange Markets under Floating Rates*. New York: Group of Thirty, 1980.

White, Lawrence H. (ed.), *The Crisis in American Banking*. New York: New York University Press, 1993.

Wilson, J. S. G., *Money Markets: The International Perspective*. London and New York: Routledge, 1993.

Zijlstra, Jelle, *Central Banking with the Benefit of Hindsight* (Per Jacobsson Lecture). Washington, DC: The Per Jacobsson Foundation, 1981.

Index